OTHER MOTHERS

Other Mothers

Beyond the Maternal Ideal

Edited by
Ellen Bayuk Rosenman
and Claudia C. Klaver

The Ohio State University Press
Columbus

Copyright © 2008 by The Ohio State University.
All rights reserved.

Library of Congress Cataloging-in-Publication Data
Other mothers : beyond the maternal ideal / edited by Ellen Bayuk Rosenman and Claudia C. Klaver.
    p. cm.
  Includes bibliographical references and index.
  ISBN-13: 978-0-8142-0286-9 (cloth : alk. paper)
  ISBN-10: 0-8142-0286-1 (cloth : alk. paper)
  ISBN-13: 978-0-8142-9047-7 (CD-ROM)
  1. English literature—19th century—History and criticism. 2. Motherhood in literature. 3. Mothers in literature. 4. Motherhood—Philosophy. 5. Femininity (Philosophy) in literature. 6. Motherhood—Social aspects—Great Britain—History—19th century. 7. Motherhood—Political aspects—Great Britain—History—19th century. 8. Sex role in literature. 9. Social classes in literature. 10. Race in literature. I. Rosenman, Ellen Bayuk. II. Klaver, Claudia C.
  PR468.M596O75 2008
  820.9'355—dc22
                                2008018816

This book is available in the following editions:
Cloth (ISBN 978-0-8142-0286-9)
CD-ROM (ISBN 978-0-8142-9047-7)

Cover design by Jenny Poff
Type set in Adobe Granjon
Text design by Juliet Williams
Printed by Thomson-Shore, Inc.

∞ The paper used in this publication meets the minimum requirements of the American National Standard for Information Sciences—Permanence of Paper for Printed Library Materials. ANSI Z39.48-1992.

9 8 7 6 5 4 3 2 1

CONTENTS

Illustrations   vii

Introduction   1
    CLAUDIA C. KLAVER and ELLEN BAYUK ROSENMAN

Part I. Beyond the Maternal Ideal

1. "How to Be a Domestic Goddess" Redux
   DEIRDRE D'ALBERTIS   25

2. "Long, Long Disappointment": Maternal Failure and Masculine Exhaustion in Margaret Oliphant's *Autobiography*
   LAURA GREEN   36

3. "Bland, Adoring, and Gently Tearful Women": Debunking the Maternal Ideal in George Eliot's *Felix Holt*
   HEATHER MILTON   55

4. Elderly Mothers and Middle-Aged Daughters in Charles Dickens's *Dombey and Son*
   TERESA MANGUM   75

Part II. "Bad Mothers": Caretaking, Class, and Maternal Violence

5. Unforgiven: Drunken Mothers in Hesba Stretton's Religious Tract Society and Scottish Temperance League Fiction
   DEBORAH DENENHOLZ MORSE   101

6. Infant Doping and Middle-Class Motherhood: Opium Warnings and Charlotte Yonge's *The Daisy Chain*
   DARA ROSSMAN REGAIGNON — 125

7. Motherhood on Trial: Violence and Unwed Mothers in Victorian England
   GINGER FROST — 145

8. A Murdering Mother: Frances Knorr
   LUCY SUSSEX — 163

Part III. Maternity and Difference: Nation, Race, and Empire

9. "My Own Dear Sons": Discursive Maternity and Proper British Bodies in *Wonderful Adventures of Mrs. Seacole in Many Lands*
   DEIRDRE H. McMAHON — 181

10. Conceiving the Nation: Visions and Versions of Colonial Prenatality
    DEIRDRE OSBORNE — 202

11. Orphan Stories and Maternal Legacies in Charlotte Brontë
    MARY JEAN CORBETT — 227

12. Distance Mothering and the "Cradle Lands": Imperial Motherhood and Lady Duff Gordon's *Letters from Egypt*
    CARA MURRAY — 248

Part IV. The Maternal Body

13. The Text as Child: Gender/Sex and Metaphors of Maternity at the *Fin de Siècle*
    BRENDA R. WEBER — 271

14. The Widest Lap: Fatness, Fasting, and Nurturance in Nineteenth-Century Fiction
    LILLIAN E. CRATON — 291

15. Mother Love: Edith Simcox, Maternity, and Lesbian Erotics
    ELLEN BAYUK ROSENMAN — 313

Contributors — 335
Index — 339

ILLUSTRATIONS

Figure 4.1.	Hablot Browne's etching "A Chance Meeting" from *Dombey and Son*.	81
Figure 4.2.	1848 portrait of Mrs. Skewton.	89
Figure 6.1	N. [William Newman], *Punch* 17 (1849): 193.	131

INTRODUCTION

Claudia C. Klaver and
Ellen Bayuk Rosenman

Who fed me from her gentle breast
And hush'd me in her arms to rest
And on my cheek sweet kisses prest?
—Ann Taylor Gilbert, "My Mother" (1805)

"Oh, Willie, my child dead, dead, dead! and he never knew me, never called me mother!" (Falls sobbing across the body . . .)
—T. A. Palmer, *East Lynne* (1874)

The phrase "other mothers" conjures up familiar images of transgression and despair: adulteresses who abandon their children, young girls seduced and forsaken, tragic figures that are the anathematized mirror of ideal motherhood. As the sanctification of motherhood gained its full ideological force in the nineteenth century, the successful or failed performance of maternity became the ubiquitous subject of social debate and textual representation. Our two epigraphs capture the fervor of mother-worship, one extolling the perfect responsiveness of maternal tenderness, the other dramatizing the pathos of maternal estrangement. Of course, no one could live up to perfect selflessness, purity, and love connoted by "mother"; in this sense, all mothers are other mothers. But this impossibility did not prevent the ideal from securing a highly visible place in Victorian culture.

In spite of its importance, however, maternity itself is one of the least-studied aspects of the Victorian era. It has been annexed to formulations of gender, the private sphere, and the consolidation of the bourgeois values. More recently, maternity has been implicated in the ideological structures of race and nation. Yet detailed explorations that range beyond these ideas are rare. Although maternity is routinely placed at the center of constructions of femininity and domesticity, it has received surprisingly little attention as a distinct conception or experience. Most often, it is collapsed into treatments of femininity and domesticity, mentioned and then subsumed into a more general analysis of gender roles. The idealization of motherhood was an unquestionable part of the Victorian landscape, even though, as we will argue, its precise meaning, reach, power, and use were far from uniform. As asserted in foundational works by Nancy Armstrong, Leonore Davidoff and Catherine Hall, Sandra Gilbert and Susan Gubar, and Martha Vicinus (*Suffer*), the Angel in the House symbolized cherished bourgeois values. She was an imaginative grounding point for femininity, just as femininity was a grounding point for domesticity. The virtues of the middle-class woman and of the home over which she was to preside emanated from an image of the mother as pure, self-sacrificing, and devoted, a spiritual influence and a moral instructress. Definitions of gender and of gender difference, particularly the reinvention of femininity as chaste, subordinate, and exempted from wage-earning labor, depended on this idealization, which in turn helped to justify the supremacy of the middle class. Similarly, as a repository of virtues and a conduit of values to the next generation, the mother functioned as both a fantasized origin and ideological touchstone for the racial and national superiority of the British nation as it extended its overseas empire. As Ann Laura Stoler asserts, "Child rearing . . . was hailed as a national, imperial, and racial duty" (72). Maternity was expected to anchor key cultural oppositions such as masculine versus feminine, bourgeois versus working class, British versus foreign, and white versus racially other, along with the more abstract oppositions underlying them: spiritual versus corporeal, pure versus impure, private versus public, and leisure versus labor.

Even as this model of the domestic ideal as the ground for an ideology of separate sphere was established, however, it was also being complicated, at times by the very same works that helped to establish it as a critical commonplace. Mary Poovey's *Uneven Developments* (1988), in particular, at once argued for the social and culture centrality of the separate spheres ideology, exposed the contradictions at its center, and demonstrated the ways in which those contradictions destabilized the gendered oppositions of Victorian culture. *Uneven Developments* emerged at the beginning of an era of revisionist gender scholarship, most of it published in about a decade between the late 1980s through the 1990s, whose scope, richness, and sheer quantity is extraordinary.[1] One could consider this the golden age of Victorian gender studies, when basic paradigms were continually qualified,

---

[1] In spite of the length of this survey, it is not intended to be exhaustive but omits important and impressive books in the interests of (relative) brevity.

reexamined, and rethought. "The Angel in the House," once shorthand for the stable constellation of qualities described above, became a complex, contradictory figure.

The titles of Elizabeth Langland's *Nobody's Angels* (1995) and Dorice Williams Elliott's *The Angel Out of the House* (2002) declare the revisionist spirit of this criticism as it deconstructs the Angel in the House, separate spheres, and the idea of a single, coherent "female nature" as unquestioned ideological and empirical norms. Such works, also including Linda Peterson's *Family, Love, and Work in the Lives of Victorian Gentlewomen* (1989), Judith Walkowitz in *City of Dreadful Delight* (1992), Mary Jean Corbett's *Representing Femininity* (1992), Deborah Nord in *Walking the Victorian Streets* (1995), Margaret Beetham's *A Magazine of Her Own* (1996), and Karen Chase and Michael Levenson's *The Spectacle of Intimacy* (2000), insist that women regularly traversed the physical boundaries between domestic and public space, that they played active roles in the so-called public sphere, and that, even in the home, they participated directly and indirectly in economic life.

Private life was not so private after all, nor was the public world exclusively populated by men. Critics traced the instability of the private/public boundary, with the governess attracting special attention as a figure who condensed many resulting ambiguities. Resembling the members of the middle-class family she served, she nevertheless stood apart from it; exhibiting her education and female accomplishments, she did so for pay rather than from the heart; theoretically protected from the stresses of the marketplace, in practice she was compelled to earn a living.[2] The scandal of her economic and social vulnerability not only questioned the patriarchal division of labor, it also called into question the nature of family responsibilities, which were both sanctified as the "natural" expression of womanhood and handed over to the help in the form of poorly remunerated labor. Once mined for their simplistic, binary definitions of femininity, conduct books became understood as sites of debates over the extent to which women should participate directly in their domestic role.[3] Religiously inspired works might exhort women to eschew idleness and take responsibility for every aspect of their homes, but other texts argued that the daily frustrations of housework and child care might compromise women's

---

[2] Poovey again provides a foundational discussion of the governess in *Uneven Development;* see also Cecilia Wadsö Lecaros's *The Victorian Governess Novel* (2001) and Kathryn Hughes's *The Victorian Governess* (2003).

[3] See Beetham (162–64), Anderson (Powers of Distance 55), and Davidoff and Hall (335–42) for scholarly treatments of this debate, as well as Regaignon's essay in this volume, "Infant Doping and Middle-Class Motherhood."

ability to model the virtues of serenity and patience; still others urged women to exercise domestic dominion by controlling their servants, fulfilling their role as apparently private angels through economic authority. Alongside this revisionist scholarship, masculinity underwent an equally dramatic reassessment that further undermined the hegemonic power of separate spheres and heterosexuality in the construction of gender.[4]

Further compromising the association of women with a tightly enclosed domestic sphere, philanthropy and nursing offered public outlets for qualities designated as feminine. Justified as a logical extension of their domestic mandate, this public femininity raised questions about women's social destiny. Studies of women such as Josephine Butler, Florence Nightingale, and Queen Victoria—that most public of feminine women—emphasized the satisfaction found in work apart from the family, sometimes revealing deep frustration with the constraints of bourgeois womanhood.[5] In doing so, they drove a wedge between "domesticity" and "femininity," uncovering Victorian critiques of the bourgeois home while performing highly valued "woman's work" outside its walls. Alison Booth's *How to Make It as a Woman* (2004) unfolds the extraordinary variety of women offered as models to Victorian female readers, from predictable choices such as Queen Victoria to eye-opening subversives such as Charlotte Corday, assassin of Jacques-Louis Marat during the French Revolution. Similarly, critics have discovered resources for self-assertion as well as service in the rhetoric of domesticity. In her analysis of Florence Nightingale, Poovey discloses the "aggressive component" of home management that underwrote Nightin-

---

[4] Masculinity studies such as James Eli Adams's *Dandies and Desert Saints* (1995), Joseph Kestner's *Masculinity in Victorian Painting* (1995), and Herbert Sussman's *Victorian Masculinities* (1995) insist on the performative nature of masculinity along with the anxieties that clustered around its multiple, socially constructed, and therefore unstable forms. In John Tosh's *A Man's Place* (1999), men cross the imaginary boundary between private and public as they struggle to fulfill a domestic role. Works on muscular Christianity, such as Donald Hall's collection *Muscular Christianity* (1994), consider the tensions between the physical dimensions of masculinity and its moral imperatives, which were frequently coded feminine. Perhaps most dramatically, scholarship has situated homoeroticism and homosexuality at the center of Victorian masculinity. Linda Dowling's *Hellenism and Homosexuality* (1994) and Christopher Lane's *The Burdens of Intimacy* (1999) are only two examples of the substantial body of work untangling the complex prohibitions, evasions, and enticements structuring a continuum of same-sex bonds. Wide-ranging books and essay collections, such as William Cohen's *Sexual Scandal* (1996) and Richard Dellamora's *Victorian Sexual Dissidence* (1999), have continued to problematize gender categories, their interrelationships, and their relationships to categories of sexuality.

[5] Adrienne Munich's *Queen Victoria's Secrets* (1996) and Munich and Margaret Homans's collection *Remaking Queen Victoria* (1997) consider the ideological contradictions of Victoria as private woman but public monarch.

gale's ruthless professionalism ("Uneven Developments" 170). Women's authority, resistance, and self-assertion both inside and outside the home now compel our attention. The subject of women's power—its nature, meaning, and extent in specific settings—has now become so thoroughly a part of our understanding that it is generating its own controversies, as in Amanda Anderson's recent critique of what she calls the "aggrandized agency" Poovey and Langland attribute to particular Victorian women.[6] Thanks to this revisionist scholarship, issues raised by public work and domestic power structures are now central problematics in the study of Victorian women and gender ideology.

Questions of agency and power have also made female display, especially in the form of sexuality, a privileged site of investigation.[7] A significant body of work has complicated the binary of purity and transgression, as women's bodies have become visible in contexts beyond traditional erotic plots and the heterosexual dyad. Representative of this scholarship is the multifaceted collection *Sexualities in Victorian Britain* (1996), whose title indicates the range of its investigations and conclusions, from the construction of the sexually pure, imputedly "classless" woman who erases the process of class formation, to the demonization of female pleasure in medical science, to the dependence of masculinity on the apparently passive Angel in the House, to a sexually and economically motivated case of cross-dressing. Dispensing with an overarching theory of female sexuality, this collection suggests the multiple contexts and aims that proliferated incompatible versions of female sexuality. Martha Vicinus uncovers a rich tradition of same-sex attachment in *Independent Women* (1985) and *Intimate Friends* (2004), while Sharon Marcus's *Between Women* (2007) charts a subtle field of female affiliations that resists the familiar binaries of homosexual/heterosexual and submissive/transgressive. Related scholarship, such as Dorothy Mermin's *Godiva's Ride* (1993), has been particularly attentive to the liminal figure of the woman writer, who, like the governess, occupied a space at once public and private. Delineating human emotions and relationships (and able to work at home, unlike other employed women), she also circulated her name in public, a form of visibility that could also be pathologized as indecent, akin to the physical display of

---

[6] See chapter 2, "Temptations of Aggrandized Agency," in Anderson's *The Way We Argue Now* (46–68).

[7] Other works developing this theme of display include Tracy Davis's *Actresses and Working Women* (1991), along with treatments of the significant trials of Caroline Norton by Poovey and of Queen Caroline by Anna Clark, whose book *The Struggle for Breeches* (1995) pays special attention to the unlikely convergence of class and gender agendas in the heroizing of Caroline.

actresses and prostitutes. As with agency, its close relation, female embodiment has taken on multiple, complex-specific meanings that complicate the imputed hegemony of male gaze, masculine sexual privilege, and patriarchal control.

Inevitably, deconstructing the Angel in the House and the ideology of separate spheres revealed their class-specific nature, urging the articulation of class as an analytical category and the study of lower-class women. Studies of urban journalism, philanthropy, and industrial reform revealed different "images of women" that challenged simple formulations of sexual difference.[8] While Victorian commentators condemned working-class women who failed to enact middle-class models, they also acknowledged the obvious fact that physical labor and economic exigency played a more insistent role in working women's lives. While not unknown to representations of middle-class life, violence, aggression, and extreme economic vulnerability became part of the vocabulary of Victorian gender studies. Moreover, even though bourgeois ideals might condemn the poor, they could also invoke melodramatic narratives of female victimhood, granting impoverished women some limited purchase in the legal and economic system. Françoise Barret-Ducrocq's controversial *Love in the Time of Victoria* (1991) and Ginger Frost's *Promises Broken* (1995) demonstrate the power of this discourse in the settings of the foundling hospital and the courtroom.[9] Images of working-class women's bodies further denaturalized the bourgeois ideal of femininity. Particularly as photography became recognized as an essential tool for constructing and manipulating identities, meanings of "the female body" multiplied. The relationship between the gentleman Arthur Munby and the maid-of-all-work Hannah Cullwick, culminating in a secret marriage, emerged as a fertile case study in these dynamics in Anne McClintock's *Imperial Leather* (1995) and Carol Mavor's *Pleasures Taken* (1995). Cullwick appears as a sturdy scullery maid, an attractive lady, a man, and, in blackface, as a slave. As this last incarnation makes literal, scholarship also reckoned with the semiotic importance of race as a marker of identity in the study of working-class women.

Similarly, as Victorian studies has embraced postcolonial theory, the

---

[8] For example, see Seth Koven's *Slumming* (2004), especially chapter 4, "The Politics and Erotics of Dirt: Cross Class Sisterhood in the Slums" (183–227).

[9] Julia Swindells, Victorian Writing and Working Women (1985); Arlene Young, *Culture, Class, and Gender in the Victorian Novel: Gentlemen, Gents, and Working Women* (1999); Patricia Johnson, *Hidden Hands: Working-Class Women and Victorian Social-Problem Fiction* (2001); Kristina Huneault, *Difficult Subjects: Working Women and Visual Culture in Britain, 1880–1914* (2002); and Lynn M. Alexander, *Women, Work, and Representation* (2003) have all contributed to our understanding of working-class women.

foreign spaces of empire divulge further complexities and ambiguities, particularly with regard to race. Imperial conquest invoked an idealized white, middle-class femininity to justify imperial missions. White middle-class women were sanctified as the source of racial purity (a claim with obvious implications for motherhood), while their imputed vulnerability authorized British violence against native men. McClintock's *Imperial Leather* and Jennifer Brody's *Impossible Purities* (1998) have shown that, as whiteness emerged as a crucial category defining Britishness and metropolitan superiority, imperialism used racial categories to stabilize the unpredictability of cross-cultural encounters. Metonymically associated with foreign landscapes, nonwhite women's bodies invited male penetration, while fantasies about native women's sexuality authorized white male predation. Within these imperialistic paradigms, however, white British and colonial women found new possibilities. Colonial settings, different cultural contexts, and varied geographies attenuated the hold of the metropolitan center, sometimes imposing greater hardships, sometimes permitting greater freedoms. Emphasizing the significance of sexual relations as part of an overarching European imperialist project, Ann Laura Stoler, in *Carnal Knowledge and Imperial Power* (2002), also urged critics to pay detailed attention to the particularities of local contexts, which forcefully inflect the workings of gender, race, and class.

In spite of their diversity, several themes and insights emerge from these studies. One theme is a focus on female subjectivity, agency, mobility, and authority as they are authorized by precisely those formulations that were originally understood to contain them. "Victorian femininity" has become an open category, generating contradictions, possibilities, and life paths in many different directions. Particularly as masculinity and heterosexuality have been displaced from their normative status, femininity is no longer locked in a simple relational dyad with masculinity. We now recognize its mutual constitution with many identities, in shifting and context-specific forms. Scholarship on class and imperialism has articulated gender in terms of class and race, charting not simply intersections—as if in other contexts women might not be classed or raced—but the inseparability of these identity categories. The interrelationship between gender and other categories further detaches femininity from the home, masculinity, and the private sphere. As we have recognized this complexity, we have also come to see femininity as a symbolic space in which a wide range of cultural anxieties can be projected, represented, and displaced. Emerging in many different cultural sites, it can be appropriated to symbolize a variety of emotionally charged values in public discourse and can anchor a variety of choices and experiences in individual lives.

This fertile period has produced a handful of outstanding works that are important exceptions to the scholarly silence around Victorian motherhood.[10] Most prominently, in *Death and the Mother from Freud to Dickens* (1998), Carolyn Dever has theorized the significance of maternal absence and death in the works of both Freud and canonical Victorian novelists. Dever links the emergence of psychoanalytic theory's preoccupation with the mother with the Victorian novel, arguing that the maternal void poses fundamental questions about origin and the development of individual identity. Dever's text provides a compelling account of cultural preoccupations with the dead mother, though its treatment of the situation, roles, representations, and experiences of mothers is necessarily limited.

Along with Dever's work, two areas of scholarship have developed important critical and historical insights into Victorian mothers and motherhood. In the field of literary and cultural studies, Jill Matus, Mary Poovey, and Sally Shuttleworth have all examined overlapping connections between maternity and sexuality. All three scholars draw upon Victorian medical discourses about the sexed female body to demonstrate Victorian anxieties about the proximity between woman's maternal role and her sexuality. Matus's examination of imbrication of Victorian motherhood with concerns about female sexuality is the most extensive of these studies. In *Unstable Bodies: Victorian Representations of Sexuality and Maternity* (1995), she charts the articulation of both "moral" motherhood and maternal deviance in relation to sexed female body, though not always to sexuality per se. Examining cultural concerns about working-class motherhood, wet-nursing and infanticide, maternal instinct, and insanity, she develops readings of maternal characters in a range of novels, providing wide-ranging representations of embodied mothers and types of maternal failure or deviance. Matus's study participates in the broader project of Victorian gender and queer studies by moving beyond conventional understandings of nineteenth-century discourses of gender and sexuality. Her goal is to

---

[10] It is worth repeating that, even in this explosion of gender scholarship, treatments of maternity are rare. Langland's *Nobody's Angels* and Nancy Armstrong's *Desire and Domestic Fiction* (1987) do not even index motherhood or maternity. Of the many works in Victorian gender/literary studies cited here, only Poovey's *Uneven Developments* (1988) and Margaret Homans's *Bearing the Word* (1986) treat maternity in an extended way. More recently, Monica Cohen's *Professional Domesticity* (1998) does not address motherhood at all. In the area of race, nation, and empire, Anne McClintock's *Imperial Leather* (1995), Catherine Hall's collection *Civilizing Subjects* (2002), Anita Levy's *Other Women* (1991), Jennifer Brody's *Impossible Purities* (1998), and Laura Ann Stoler's *Carnal Knowledge and Imperial Power* (2002) do not offer substantive discussions. Treatments of class such as Regenia Gagnier's *Subjectivities* (1991) and Hall's *Defining the Nation: Class, Race, Gender and the British Reform Act of 1867* (2000) are also silent.

demonstrate that sexual difference was not fixed in a rigid binary either in Victorian biomedical discourse or in the novel, but was rather characterized by slippage and approximation. Fraught sites of instability, these maternal aberrations generate both anxieties and discursive possibility.

Where Matus identifies the slippages and instabilities that challenge hierarchical gendered power structures, Sally Shuttleworth and Mary Poovey identify such challenges in the operation of ideological contradiction. As Shuttleworth writes in "Demonic Mothers" (1992):

> [T]he very ideological centrality of these [sacred maternal ideals] ensured that motherhood was not the still point around which other contradictions might turn, but rather a field of potent conflict in itself. Far from guaranteeing, by its seemingly unchallengeable status, areas of agreement over ideological conflict, it acted as a focal point for many of the most problematic areas of Victorian ideology. (31)

Thus the image of the idealized mother was continually threatened and displaced by that of the demonic mother. As in Matus's study, Shuttleworth's examination of ideology centers on constructions of the female body. Looking at advice books, medical texts, and novels, she demonstrates the multiple ways in which the maternal body is also always a sexual body. Even apparently nonsexual concerns such as maternal health and breastfeeding are informed by concerns about self-regulation, indulgence, and excess that have dense sexual connotations. Mary Poovey's chapter "Scenes of an Indelicate Character: The Medical Treatment of Victorian Women" in *Uneven Developments,* while much narrower in its focus, also locates the disruption of rigid binaries of gender and the images of maternity in ideological contradictions. Poovey's chapter examines the medical debate about the use of anesthesia in childbirth, as well as the competition between medical and religious accounts of childbirth. In particular, she discusses how women's apparent sexual excitation while under anesthesia during childbirth exposed conflicting definitions of women as at once fundamentally maternal, and hence necessarily embodied, and essentially moral and asexual.

Matus, Shuttleworth, and Poovey all show that the popular image of the ideal mother was not a simple orthodoxy. Their research into medical and advice literature also makes visible the many aspects of motherhood that concerned the Victorian public, not just caregiving, but also breastfeeding, the question of maternal instinct, heredity legacies, and the very act of giving birth. This scholarship has provided an important resource for other critics, ensuring that motherhood is not defined solely in terms of the idealized images and prescriptions made famous by such texts as Coventry Patmore's "Angel in the House," Sarah Ellis's *Mothers of England,* and John Ruskin's *Sesame and Lilies.* The concentration of this scholarship around medical texts, including medical advice books and articles, charts a specific archive addressing a particular range of issues that, focusing on the maternal *body,* inevitably ties motherhood to issues associated with sexuality. Such focused investigations encourage scholars to seek out other sources to extend our understanding of motherhood as a multifaceted phenomenon in which the broad category of "sexuality" can be developed in many directions. In *Between Women* (2007), for instance, Sharon Marcus examines the mother/daughter relationship in her treatments of fashion magazines and doll stories, which provide surprising representations of desire and aggression that elude conventional categories. Marcus argues forcefully that maternal relations need to be understood in relation to broad definitions of eroticism that range beyond the familiar theme of sexual transgression.

Other sources, generated by historians, engage issues besides sexuality by examining maternity in specific periods and geographical settings. Ellen Ross's *Love and Toil: Motherhood in Outcast London, 1870–1918* (1993) emphasizes the stresses of working-class motherhood, paying detailed attention to the remunerative and domestic labor that played a vital role in the family's economic survival, and to the economic hardship that infiltrated the family's affective life. In her account, the experiences and expectations of motherhood are emphatically class specific, with little reference to the separate spheres or delicacy of womanhood. Leonore Davidoff and Catherine Hall's *Family Fortunes: Men and Women of the English Middle Class, 1780–1850* (1987), which focuses on Birmingham and the rural counties of Essex and Suffolk, has provided a crucial resource for Victorian scholars seeking to understand the way gender structured virtually all aspects of belief and everyday life for provincial bourgeois Evangelicals in the late eighteenth through mid-nineteenth centuries. Davidoff and Hall's treatment of motherhood itself is relatively condensed, but does cover important issues such as childbearing patterns, domestic management, children's illnesses and mortality, surrogate mothering of nieces, and aging. These works by Ross and Davidoff and Hall make an invaluable contribution to our understanding of Victorian motherhood by examining the material realities of specific groups of mothers in particular contexts and will continue to serve as resources for Victorian scholars. At the same time, however, their focus on specific populations should encourage detailed exploration of other groups and locations in order to extend our understanding of the diversity and range of maternal experience and representation in the nineteenth century. These three areas of scholarship—on maternal absence, on maternity and sexuality, and on specific historical and geographical sites—have each examined Victorian motherhood as involved in a specific set of concerns, rather than as coextensive with bourgeois femininity and domesticity.

This revisionist scholarship on both maternity and the construction of gender has accumulated to the point where the field as a whole seems poised for reorientation. In a recent article, Caroline Levine asserts, "We are at a turning point, it seems, when it comes to thinking about nineteenth century gender norms" (627). The idea of a hegemonic ideology or discourse seems increasingly reductive, even unproductive. Scholars have identified so many contradictions and transgressions that we cannot help but question the extent to which the familiar ideal of the female domestic angel constituted an article of faith, whether empirical or ideological. Further, we have enumerated so many different *kinds* of transgressions that they cannot be traced to a small constellation of values. We need to return to the very idea of Victorian norms and question the extent to which recurring declarations about women's roles constituted a discursive regime or hegemonic ideology that controlled the social and cultural field. As the trend of this revisionist scholarship implies, such assumptions can oversimplify the complexity of power as well as the diversity and uneven texture of human social and subjective experience. To draw again on Levine's analysis, "crude, binary ideologies—such as separate spheres—can dominate the social, cultural, and economic world at some moments, while at others, pressed by alternative and competing ... imperatives, they also falter, are transformed, or even temporarily disappear" (629). Whether destabilized by internal inconsistencies or challenged by external resistance, the domestic femininity of the Angel in the House cannot serve as an unquestioned heuristic for scholarship.

This reorientation of the field has created a propitious moment to dislodge maternity from its imbrication in conventional formulations of domestic femininity. If scholarship no longer conceives of the domestic ideal as the linchpin of Victorian culture and society, then motherhood, too, can—and needs to—be reconceptualized.[11] This is the aim of our

---

[11] Indeed, two recent essays demonstrate the possibilities for such a reconceptualization. In "'Their Calling Me "Mother" Was Not, I Think, Altogether Unmeaning': Mary Seacole's Maternal Personae," Nicole Fluhr examines the way Mary Seacole's autobiographical narrative constructs narrative personae out of a range of seemingly incompatible maternal ideals—middle and working class, black, mixed race, and white. Not only do the terms of Seacole's maternal personae seems to be at odds, but there is also a tension between that textual personae and extratextual references to Seacole's own biological daughter, about

collection: to open a conversation about Victorian motherhood in its diverse enactments and representations. The Victorian maternal ideal was at once more complex, less stable, less coherent, and less universal than the iconic simplicity it connoted. Although it has compelled attention because it has been presumed to have a regulative force, we see now that it did not play such a coercive cultural role. Certainly it was articulated often and in many forms, both directly and indirectly. But this widespread articulation does not automatically denote its hegemony. Nor does it limit alternatives to a systematic set of transgressions performed by a conventional cast of sinners. The essays in this collection ask what specific articulations of this ideal mean and how they function. Although it could operate powerfully in local and strategic ways, supplying an influential rhetoric or making available a compelling persona, the maternal ideal did not exhaust the possibilities of motherhood. In dialogue with a range of experiences and expectations, it is repeatedly revised when it came into contact with competing claims, such as the recognition that concrete economic exigencies, rather than or in addition to biological and spiritual ones, shape maternal behavior, or when individual mothers consciously fashioned alternative relationships with their children. Moreover, when understood as part of a complex field of experiences, beliefs, and identity categories, it is clear that the very force of the ideal provided metaphorical material that could be loosened from its intended aims and directed to other ends, generating new cultural and erotic forms.

In short, no single assertion can accommodate these highly variegated effects. Although we have attempted to achieve some coherence in this collection by using thematic rubrics to suggest shared concerns, we have not sought even local conclusions within these groupings. In *Touching/Feeling* (2003), Eve Sedgwick urges scholars to "specify and pluralize" our ignorance, recognizing how much we do not know and approaching these gaps with detailed local investigations that may well resist overarching generalizations (25). She playfully figures this diversity as siblings sharing a bed, an experience that may involve warmth, attachment, antagonism, incompatibility, thrashing, comfort—almost any possible relationship (8).

---

whom Seacole herself remains completely silent. Another recent essay, Andrea Bobotis's "Rival Maternities: Maud Gonne, Queen Victoria, and the Reign of the Political Mother," "argues that Gonne both petitioned for Irish mothers' involvement in nationalist politics and sustained her own elite class position by challenging Victoria's embodiment of maternal sovereignty. Through her literary and dramatic personifications of Cathleen ni Houlihan and Mother Ireland, Gonne crafted a model of nationalist motherhood that, when placed alongside the Queen's representations of imperial maternity, worked to promote Ireland's divestiture of English governance" (63).

The range of our essays, along with the format of an essay collection itself, attempts to put this model into practice. Historically, the essays span Victoria's range from the 1840s to the early twentieth century; geographically, they consider Australia and Egypt as well as Britain; in terms of genre, they engage an array of texts ranging from court reports and temperance tracts to autobiographies and novels. They examine maternal figures of diverse races, classes, ages, and even genders, in contexts that range from the frontlines of war and the scaffold to the domestic interiors of provincial England. These varied accounts take the collection "beyond the maternal ideal" to consider the multiple, unpredictable ways in which motherhood was experienced and imagined in this formative historical period.

We have organized these essays into four categories to provide a shorthand of the volume's range and to suggest ways in which individual essays might be read in relation to each other. It will be obvious, however, that some threads, such as social class, cut across these divisions and that other organizational rubrics would create different interconnections. The ones we have chosen, however, highlight the most important relationships among the essays. Our organization places individual essays within the framework of current issues in Victorian studies, foregrounding the familiar categories of race, class, and gender, while individual essays and the divergent conclusions within each grouping demonstrate how complex such formations remained even in the historical moment when they were allegedly being consolidated.

The collection's first group of essays, which we have titled "Beyond the Maternal Ideal," addresses the discursive construction and playing out of the ideal itself, as attempts to fulfill that ideal reveal its impossibility, its unforeseen implications, or its destructiveness for mothers and children. The essays in this section take as their starting point the cultural importance of this idea, but then demonstrate the complexity of its functions in the texts and experiences of a broad range of Victorian, and even contemporary, writers. In "'How to Be a Domestic Goddess' Redux," Deirdre d'Albertis looks at one way in which the internal logic of the ideal is played out in fiction to produce a version of maternity that seems fundamentally at odds with its hegemonic image. In particular, she compares the way in which seeming and feeling like a good mother substitute for "being" one (possessing some maternal essence) in Thackeray's *Vanity Fair* and Allison Pearson's contemporary novel *I Don't Know How She Does It*.

The essays by Laura Green and Heather Milton, in contrast, explore the ideal in terms of maternal potency. In "'Long, Long Disappointment': Maternal Failure and Masculine Exhaustion in Margaret Oliphant's *Autobiography*," Laura Green finds in Oliphant a figure who combines the public and the maternal in complicated ways. Writing to support her family, Oliphant does not feel the conventional conflict about neglecting her children for her career, but rather regrets the toll economic pressure takes on her art and shakes off guilt when confronting her sons' disappointing lives, diluting the notion of all-powerful maternal influence. Heather Milton turns to Eliot's novel *Felix Holt* to expose maternal influence as a profoundly negative rather than a positive force. In "'Bland, Adoring, and Gently Tearful Women': Debunking the Maternal Ideal in George Eliot's *Felix Holt,*" Milton measures the costs of "successful" maternity, as the self-sacrificing mother both frustrates herself and damages her son by raising him to perpetuate the destructive operations of male privilege. Together, the essays of Green and Milton call into question both the influence and the value of the maternal ideal.

In "Elderly Mothers and Middle-Aged Daughters in Charles Dickens's *Dombey and Son,*" Teresa Mangum approaches the maternal ideal through the relationship between aging mothers and middle-aged daughters, showing how the mothering failures of the paired characters "Cleopatra" and "Good Mrs. Brown" actually provide their adult daughters with crucial opportunities for human development. The very failure of these mothers to dispense unselfish love creates the narrative space for Edith Dombey and Alice Brown to move beyond their own narrowly self-centered emotional paradigms. Thus while Milton's reading of *Felix Holt* reveals the destructiveness of the "ideal," selfless mother, Mangum's reading of *Dombey and Son* reveals the narrative and moral potentialities of maternal failures.

The collection's second section—"'Bad Mothers': Caretaking, Class, and Maternal Violence"—takes destructive motherhood itself as its focus, concentrating specifically on literary and historical examples of maternal failure. The four essays in this section present spectacular departures from the ideal of maternal nurturance, exploring transgressions that do not involve the familiar theme of deviant sexuality. Presenting caretaking in concrete contexts rather than relying on abstract claims about mothers as spiritual guides, these essays reveal a surprising range of cultural attitudes toward failed mothers. Analyzing the portrayal of maternal alcoholism in religious fiction in "Unforgiven: Drunken Mothers in Hesba Stretton's Religious Tract Society and Scottish Temperance League Fiction," Deborah Denenholz Morse traces the bourgeois narrative conventions that consign working-class mothers to death while granting middle-class mothers a second chance at maternity. In "Infant Doping and Middle-Class Motherhood: Opium Warnings and Charlotte Yonge's *The Daisy Chain,*" Dara Rossman Regaignon uncovers a complex, perhaps unconscious ambivalence about middle-class mothers' actual duties in the home. Focusing on the mediation of the working-class nurse's paid daily care, Regaignon demonstrates the novel's unexpected if unstated conclusion that the middle-class mother is toxic to her children, both physically and psychologically.

The essays in this section also demonstrate the ways in which class identities placed the maternal ideal in dialogue with other claims and narratives. In this vein, Frost's and Sussex's essays restore an economic dimension to motherhood. In "Motherhood on Trial: Violence and Unwed Mothers in Victorian England," Ginger Frost examines trials involving violence and unwed mothers, both as victims and perpetrators, finding that working-class status and an idealized conception of maternal instinct actually worked together to aid women on trial, even those accused of infanticide. Similarly, Lucy Sussex's essay, "A Murdering Mother: Frances Knorr" examines the issue of infanticide through the trial of a working-class woman executed in Australia. Although the trial itself indicted her as a failed mother, the public sympathized with her extreme emotional and economic distress. Taken together, these essays demonstrate that class does not operate consistently across narratives, contexts, and settings, but takes on different meanings and leads to different outcomes. The familiar opposition between the good middle-class mother and the bad working-class one is upheld in Morse's essay, challenged in the sympathetic reception of Frost's and Sussex's violent working-class mothers, and overturned in *The Daisy Chain*, in which the working-class nurse actually provides superior care.

In the collection's third section, "Maternity and Difference: Nation, Race, and Empire," foreign places and other races refigure maternity, while maternity alters expected power structures on a small scale, complicating hierarchical relations between individuals of different races and rewriting the authority of the English narrator in travel narratives. In "'My Own Dear Sons': Discursive Maternity and Proper British Bodies in *Wonderful Adventures of Mrs. Seacole in Many Lands*," Deirdre H. McMahon analyzes the representation of Mother Seacole, a black, childless woman who practiced a version of the public mothering of nurses and philanthropists in her support of Crimean troops. McMahon considers both the challenge Mother Seacole poses to the ideal's biological and racial origin and the consolidation of the ideal as Seacole's symbolic maternity masks the privations of actual women and children on the front. Similarly, in "Conceiving the Nation: Visions and Versions of Colonial Prenatality," Deirdre Osborne examines short stories by white Australian authors to argue that colonial women's displacement from the British imperial center allows them to revise representations of gender, racial, and class identities.

The remaining two essays in this section examine models of motherhood in which the bonds between mother and child are nonbiological and emphatically marked by racial difference. In "Orphan Stories and

Maternal Legacies in Charlotte Brontë," Mary Jean Corbett looks at the difference race makes in Brontë's adult fiction and juvenilia, exploring the role of the elusive, imagined birth mother in ambivalent representations of adoption as rescue, transformation, and colonization. Race and maternity are also imbricated with Britain's colonial project in Cara Murray's essay, "Distance Mothering and the 'Cradle Lands': Imperial Motherhood and Lady Duff Gordon's *Letters from Egypt.*" Through an examination of Duff's published letters, Murray explores the paradoxical experience of the mother who leaves her children in England to mother and be mothered by a racial other in a foreign setting. In these essays, the power of whiteness is apparent, though in different ways. As in part 2, this grouping both reflects familiar maternal oppositions, now extended to the categories of race and empire, and shows how their apparent fixity was reworked in specific contexts. Identity and power do not line up neatly and predictably within these dyads—white versus black, British versus non-British. Rather, power operates in complex ways and subjective categories are revealed as plastic, as black and colonial women in McMahon's and Osborne's essays both fulfill and revise the maternal ideal, and as the unseating of biological maternity as the privileged form of motherhood ruptures the racial boundaries of the family in essays by Corbett and Murray.

The final section of the collection focuses on the maternal body. The maternal body is a critical point of intervention, because it is the site that at once naturalizes maternity, identifying it with biological femininity, and challenges the spiritual essence of maternity. These essays reimagine the angelic, ethereal mother as an embodied presence, exploring the material, erotic, and figurative possibilities of the maternal body. In "The Text as Child: Gender/Sex and Metaphors of Maternity at the *Fin de Siècle,*" Brenda R. Weber returns the collection to the role of the woman writer, exploring attempts to unify maternity and artistic ambition. Examining the use of gestation and childbirth as metaphors for the creative process in the novels of three late-century women authors—Elizabeth Robins, Mary Cholmondeley, and Rhoda Broughton—Weber concludes that this rhetoric both normalized and limited their artistic ambitions, disciplining the possibilities of the mind by restricting the representations of the physical body. While Weber explores the complicated metaphorics of female creativity, Lillian E. Craton and Ellen Bayuk Rosenman read the maternal body as an enticing physical presence. In "The Widest Lap: Fatness, Fasting, and Nurturance in Nineteenth-Century Fiction," Craton analyzes literary celebrations of ample maternal figures, generally of the working class, as a critique of the bourgeois emphasis on self-denial, discovering a tacit argument connecting literal self-nourishment with the ability to care emotionally for others. Rosenman examines a different form of embodied maternal desire in her essay, "Mother Love: Edith Simcox, Maternity, and Lesbian Erotics," which takes up the subject of same-sex eroticism. Detaching maternity from heterosexuality, Simcox's *Autobiography of a Shirtmaker* and *Episodes in the Lives of Men, Women, and Lovers* use mother-worship to both mask and authorize lesbian desire, altering the conventions of Victorian life writing in the process.

The wide-ranging scope of these essays, along with the shifting theoretical underpinnings of this collection as a whole, precludes the emergence of any single conclusion about Victorian motherhood. Paradoxically, this lack of a conclusion is perhaps the most important contribution of the collection. We hope it will encourage scholars to consider motherhood a "live" issue, posing a surprising range of questions and challenges in its many incarnations. As even these brief summaries should suggest, motherhood cannot be understood apart from its emergence through and with other categories, particularly race, class, and national/geographical setting. It takes on distinct meanings in specific contexts that this collection can only begin to explore.

Moreover, while our groupings suggest obvious contributions to familiar areas of study, demonstrating the multiple articulations of motherhood in relation to the crucial categories of class, race, and the body, it should also be obvious that these essays also connect along other axes. These alternative connections underscore and extend the manifold and context-specific nature of Victorian motherhood. Readers might consider the relationships among essays that deal with adoptive, constructed, or symbolic families, for example. Such familial ties cross not only class lines, as Mangum and Craton show in their readings of Dickens's novels, but also racial boundaries, as demonstrated in McMahon's analysis of Mary Seacole's memoir, Corbett's reading of Brontë's adoption fictions, and Murray's account of Lady Duff Gordon's letters. Also represented in these essays are a few of the many examples of gender-crossing motherhood—the many male figures who stand in for absent or delinquent biological mothers to provide maternal nurture and domestic security for needy children. Morse's readings of Hesba Stretton's fictions reveal several such male mothers, as does Mangum's portrait of Captain Cuttle and Sol Gills. The families created through these crossings are bound together by interest, emotion, shared experience, and the imaginations of the authors who describe them. When biological motherhood fails or loses its hold, other forms of maternity, other motherlike forms of nurturance, and other definitions of "family" come into being. Concomitantly, these new formations wash back onto biological maternity, questioning its emotional claims and cultural cogency.

Alternatively, readers might explore the diverse representations and self-representations of women writers to move beyond the simple, uniform tension between "mother" and "writer." Perhaps surprisingly, Oliphant, often associated with mid-Victorian culture, found little gender dissonance in her professional identity, while Weber's *fin-de-siècle* authors worked strenuously to recuperate their writing as a form of motherhood. Writing from unconventional subject positions, lesbian Edith Simcox and the Australian authors of Osborne's essay remake narrative conventions as they consciously rethink gender roles, departing from the traditions of realism, the erotic plot, the family romance, and the female bildungsroman, while Duff Gordon's maternal perspective alters the conventions of travel writing. Their artistic experiments point to the active relationship between literary forms and cultural values, expanding the category of "Victorian literature" in terms of both subject matter and literary technique.

Essays by d'Albertis, Regaignon, and Craton can be read together as investigations of the relationship between maternity as a cultural ideal and mothering as a set of physical practices. While d'Albertis untangles the ways in which the actual work of mothering can be refigured as "mere" appearance, Regaignon and Craton uncover a thread of doubt about the ways in which bourgeois womanhood—apparently the model for ideal maternity—might in fact be entirely unsuited for the job because of the very characteristics that underlie its idealization. One might also include Rosenman's essay, which argues that physical acts of mothering made the mother's body erotically available for distinctly unconventional uses. These essays also intersect with those of McMahon and Murray, in which actual caretaking is successfully carried out by a woman who is not the actual mother of her charges. While Regaignon's and Craton's texts imply that mothering is best performed by working-class surrogates, who have the bodily strength and the knowledge to discharge it more successfully than actual middle-class mothers, McMahon's and Murray's essays present the unexpected successes of voluntary and symbolic mothers who, unlike domestic employees, found forms of agency in these roles.

While attention to the dynamic interplay of identities yields new insights into even the best-known canonical novels, as Mangum and Corbett show us, this collection also benefits from the recovery of unfamiliar texts and sources. Moving beyond the canon, which by now includes familiar social historical sources such as Sarah Stickney Ellis's conduct books and John Ruskin's *Sesame and Lilies,* our authors canvas new cultural spaces, revealing heterogeneous fields of thought and practice. By rethinking the colonies as distinctive environments rather than as subordinate extensions of the British imperial center, several essays analyze the ways in which different colonial and national settings changed the experience of motherhood. In others, the courtroom and the scaffold reveal sympathetic recognitions of the stresses and responsibilities of the lived experience of motherhood. We seek to open up new textual spaces as well. Forgotten novels and short stories, letters and diaries, claim authority alongside more familiar texts. In spite of decades of Victorian studies, in which literary and cultural sources have been read in tandem, an enormous amount of material awaits serious investigation.

For some, the work of recovery driven by questions of female agency and transgression might seem to have run its course.[12] Mary Poovey, for instance, has recently parodied her own earlier work in the mock recovery of the writer Ellen Pickering. According to Poovey, while Pickering's forgotten novels can be shown to demonstrate the requisite mix of convention and subversion to attract critical attention, they are uninteresting and derivative because of their very display of these overly familiar themes. While, like Poovey, we wish to avoid recycling predictable stories, our collection attests to the value of recovery work. Alison Booth's *How to Make It as a Woman* and Sally Mitchell's *Frances Power Cobb: Victorian Feminist, Journalist, Reformer* (2004) represent only two examples of recent scholarship whose recovery of lesser-known women has expanded our sense of Victorian norms. It is hard to underestimate the importance of archival research in providing a full, complex understanding of the nineteenth century. Poovey's characterization of Pickering's lack of originality points, paradoxically, to the need for such work. To underscore the predictability of the submission/transgression binary, Poovey uses the trope of maternity: Pickering the good mother-author supports conventional female characters and the happy ending of the marriage plot, while Pickering "the bad mother" is also drawn to rebellious characters and stories (447). As Poovey recognizes, maternity has automatically invoked—and quintessentially expressed—simple binaries of femininity. We hope that *Other Mothers* will begin to undo this apparent inevitable association, defamiliarizing maternity to invite new investigations into its uncharted complexities.

---

[12] See also "Gender Studies in the Twenty-First Century: An Interview with Christopher Lane and Alison Booth," in which Lane and Booth acknowledge and dispute the idea that the recovery of lesser-known women writers is outmoded.

Works Cited

Adams, James Eli. *Dandies and Desert Saints: Styles of Victorian Manhood*. Ithaca: Cornell University Press, 1995.

Alexander, Lynn M. *Women, Work, and Representation: Needlewomen in Victorian Art and Literature*. Athens: Ohio University Press, 2003.

Anderson, Amanda. *The Way We Argue Now: A Study in the Cultures of Theory*. Princeton: Princeton University Press, 2006.

———. *The Powers of Distance: Cosmopolitanism and the Cultivation of Detachment*. Princeton: Princeton University Press, 2001.

———. *Tainted Souls and Painted Faces: The Rhetoric of Fallenness in Victorian Culture*. Ithaca: Cornell University Press, 1993.

Armstrong, Nancy. *Desire and Domestic Fiction: A Political History of the Novel*. Oxford: Oxford University Press, 1987.

Barret-Duchcrocq, Françoise. *Love in the Time of Victoria: Sexuality and Desire among Working-Class Men and Women in Nineteenth-Century London*. Trans. John Howe. New York: Penguin, 1989, 1991.

Beetham, Margaret. *A Magazine Of Her Own: Domesticity and Desire in the Woman's Magazine*. London: Routledge, 1996.

Bobotis, Andrea. "Rival Maternities: Maud Gonne, Queen Victorian, and the Reign of the Political Mother." *Victorian Studies* 49 (2006): 63–84.

Booth, Alison. *How to Make It as a Woman: Collective Biographical History from Victoria to the Present*. Chicago: University of Chicago Press, 2004.

Brody, Jennifer. *Impossible Purities: Blackness, Femininity, and Victorian Culture*. Durham: Duke University Press, 1998.

Chase, Karen, and Michael Levenson. *The Spectacle of Intimacy: A Public Life for the Victorian Family*. Princeton: Princeton University Press, 2000.

Clark, Anna. *The Struggle for Breeches: Gender and the Making of the British Working Class*. Berkeley: University of California Press, 1995.

Cohen, Monica. *Professional Domesticity in the Victorian Novel: Women, Work and Home*. Cambridge: Cambridge University Press, 1998.

Cohen, William A. *Sexual Scandal: The Private Parts of Victorian Fiction*. Durham: Duke University Press, 1996.

Corbett, Mary Jean. *Representing Femininity: Middle-Class Subjectivity in Victorian and Edwardian Women's Autobiographies*. Oxford: Oxford University Press, 1992.

Davidoff, Leonore, and Catherine Hall. *Family Fortunes: Men and Women of the English Middle Class, 1780–1850*. Chicago: University of Chicago Press, 1987.

Davis, Tracy. *Actresses and Working Women: Their Social Identity in Victorian Culture*. London: Routledge, 1991.

Dellamora, Richard, ed. *Victorian Sexual Dissidence*. Ithaca: Cornell University Press, 1999.

Dever, Carolyn. *Death and the Mother from Freud to Dickens: Victorian Fiction and the Anxiety of Origins*. Cambridge: Cambridge University Press, 1998.

Dowling, Linda. *Hellenism and Homosexuality in Victorian Oxford*. Ithaca: Cornell University Press, 1994.

Elliott, Dorice Williams. *The Angel Out of the House: Philanthropy and Gender in Nineteenth-Century England*. Charlottesville: University Press of Virginia, 2002.

Fluhr, Nicole. "'Their Calling Me "Mother" Was Not, I Think, Altogether Unmeaning':

Mary Seacole's Maternal Personae." *Victorian Literature and Culture* 34.1 (2006): 95–113.

Frost, Ginger. *Promises Broken: Courtship, Class, and Gender in Victorian England.* Charlottesville: University Press of Virginia, 1995.

Gagnier, Regenia. *Subjectivities: A History of Self-Representation in Britain, 1832–1920.* Oxford: Oxford University Press, 1991.

"Gender Studies in the Twenty-First Century: An Interview with Christopher Lane and Alison Booth." *Nineteenth-Century Gender Studies* 3.1 (2007). http://www.ncgsjournal.com/issue31/rosenman.htm.

Gilbert, Sandra, and Susan Gubar. *The Madwoman in the Attic: The Woman Writer and the Nineteenth-Century Literary Imagination.* New Haven: Yale University Press, 1979.

Hall, Catherine. *Civilizing Subjects: Metropole and Colony in the English Imagination.* Chicago: University of Chicago Press, 2002.

———. *Defining the Nation: Class, Race, Gender and the British Reform Act of 1867.* Cambridge: Cambridge University Press, 2000.

Hall, Donald, ed. *Muscular Christianity: Embodying the Victorian Age.* Cambridge: Cambridge University Press, 1994.

Homans, Margaret. *Bearing the Word: Language and Female Experience in Nineteenth-Century Women's Writing.* Chicago: University of Chicago Press, 1986.

Hughes, Kathryn. *The Victorian Governess.* Hambledon and London: Continuum International Publishing Group, 2003.

Huneault, Kristina. *Difficult Subjects: Working Women and Visual Culture in Britain, 1880–1914.* Aldershot, UK: Ashgate, 2002.

Johnson, Patricia. *Hidden Hands: Working-Class Women and Victorian Social-Problem Fiction.* Athens: Ohio University Press, 2001.

Kestner, Joseph. *Masculinities in Victorian Painting.* Aldershot, UK: Scolar Press, 1995.

Koven, Seth. *Slumming: Sexual and Social Politics in Victorian London.* Princeton: Princeton University Press, 2004.

Lane, Christopher. *The Burdens of Intimacy: Psychoanalysis and Victorian Masculinity.* Chicago: University of Chicago Press, 1999.

Langland, Elizabeth. *Nobody's Angels: Middle-Class Women and Domestic Ideology in Victorian Culture.* Ithaca: Cornell University Press, 1995.

Lecaros, Cecilia Wadsö. *The Victorian Governess Novel.* Lund, Sweden: Lund University Press, 2001.

Levine, Caroline. "Strategic Formalism: Toward a New Method of Cultural Studies." *Victorian Studies* 48.4 (2006): 625–57.

Levy, Anita. *Other Women: The Writing of Class, Race, and Gender, 1832–1989.* Princeton: Princeton University Press, 1991.

Marcus, Sharon. *Between Women: Friendship, Desire, and Marriage in Victorian England.* Princeton: Princeton University Press, 2007.

Matus, Jill. *Unstable Bodies: Victorian Representations of Sexuality and Maternity.* Manchester: Manchester University Press, 1995.

Mavor, Carol. *Pleasures Taken: Performances of Sexuality and Loss in Victorian Photographs.* Durham: Duke University Press, 1995.

McClintock, Anne. *Imperial Leather: Race, Gender and Sexuality in the Colonial Contest.* New York and London: Routledge, 1995.

Mermin, Dorothy. *Godiva's Ride: Women of Letters in England, 1830–1880.* Bloomington: Indianapolis University Press, 1993.

Miller, Andrew, and James Eli Adams, eds. *Sexualities in Victorian Britain*. Bloomington: Indiana University Press, 1996.

Mitchell, Sally. *Frances Power Cobb: Victorian Feminist, Journalist, Reformer*. Charlottesville: University Press of Virginia, 2004.

Munich, Adrienne. *Queen Victoria's Secrets*. New York: Columbia University Press, 1996.

Munich, Adrienne, and Margaret Homans. *Remaking Queen Victoria*. Cambridge: Cambridge University Press, 1997.

Nord, Deborah Epstein. *Walking the Victorian Streets: Women, Representation and the City*. Ithaca: Cornell University Press, 1995.

Peterson, M. Jeanne. *Family, Love, and Work in the Lives of Victorian Gentlewomen*. Bloomington: Indiana University Press, 1989.

Poovey, Mary. "Recovering Ellen Pickering." *Yale Journal of Criticism* 13.2 (2000): 437–52.

———. *Uneven Developments: The Ideological Work of Gender in Mid-Victorian England*. Chicago: University of Chicago Press, 1988.

Ross, Ellen. *Love and Toil: Motherhood in Outcast London, 1870–1918*. Oxford: Oxford University Press, 1993.

Sedgwick, Eve Kosofsky. *Touching/Feeling: Affect, Pedagogy, Performativity*. Durham: Duke University Press, 2003.

Shuttleworth, Sally. In "Demonic Mothers: Ideologies of Bourgeois Motherhood in the Mid-Victorian Era." *Rewriting the Victorians: Theory, History and the Politics of Gender*. Ed. Linda M. Shires. New York: Routledge, 1992. 31–51.

Stoler, Ann Laura. *Carnal Knowledge and Imperial Power: Race and the Intimate in Imperial Rule*. Berkeley: University of California Press, 2002.

Sussman, Herbert. *Victorian Masculinities; Manhood and Masculine Politics in Early Victorian Literature and Art*. Cambridge: Cambridge University Press, 1995.

Swindells, Julia. *Victorian Writing and Working Women*. Minneapolis: University of Minnesota Press, 1985.

Tosh, John. *A Man's Place: Masculinity and the Middle-Class Home in Victorian England*. New Haven: Yale University Press, 1999.

Vinicus, Martha. *Intimate Friends: Women Who Loved Women, 1778–1928*. Chicago: University of Chicago Press, 2004.

———. *Independent Women: Work and Community for Single Women, 1850–1920*. Chicago: University of Chicago Press, 1985.

———. *Suffer and Be Still: Women in the Victorian Age*. Bloomington: Indiana University Press, 1973.

Walkowitz, Judith. *City of Dreadful Delight: Narratives of Sexual Danger of Late-Victorian London*. Chicago: University of Chicago Press, 1992.

Yeazell, Ruth Bernard. *Fictions of Modesty: Women and Courtship in the English Novel*. Chicago: University of Chicago, 1991.

Young, Arlene. *Culture, Class, and Gender in the Victorian Novel: Gentlemen, Gents, and Working Women*. New York: St. Martin's Press, 1999.

PART I

Beyond the Maternal Ideal

CHAPTER 1

"How to Be a Domestic Goddess" Redux

Deirdre d'Albertis

> We want to feel not like a postmodern, post feminist, overstretched modern woman, but rather, a domestic goddess, trailing nutmeggy fumes of baking pie in our languorous wake. So what I am talking about is not being a domestic goddess, exactly, but feeling like one.
> —Nigella Lawson, *How to Be a Domestic Goddess: Baking and the Art of Comfort Cooking* (2001)

Domesticity is on an upswing. Again. The phenomenal success of British sexpot/media chef Nigella Lawson points to a series of paradoxes that seem particularly impossible for contemporary middle-class women to negotiate. Lawson, who avowedly loves to eat, presents her own body as an object of delectation—desirable even as it indulges in "forbidden" carbohydrates and sweets denied to less divinely corporeal women. Like her more matronly forerunner, Martha Stewart, Lawson purveys a "feeling"—or what Walter Benjamin would have described as the auratic effect—of domesticity. She markets the fumes rather than fundaments of a by-now fetishized art of household management, much the same sort of recondite and increasingly unfamiliar body of knowledge offered to the tyro by Cheryl Mendelson, author of the 1999 publishing sensation *Home Comforts: The Art and Science of Keeping House*. The rhetorical stress in Lawson's paean to the art of "comfort cooking" is on a rejection of modernity (along with its avatar, "the overstretched modern woman"). Feminism brings middle-class (read professional, consumerist) women not liberation but an oppressive regime of "post"-living in every sense. The answer to the contradictions of twenty-first-century gender politics, it would seem, is to return to a time when feminism didn't obtain, but to return via a carefully orchestrated—and admittedly illusionistic—sense of embodiment rather than action, being rather than doing.

One might observe, optimistically, that the marketing of home comforts today addresses a more diverse public than did the tomes of Sarah Stickney Ellis and Isabella Beeton. Celebrity chefs—both male and female—appeal to single, upwardly mobile consumers of both sexes, for instance, and—as the Stewart Omnimedia empire makes clear—a new aesthetics and indeed demographics of domesticity has exceeded the heteronormative assumption of such mid-twentieth-century housewifery guides as *Redbook* and *Good Housekeeping*. Yet it is my contention here that despite the apparent uncoupling of home and gender, or of home and marriage, it is still the unholy trinity of domesticity, maternity, and feminism that continues to bedevil our thinking about what it means to produce, as well as to maintain, an affect of domesticity—the complex of feeling we continue to associate with private life. It still takes a wife or mother (even if it is a man who chooses to fill the role) to make a home of the archetypal sort. The very fact that mothering remains such a huge source of conflict within feminism, as well as in the larger culture (Judith Warner, for example, has received a lot of press lately for her protest against the "perfect madness" of a middle-class "Mommy Mystique"), reinforces the ongoing ideological centrality of what philosopher Patrice DiQuinzio usefully refers to as "the impossibility of motherhood."[1]

What interests me about this moment is the fact that we have seen it before.[2] The Victorian household economy, so frequently invoked by present-day ideologues as the prototype of authentic domesticity, was also a fragile construct, one equally oriented toward feeling (rather than actually behaving) like a domestic goddess. The term itself is an oxymoron (as Roseanne Barr surely recognized a few years ago when she tried to pitch a network series bearing the same title): true domestics are workers, members of a distinctly unglamorous service economy, and—as such—hardly goddess material.[3] Domesticity encompasses both the pragmatic and the

---

[1] DiQuinzio examines how "the resurgence of the woman's movement in the second half of the twentieth century has intensified the contention surrounding mothering," pointing out how "it is impossible to be a mother in the sense implied by mother*hood,* which suggests an essential identity or state of being." "Essential motherhood" as such cannot be said to exist, in other words (vii).

[2] In discussing the continuity between Victorian and contemporary conceptions of consumer domesticity, I want to bear in mind Jay Clayton's suggestion that "cultural studies should not shy away from tracing long historical relationships between the past and present. In doing so, however, it must always attend equally to both the anomalous and the analogous. Continuity is a part of historical experience, but it exists side by side with zones of difference, areas of discontinuity and rupture" (36).

[3] For a thorough discussion of how "the lifestyles of the First World are made possible by a global transfer of the services associated with a wife's traditional role—child care, home making, and sex—from poor countries to rich ones," see Ehrenreich and Hochschild (40).

ideal, the state of being intimately known and located within a network of (largely involuntary) relations, as well as a concept of the most hallowed meanings one might wish to attach to such relations.

In this essay I would like to begin by invoking the example of one representative contemporary "social problem" novel, Allison Pearson's 2002 best seller *I Don't Know How She Does It* ("the definitive social comedy of working motherhood," according to the *Washington Post*), before turning to the "domestic goddess" in an earlier incarnation: William Makepeace Thackeray's *Vanity Fair* (1847–8) with its highly equivocal treatment of domesticity, maternity, and heterosexual power relations. Pearson's and Thackeray's texts may be read as symptomatic of a frustrated desire for an elusive "bread-and-butter paradise" of domesticity (Thackeray 584) stimulated in both twenty-first and nineteenth-century writers by the face-off between liberal feminism—with its resort to a rhetoric of individualism and rights—and a continually regenerating "cult of true womanhood."

It is around maternity, in particular, that both Pearson and Thackeray locate their critique of domesticity.[4] After numerous mishaps, Pearson's heroine, Kate Reddy, ends up renouncing her career as a hedge-fund manager in order more seriously to mother her two children, as well as to save her foundering marriage. Contrary to such a conclusion, much of the humor of the book arises from the protagonist's failure to live up to her own internalized standards of domesticity (even as she resists and lampoons them). Although Pearson attempts to rectify the home/work imbalance formally (just as mid-Victorian social problem novelists attempted to overcome the contradictions of industrial capitalism via the marriage plot), her narrative is largely animated by Kate's attempts to buy or simulate "domestic bliss," rather than actually conjure it up "from scratch."[5] The novel opens in the middle of the night with the harried, jet-lagged narrator "distressing" store-bought mince pies as a ploy to convince stay-at-home mothers and teachers at her daughter's school that they are her own: "Discarding the Sainsbury luxury packaging, I wrinkle the pies out of their pleated foil cups, place them on a chopping board and bring down a rolling pin on their blameless floury faces. This is not as easy as it sounds, believe me. . . . [H]ome-made is what I am after here. Home is where the heart is. Home

[4] The ambivalent equation of domesticity with maternity in both texts runs counter, in an important sense, to Carolyn Dever's recent claim that "the maternal ideal in fiction thus takes its shape and power in the context of almost complete maternal absence, and . . . through the necessary vehicle of such a void" (xi). Rather than investigate a poetics of maternal loss, I am interested here in examining an illusion—the "domestic goddess"—in relation to actual mothering practices in these narratives.

[5] A recent manual, *Domestic Bliss: Simple Ways to Add Style to Your Life,* speaks to this same desire (see Konig).

is where the good mother is, baking for her children" (3). Meant to stand as a testament to maternal virtue, the "blameless" if provoking pies actually represent Kate's striving after an unrealizable experience: *being* (rather than merely appearing as) a good mother. Her labor, concentrated on the unmaking of commercially produced comfort food, is paradoxical in that it is work dedicated to manufacturing a sign (rather than an artifact) of authentic maternity. Why not simply bake the pies themselves? Domesticity, the arrangements one can actually see in the temporal and spatial organization of a home, is made to stand in for the invisible work of nurturance associated with raising children. Any elision between the two leads to problems of representation, of course, for a well-kept house is no true indication of well-parented offspring. Thus the tension between seeming and being most reliably crops up in this confusion between homemaking and caregiving in both texts.

Pearson suggests that it is this sort of work which best typifies contemporary motherhood, blurring the boundaries between "good" and "bad" mothering by focusing on how a "feeling" of domesticity has become increasingly dislocated from traditional reproductive tasks. In order to feel like a "good" mother, Kate Reddy must persuade someone (other than herself) that her contribution to the school's annual carol concert is authentic. The commodification of domesticity is experienced less as alienating than as necessary within a social domain that valorizes the "home-made," even as it supports a market predicated upon the decline of domestic production. In Pearson's novel, domestic authority is expressed largely through consumer taste and preference, a twenty-first-century version of what Ruskin praised as the Victorian woman's power of "sweet ordering, arrangement, and decision" (77). Even if the novel finally rejects this way of life and subscribes to a fairly conservative account of maternity (as I believe it does), it nevertheless operates on the premise that the tension between seeming and being drives most women's experience of mothering, regardless of their choices. Indeed, the current proliferation of advice literature designed to guide upper-middle-class women in their purchasing of affect bears out a widespread conflation of commerce and domesticity in contemporary Britain and America.

It may come as a shock, then, to realize that such confusion of commerce with domesticity is as persistent as Anglo-American notions of home itself. Judith Flanders writes in her compendious history, *Inside the Victorian Home,* that "the Victorian house became defined as a refuge, a place apart from the sordid rules of commercial life, with different morals, different rules, different guidelines to protect the soul from being consumed by commerce. Or so it seemed" (5). In fact, as both Warner and Thad Logan have demonstrated, the moral dimension of Victorian domesticity was bound up from the outset with "the growth of a commodity culture and the development of consumer desire" (Logan 26). If, in the domestic sphere, women "were, in some sense, its inmates," Logan points out, "they were also its producers, its curators, and its ornaments" (26). As producers, curators, and ornaments of the middle-class home, women were required to manage an empire of things, including their own persons, all the while effacing the materiality of its origins. When Nigella Lawson promises her reader the experience of "feeling" like a domestic goddess, she also promises to overcome an imprisoning prospect of stasis—surely the essence of "home"—in favor of performance and multiple subject positions: one might choose first to produce, and then to curate, one's appearance as ornament. Nothing is fixed or constraining in such an account of domesticity. Also, one might argue, nothing is "real": all that is solid melts in air.

Thackeray forcefully portrays the production and curation of domesticity as a morally legible process, albeit in a negative register: "[I]f you are not guilty have a care of appearances," warns the narrator of *Vanity Fair*, "which are as ruinous as guilt" (445). He acknowledges the imperative to seem virtuous, even as he enforces as meaningful a distinction between mere reputation and actual conduct. Alternating between satire at the expense of cynical worldlings and sentimental celebration of those whom Becky Sharp derides as "children and child-lovers" (455), Thackeray's narrator promotes a specific model of domestic virtue in the form of Amelia Sedley:

> [V]ery likely the Heroic Female character which ladies admire is a more glorious and beautiful object than the kind, fresh, smiling, artless, tender little *domestic goddess,* whom men are inclined to worship—yet the latter and inferior sort of women must have this consolation—that the men *do* admire them after all:—and—that, in spite of all our kind friends' warnings and protests, we go on in our desperate error and folly, and shall to the end of the chapter.... I am tempted to think that to be despised by her sex is a very great compliment to a woman. (115–16; emphasis added)

Amelia is identified, at least initially, as the heroine of *Vanity Fair,* and this is because, as the above passage makes clear, she is described, however ironically, as a genuine incarnation of the "domestic goddess." Unlike the "Heroic Female," she truly is a "glorious and beautiful object," much admired by men, even as she is denigrated by women. Distinguished by a lack of worldliness, Amelia's domesticity is rooted not in capable household management (or doing anything at all), but in obliviousness to anything beyond her strictly limited family circle. In this sense, we might say that Thackeray, like Lawson, is interested not so much in Amelia "being a domestic goddess," as in "feeling like one." Yet feeling for Thackeray denotes an outward orientation, unlike Lawson's unabashedly autotelic one. A woman's capacity for feeling—without hope of reciprocity—first for her husband, and then more importantly for her son, is what is at stake, not self-delighting, sensual enjoyment of home pleasures. In a novel dedicated to anatomizing the human condition as synonymous with avarice and ambition, "the bootless love of women for children in Vanity Fair" (497) marks maternal virtue as the sine qua non of domestic exceptionalism. By definition, Amelia's love can never be compensated for or repaid; indeed, it is the one indispensable trait of domesticity that it must explicitly transcend market relations.

In contrast to Amelia's self-sacrificing, apparently disinterested maternity, Becky Sharp would seem to stand for every kind of falseness of which human beings are capable. "Unsurpassable in lies" (524), Becky's character is predicated upon a spectacular disregard for domestic virtue. She is exposed repeatedly, both by Thackeray's narrator and his characters, as "a wicked woman—a heartless mother, a false wife" (549). Yet she, too, has the power to inspire worship. In the *role* of wife and mother, she fascinates Rawdon Crawley as well as their son with her mastery of appearances. She knows, in other words, how to make people "feel" for her:

> Sometimes—once or twice a week—that lady visited the upper regions in which the child lived. She came like a vivified figure out of the *Magasin des Modes*—blandly smiling in the most beautiful clothes and little gloves and boots. . . . She nodded twice or thrice patronisingly at the little boy, who looked up from his dinner or from the pictures of soldiers he was painting. When she left the room, an odour of rose, or some other magical fragrance, lingered about the nursery. She was an unearthly being in his eyes, superior to his father—to all the world: to be worshipped and admired at a distance. . . . Oh thou poor lonely little benighted boy! Mother is the name for God in the lips and hearts of little children; and here was one who was worshipping a stone! (380)

Thackeray recognizes that Becky functions in *Vanity Fair* as another kind of domestic goddess, a foil to Amelia's brand of divinity: "like a vivified figure out of the *Magasin des Modes*," she represents the perfectly self-curated ornament "worshipped and admired at a distance" not only by little boys, but also by most of the grown men she encounters and seduces for her own purposes. Yet this domestic ornament is furiously denounced by Thackeray's narrator as nothing more than stone, not a feeling creature—something Amelia is to a fault—but rather a false idol, insentient, defined in terms of sensational surfaces rather than feeling depths. If Amelia's domestic goddess is "kind, fresh, smiling, artless, tender," and "little," Becky's is "unearthly," "superior," and "distant."

Thackeray emphatically insists upon the difference between Amelia and Becky. Even so, the novel unwittingly dramatizes the difficulty of penetrating beneath the "odour of rose, or some other magical fragrance" that lingers about maternity to distinguish one domestic apparition from the other. In the case of each woman, a heady mixture of desire and wish fulfillment complicates not only the perspective of most characters, but of the narrator himself. Adult male desire is repeatedly figured as formed most powerfully within the mother-child dyad. The unrequited yearning of Major Dobbin for Amelia, for instance, is expressed principally in terms of childish appetite: "[A]nd so William was at liberty to look and long: as the poor boy at school who has no money may sigh after the contents of the tart-woman's tray" (597). Amelia is represented both in terms of the tantalizing "contents" of the tray and the prohibitive "tart-woman" herself, someone who must be paid before a "poor boy's" desired object may be attained. Too much feeling, it would seem, leads to such rhetorical doublings throughout *Vanity Fair*. With both Becky and Amelia, domestic power is ultimately organized around unstable congeries of affect, whether produced from within the woman or without.

Despite his efforts to play them off one another, Thackeray ultimately acknowledges that the economics of any "little domestic establishment" (544) in a "ready-money society" (204) is predicated on such dissonance between appearance and reality:

> The best of women (I have heard my grandmother say) are hypocrites. We don't know how much they hide from us: how watchful they are when they seem most artless and confidential: how often those frank smiles which they wear so easily, are traps to cajole or elude or disarm—I don't mean your mere coquettes, but your domestic models, and paragons of virtue.... We accept this amiable slavishness, and praise a woman for it: we call this pretty treachery truth. A good housewife is of necessity a humbug. (175)

If even "your domestic models" and "paragons of virtue" dissimulate in order "to cajole or elude or disarm" the ones they love, as the narrator (and his grandmother!) suggest, all members of society are complicit in "this amiable slavishness." And to assert, as Thackeray's narrator does, that "a good housewife is of necessity a humbug" is to undermine carefully constructed antinomies within the text: good versus bad mother, domestic goddess versus stone idol.

In Becky Sharp, the consummate professional whose art consists endlessly in inventing "a character for herself" (641), Thackeray explores motherhood as performance with almost clinical detachment. Relentlessly exposed in her lack of maternal affection, Becky is described as utterly indifferent to little Rawdon's physical and emotional needs. As he grows more critical of his mother, her behavior toward him also becomes more hostile: "[T]he consciousness that the child was in the house was a reproach and a pain to her" (444). She notices him chiefly in the presence of others with whom "tenderness [is] the fashion" (451). Eventually losing custody of her son, Becky maintains an interest in Rawdon insofar as he features in narratives retailed for personal gain to would-be sympathizers, "bursting into tears about her boy, and exhibiting the most frantic grief when his name was mentioned, or she saw anybody like him" (641–42). Becky's performance of motherly grief is powerful enough to win over supporters to her cause; only when her nemesis Wenham disabuses a believing Mrs. Alderney is the truth of her maternal ignominy published abroad. Reunited with Amelia after years of vagabondage, Becky finds common ground in their shared experience of motherhood as loss. Becky has given up her son; so has Amelia. Becky's family has disintegrated; so has Amelia's. Both women are unable to maintain their own desires within the prevailing system of domestic values. Economic constraints govern their choices; both women give up a child (whether willingly or not) in response to pressures codified as duty. When each faces the other, childless, she sees reflected a version of herself and the act whereby her motherhood negates itself as an active practice, becoming purely discursive or symbolic: "'The child, my child? Oh yes, my agonies were frightful,' Becky owned, not perhaps without a twinge of conscience. It jarred upon her, to be obliged to commence instantly to tell lies in reply to so much confidence and simplicity" (660).

Pairing female protagonists, Thackeray foregrounds the narcissistic investment of the women who represent both "good" and "bad" mothers in *Vanity Fair*, examining what may well be "selfish" extremes of parental devotion on the one hand and negligence on the other. Neither position is naturalized for Thackeray; both are understood as excessive, perhaps even pathological. If Becky's relations with her child are cold and abusive, Amelia's attachment to her infant clearly borders on fanatical:

> How his mother nursed him, and dressed him, and lived upon him; how she drove away all nurses, and would scarce allow any hand but her own

to touch him . . . need not be told here. This child was her being. Her existence was a maternal caress. She enveloped the feeble and unconscious creature with love and worship. It was her life which the baby drank in from her bosom. Of nights, and when alone, she had stealthy and intense raptures of motherly love, such as God's marvellous care has awarded to the female instinct—joys how far higher and lower than reason—blind beautiful devotions which only women's hearts know. (358, 360)

While Becky's sense of self eclipses that of her offspring, Amelia can be said to exist only insofar as "the child [is] her being." Exalted for her "blind beautiful devotions," she is also shown to be ruled by "female instinct," a faculty described as both "higher and lower than reason" (360). When alone, and given over to the "stealthy and intense raptures of motherly love," Amelia's hyperbolic maternity produces an answering hysterical excess in Thackeray's prose. In this sense, Amelia stands in every bit as troubling a relation to emergent nineteenth-century ideals of impersonal motherhood as does Becky. The domestic goddess excites a surfeit of feeling—too much rapture—either in the mother herself (enveloping as she does an unresponsive, "feeble and unconscious creature") or in her beholders (little Rawdon, Dobbin, and—at times—the narrator). If, as Amanda Anderson has suggested, objective or "professional" conceptions of maternity at midcentury held out the prospect of "far-reaching forms of guardianship and influence, which in turn depended on cultivated practices of moral discernment, impersonal judgment, and even self-crafting" (35), Thackeray's domestic goddesses are strongly allied with what Anderson terms an oppositional "non-reflective femininity" (46). Both Becky and Amelia feel ill at ease in their maternal skin: it is a role that invites excesses both of autonomy and self-sacrifice that are hard to reconcile with forms of "guardianship and influence" ideally attributed to Victorian motherhood.

Thackeray's awareness of the performative dimensions of femininity for both Becky Sharp and Amelia Sedley mobilizes two dominant narratorial modes in *Vanity Fair:* satire and sentiment. Defined as a privileging of feeling over reason, sentiment asserts itself sporadically throughout the novel in passages such as the narrator's hymn to mother and child quoted above. Satire rules the rest. Thackeray's customary mode is satirical; writing to Robert Bell about the reception of *Vanity Fair,* he vows: "I want to leave everybody dissatisfied and unhappy at the end of the story—we ought all to be with our own and other stories. Good God don't I see (in that may-be cracked and warped looking-glass in which I am always looking) my own weaknesses wickednesses lusts follies short-comings?" (qtd. in Shillingsburg 762). According to his own conception of the novel, Thackeray believed that "pathos . . . should be very occasional indeed in humorous works and indicated rather than expressed or expressed very rarely" (762). Yet, for Thackeray, both pathos and humor, or sentiment and satire, aim to influence the reader in a register far from rational. "If you detect the ridicule, and your kindliness is chilled by it, you are slipping into the grasp of Satire. . . ." George Meredith hypothesized in 1897, "the Satirist is a moral agent, often a social scavenger, working on a storage of bile" (73, 76).[6] As a novelistic "moral agent" and "scavenger," Thackeray deliberately affronts his public with bilious misanthropy: "we must lift up our voices about these and howl to a congregation of fools" (762).

Satire and sentiment continue to shape readerly desires for a domesticity of affect, rather than essence, I would argue, in response to threats consistently associated with the politics of liberal feminism. As textual strategies designed to manipulate feeling, rather than to address reason, satire and sentiment are still the preferred rhetorical tools of writers seeking to enshrine, as well as to debunk, a renaissant myth of the domestic goddess in contemporary culture (see de Marneffe; Warner). Becky Sharp anticipates Nigella Lawson's blithe uncoupling of being and seeming by offering a much earlier, and ultimately more radical, account of the origins of virtual domesticity:

> "I think I could be a good woman if I had five thousand a year. I could dawdle about in the nursery, and count the apricots on the wall. I could water plants in a green-house, and pick off dead leaves from the geraniums. I could ask old women about their rheumatisms, and order half-a-crown's worth of soup for the poor. I shouldn't miss it much, out of five thousand a year." . . . And who knows but Rebecca was right in her speculations—and that it was only a question of money and fortune which made a difference between her and an honest woman? (422)

Thackeray's narrator places himself in the bizarre position of critiquing, and yet grudgingly affirming Becky's opportunistic theory of domestic virtue as performance. An honest woman can be made, a domestic goddess can be had—all for the right price.

---

[6] Meredith sees the English as particularly prone to vacillating between satire and sentiment, both terms he opposes to his own preferred notion of the Comic spirit: "Generally, however, the English elect excel in satire, and they are noble humorists. The national disposition is for hard-hitting, with a moral purpose to sanction it; or for a rosy, sometimes a larmoyant, geniality, not unmanly in its verging upon tenderness, and with a singular attraction for thick-headedness, to decorate it with asses' ears and the most beautiful sylvan haloes" (72).

Works Cited

Anderson, Amanda. *The Powers of Distance: Cosmopolitanism and the Cultivation of Detachment.* Princeton: Princeton University Press, 2001.

Clayton, Jay. *Charles Dickens in Cyberspace: The Afterlife of the Nineteenth Century in Postmodern Culture.* New York: Oxford University Press, 2003.

deMarneffe, Daphne. *Maternal Desire: On Children, Love, and the Inner Life.* New York: Little, Brown and Co., 2004.

Dever, Carolyn. *Death and the Mother from Dickens to Freud: Victorian Fiction and the Anxiety of Origins.* New York: Cambridge University Press, 1998.

DiQuinzio, Patrice. *The Impossibility of Motherhood: Feminism, Individualism, and the Problem of Mothering.* New York: Routledge, 1999.

Ehrenreich, Barbara, and Arlie Russell Hochschild. *Global Woman: Nannies, Maids, and Sex Workers in the New Economy.* New York: Henry Holt and Co., 2002.

Flanders, Judith. *Inside the Victorian Home: A Portrait of Domestic Life in Victorian England.* New York: W.W. Norton & Co., 2004.

Konig, Rita. *Domestic Bliss: Simple Ways to Add Style to Your Life.* New York: Fireside, 2003.

Lawson, Nigella. *How to Be a Domestic Goddess: Baking and the Art of Comfort Cooking.* New York: Hyperion, 2001.

Logan, Thad. *The Victorian Parlour.* Cambridge: Cambridge University Press, 2001.

Mendelson, Cheryl. *Home Comforts: The Art and Science of Keeping House.* New York: Scribner, 1999.

Meredith, George. *An Essay on Comedy and the Uses of the Comic Spirit.* New York: Charles Scribner's Sons, 1915.

Pearson, Allison. *I Don't Know How She Does It: The Life of Kate Reddy, Working Mother.* New York: Anchor Books, 2003.

Ruskin, John. *Sesame and Lilies.* Ed. Deborah Epstein Nord. New Haven: Yale University Press, 2002.

Thackeray, William Makepeace. "Letter to Robert Bell, September 3, 1848." In *Vanity Fair.* Ed. Peter L. Shillingsburg. New York: W.W. Norton & Co., 1994.

———. *Vanity Fair.* Ed. Peter L. Shillingsburg. New York: W.W. Norton & Co, 1994.

Warner, Judith. *Perfect Madness: Motherhood in the Age of Anxiety.* New York: Riverhead Books, 2005.

Wood, Mrs. Ellen. *East Lynne.* Ed. Andrew Maunder. Broadview Press, 2000.

CHAPTER 2

"Long, Long Disappointment"

Maternal Failure and Masculine Exhaustion
in Margaret Oliphant's *Autobiography*

LAURA GREEN

While mothers populate the background of Victorian domestic fiction, its protagonists are most frequently daughters—often, indeed, motherless daughters. As Carolyn Dever has argued, "To write a life, in the Victorian period, is to write the story of the loss of the mother" (1).[1] Given that so many Victorian novels about women are structured as "lives," unfolding from youth to a threshold of adulthood signaled, usually, by marriage, it is perhaps inevitable that their dominant point of view should be filial rather than maternal. Premarital motherhood, after all, is a contradiction in terms in the plots of Victorian literature or culture, except as crime or *cause célèbre*.[2]

What is perhaps more surprising is that maternal narratives are largely absent from the smaller canon of Victorian women's autobiographical writings and from critical discussion of that canon. For example, in *Represent-*

---

[1] See also Thaden 3–8. For another influential discussion of the "central myth of our culture's dependence on the mother's absence" as "sorrowfully but fortunately [making] possible the construction of language and culture," see Homans, particularly chapter 1.

[2] Novels in which premarital maternity appears as crime or sensation include Charles Dickens, *Bleak House* (1853); Elizabeth Gaskell, *Ruth* (1853); Elizabeth Barrett Browning, *Aurora Leigh* (1857); George Eliot, *Adam Bede* (1859) and *Felix Holt* (1866); and Thomas Hardy, *Tess of the D'Urbervilles* (1891). In two of these novels—Gaskell's and Hardy's—the mother is also the protagonist, but in both her extramarital maternity leads to her death. Discussing three novels with mother-protagonists—Anne Brontë's *The Tenant of Wildfell Hall* (1848); Mrs. Henry Wood's *East Lynne* (1861); and Caroline Norton's *Lost and Saved* (1863)—Elisabeth Gruner calls them "two generic misfits and one popular sensation novel" (304)—marginal to the mainstream of the daughter's story.

ing Femininity, Mary Jean Corbett's wide survey of middle-class women's autobiography, maternity appears infrequently as one part of the domestic milieu with which such autobiographies must reckon. Linda Peterson's *Traditions of Victorian Women's Autobiography* finds three generic sources for women's autobiography adapted by Victorian writers: spiritual autobiography; domestic memoir; and *"chroniques scandaleuses,"* or (in their later incarnation) artists' lives, among which detailed representations of maternity are rare.

Maternal narrative is missing in these places where one might most expect to find it—in women's domestic novels and autobiographical writings—precisely, I think, because the mother functioned within domestic ideology not only as an ideal but as the icon of an ideal, the apex of the triangle of roles (daughter, mother, wife) that figured womanhood. An icon represents, but cannot possess, a point of view. "The happiest women, like the happiest nations, have no history," George Eliot opines in one of her high-patriarchal moments (*The Mill on the Floss* 494); if domestic ideology posits mothers as the happiest women, then they must be outside of the "histories" of the domestic novel and of autobiography. In the scheme of domestic ideology, the frictionless (history-less) maternal figure was supposed not only to anchor but also to reproduce the gendered division of labor according to which "female nature, which was governed by maternal instinct, was supposedly noncompetitive, nonaggressive, and self-sacrificing—that is, internally consistent and not alienated; male nature, the counterpart, was competitive, aggressive, and acquisitive" (Poovey 77). As for unhappy or unsuccessful mothers—mothers who are inconsistent or alienated, or who, in producing wayward sons and daughters, fail to reproduce masculine and feminine gender roles—the less said, or written, about them, the better.[3] Elizabeth Langland suggests that the "story of the marginal mother" undermines not just representations of gender but also the very genre—the novel—in which they are represented, because "the movement toward narrative closure in the daughter's story is contradicted

---

[3] Perhaps the most striking representations of maternal resistance and disillusion are Eliot's. *Felix Holt*'s Mrs. Transome, for example, is "certainly not one of those bland, adoring, and gently tearful women. After sharing the common dream that when a beautiful man-child was born to her, her cup of happiness would be full, she had travelled through long years apart from that child to find herself at last in the presence of a son of whom she was afraid, who was utterly unmanageable by her, and to whose sentiments in any given case she possessed no key" (198). For an extended analysis of *Felix Holt* as posing a radical challenge to conventional Victorian ideals of motherhood, see Milton in this volume. In *Daniel Deronda,* Daniel's mother, the Princess Halm-Elberstain, notoriously rejects the "common dream" entirely; she "wanted to live out the life that was in me, and not to be hampered with other lives" (536–37).

by the opposing impulse toward radical instability and openness in the mother's tale" ("Patriarchal Ideology" 384).

But if, like the wage-earning middle-class woman, the failed mother was an ideological impossibility and a narrative contradiction, then also like the wage-earning middle-class woman she was nevertheless a historical fact. Given the discomfiting implications for gender ideology of the figure of the failed mother, it is perhaps not surprising that one of the most extended representations of Victorian maternal failure that we have should occur in a document whose relation to publication was ambiguous from the start: Margaret Oliphant's *Autobiography,* which was written in fits and starts over decades and unpublished in her lifetime. The *Autobiography* is also the work of a novelist who, as Barbara Thaden argues, does frequently depict mothers in her novels and "clearly identifies with mothers in her fiction . . . even dead mothers" (20); perhaps not coincidentally, Oliphant was in her lifetime, and largely remains now, a minor and popular rather than a canonical Victorian novelist.

The issue of failure has dominated the reception of Oliphant's work since the publication of her first novel, which a reviewer for the *Athenaeum* characterized in terms of unrealized potential: "Had the passages been condensed within a single volume, the tale would have taken a very high rank" (qtd. in Williams 9). That Oliphant's literary career emphasized quantity at the expense of quality (she published ninety-eight novels as well as biographies, literary histories, reviews, and essays) is an oft-repeated view fostered by Oliphant's own representations of herself in the *Autobiography* as compelled to write furiously to support her extended family. She also repeatedly claims that her children were a much more important production than her writing, and her failure to preserve them more devastating than that of her literary reputation. "At my most ambitious of times I would rather my children had remembered me as their mother, and my friends as their friend. . . . And now that there are no children to whom to leave any memory; and the friends drop day by day, what is the reputation of a circulating library to me?" (136).

Despite such assertions, the figure of Oliphant the author rather than Oliphant the mother has taken center stage in recent feminist reconsiderations. Feminist scholarship has reevaluated her career as shaped by the pressures created by the gender ideologies of Victorian literary production and reception. Recent readings of the *Autobiography* itself have emphasized the gender- and genre-challenging ambivalence, indeterminacy, and nonlinearity of its narrative.[4] In this essay, I take seriously Oliphant's claim

---

[4] Corbett argues that the narrative is shaped by the impossibility "even for middle-class women of the nineteenth century [of] living 'a literary life,' in the sense that term might hold for Mill or Dickens or Trollope" (106); Barros, also comparing Oliphant's *Autobiog-*

in the *Autobiography* that the experience of maternity was at least as important, and as vexed, for her as the experience and representation of a literary life. I analyze the *Autobiography* as representing that experience not only through its moving "outpourings of grief" over her maternal losses but also through its reticence and opacity about the implications of her experience of maternal failure.

Oliphant's autobiographical narrative suggests the weakness of the maternal ideal as an agent of gendered social reproduction even as it celebrates that ideal. The *Autobiography* can be read as a record of the consumption of Oliphant's enormous energies by her doomed efforts to keep several generations of sickly, impecunious brothers, husband, and sons afloat and alive. Oliphant was widowed after seven years of marriage; during her marriage as well as after her husband's death she took on financial (conventionally paternal) as well as emotional (conventionally maternal) responsibilities in order to support not only her own children (of whom two sons, Cyril and Cecco, lived to early adulthood), but also two adult brothers (Willie, whom alcoholism rendered incapable of steady employment, and Frank, who came to live with her after he suffered financial ruin, the loss of his wife, and a nervous breakdown) and her brother Frank's three children.

Despite the extravagance of Oliphant's experience of masculine illness, impecuniousness, and dependency and what Jay calls her "readiness to publicize her view of men as a separate and inferior race" (*Fiction to Herself* 73), she retained an admiration for masculinity in the abstract. "I have learned to take perhaps more a man's view of mortal affairs," she asserts early in the *Autobiography,* comparing herself to Charlotte Brontë and projecting a posthumous reputation for "courage ... and for honesty and honourable dealing" (11). Her sons, whom she educated at Eton and Oxford, became the receptacles of her hopes for the embodiment of these masculine values. But Cyril was apparently an alcoholic (see Williams 146

---

raphy to those of male contemporaries, suggests that "Margaret Oliphant interrogates and problematizes the autobiographical persona as she presents her life narrative. The certitude about the persona that is manifest in the autobiographies of Newman, Darwin, and Mill is absent from the Oliphant persona" (151). Peterson, Langbauer, and d'Albertis all represent the *Autobiography* as a successful exposition of Oliphant's own personal and aesthetic values—a celebration of "personal taste and aesthetic judgment" (Peterson 169) and of the "importance of the commonplace" (Langbauer 132) in autobiography and in life; and a "critique of the restrictive plots of domestic fiction" (d'Albertis 809). Jay emphasizes the "literariness of the *Autobiography* ... to dispel the long-held notion that this fragmented self-disclosure is merely a naïve compilation of diary, chronicle, and anecdote" (Introduction x). Barbara Thaden does analyze Oliphant's fictional representations of maternity in her book on the "maternal voice"; and Jay discusses Oliphant's "obsessive interest in the mother-child relationship" in *Fiction to Herself* (126–33).

and Trela 23); Cecco, like his father, suffered from tuberculosis; and both were unable or unwilling to assume the valorized masculine role as adults. They remained financially dependent upon Oliphant until their early deaths (Cyril's at thirty-four, Cecco's at thirty-five) and themselves produced neither children nor books. Though it repeatedly stages and mourns such masculine decline and failure, the *Autobiography* is ambivalent about acknowledging Oliphant's own transgressions against the maternal ideal (in her "man's view of mortal affairs") or the contradictions and limitations of Victorian gender norms that it reveals.

As a middle-class woman who moved in literary circles and educated her sons as gentlemen, Oliphant cannot be taken as typical in her negotiations with the maternal ideal. But her experience and representation of maternity, shaped as much by the brute facts of Victorian mortality as by the complexities of Victorian domestic ideology, make the *Autobiography* exemplary of the pluralist account of Victorian gender ideologies that feminist scholars have been building for the past several decades. In this account, the ensemble of beliefs, representations, and admonishments that we have come to call "domestic ideology," strikingly prescriptive though its representation of womanhood could be, is most usefully viewed not as a rigid grid by which subjects were firmly positioned, but as the shifting matrix of negotiations with dominant discourses experienced by subjects who varied in their degree of opposition to or articulation with social norms, access to socioeconomic resources, and cultural authority.[5] As Merryn Williams and others have argued, for example, Oliphant's reputation for conservatism on the "Woman Question," based on her dismissive responses to the writings of reformers such as Barbara Bodichon and John Stuart Mill, is belied both by the representations of clever, ambitious young women in novels such as *Miss Marjoribanks* (1865–66) and by her later, cautious support for some forms of woman's suffrage.[6] Oliphant's

---

[5] As Mary Poovey influentially stated this position several decades ago, "This ideological formulation [of gender] was uneven both in the sense of being experienced differently by individuals who were positioned differently within the social formation (by sex, class, or race, for example) and in the sense of being articulated differently by the different institutions, discourses, and practices that it both constituted and was constituted by. For some groups of people some of the time, an ideological formulation of, for example, maternal nature might have seemed so accurate as to be true; for others, it probably felt less like a description than a goal or even a judgment—a description, that is, of what the individual should and has failed to be" (3). Other important discussions of the role and representation of women within domestic ideology include those by Armstrong and Langland, *Nobody's Angels,* both of whom emphasize the forms of power (ideological, for Armstrong; political and institutional, for Langland) accruing to the figure of the domestic angel in the nineteenth century.

[6] See Williams in Trela.

representation in her autobiography of the relationship between maternity and authorship is similarly shifting: she represents maternity at different moments as the impetus for her writing, as the impediment to a career of greater literary value, as more important than her literary career, and as a source of pleasure and pain parallel with writing. These shifts create simultaneously a celebration of the maternal ideal, a record of its unintended consequences, and a reluctant elegy for its failure.

Although it is customary to refer to this text as "Oliphant's *Autobiography*"—a custom I will follow—the implication of a consistent authorial intention expressed in linear life narrative is somewhat misleading. The first and until recently standard edition of the *Autobiography* was edited in 1899 from Oliphant's manuscript by her second cousin and amanuensis Annie Coghill, who organized manuscript sections chronologically; omitted "well over a quarter of the original manuscript," including Oliphant's "outpourings of grief" (Jay, "Introduction" ix, x) for her dead children; and concluded with a selection of Oliphant's letters to fill in the record of her later years. In 1990, Elisabeth Jay returned to the manuscript and produced an edition whose parts are organized by date of composition rather than narrative chronology and which includes material that Coghill omitted.[7] Both editions thus reflect not only the temporal lapses and changing contexts of Oliphant's impulses toward first-person narrative, but also the judgment of her editors about how best to represent those lapses and changes and through them Oliphant herself. In both arrangements, a logically rebarbative narrative structure announces itself to the reader on the first page: "Twenty-one years have passed since I wrote what is on the opposite page" (Coghill 3); and "To return to the idea with which I started that it was better when I steadily made up my mind in Edinburgh to enter without any props upon my natural lonely life—I am not sure that it was a good idea after all" (Jay, *Autobiography* 3). Although parts of the narrative progress chronologically, the work as a whole has a contrapuntal rather than a linear organization, combining straightforward retrospective life narrative with anecdotes of Oliphant's literary milieu and present-tense lamentations for her dead children. Each of these strands is frequently introduced or qualified by negation, as when Oliphant begins her account of childhood by claiming to "remember nothing of Wallyford, where I was born" (18); deprecates the anecdotes as "making pennyworths of myself" (95); or (having interrupted her narrative with mourning) admonishes

---

[7] In this article I quote from Jay's edition unless otherwise noted. A reprint of Coghill's arrangement, with a foreword by Laurie Langbauer, was published by the University of Chicago Press in 1988. See Jay, "Introduction," and Jay in Trela for discussions of Oliphant's manuscript and the issues involved in editing it.

herself: "I must try to change the tone of this record" (86) and "I must try to begin again" (95). Part of what makes the *Autobiography* arresting, then, is how frankly it reveals the difficulty of, and mixed motives inherent in, self-representation.

But the *Autobiography* is marked by opacity as well as revelation, by self-concealment as well as self-expression. As Jay writes, by 1885, when Oliphant began thinking seriously about constructing an autobiography, "she had already written two full-length biographies, reviewed numerous biographies and autobiographies, and recently written a series of articles for *Blackwood's* on interesting examples of the autobiographical genre" (*Fiction to Herself* 25). She had a strong preference for domestic detail and what might be called human interest in life writing. A biography, she asserts in a *Contemporary Review* essay, ought not to be a "mere record of facts" but to set out "the whole course and progress of a life . . . according to the real scope and meaning which pervade and inspire it" (83). Yet as an author, Oliphant is often reluctant to pursue very far the question of the "real scope and meaning" of a life, whether hers or another subject's. At the opening of *Jeanne d'Arc* (1896), for example, she asserts that her subject

> can neither be classified, as her countrymen love to classify, nor traced to any system of evolution as we all attempt to do nowadays. . . .
>
> How did she come out of that stolid peasant race, out of that distracted and ignoble age, out of riot and license and the fierce thirst for gain, and failure of every noble faculty? Who can tell? By the grace of God, by the inspiration of heaven, the only origins in which the student of nature, which is over nature, can put any trust. No evolution, no system of development, can explain Jeanne. (7–8)

The claim that a subject cannot be explained—the pejorative association of explanation with either French metaphysics or scientific reductionism—is on its face a startling one for a biographer (as well as autobiographer and domestic novelist) to make. Although she emphasizes her use of historical sources (the book includes footnotes, maps, and an index of proper names), Oliphant prefers to celebrate rather than analyze the origins of the heroic womanhood of Jeanne, "the finest emblem in the world in general of that noble, fearless, and spotless Virginity which is one of the finest inspirations of the medieval mind" (8).

In the latter part of the *Autobiography,* Oliphant generalizes this polemical preference for presentation over explanation: "I have never, I am glad to say, been 'a student of human nature' or any such thing. . . . My own opinion has always been . . . that to study human nature was the greatest impertinence, to be resented whenever encountered" (98). The "study" of "human nature" seems to be particularly impertinent when it appears as the study of the nature of gender. In a review of Anna Jameson's memoirs, Oliphant remarks that "from the beginning of history, . . . whenever it has been necessary, women have toiled, have earned money . . . in total indifference to all theory" (qtd. in Peterson 153). "Theory," "system," and "classif[ication]" all connote for Oliphant an improper (in the sense of scandalous as well as misapplied) reification of what she understands as individual, improvisational negotiations of natural gender roles. To denaturalize these roles as systemic rather than essential, even from a feminist point of view, is to denigrate the domestic heroism of the kinds of negotiations so familiar to Oliphant herself: "I have always had to think of other people, and to plan everything—for my own pleasure, it is true, very often, but *always in subjection to the necessity which bound me to them*" (16; emphasis added). It is this sense of "subjection to . . . necessity" that preserves for Oliphant the dignity and meaning of her maternal labors in the face of failure and loss; but the assertion of "necessity" marks the limits of inquiry.

The *Autobiography* begins with Oliphant's comparison of herself to a heroic female figure closer to her than Joan of Arc—George Eliot, whose *Life as Related in Her Letters and Journals,* edited by John Cross, she had recently reviewed and disliked for what she took to be its subject's self-importance.

> I have been tempted to begin writing by George Eliot's life. . . . I wonder if I am a little envious of her? I always avoid considering formally what my own mind is worth. I have never had any theory on the subject. I have written because it gave me pleasure, because it came natural to me, because it was like talking or breathing, besides the big fact that it was necessary for me to work for my children. That, however, was not the first motive, so that when I laugh inquiries off and say that it is my trade, I do it only by way of eluding the question which I have neither time nor wish to enter into. (14)

Again, we see the dismissal of "theory" and an ambivalent representation of her own behavior as part of her nature ("it came natural to me"). Structural (economic) necessity is conceded ("I had to work for my children")— but then partially retracted ("That, however, was not the first motive"). Similarly, Oliphant simultaneously disclaims introspection ("I always avoid considering formally what my own mind is worth"), exhibits her own self-knowledge ("I wonder if I am a little envious of her"), and frankly admits to employing a rhetorical stratagem ("eluding the question [of why she writes]") at the moment of continuing to employ it. In this passage (written before the deaths of her sons), her ability to "avoid" and "elude" is almost playful, proffering to the reader an "involuntary confession" (15) of conflict and ambivalence only to circumscribe it with reticence.

Playfulness in other ways informs the part of the *Autobiography* written before her sons' deaths or recollecting that time. A number of Oliphant's social comedies, such as *Miss Marjoribanks* and *Phoebe, Junior* (1876), feature strong heroines who ally themselves with weaker men through whom they will be able to realize their own social ambitions. Similarly, in the *Autobiography,* Oliphant depicts her maternal, head-of-the-household persona as a figure of almost slapstick vitality. She "loved the easy swing of life, without taking much thought for the morrow, with a faith in my own power to go on working" (117) and emphasizes the "spirit almost criminally elastic [that] ought to have been worn out by work, and crushed by care, half a hundred times by all rules" (135). Her husband, by contrast, is a shadowy presence even while alive, marked by "worries and troubles with his workmen" (62). While Oliphant is "writing steadily all the time, getting about £400 for a novel," her artist husband's glassmaking business is turned down by a potential investor who satirically "congratulated my husband that his circumstances permitted him to be so indifferent to profit" (63).[8]

Although, as Linda Peterson suggests, the *Autobiography*'s most blissful recollections are of harmony between her literary and domestic responsibilities ("As Oliphant reconstructs her life, professional work seems naturally and necessarily to proceed from the domestic context" [155]), it is Oliphant's role as mother more than as wife that creates that "domestic context." In her recollections, one "good time" occurs early in her widowhood:

> This [1862–63, the year of the publication and success of *Salem Chapel*] was also the time when I wrote the [biography] "Edward Irving." It must have been my good time, the little boat going very smoothly and all promising well, and, always my burden of happiness, the children all well. They had the measles, I remember.... It was a day on which Mrs. Carlyle was coming for the afternoon.... [She] sat by me, so kind and

---

[8] The Oliphants' short marriage suffered first from tensions between Frank and Oliphant's mother; then perhaps, as these lines suggest, from financial strain; and finally from Frank's rapidly failing health. See Jay, *Fiction to Herself* 14–17.

tender and full of encouragement. . . . [A]nd by the first post possible that same evening, I got a letter from her telling me that Mr. Carlyle had made her sit down at once and write to tell me that a sister of his had once had just such an attack, which never was repeated. God bless them, that much maligned, much misunderstood pair! That was not much like the old ogre his false friends have made him out to be. (103)

In this scene, harmonies multiply: the activity of nursing sick children not only coexists with, but is also eased by, intercourse with prominent representatives of the "literary life" that Oliphant elsewhere denies living (137); that harmony is not only facilitated by but also extends to include the notoriously unharmonious Carlyles. Even the additional responsibility that later devolves upon the widowed Oliphant for her brother's family does not immediately disturb her representation of a familial scene in which maternity anchors rather than constrains all kinds of productivity—of text as well as children: "There is no doubt that it was much more congenial to me to drive on and keep everything going, with a certain scorn of the increased work, and a metaphorical toss of my head, as if it mattered! than it ever would have been to labour with an artist's fervour and concentration to produce a masterpiece" (132). For a time, each new burden produced by masculine failure or death increases Oliphant's domestic energy and careless bounty.

Yet a warning note, of a less harmonious and more tragic relation between the financial and the more conventionally maternal responsibilities of Victorian domesticity, sounds early in the narrative, when Oliphant describes the friendship of her and her husband with another literary couple, the writers Mary and William Howitt. Unlike Oliphant, Mary Howitt seems to have been vividly attuned to a conventional ideological conflict between authorship and domesticity. Mary Jean Corbett suggests that Howitt's representation of her writing in her own autobiography "underwrites an unequal and gendered difference between her writerly identity and her husband's" because "only William's work must be uninterrupted, sustained over time as his proper occupation" (Corbett 86), while Howitt, like Oliphant, rapidly and without protection from interruption produces ephemera to sustain the household. Howitt's self-representation prevents Oliphant from recuperating this couple—with its parallels to her own marriage—for her model of domestic and professional harmony; she emphasizes that she "liked [Mary Howitt] greatly" but "not so her husband, who did not please me at all"; characteristically, she does not explain why William Howitt failed to please. Mary Howitt "frightened me very much, I remember, by telling me of many babies whom she had lost through some defective valve in the heart, which she said was somehow connected with too much mental work on the part of the mother—a foolish thing, I should think, yet the same thing [i.e., the loss of children in infancy] occurred twice to myself. It alarmed and saddened me terribly—but I liked her greatly" (40).[9]

The Howitt household darkly parodies Oliphant's own—domestic *dis*harmony, between husband and wife, literary and maternal activity, is all too apparent. But Oliphant does not entirely accept this representation of a conflict between maternal and "mental" work; her attitude both within and toward Howitt's anecdote is equivocal. As a young mother, she is understandably "frightened," "alarmed," and "saddened" by Howitt's account, given her own recent losses (of two children in infancy in her first three years of marriage); yet she does not go so far as to concede the truth of a proposition that she calls "foolish," finally substituting a judgment of Howitt herself ("I liked her greatly") for a firm evaluation of her claims about maternity and mental labor. The close of the anecdote (after which the Howitts disappear from the narrative) describes Oliphant's bemusement at Howitt's enthusiasm for her eldest daughter's experience as a spiritual medium—"the Howitts' eldest daughter was an art medium producing wonderful scribble-scrabbles, which it was the wonder of wonders to find her mother . . . full of enthusiasm about" (41)—and so further undermines Howitt's doom-prophesying authority as an expert on motherhood.

Loss and disappointment, however, erode Oliphant's vision of domestic harmony and vigorous productivity. In addition to the infant deaths of the 1850s, she loses her ten-year-old daughter, Maggie, in 1864, and her nephew Frank some fifteen years later. While Maggie's death provokes the passionate lamentation with which Jay's edition begins, and causes Oliphant uncharacteristic "upbraiding and reproaching [of] God" (9), it lacks the finality of the much later deaths of Cyril, in 1890, and Cecco, in 1894: "My own children, my very own, born of me, have all been taken away from me"; she is now "a mother childless" (79). In the face of this terrible oxymoron Oliphant's continued energy finally comes to seem to her not comically productive but uncannily torturous: "All this misery does not give me even a headache. I neither eat nor sleep for days together and I am as well at the end of them as I am at the beginning. What is to become of me, shall I never die?" Looking back she sees not bounty but lack. "My three

---

[9] For a discussion of Howitt's autobiographical representation of the relation between maternity and writing, see Corbett 86–89. On the argument that intellectual labor could harm women's reproductive systems, see Russett 104–29.

boys, for Frank [her nephew] was mine too all now gone.... Madge [her niece] married too and in an unfortunate way. All failure, failure everything, and I am thought a successful woman, but everything I touch seems to go wrong" (81).[10]

These words come from one of three lamentations written during the month of Cecco's death. It is in these grief-stricken entries—for they read like diary entries rather than autobiographical retrospect—that Oliphant confronts her own sense of maternal failure. She begins one meditation by confessing that "[o]ne cruel man the other day told me I had ruined my family by my indulgence and extravagance" (79). Oliphant vacillates in her response to this charge. First, she reasserts her beneficent intentions: "I do not honestly before God think so ... I meant, having no money to leave [Cyril and Cecco], to endow them with the best education, and a happy youth" (79). She acknowledges that "this education has not come to much, in any case...." But she rejects the possibility that the education was misguided: "My Tiddy [i.e., Cyril], God forgive and bless him, partly by his own fault, my Cecco by the long burden of illness which has kept him back, have not achieved those high hopes which I seemed so fully justified in forming." She reiterates the blamelessness of her intentions—"What was wrong was done in love and not wrongly meant. And now my work is accomplished, and my trust fulfilled however badly" (82). Even as these words contain the saving reminder of the seriousness of her efforts, the next bitter turn undermines that seriousness: "If I had broken down as many women might in that sad Time [*sic*] after my husband died, before Cecco was born, how very, very little difference it would have made.... [N]obody thinks that the few books I will leave behind me count for anything. I have no such thought" (82). On the one hand, Oliphant seems to dismiss her authorial as well as her maternal efforts; on the other, once again she reminds herself, if only by denegation, of her own productivity—the more than "few books" that she will leave behind. Through these vacillations she arrives at a slightly more hopeful conclusion: "Cecco would have gone unborn had that [i.e., her earlier death] been so—I am wrong to say it—his dear life ... could not have been left out" (83). She will, despite the obliterating intensity of her grief at the present-tense moment of this writing, return to the retrospective narrative of the *Autobiography*—half of which, Jay points out, was written after Cecco's death (*Fiction to Herself*

---

[10] Oliphant's nephew Frank became an engineer and died of typhoid in India at the age of twenty-five (Williams 119). Her niece Madge, whom she trained as an artist, made a marriage to a businessman fourteen years her senior that Oliphant considered "unfortunate" (81); she died of scarlet fever less than two months after Oliphant's own death (Williams 185).

30)—recharacterizing it as directed "consciously for the public, with the aim (no evil aim) of leaving a little more money for [her niece] Denny" (95). Repeatedly, it is the return to her persona not singly as author or as mother but as *woman working for her children* that allows Oliphant to move past self-recrimination and complete despair.

To the extent that she entertains self-reproach, Oliphant does so in a way that turns the "cruel man's" image of maternal excess on its head. She mentions a "sadder theory" about "the great sorrows that have clouded the end of [her] life," and elaborates this "theory" in a footnote:

> This is what I thought—that I had so accustomed them to the easy going on of all things, never letting them see my [financial] anxieties or know that there was a difficulty about anything, so that . . . it took all thought of necessity out of my Tiddy's mind, who had always, I am sure, the feeling . . . that nothing was likely ever to go far wrong so long as I was there. The sentiment was not ungenerous. . . . And my Cecco, . . . who was stricken by the hand of God [i.e., illness], until that too rendered further going on impossible, by the drying up of my sources and means of getting [literary commissions] for him—so that I seem sometimes to feel as if it were all my doing, and that I had brought by my heedlessness both to an impasse from which there was no issue but one. . . . Who can tell? God alone over all knows, and works by our follies as well as our better ways. Must it not be at last to the good of all? (117)

Though the self-doubt is grave, it is literally marginal to her main narrative, and again, the excesses to which Oliphant admits are those of generosity and energy. Again, too, questions perform the role of a conclusion, putting determination of cause and effect beyond human comprehension. These questions, particularly the last, echo Tennyson's *In Memoriam* (which Oliphant came to appreciate during her mourning for Maggie): "Behold, we know not anything / I can but trust that good shall fall / At last—far off—at last, to all, / And every winter change to spring" (LIV 13–16). The echo is not confined to the language, for Tennyson's, too, is an elegy in which doubt is finally answered by assertion rather than by argument or explanation.

Nevertheless, at the end of the *Autobiography,* Oliphant returns to the question of the disparity between her "high hopes" for her sons in their youths and their subsequent declines. "My dearest, bright delightful boy somehow missed his footing, how can I tell how?" she writes of Cyril, who "took a second-class [degree] at Oxford,—a great disappointment, yet not disgraceful after all." Briefly she contemplates answers, adducing conflicting possibilities such as "inherited tendencies" (presumably toward alcoholism); the "perversity of youth, which he never outgrew"; a dislike of hard work; and the influence of her own tendency to "laugh at the superior people." Again, however, she finally dismisses the attempt at explanation with a question, concluding with the irreducible fact of her own loss: "Why should I try to explain? He went out of the world, leaving a love-song or two behind him and the little volume of 'De Musset,' of which much was so well done, and yet some so badly done, and nothing more to show for his life. And I to watch it all going on day by day and year by year!" (152–53). Jay suggests that Oliphant has a "fatalis[tic]" sense of character—her own and others'—as she often has recourse to concluding "phrase[s] such as 'It was my way' or 'But so it was' or 'I could have done no other'" (*Fiction to Herself* 31). These assertions have, paradoxically, the same effect as her questions ("Why should I try to explain?" "How can I say how?") and vacillations (great disappointment/no disgrace; inherited tendencies/maternal influence; well done/badly done): assertions of necessity, mutually canceling descriptions, and dismissive questions all serve to render explanation nugatory. In doing so, they mark, for Oliphant, the limit of what can be discussed: while her personal suffering falls within that limit, the systems, theories, and classifications of gender ideology fall without.

Yet the (continuing) centrality of motherhood to gender ideology means that the personal experience of maternal failure cannot easily be separated from its social implications. According to Jay, not only the one "cruel man" but "many of Oliphant's acquaintance felt that she had been an over-devoted mother" (*Autobiography* 171).[11] As Sally Shuttleworth suggests in an essay on the Victorian "demonic mother," the threat of overdevotion or "maternal excess" (43) was one of the contradictions built into the maternal ideal. Through maternal excess, "The sacred passion [i.e., maternal love] can itself be demonized, turned into an avenging force which destroys both the angelic mother herself and the concord of the domestic hearth, revealing all too clearly the precarious balance of the patriarchal bourgeois order" (44). Shuttleworth quotes one advice-writer on the "relaxing effeminacy" that "emotional immoderation" can produce (43). Some contemporaries of Oliphant apparently viewed her sons as effete if not effeminate: "He lived at home an idle and self-indulgent life," one acquaintance observed about Cyril, " . . . and no more melancholy decadence than that of the vivid sparkling Eton boy into the elderly and deprecating loafer . . . could be

---

[11] For an argument, however, that most critical and biographical representations overstate the failure of Oliphant's sons, see Peterson 160–64.

imagined" (qtd. in Williams 145). Another wrote of Cecco that his presence seemed to impose the necessity "to moderate and hush our talk when he was by, as one does for a much older person who must not be disturbed or worried" (qtd. in Williams 174). The explicit distortion in each case is one of age rather than gender: Cyril has become "an elderly and deprecating loafer"; Cecco is like "a much older person." But the "decadence" of these images and their emphasis on delicacy and incapacity suggests a more generally flawed masculinity.[12]

Oliphant sometimes represents herself as troubled by her children's continued dependence on her and by their apparent rejection of the conventional structures of heterosexual adulthood: "My heart fails me when I think how entirely I represent home to [Cecco, Denny, and Madge]. . . . I think now it would be nothing but blessedness, that one of the girls at least, and my Cecco, should each find some one who would be the partner of their lives—and so be weaned from me" (59), she writes. When faced with this "blessedness" in Madge's case, however, she considered the outcome "unfortunate" (81; see Williams 172–73). And the *Autobiography*'s closing image of Cecco suggests her unwillingness to lose the only familial intimacy and fulfillment (however diminished) of her maternal expectations remaining to her:

> My Cecco took the first steps in the same way [as Cyril]; but, thanks be to God, righted himself and overcame—not in time enough to save his career at Oxford, but so as to be all that I had hoped—always my very own, my dearest companion, choosing me before all others. . . . When he was absent he wrote to me every day. I never went out but he was there to give me his arm. . . . I can hear myself saying "Cecco and I." It was the constant phrase. But all through he was getting weaker: and I knew it, and tried not to know. (153–54)

[12] A. C. Benson made this comment in 1888, just before the decade in which the word "decadence" became associated with illicit sexual styles, including homosexuality. Jay also quotes Benson as remarking on "something 'morbidly passionate' in her love for her boys" (*Fiction to Herself* 42). An Eton man himself, the "semi-official biographer" (Dellamora 59) of Walter Pater and an associate of the "Decadents" of the 1890s, Benson would surely have been aware of this connotation, but how specifically he intends it here seems impossible to determine. The conjunction of language such as Benson's, Oliphant's cryptically expressed anxieties about Cyril's misbehavior, and both Cyril and Cecco's lack of apparent heterosexual ties might lead the twenty-first-century reader to wonder where their own self-definitions fall within what Richard Dellamora investigates as "masculine experience during the [Victorian] period, experience not only of men who appear recognizably 'homosexual' but [of] a wider and more varied range of men" (5). The sexual attitudes and experiences of the Oliphant sons are, however, unrecoverable, certainly without research beyond the scope of this essay and possibly at all.

In the context of the ideological matrix that Shuttleworth discusses, this uxorious image might seem to put Oliphant in the category of the "demonic mother" transgressing the boundary between maternal and romantic passion. The practice of blaming mothers for perceived failures of masculine subjectivity would develop in a more virulent strain in some of Freud's theories. In his speculative essay on Leonardo da Vinci (1909), for example, published only a decade after Oliphant's *Autbiography,* Freud claims that the subjects in all of his "male homosexual cases" had in childhood had a very strong maternal attachment that "was evoked or encouraged by too much tenderness on the part of the mother herself" (99).[13] For Oliphant, however, this representation is neither transgressive nor blameworthy; on the contrary, it is part of her increasing idealization of Cecco after the more actively unsatisfactory Cyril's death. Unlike Cyril's degeneration, Cecco's devotion repays Oliphant's own and partly makes good her losses. Cecco was also more successful than Cyril in inheriting Oliphant's literary mantle. As Peterson writes, "By the end of 1885 Cecco's story 'Grateful Ghosts' was in proofs for *Blackwood's Magazine,* and Oliphant was writing happily to the publisher: 'I trust too that your last new contributor, Cecco, will give you and the public satisfaction, and that this may be the beginning of a long connection'" (Peterson 163). Cecco is the last man standing in the *Autobiography;* but in the end, like Cyril, he dies leaving little literary—and no human—progeny.

The *Autobiography*'s theme of exhausted, unproductive masculinity and energetic female productivity is all the more ominous because it is not confined to Oliphant's family but is amplified in the narrative's marginal and secondary male figures: William Howitt; the painter Robert Macpherson, whose wife, Geraldine, according to Oliphant, "work[ed] like a slave—nay, as no slave ever worked—at the common trade, the photographing, at which she did quite as much, if not, people said, more than, he did" (75) and who, according to Williams, was left, after his death, with four children and debts to pay off, while suffering from rheumatism and heart disease (102); and Oliphant's good friend (and biographical subject) John Tulloch, principal of St. Andrew's College, who suffered from depression. Oliphant admired him greatly, but she wrote to him on one occasion, "But think, please if it had been me who had been ill, what would have become

---

[13] The complete absence of information about Leonardo's unmarried mother, Caterina, which Freud acknowledges, does not inhibit him from concluding that "like all unsatisfied mothers, she took her little son in place of her husband, and by the too early maturing of his erotism robbed him of a part of his masculinity" (117). Freud however left undeveloped, and often expressed uncertainty about, the now discredited connection he asserts here between what he represents as two forms of gender deviance.

of me?—no income going on whether one could work or not—no wife to take care of me" (qtd. in Williams 140). Reading, in the wake of Cecco's death, a biography of Archbishop Campbell Tait, whose children and wife died in an outbreak of scarlet fever (172n 84), she writes, "Oh good archbishop you are better than I, only three years and a half off 70 and surely one can't be made to live longer than that.... I could turn to and work or write a love story or draw or skate or walk a mile—anything, anything—but my burden is more than I can bear" (86). In Oliphant's experience and in her writing, the debt, depression, and death that men suffer almost appear as indulgences that women, who carry the burdens of planning and acting, cannot afford.

Like Thomas Hardy, whose representation of marital relations in *Jude the Obscure* (1895) she notoriously attacked, Oliphant could see to the end of Victorian gender ideology without welcoming what might lie beyond it. And so the *Autobiography* ends with an emphasis on loss—the loss of what Oliphant has created, children and text:

And now here I am all alone.
I cannot write any more. (154)

Jay suggests that this cadenced closing "was as carefully contrived as any of her deliberately unconventional endings to novels" (*Fiction to Herself* 30), and it is not accurate in broad reference to Oliphant's professional writing, which continued up to her death in 1897. But it captures a truth of the autobiographical narrative, which has gone as far as it can in representing Oliphant's negotiations of the maternal ideal and her sons' deviations from the masculine ideal. The *Autobiography* remains suspended between recognition and denial of the limitations of these ideals. If that suspension is evasive, it also allows Oliphant to resist implication in the cultural double binds that make women responsible for the reproduction of gender roles that at the same time constrain their efforts to meet those responsibilities. Why, indeed, should Oliphant try to explain?

Works Cited

Armstrong, Nancy. *Desire and Domestic Fiction: A Political History of the Novel.* New York: Oxford University Press, 1987.
Barros, Carolyn. *Autobiography: Narrative of Transformation.* Ann Arbor: University of Michigan Press, 1998.
Coghill, Mrs. Harry [Annie], ed. and arr. *Autobiography and Letters of Mrs. Oliphant.* Foreword by Laurie Langbauer. Chicago: University of Chicago Press, 1988.

Corbett, Mary Jean. *Representing Femininity: Middle-Class Subjectivity in Victorian and Women's Autobiographies.* New York: Oxford University Press, 1992.

d'Albertis, Deirdre. "The Domestic Drone: Margaret Oliphant and a Political History of the Novel." *SEL: Studies in English Literature, 1500–1900* 37 (Autumn 1994): 805–29.

Dellamora, Richard. *Masculine Desire: The Sexual Politics of Victorian Aestheticism.* Chapel Hill: University of North Carolina Press, 1990.

Dever, Carolyn. *Death and the Mother from Dickens to Freud: Victorian Fiction and the Anxiety of Origins.* Cambridge: Cambridge University Press, 1998.

Eliot, George. *Daniel Deronda.* Ed. Graham Handley. New York: Oxford, 1984.

———. *The Mill on the Floss.* Ed. and intro. A. S. Byatt. New York: Penguin, 1979.

———. *Felix Holt.* Ed. and intro. Peter Coveney. New York: Penguin, 1972.

Freud, Sigmund. "Leonardo da Vinci and a Memory of His Childhood." In *The Standard Edition of the Complete Psychological Works of Sigmund Freud.* Vol. XI. Gen ed. and trans. James Strachey et al. London: Hogarth Press, 1957. 59–137.

Gruner, Elisabeth. "Plotting the Mother: Caroline Norton, Helen Huntingdon, and Isabel Vane." *Tulsa Studies in Women's Literature* 16 (Autumn 1997): 303–25.

Homans, Margaret. *Bearing the Word: Language and Female Experience in Nineteenth-Century Women's Writing.* Chicago: University of Chicago Press, 1986.

Jay, Elisabeth. *Mrs. Oliphant: 'A Fiction to Herself.' A Literary Life.* New York: Oxford University Press, 1995.

———. "Freed by Necessity, Trapped by the Market: The Editing of Oliphant's *Autobiography.*" In Trela 135–46.

———. "Introduction." In *The Autobiography of Mrs. Oliphant: The Complete Text.* New York: Oxford University Press, 1990.

Langbauer, Laurie. "Absolute Commonplaces: Oliphant's Theory of Autobiography." In Trela 124–34.

Langland, Elizabeth. *Nobody's Angels: Middle-Class Women and Domestic Ideology in Victorian Culture.* Ithaca: Cornell University Press, 1995.

———. "Patriarchal Ideology and Marginal Motherhood in Victorian Novels by Women." *Studies in the Novel* 19 (Fall 1987): 381–94.

Oliphant, Margaret. *The Autobiography of Mrs. Oliphant: The Complete Text.* Ed. Elizabeth Jay. New York: Oxford University Press, 1990.

———. *Jeanne D'Arc: Her Life and Death.* New York and London: G. P. Putnam's Sons, 1896.

———. "The Ethics of Biography." *Contemporary Review* 44 (1883): 76–93.

Peterson, Linda H. *Traditions of Victorian Women's Autobiography: The Poetics and Politics of Life Writing.* Charlottesville: University Press of Virginia, 1999.

———. "The Female *Bildungsroman*: Tradition and Subversion in Oliphant's Fiction." In Trela 66–89.

Poovey, Mary. *Uneven Developments: The Ideological Work of Gender in Mid-Victorian England.* Chicago: University of Chicago Press, 1988.

Russett, Cynthia Eagle. *Sexual Science: The Victorian Construction of Womanhood.* Cambridge: Harvard University Press, 1989.

Shuttleworth, Sally. "Demonic Mothers: Ideologies of Bourgeois Motherhood in the Mid-Victorian Era." In *Rewriting the Victorians: Theory, History and the Politics of Gender.* Ed. Linda M. Shires. New York: Routledge, 1992. 31–51.

Thaden, Barbara. *The Maternal Voice in Victorian Fiction: Rewriting the Patriarchal Family.* New York: Garland, 1997.
Trela, D. J., ed. *Margaret Oliphant: Critical Essays on a Gentle Subversive.* Cranbury, NJ: Associated University Presses, 1995.
Williams, Merryn. *Margaret Oliphant: A Critical Biography.* London: MacMillan, 1986.

CHAPTER 3

"Bland, Adoring, and Gently Tearful Women"[1]

Debunking the Maternal Ideal in George Eliot's *Felix Holt*

HEATHER MILTON

Although the discourse about fallenness in the mid-nineteenth century was mixed and riddled with internal contradictions, Victorians involved in the rescue of "fallen" women believed that the power of maternity could potentially redeem these women. According to this discursive construction, a woman could atone and compensate for her selfishness in fulfilling her illicit sexual desires by living for her child, as novels such as Elizabeth Gaskell's *Ruth* and Elizabeth Barrett Browning's *Aurora Leigh* exemplify.[2] In *Felix Holt, the Radical* (1866), however, George Eliot complicates the redemptive possibilities of the maternal ideal, showing the conflicted relationship between maternity and recovery from a "fall." Perhaps nowhere in the Victorian novel is the ideology of motherhood as a purifying, ennobling condition so thoroughly debunked as in *Felix Holt*. Eliot suggests that the punishment fallen women receive is unfair and also insists that neither women nor children benefit from mothers attempting to live for and through their children. For Eliot, the maternal ideal involves a self-replicating misogyny: living completely for one's sons only produces

---

[1] George Eliot, *Felix Holt, the Radical*. Ed. Linda Mugglestone. London: Penguin Books, 1995, 111. All parenthetical references are to this edition.

[2] Ruth redeems herself through her self-sacrificing behavior not only in nursing the sick, but also in putting her child's needs before her own. Her fundamental reason for not marrying Bellingham and making her son legitimate when she has the opportunity to do so is the fear that Bellingham's immorality will corrupt Leonard and that she will lose her control over his upbringing.

selfish sons who then grow up to oppress their mothers and their wives. She advocates that men develop qualities, self-control and sympathy, that they ought to learn in the home and that mothers should not live through their children. Eliot's attitude toward mothering in *Felix Holt* is complex: she both critiques the self-denial required by the maternal ideal, yet also suggests that proper, moderated mothering is integral to the production of good character necessary to participate in the public sphere.

My analysis of Eliot's representation of maternity and its importance to the development of character helps reconcile the novel's seemingly disparate plot lines. Written on the eve of the Second Reform Act, which extended the franchise, *Felix Holt, the Radical,* ostensibly a "Condition of England" novel questioning the value of greater political rights for the working class, has surprised readers with its two plots about political life and the private lives of two central female characters, Mrs. Transome and Esther Lyon. Critics have tended to approach the schism in the novel's plot in one of two ways: by arguing that there is no connection between them, or, more recently, by pointing out that Eliot politicizes the domestic sphere by questioning the patriarchal domination of women.[3] Feminist scholars have noted that Eliot emphasizes that "there is no private life which has not been determined by a wider public life" (50). Yet I will also argue that *Felix Holt* and "The Address to Working Men, by Felix Holt," a corollary to the novel that appeared in *Blackwood's Edinburgh Magazine* in January 1868, illustrate that the opposite is equally true: public life is also determined by private life. In addition to politicizing the private sphere, Eliot domesticates the public sphere. The "Address" argues that parents must educate their children with great care to prepare them to assume the responsibility of citizenship, while the novel dramatizes the negative impact of the maternal ideal on the formation of men's morality and character. As the novel details, maternal self-denial allows sons to indulge their narcissism, inhibiting the development of self-discipline and fellow feeling necessary for good citizenship and good governance. Through her reworking of the maternal narrative, Eliot argues that an all-consuming, self-denying love is unhealthy for the mother, child, and, ultimately, the state.

Eliot's political beliefs emphasize that personal development must occur before broader structural changes, such as the expansion of suffrage, can take place. *Felix Holt* and the "Address" suggest that the workers' problems result from their lack of moral development: they are unruly

---

[3] Lynda Mugglestone writes, "[I]n Eliot's text the personal can be political in ways which transcend the narrow definitions of party and its associated patterns of allegiance" (xi). See also Alison Booth, who states, "That politics are personal, that reform depends on private more than public changes, is the argument of *Felix Holt*" (212).

children in need of good parenting to become proper middle-class subjects and thus worthy of the vote. Although the "Address," unlike *Felix Holt,* is set after the passage of the Second Reform Act and the expansion of the franchise, the workers, according to Eliot, still have not changed their tendencies toward drunkenness and vice. The franchise is a good thing, Eliot argues, only if an individual has "the knowledge, the foresight, and conscience, that will make him well-judging and scrupulous in the use of it" (791). Represented as acting upon immediate impulses, as in the riot, the infantilized workers lack self-control, a fundamental barrier to personal development according to a bourgeois paradigm. The "Address" explicitly states what the novel depicts through a more elaborate representation of character: it posits the workers' political problems as personal ones—that is, the workers must change their personalities and develop their inner lives to become their best selves before expecting political change to occur. Political change is reduced to the fundamental problem of "human nature . . . and nothing else" (490).

According to the "Address," proper child rearing ought to be the chief object of moral reform that must precede political reform, and Felix lectures the workers for neglecting their responsibilities as parents: "It is true enough that there is a low sense of parental duties in the nation at large, and that numbers who have no excuse in bodily hardship seem to think it a light thing to beget children . . . and then take little heed how they are disciplined and furnished for the perilous journey they are set on" (496). He urges the workers to "rouse to the utmost the feeling of responsibility in fathers and mothers" as the real means to improve their children's lives (496–97). According to Eliot, the workers must rear their children with greater care to form a morally improved subjectivity: sympathetic, virtuous, and self-disciplined.

However, the development of character and morality that is so influential on politics at large is largely represented through women's private lives. As Nancy Armstrong has demonstrated, the middle-class woman is the site of sympathy in the Victorian novel and mediates the displacement of political issues into personal ones. *Felix Holt* is the story of Esther's bildungsroman, not Felix's: she changes partly through Felix's tutelage and partly through her relationship with her surrogate mother, Mrs. Transome. Although sympathy is clearly not uniquely experienced by women in Eliot's novels, it is Esther's sympathetic awakening and moral education, and to a lesser extent Mrs. Transome's, that the novel represents.[4] Colene

---

[4] Many critics have noted that Felix Holt plays a minor role in the novel named after him. Although Felix does undergo moral growth prior to the events of the novel, according to

Bentley points out that the workers need to develop self-awareness and the ability to determine sincerity: "Because the working classes are susceptible to manipulation and blind imitation, that is to say, because they impulsively follow both true (Felix) and false (Harold, Johnson) prophets, they need proper education to sharpen their powers of discernment before entering a democratic world marked by deep conflict" (283).[5] Ultimately, it is Esther who actually develops this discernment over the course of the novel. She interprets and communicates the other characters' inner lives (Felix, Mrs. Transome, and Harold) and inspires sympathetic fellow feeling in them and for them.[6] Through focusing on Mrs. Transome's and Esther's moral improvement and development of sympathy and self-discipline, Eliot promotes a feminized subjectivity as one for the working classes to emulate and explores the political implications of improving the self internally rather than externally through the attainment of greater rights. *Felix Holt* foregrounds the primacy of the mother-child relationship to this development of good character. The novel opens with Mrs. Transome contemplating her future with her illegitimate son, Harold, returning after being abroad for fifteen years, and thus maternity and Mrs. Transome's secret of her lack of self-control frame the novel.

One indication of the centrality of maternal ideology to the Victorians is how mothering permeates the discourse relating to both the causes and remedies of fallenness. While becoming a mother might be a powerful enough force to save a fallen woman, the lack of a mother could also cause a young woman to fall. In *Tainted Souls and Painted Faces: The Rhetoric of Fallenness in Victorian Culture,* Amanda Anderson notes that the discourse regarding fallen women's agency and whether they are responsible for their fall or merely victims is mixed. Women were regarded as having lost their virtue for a variety of reasons, including lack of self-discipline, love of

---

the sexual double standard in Victorian culture, he cannot "fall" and be ruined, nor does he require forgiveness from someone in a position of social authority to reenter the community—his actions neither isolate nor alienate him from others. Unlike a man, a woman's sexual transgressions typically have a much greater detrimental impact on her life and threaten to destroy her morally, psychologically, and socially. Thus, while Felix's relatively minor role in the novel is initially surprising, the novel cannot center on him because he is incapable of sustaining the same kind of narrative interest for a middle-class audience as Mrs. Transome and Esther.

[5] Sally Shuttleworth notes that women and workers, politically and economically vulnerable, were united in the Victorian cultural imagination: "Like the working classes, women represented to the bourgeois male imagination an ever-present threat to their dominance, a threat, moreover, that was enshrined within their own home" (33).

[6] Laura Struve also argues that sympathy is sexualized and feminized in *Felix Holt,* which is best exemplified in the trial scene in which the magistrates have a romantic reaction to Esther's appeal to pardon Felix (10–12).

finery, and vanity and susceptibility to flattery. Philanthropist Ellice Hopkins, who wrote extensively about the sexual reform movement, argues in 1870 that "the mother, early lost, and the miserable unshielded home" is one of the primary reasons young women lapse in virtue and begin to lead an immoral life (56).[7] Philanthropists frequently attributed the flaws in a young woman's character that led to her fall to the absence of a maternal figure who could teach her daughter proper middle-class morality and self-control and guide her through courtship to marriage.

While many midcentury Victorian novels represent fallen women as socially outcast and incapable of surviving their shame, let alone remaining in their homes and communities, other Victorian texts dealing with fallen women, such as Gaskell's *Ruth* and Browning's *Aurora Leigh,* and the literature from the popular midcentury movement to rescue fallen women, offer a counterdiscourse to the idea of the inevitable downward trajectory of fallenness. These texts suggest that maternity is a powerful tool of women's salvation. According to one 1885 *Fortnightly Review* article, "Helping the Fallen," by Mary Jeune, "the most softening and powerful influence with many women is the love of their child. With some it is all-absorbing, and when it is so, one need never fear for the mother's future" (679). Fallen women could potentially attain redemption through mothering because taking care of their babies would give the women an incentive to change their sinful ways.

That is, according to this ideology, living for another necessitates the annihilation of the self and the selfish desires that landed women in trouble in the first place. Jeune acknowledges that while some fallen women might be upset by having a child to mark their shame as a result of their loss of virtue, it is still in the best interest of their mothers that the children live: "To the mother who is careless, it protects her against herself; and to the mother who loves it, it is the one being in the world, shameful though its existence be, on whom she can lavish all the affection of her heart" (680). In *A Woman's Thoughts about Women* (1858), Dinah Mulock Craik argues that an illegitimate child can actually be a blessing given by God

---

[7] Hopkins wrote prolifically about rescuing fallen women in the mid- to late-nineteenth century and specifically advocated fostering maternal bonds between young fallen women and their middle-class rescuers as a means of "saving" and reeducating them according to a middle-class paradigm. According to Susan Mumm, "Hopkins's books and pamphlets were widely read; some titles went into anything from twenty to seventy-five editions, with a few remaining in print until the 1940's. By her death in 1904, well over two million copies of her works had been distributed" (209). Although not all of these publications deal specifically with fallen women, their sheer numbers indicate Hopkins's popularity and the public's widespread interest in sexual reform.

as a "sign of hope and redemption" and give a fallen woman something to live for (310).[8] To the philanthropists involved in sexual rescue, children not only prevent deviant women from committing suicide, they also serve an important function in the regulation of desire. Because fallen women lack self-discipline and are excessively emotional, children provide a safe way for them to redirect "lavish" affection, both to replace riskier feelings for men and to avoid their own tendencies toward narcissism. Therefore, paradoxically, through the evacuation of identity required by Victorian maternity, a self-denying, self-disciplined subjectivity is produced.

However, the idea that devoting oneself to a child would discipline inappropriate passions was not uniform. Although Deborah Anna Logan notes that "middle-class maternal ideology" is "believed to be the most effective avenue of appeal by writers promoting reclamation of the fallen" (32), the nature of maternal ideology in Victorian novels and rescue literature is also mixed: "Evidence of the 'maternal instinct' in fallen mothers raises complex and contradictory issues: maternity is promoted as the greatest of all woman's accomplishments, but illegitimate motherhood is as great a perversion of sexual ideology as prostitution, which is why its use as a medium for redemption is so potent" (115). Shuttleworth points out that an excessive amount of maternal devotion was also considered potentially dangerous: "[M]aternal emotion partakes of the same volatile, disruptive nature as female sexual passion, or insanity, which, women were warned, was liable to burst forth suddenly if not kept under constant watchful guard" (43). Because of the centrality of the anxiety over motherhood in mid-Victorian culture, maternity performed many different ideological functions at once, making it highly contested terrain, yet philanthropists believed that bourgeois values of bodily and emotional self-control could temper excess. Within the movement to rescue fallen women, class was also a significant determining factor in whether a woman was capable of redemption. One commentator in *The Magdalen's Friend and Female Homes' Intelligencer,* a periodical devoted to rescue work, says about women of "education and refinement" that "our sympathies are at once enlisted; all our interest is awakened. We think, what a prize such a woman would be if reclaimed and restored to society!" (37–38). *Felix Holt* depicts both upper- and lower-class mothers, Mrs. Transome and Mrs. Holt, as unable to restrain themselves and in need of adopting the more acceptable middle-class values of self-control, discernment, and sympathetic identification that Esther develops over the course of the novel.[9]

---

[8] See also "Rescue Work by Women among Women" (1893), in which Mary H. Steer argues that "the most hopeful class in rescue work are the women with illegitimate children" (152).

[9] Of course, Mrs. Transome learns self-discipline while Mrs. Holt does not, and her lack

Although in *Felix Holt* Eliot participates in an alternate discourse about fallenness that challenges the strictly downward path of the "fall," she also clearly distinguishes her views from those who urge women to subordinate their own needs to their children's to atone for the past and attain redemption. While, as Carolyn Dever has pointed out, the Victorian novel typically idealizes and mythologizes the potent psychic presence of the dead or missing mother, Eliot departs from that literary tradition. Instead of removing the mother from the narrative and infusing her memory with nostalgia, Eliot strips all sentimentality from her representation of motherhood and addresses the painful reality of a fallen woman: Mrs. Transome, reconstructing a relationship with her long-absent son, Harold. Mrs. Transome has sacrificed greatly for her illegitimate child, hoping that their relationship will compensate for the shame and loneliness resulting from her adulterous affair, yet her son believes women to be subordinate to men and lacks the fellow feeling necessary to forgive his mother. Eliot notes not only that the unequal standards of sexual behavior unfairly leave mothers bearing the burden of fallenness, but also that motherhood does not necessarily offer fallen women the possibility of redemption for a loss in virtue or compensate for a lack in their own lives. The extent of Mrs. Transome's bitterness conveyed in the sentiment "God was cruel when he made women" has impressed critics both contemporary and modern (374), and while *Felix Holt* is conservative in its class politics, it may well be Eliot's most radical critique of the oppression of women.

The novel attributes Mrs. Transome's poor mothering skills to the poor mothering she received as a child, which did not teach her how to control her inappropriate desires. As a product of an earlier, more lax era and a degenerate aristocracy, she did not have an upbringing that encouraged moral improvement or an appreciation of sincerity. As a young woman, Mrs. Transome was silly, frivolous, and self-centered, and the novel suggests that she has fallen because she never developed self-discipline and good judgment. Because her education was not seriously undertaken, she read "dangerous French authors" in lieu of more serious fare (29). Hence, she failed to develop a moral compass and did not learn to value chastity: "[M]any sinful things were highly agreeable to her, and many things which she did not doubt to be good and true were dull and meaninglessness. She found ridicule of Biblical characters amusing, and she was interested in stories of illicit passion" (29). Consequently, she was not equipped to weigh the consequences of her actions.

---

of self-control and inability to understand the value of discretion mark her as lower class. Her willingness to reveal her emotions publicly is explicitly juxtaposed to Mrs. Transome's appreciation of reticence: "Mrs. Holt, unlike Mrs. Transome, was much disposed to reveal her troubles" (51).

Although Eliot acknowledges the importance of motherhood to women, *Felix Holt* provides a more nuanced and ironic view of motherhood and the complex, often competing social demands that mothers must negotiate than Gaskell's *Ruth,* and Eliot exposes the Victorian maternal ideal as such—an ideal—not a reality.[10] As Laura Green points out in her essay in this volume, Margaret Oliphant's *Autobiography* also demonstrates how slavish mothering required by the maternal ideal produces unintended consequences: though Oliphant devotes herself to her children, she ends up with sons both infantilized and emasculated. Although the degree to which Oliphant did, in fact, devote herself to her children may be questionable given her extensive output of writing, it is significant that she depicts herself as having devoted all of her emotional energy to them, suggesting that the representation of a self-sacrificing mother resonated in the culture. While Eliot depicts a different outcome resulting from this kind of smothering mothering—Harold is dynamic in his tyranny and selfishness rather than indolent—both *Felix Holt* and Oliphant's *Autobiography* reveal the logical end point of the maternal ideal and, in particular, its worship of sons, which neither fulfills women nor produces the type of sons mothers might actually want to have.

Eliot concedes that maternity is a powerful force in women's lives, noting that motherhood is initially an all-consuming, almost intoxicating experience and that it is a "common dream" that having a child will make women completely happy (111). However, the intoxicating effects of having a child cannot be sustained for the long term and form only one component of women's identities—identities that Eliot takes pains to point out are multifaceted. The narrator emphasizes that many women do not want to live exclusively for their children and satirizes the representation of motherhood as all-consuming:

> [I]t is a fact perhaps kept a little too much in the background, that mothers have a self larger than their maternity, and that when their sons have become taller than themselves, and are gone from them to college or into the world, there are wide spaces of their time which are not filled with praying for their boys, reading old letters, and envying yet blessing those who are attending to their shirt-buttons. Mrs. Transome was certainly not one of those bland, adoring, and gently tearful women. (111)

Eliot lampoons the conception of "gently tearful" mothers as perpetually

---

[10] Pauline Nestor notes that motherhood in Eliot's novels frequently involves failure and argues that her challenge of the maternal role is much more disturbing than that of Gaskell (180).

occupied with their children long after they are grown, proposing that these types of mothers are dull indeed. Instead, she suggests that women fulfill their needs other than solely through their children.

Felix Holt also demonstrates that not every woman feels nurturing maternal impulses, and that mothers do not necessarily ensure their children's well-being. Mrs. Transome may love one son, but she despises the other. Not even in *Adam Bede,* when Hetty abandons her baby, is the urge for infanticide so clearly and consciously articulated as it is in *Felix Holt* when Mrs. Transome hopes that her weak firstborn son will die so that Harold may become heir:

> [T]he mother's early raptures had lasted but a short time, and even while they lasted there had grown up in the midst of them a hungry desire, like a black poisonous plant feeding in the sunlight,—the desire that her first, rickety, ugly, imbecile child should die, and leave room for her darling, of whom she could be proud. (23)

Whereas in *Adam Bede* Hetty is represented as something of a lower order of being who acts upon impulses that are not entirely clear to her, Mrs. Transome is an intelligent, wellborn lady who is grateful when her child finally dies so that she can gratify her own desires by seeing her favorite son become heir—quite a departure from the idea that motherhood is purifying and ennobling.

However, bearing a child as the result of her adulterous affair with Matthew Jermyn has not vindicated Mrs. Transome's illicit liaison, nor does a relationship with her son compensate for her many years of self-recrimination and social isolation resulting from speculative gossip about the affair. Eliot depicts Mrs. Transome as initially believing in the Victorian maternal ideal that living for Harold will make up for what she has suffered as a fallen woman; yet despite her desire for a fulfilling relationship with him upon his return from abroad, she is forced to accept that she has deluded herself: "[S]he had thought that the possession of this child would give unity to her life, and make some gladness through the changing years that would grow as fruit out of these early maternal caresses. But nothing had come just as she wished" (23). Part of what Eliot points out through the gulf between Mrs. Transome's hopes and the crushing reality is that given the high expectations Victorian culture places upon motherhood to enrich and unify a woman's life, it is no surprise that motherhood could not possibly live up to them.

According to Eliot, the reality of motherhood is just as likely to be an alienating experience, as it is for Mrs. Transome. Like so many of Eliot's other women characters limited by the bounds of acceptable behavior and occupation for their gender and class, Mrs. Transome longs to lead an active life. Married to a feebleminded husband, she has managed the estate, negotiated with tenants, and acted as bailiff for years while Harold has been abroad, and he automatically assumes these jobs upon his return to England. She initially hopes that she and her son will manage the estate together and that he will acknowledge her intelligence and expertise:

> [S]he cared especially that her son, who had seen a strange world, should feel that he was come home to a mother who was to be consulted on all things, and who could supply his lack of the local experience necessary to an English landholder. . . . [L]ife would have little meaning to her if she were to be gently thrust aside as a harmless elderly woman. (17)

Mrs. Transome expects to be consulted on business matters and particularly wants to advise Harold on his participation in the election, knowing that his rash foray into Radical politics will alienate the conservative, rural area and is unlikely to be successful. However, Harold stops any attempt by his mother to guide him in politics, arguing that women's viewpoints on political matters are irrelevant since they play no part at all in life beyond raising children. Mrs. Transome resents Harold's attempt to reduce her solely to a passive maternal role as a "grandmamma on satin cushions" (21), yet comes to the painful realization that she is "as unnecessary as a chimney ornament" to Harold in his political ambitions and management of the estate (116). Instead of appealing to his mother's political savvy, Harold acts on his own impulses and blunders. Ultimately, the logic of the novel vindicates Mrs. Transome's Tory politics, not Harold's radicalism, which only incites the uneducated workers to riot.

The narrator notes that the happiness of having children is difficult to sustain once they are grown precisely because even as adults they continue to expect that their mothers will deny their own needs and identities in perpetuity: "[I]n after years it can only continue to be joy on the same terms as other long-lived love—that is, by much suppression of self, and the power of living in the experience of another" (23). However, Eliot repeatedly asserts that mothers cannot live exclusively for their children because they end up limiting themselves. Clearly, Mrs. Transome does not entirely suppress her own desires. While Mrs. Transome lives for Harold, she also quite lives through him, hoping to be an active part of the community through Harold's involvement in politics. Yet, it is the problem raised by not maintaining enough of a separate identity that Eliot explores. Mrs. Transome is not only prevented from managing the estate and advising her son on his political career, she also stunts her own internal moral and spiritual growth so that while she grows in wisdom during the course of the novel, she never becomes one of Eliot's admirable characters.

For Eliot, mothers who live entirely for and through their children create self-absorbed sons. The novel illustrates how Mrs. Transome has participated in constructing the conditions of her own oppression through her inadequate mothering, which encourages Harold to be tyrannical, thus perpetuating the patriarchal domination of women.[11] Elizabeth Langland points out that *Felix Holt* belongs to a recurring representation of marginalized mothers in mother-son relationships in Victorian novels by women: "A mother's yearning love for her son within a patriarchal structure dictates a self-suppression that the son, socialized by the same ideology, will happily escape, and we witness the pain and poignancy of the ways mothers have been implicated in enforcing their own marginalization" ("Patriarchal Ideology" 388). Mrs. Transome has reared Harold to be selfish and encouraged him to fulfill his ambitions regardless of the cost to others.

> After sharing the common dream that when a beautiful man-child was born to her, her cup of happiness would be full, she had travelled through long years apart from that child to find herself at last in the presence of a son of whom she was afraid, who was utterly unmanageable by her, and to whose sentiments in any given case she possessed no key. (111)

Through her failure to teach him respect and sympathy for others, Harold has become a tyrant, and Mrs. Transome's inadequate mothering sustains the continuation of male oppression of women into the next generation.

Although as a second son Harold has worked hard abroad to earn a fortune, he has much in common with the spoiled firstborn son ubiquitous to the Victorian novel, who expects all others to bend to his will, knowing that because he is at the top of the social order, his actions—no matter how egregious—are unlikely to have serious, life-altering repercussions for himself. In addition to rejecting his filial duty, Harold also married a slave, declaring his distaste for English wives because they are too independent and express themselves when they ought to let men do the

---

[11] Although Felix has developed self-discipline and a sound morality, it is in spite of his mother, not because of her. Although Mrs. Holt is a loving mother, exemplified by her adoption of the sickly Job Tudge, her lack of moderation and self-control, used throughout the novel for comic effect, is endemic to the working class, which always risks erupting into chaos and poses a threat to social stability. Felix tells Rufus Lyon that he learns self-control only after he leaves home and undergoes a conversion experience that occurs before the events of the novel.

thinking: "Western women were not to his taste: they showed a transition from the feebly animal to the thinking being, which was simply troublesome. Harold preferred a slow-witted large-eyed woman, silent and affectionate, with a load of black hair weighing much more heavily than her brains" (344–45). His arrogance and domination of women also indicate how he would govern those with less power than himself and implicitly undermine any Radical claims to change through political means. Michelle Weinroth points out the implications of Harold's tyranny, noting that "the portrait of Mrs. Transome—a mother mistreated at the hands of her irreverent and opportunistic son—implies that the most progressive of politics is hollow and futile if it is oblivious to the subjectivity of those upon whom societal change is foisted" (19). Harold has become just like his biological father, Jermyn, lacking the ability to perceive pain and sympathize with others, because as a child he was never taught to do so by his mother. Hence, Harold has failed to learn in the feminine private sphere the qualities necessary to operate justly in the public sphere.

Because Harold has been taught by his mother to think only of himself, Mrs. Transome also cannot obtain forgiveness from him for having had an affair. Hence, Mrs. Transome's emotional investment backfires on her. She refuses to confess her affair with Jermyn to Harold because she knows that he is incapable of the sympathy necessary to feel for her and, consequently, to forgive her. Although Mrs. Transome does not deny the truth about his illegitimacy when Harold asks her point-blank, this does not satisfy him because what he wants is what he expects from all women—submission.

While Eliot complicates the narrative of the fallen mother's salvation through her child, she does suggest that fallen women can and should be redeemed. One of the most striking aspects of the novel is the limited punishment that Mrs. Transome receives as a result of her sexual deviance. What is surprising about the depiction of Mrs. Transome's adultery is not so much her lapse of virtue itself, but the lack of narrative judgment about it in comparison to many other mid-Victorian novels with fallen women. Eliot, herself a fallen woman who experienced firsthand how George Henry Lewes was invited to dine while she was not, was acutely aware of how Victorian culture condoned sexual transgressions in men and condemned them in women. She repeatedly draws attention to the inequity of punishment Mrs. Transome has endured because of the sexual double standard. Although Mrs. Transome is not openly known to have an illegitimate child, everyone in the community has speculated about it, and she is socially isolated as a result of the suspicion while her former lover, Jermyn, has flourished in his career:

[T]he memory of those years all came back to her now with a protest against the cruelty that had all fallen on *her.* She started up with a new restlessness from this spirit of resistance. She was not penitent. She had borne too hard a punishment. Always the edge of calamity had fallen on *her.* Who had felt for her? (468; emphasis in original)

The novel emphasizes that while men typically escape their infidelities without any toll, women are left to suffer the psychic and material burdens of illicit affairs alone.

Instead of punishing Mrs. Transome, Eliot both acknowledges and subverts the conventions of melodrama that surround the representation of fallen women in the Victorian novel and in the philanthropic literature from the sexual rescue movement, thereby exposing the absurdity of the extreme punishment they receive. Although quite conscious of what is expected of her as a fallen woman, Mrs. Transome refuses to play her designated part. To understand just how radically Eliot revises the representation of fallen women, it is worth remembering that the archetypal fallen woman in the Victorian novel is more akin to Dickens's Lady Dedlock of *Bleak House,* who dies alone in the snow, socially outcast, than to Mrs. Transome. Even Ruth, a victim of seduction, who is redeemed at the end of that novel through her self-sacrificing behavior, still dies, while in *Aurora Leigh,* Marian Erle, a victim of rape, is exiled to Italy; they cannot be completely redeemed and restored to the community. Although Mrs. Transome clearly fears abjection and death as the consequence of the revelation of her affair and illegitimate child, she neither commits suicide nor emigrates. At the end of the novel, when Harold learns the truth, she emphatically refuses to enact the trope of the fallen woman in Victorian culture and participate in her self-destruction. She declares, "I am not ill. I am not going to die! I shall live—I shall live!" (467). Clearly, her death is expected according to narrative convention.

As Winifred Hughes points out, Mrs. Transome's plot line contains elements common to sensation fiction, and to a certain degree a woman's sexual sins were inherently and inevitably sensational; however, Eliot deflates the melodramatic expectations of that genre and gives Mrs. Transome a rather ordinary death that is represented as matter of fact rather than spectacular.[12] Significantly, Eliot insists on Mrs. Transome's return and reinte-

---

[12] Shuttleworth notes that sensation fiction contains numerous representations of excessive, undisciplined mothering, which was equated in Victorian culture with excessive, undisciplined sexuality and therefore fallenness: "The pages are full of unregulated motherhood: women who abandon their children or destroy them through love, who lash out in excesses of both sexual and maternal emotion, overturning all domestic peace around

gration into society: "[T]he Transome family were absent for some time from Transome Court.... After a while the family came back, and Mrs. Transome died there" (477). Mrs. Transome retains outward manifestations of respect from her neighbors, who follow her lead in handling the scandal by refusing to acknowledge it: "Sir Maximus was at her funeral, and throughout that neighborhood there was silence about the past" (477). Moreover, in a surprising reversal of the more typical outcome for sins of a sexual nature in Victorian fiction, it is Mrs. Transome's lover, Jermyn, who ends up having his reputation destroyed, and he is forced to leave the community permanently.[13]

Eliot rewrites the narrative of fallenness to include fathers as well as mothers and repeatedly emphasizes men's participation in lapses in virtue and the bearing of illegitimate children. Mrs. Transome knows that Jermyn simply expects that she will take upon herself the role of the mother who has sinned and now must account for herself to their son while Jermyn's pride remains intact. She pointedly reminds him of his part in their affair and his refusal to accept any responsibility for it: "I have caused you to strain your conscience, have I?—it is I who have sullied your purity? ... I would not lose the misery of being a woman, now I see what can be the baseness of a man" (401). Though many critics have commented on the bitterness of this last oft-quoted sentence, Mrs. Transome's refusal to capitulate to unfair standards and the narrative insistence on Jermyn's responsibility that follow it are not as often noted. Mrs. Transome forces Jermyn to reveal their secret to Harold himself, and by assuming responsibility for his paternity, insists that Jermyn share the burden of the consequences of their joint actions. Eliot thereby restructures the economy of sexual deviance through the displacement and redistribution of guilt to emphasize the father's role in the production of an illegitimate child and the mother's marginalization.

Although Mrs. Transome's social status and her subjective development allow her to be restored, her reintegration to the community is largely the result of Esther's intervention. While Mrs. Transome is not redeemed by her relationship with her son, Eliot does revise the maternal narrative so that the motherless Esther Lyon, a potential daughter-in-law to Mrs. Transome, mediates forgiveness between mother and son. The novel suggests

them. Yet the true villains of the piece, despite the 'safe' moral commentary offered by the narrators, tend to be the calculating and colorless males who pursue these women to their doom, a pursuit frequently tied to their own economic or social advantage" (49–50).

[13] Elizabeth Langland observes that even when forgiveness might be expected from a novelist who advocated sympathy and tolerance for human failure, Eliot tends to punish men who betray women: "[T]he compassion and forgiveness that shape the narrator's voice and infuse the lives of many of her characters are absent for these men" ("Promises Not Kept" 59).

that only a daughter and not a son could understand a woman's unique temptations and social vulnerability caused by the loss of virtue because women share an understanding of the precarious nature of their identity and social standing, knowing that even a small slip could have great and lasting consequences. Esther identifies with Mrs. Transome's suffering, and instead of forcing her supplication, offers compassion: "[T]here was mercy in her young heart; she might be a daughter who had no impulse to punish and to strike her whom fate had stricken. . . . The proud woman yearned for the caressing pity that must dwell in that young bosom" (469). Although Esther's forgiveness is predicated on ignorance of Mrs. Transome's sin, as Eliot cannot narrate Mrs. Transome's tale of illicit sexual relations to a pure, young virgin, Esther also does not require a humiliating confession in order to bestow it. This reversal of roles also suggests the kind of sympathetic, wise mother that Esther herself will become.

Significantly, it is Esther's powers of discernment that enable her to effect a reconciliation between mother and son by tapping Harold's anxieties about his newly liminal class status as an illegitimate child of a social upstart with an unsavory reputation. Harold eagerly desires to prove his true worth to Esther, whom he hopes to marry, and she appeals to his sense of honor and decency as a gentleman to forgive his mother by saying, "I know you would have come. I know you meant it" (471). Esther thereby gives Harold credit in advance for forgiving his mother, when in actuality it is not at all clear that he intends to do so, and he cannot refuse her request. By showing compassion, Harold can prove to Esther that his character, if not his birth, is gentlemanly and therefore reassert his former class status. Consequently, Esther becomes the medium for Harold to express his interiority, and although Mrs. Transome is a fallen woman, she evades the disciplinary effects of a sexual economy that punishes women's deviant behavior.

Therefore, although *Felix Holt* highlights women's unequal social vulnerability, it also explores the possibilities of women's agency, albeit of a limited kind, through the extension of the moral influence of that feminine best self that transcends politics and patriarchal custom. For Eliot, women's greatest agency lies in their ability to manipulate affect, and she subscribes to what Alison Booth has termed an "ideology of influence" that uses "the refined private insight of cultivated women" to implement positive change for women (36). By interpreting events and authorizing the truth about others (including intervening to obtain a pardon for Felix for his role in the riot),[14] Esther fulfills a hermeneutic function in the novel

---

[14] Only Esther can present Felix's intentions positively in the public domain for a middle-class audience, and she translates his behavior and interiority to the bourgeois magistrates. Felix and Harold, tainted by violence and corruption, cannot generate affect and lack the

at which the men fail. By mediating Harold's forgiveness of his mother through her skillful handling of complex representations of interiority and affect as signifiers of class, Esther not only absolves sins, she also controls the representation of subjectivity.[15]

Esther not only engineers Mrs. Transome's reintegration into the community, she avoids her own moral compromise through her relationship with her mother figure. Carolyn Dever notes that in Victorian fiction the absence or death of the mother can provide a source of empowerment or liberation for heroines and that frequently the loss of the mother is integral to subjective development, yet Eliot replaces a lost mother as a catalyst for Esther's personal and moral growth. Because Esther lacks a mother to guide her through courtship and marriage, she is consequently in danger of a moral lapse that Eliot equates to Mrs. Transome's when she considers marrying Harold for the wrong reasons—social position and fortune—when she does not love him. Although her adoptive stepfather, Rufus Lyon, has attempted to instill in Esther sound moral values, he cannot substitute for a mother and teach Esther how to negotiate courtship to guard her chastity and pick an appropriate marriage partner. Like Mrs. Transome, Esther has read all of the wrong books and admires dangerous Byronic heroes and their passionate outbursts, which does not prepare her to practice self-control over her desire.

However, Esther does not actually "fall"; she falls by proxy via Mrs. Transome, who is held up as an example of what Esther might become if she does not subdue her vanity and love of finery and make the correct choice in marriage. Although Esther technically never loses her virtue, nor by marrying Harold would she, Eliot clearly implies that marrying Harold for love of rank and luxury would require a moral compromise equal to a loss of virtue; marrying without love "seemed nothing less than a fall and a degradation" (465). Esther must undergo a disciplinary process of her own to develop sympathy and wisdom in order to avoid what would be a hollow, meaningless exercise in vanity.

While the Victorians frequently attributed a young woman's fall to the loss of her guiding influence at an early age, an ennobling love for a new mother figure also indicated her potential for redemption by revealing her better nature. Esther both loves Mrs. Transome and wishes to emulate her gracefulness and sense of decorum as part of her aspirations to become a lady, yet also recognizes Mrs. Transome's suffering and its relation to her

---

credibility to be believable. Esther's "confession of faith" in Felix during the trial conveys her sincere approbation of him as possessing a middle-class subjectivity, and she thereby constructs his identity in addition to Harold's (448).

[15] Struve makes a similar point (7).

past mistakes. Esther has ample opportunity to observe Mrs. Transome's unhappiness and realizes that her "youthful brilliancy" has been replaced with "a joyless, embittered age" (459). Therefore, her mother figure's example warns Esther that she must choose wisely to avoid a similar fate: "[T]his daily presence of elderly dissatisfaction amidst such outward things as she had always thought must greatly help to satisfy, awaked, not merely vague questioning emotion, but strong determining thought" (460). Much as Harold sees his likeness to his father in the mirror, so, too, does Esther recognize her future self in her surrogate mother and realizes that "Harold had a padded yoke ready for the neck of every man, woman, and child that depended on him" (419). She would not only "fall" by marrying Harold, she would also end up just as subordinate to him as his mother. Moreover, Esther learns to value the personal qualities over material possessions, and the novel emphasizes that psychology and personality transcend social status. Like the workers, Esther ought not aspire to wealth but to personal worth.

Therefore, Esther's decision not to marry Harold breaks the cycle of women participating in their own oppression. Although critics have argued that the narrative closure of the ending with Esther's marriage to Felix conflicts with the critique of patriarchy embodied in Mrs. Transome's bitterness, arguing that Felix is just as domineering as Harold, I disagree that the ending of *Felix Holt* suggests that Esther submits to his will.[16] Rather, I agree with Rita Bode, who argues that Esther's influence over Felix is substantial. Bode states, "Esther likes the idea of Felix's superiority to her; but despite Esther's embracing of her inferiority, the novel presents the possibility that she chooses Felix because he is open to her influence, whereas Harold Transome is not" (779).[17] The logic of the novel supports the argument that Esther has more influence over the men in her life than Mrs. Transome and will not replicate her condition of supplication. It is Esther who engineers Felix's pardon, convinces him to abandon his objection to marriage, and supports him with her money, while it is Felix who "grumbles" at the end of the novel that he is at risk of becoming a "sleek dog" (477) from adapting too much to his wife's aspirations and lifestyle (478). Thus, instead of reading the ending of the novel as about one more woman about to be subsumed into an inevitable stifling cycle of self-denial in marriage and maternity, I would argue that Eliot rewrites the maternal narrative to make it the story of the daughter's and the mother's redemption through each other.

[16] See Langland, "Patriarchal Ideology" (392).
[17] Struve also emphasizes Esther's agency (10–12). See also Elizabeth Starr, who argues that Esther's influence is greater than Felix's by the end of the novel: "In the spectacle of her [Esther's] wedding to him . . . Felix figures only as a minor character" (72).

Mrs. Transome and Esther undergo the kind of personal, moral transformation in the novel that Eliot advocates for the workers in *Felix Holt* and, more explicitly, in "The Address to Working Men." They demonstrate the process that the workers must experience to become their best selves—morally improved, self-disciplined, and capable of compassion. However, while Eliot at times seems to ally the disempowered middle-class women with that of working-class men, structurally and thematically, she ultimately makes a significant distinction between them. While the working classes are encouraged to improve themselves and the lives of their children by becoming educated and learning self-control, it is only by adopting middle-class values, and not by attaining the status of the middle class economically or politically, which would indeed require more radical measures than *Felix Holt* advocates.

Hence, through this process of moral growth in *Felix Holt,* Eliot posits the development of the self, which achieves its apogee in the attainment of sympathy combined with self-discipline, as an antidote to one's material conditions in life. The "best life [is] that where one bears and does everything because of some great and strong feeling—so that this and that in one's circumstances don't signify" (253). That best self, of course, is both a middle-class and a feminized one, but workers only need to emulate the values and behavior of the middle class to avoid the disquieting excess of rioting and mayhem. Of course, the focus on moral development through good parenting, particularly good mothering, instead of aspiring to more ambitious structural reform, defuses the potential for violent social change and collective political action. Thus, becoming one's best self elides the need to change one's "circumstances"—political and material conditions—and the domestic plot deflects attention from collective struggle for greater rights to emphasize subjectivity and individuality. *Felix Holt* ultimately uses individual relations to solve political problems, thereby obfuscating what initially appear to be radical critiques of class domination.

Although *Felix Holt* is conservative in its class politics, it is much more radical in its revision of the maternal narrative. Eliot critiques the debilitating effects of the maternal ideal with its encouragement to eradicate the self, which only perpetuates the domination of women. Rather, good mothering requires having a range of interests outside of one's children. Investing all of one's energy into children only teaches sons to expect the same slavish devotion from all women and also does not prepare them to exercise good judgment and behave sympathetically to members of the body politic. In order for men to become better at governing, they need to be reared by mothers who do not deny their own needs and identities, thereby discouraging men's narcissism and encouraging their ability to empathize with others.

Works Cited

Anderson, Amanda. *Tainted Souls and Painted Faces: The Rhetoric of Fallenness in Victorian Culture.* Ithaca: Cornell University Press, 1993.
Anon. "Christian Charity Not Sentiment." *Magdalen's Friend and Female Homes' Intelligencer* 4 (1863): 35–39.
Armstrong, Nancy. *Desire and Domestic Fiction: A Political History of the Novel.* New York: Oxford University Press, 1987.
Bentley, Colene. "Democratic Citizenship in Felix Holt." *Nineteenth-Century Contexts* 24.3 (2002): 271–89.
Bode, Rita. "Power and Submission in *Felix Holt, the Radical.*" *Studies in English Literature, 1500–1900* 35.4 (Fall 1995): 769–88.
Booth, Alison. *Greatness Engendered: George Eliot and Virginia Woolf.* Ithaca: Cornell University Press, 1992.
Browning, Elizabeth Barrett. *Aurora Leigh.* Ed. Kerry McSweeney. Oxford: Oxford University Press, 1993.
Craik, Dinah Mulock. *A Woman's Thoughts about Women.* London: Hurst and Blackett, Limited, 1858.
Davidoff, Leonore, and Catherine Hall. *Family Fortunes: Men and Women of the English Middle Class, 1780–1850.* 2nd ed. Chicago: University of Chicago Press, 1991.
Dever, Carolyn. *Death and the Mother from Dickens to Freud: Victorian Fiction and the Anxiety of Origins.* Cambridge: Cambridge University Press, 1998.
Dickens, Charles. *Bleak House.* Ed. George Ford and Sylvere Monod. New York: W. W. Norton & Company, 1977.
Eliot, George. *Adam Bede.* Ed. Valentine Cunningham. Oxford: Oxford University Press, 1996.
———. *Felix Holt, the Radical.* Ed. Linda Mugglestone. London: Penguin Books, 1995.
Gaskell, Elizabeth. *Ruth.* Ed. Angus Easton. London: Penguin Books, 1997.
Hopkins, Ellice. *Work among the Lost.* London: Hatchards, 1877 (1870).
Hughes, Winifred. *The Maniac in the Cellar: Sensation Novels of the 1860s.* Princeton: Princeton University Press, 1980.
Jeune, Mary. "Helping the Fallen." *Fortnightly Review* 44 (November 1, 1885): 669–82.
Langland, Elizabeth. "Patriarchal Ideology and Marginal Motherhood in Victorian Novels by Women." *Studies in the Novel* 19 (Fall 1987): 381–94.
———. "Promises Not Kept: Sexual Infidelity and the Vengeful George Eliot." *Postscript* 3 (1986): 53–60.
Logan, Deborah Anna. *Fallenness in Victorian Women's Writing: Marry, Stitch, Die, or Do Worse.* Columbia: University of Missouri Press, 1998.
Mugglestone, Lynda. "Introduction." In *Felix Holt, the Radical.* London: Penguin Books, 1995. vii–xxviii.
Mumm, Susan. "'I Love My Sex': Two Late Victorian Pulpit Women." In *Women, Scholarship, and Criticism: Gender and Knowledge, c. 1790–1900.* Ed. Joan Bellamy, Anne Laurence, and Gill Perry. Manchester: Manchester University Press, 2000. 204–21.
Nestor, Pauline. *Female Friendship and Communities: Charlotte Brontë, George Eliot, Elizabeth Gaskell.* Oxford: Clarendon Press, 1985.
Shuttleworth, Sally. "Demonic Mothers: Ideologies of Bourgeois Motherhood in the Mid-Victorian Era." In *Rewriting the Victorians: Theory, History.* Ed. Linda M. Shires. New York: Routledge, 1992. 31–51.

Starr, Elizabeth. "'Influencing the Moral Taste': Literary Work, Aesthetics, and Social Change in *Felix Holt, the Radical.*" *Nineteenth-Century Literature* 56.1 (2001): 52–75.

Steer, Mary H. "Rescue Work by Women among Women." In *Woman's Mission: A Series of Congress Papers on the Philanthropic Work of Women by Eminent Writers.* Ed. Baroness Burdett-Coutts. New York: Charles Scribner's Sons, 1893. 149–59.

Struve, Laura. "Expert Witnesses: Women and Publicity in Mary Barton and Felix Holt." *Victorian Review* 28 (2002): 1–24.

Weinroth, Michelle. "Engendering Consent: the Voice of Persuasion in *Felix Holt, the Radical.*" *Victorians Institute Journal* 32 (2004): 7–44.

CHAPTER 4

Elderly Mothers and Middle-Aged Daughters in Charles Dickens's *Dombey and Son*

TERESA MANGUM[*]

Charles Dickens's title *Dombey and Son: Wholesale, Retail, and for Exportation* provocatively misleads readers. The novel does indeed open with Mr. Dombey's ecstatic welcome of his male heir. Yet in directing attention to father and son, the title also diverts readers' attention from the centrality of a second narrative launched in those first few pages: the story of mother and daughter. "Son"—named Paul like his father and grandfather before him—appears aged and frail in infancy and dies before reaching either adolescence or the midpoint of the novel. The daughter not only quietly dominates the novel, as many critics have pointed out; she also introduces a series of mothers and daughters. Destined to be divided from both her biological mother and stepmother, Florence Dombey assuages the trauma of maternal loss by assuming the role of mother herself—nurturing her beloved brother Paul, her own children, and ultimately her father. The other daughters in the novel face quite different challenges.

From the first serial installment in 1846 until the conclusion appeared in 1848, the novel divided readers' attention between the father/son focus of the title and the mother/daughter iterations in the plot. The opening paragraphs show as well as tell readers that Dombey senior has long

---

[*] I wish to thank the University of Iowa Provost's Office and the Obermann Center for Advanced Studies for supporting the writing of this essay. I am also grateful to members of the Dickens Project for inviting me to give an earlier version at the "Dickens Universe" in Santa Cruz and for offering helpful suggestions.

neglected his wife and daughter Florence. When Mrs. Dombey dies just after Paul's birth, the heartbroken six-year-old daughter is forever divided from the mother whom she adores. Later, as a young girl still grieving for her biological mother's death, Florence nevertheless thrills to the possibility of having a second mother. This stepmother—the seething, imperious, vengeful Edith—succumbs to a social demise as decisive as the first Mrs. Dombey's material death. The second Mrs. Dombey punishes her would-be conqueror, Mr. Dombey, and her would-be seducer, Dombey's manager Carker, first by absconding to France with Carker and then by abandoning the double-crossed double-dealer to the consequences of his professional suicide. In both cases, Florence labors as diligently throughout the novel to absolve these absent mothers of their seeming abandonment of their daughter as she does to forgive the far more prominent father figure's cruelty and neglect. While a father's eventual recognition of a daughter's worth forms the bathetic resolution of the ironically titled *Dombey and Son,* Mrs. Dombey's death motivates the novel's complementary fascination with daughters who struggle toward reconciliation with their mothers. This sometimes submerged mother/daughter plot surfaces in two crucial secondary plots that interrupt and obliquely comment upon the Dombey family saga. Two pairs of pimping mothers and violated, vengeful daughters—Mrs. Brown and her daughter Alice Marwood, on one hand, and the formerly wealthy Mrs. Skewton and her daughter Edith, on the other—concentrate tensions between parents and children into the often lived but seldom told story of grown daughters and their elderly mothers. Rather than facing maternal loss as Florence does, these daughters must make their peace with the overwhelming, unjust, and even injurious demands of long-lived mothers whose age and rage position them as deeply Other to sentimental portraits of radiant new mothers or reassuring middle-aged mothers, much less to the sweetly melancholy memory of dead mothers.

In the father/daughter plot of *Dombey and Son,* filial self-abnegation and masochism win praise; in the mother/daughter plot mothers are sternly called to account for the home truths coming to haunt their midlife daughters.[1] At the same time, these midlife daughters learn to master not their mothers but their own anger, blame, and self-pity. The novel rewards the youthful Florence for turning her father into a man emotionally dependent upon her and a loving grandfather to her children. The two middle-aged daughters are also rewarded, but in a far more qualified fashion. Rather

---

[1] The ages defined as midlife are as flexible then as now. I am using the term loosely to encompass adult daughters. Both of these daughters are not only past girlhood, but they are prematurely matured and aged by their unprotected, exploited youths.

than winning love and pity, these bitter, unsentimental, yet conscientious daughters choose to take responsibility for their intractable elderly mothers. The learning process each midlife daughter undergoes rewards readers with what might be the greatest achievement, given the value system of Victorian fiction—genuine character development leading to greater psychological complexity and maturity. As with so many Victorian fallen female characters, the "ruined" daughter is inevitably punished with literal or social death, but not before she fully acknowledges the forces that shaped her mother. Pitted against one another by class but linked as victims of dominating men and manipulating mothers, these two adult daughters rewrite sentimental Victorian narratives of mother/daughter love in order to survive the selfish parents whom they must now unselfishly mother.[2]

Critical studies of mothers and maternity very often focus on childbirth, on the early years of child rearing, or on the relationship between a young woman struggling through her courtship years and her supportive (or problematic) mother. But how do we study, much less judge, elderly mothers whose authority and judgment are overthrown by such illnesses as strokes, Alzheimer's disease, or dementia? Literary critics, sociologists, and psychologists alike scrutinize younger mothers for characteristics such as maternal devotion, evidence of responsibility, endurance in the face of hardship on their children's behalf, self-sacrifice (or, alternatively, the capacity to balance maternal and other roles), as well as for their patience, understanding, and empathy. Yet these already unfairly high standards are clearly unreasonable expectations for enfeebled elderly women who are themselves no longer capable of reason or judgment. A novel like *Dombey and Son* suggests that when it comes to such maternal figures, we are driven to examine and even to judge mothers through the character, choices, and actions of their daughters. The daughter is the remaining trace of the mother, not only in a biological sense, but also in social, emotional, and ethical senses as well. Forbidden to judge the mother in her shattered old age—however vicious she might have been in her own youth

---

[2] In her essay on the suppression of the "woman's story," that is, the sexual pasts of female characters in the novel, Joss Marsh similarly argues for this same internally conflicted plot structure but in regards to sexual stories. Just as I see the novel quite uniquely first tell the story of elderly mothers and middle-aged daughters and then suppress it, Marsh brilliantly demonstrates that the novel "both gives woman a voice and silences her" (405) in what she ultimately describes as a logic not of silencing but of displacement. She argues that this displacement moves the stories of fallen women into the knowledge of pure women (Edith's story is a gift to Florence while Alice tells the story of her birth and her fall to Harriet Carker). Thus, in her own distinctive argument, Marsh joins numerous critics who argue in one way or another that the core of Dombey and Son "may in fact be a woman's story" (406).

and midlife—the reader must rely on the daughter, who judges for us and in whom the mother continues to live and so to be judged. The degree to which the daughter accepts, rejects, or abandons the mother is therefore crucial to readers' response *to* the mother. In effect, the daughter's actions form a judgment upon the mother, but the person the daughter is or becomes—how she thinks, feels, and acts—also enacts a judgment *of* her mother's past mothering.

Perhaps today more than ever the seldom-recounted stories of elderly mothers and adult daughters need telling. Kathleen Buckwalter, a professor of nursing trained in psychiatry and geriatric medicine, has done fascinating research on the many middle-aged women who—like the fictional Edith and Alice—unexpectedly find themselves the caretakers of feeble, failing mothers whom the daughters believe have done them great wrong. In "Negotiating Family Relationships: Dementia Care as a Midlife Developmental Task," Buckwalter and her collaborators Kathleen Sherrell and Darby Morhardt discuss the path to what Margaret Blenkner labeled "filial maturity" in the title of a 1965 article on the topic. In response to innumerable representations of bristling, burdened, middle-aged children who care for their elderly parents only under duress, these multidisciplinary gerontological researchers seek more hopeful stories of caregiving. Their years of interviewing caregivers suggest that parent care is "a developmental task that provides opportunities for psychological growth and the potential for positive rewards from the care-giving experience" (Sherrell, Buckwalter, and Morhardt 383). Until fairly recently, they argue, researchers have overlooked the ways painful family histories "adversely affect the degree of concern adults feel toward their aging parents as well as the quality of their contemporary relationships" (385). The researchers' alternative view of caregiving focuses on the midlife caregiver's version of her (and occasionally his) family history and the plot twist—or "filial crisis"—that converts oppression into opportunity for those caregivers who make peace with familial pasts (386). They believe that to reconstruct a sense of intractable victimization as a narrative of development the adult child must overcome at least three obstacles to empathy and maturity. Those obstacles are the tendency to become trapped in reviews of perceived past injustices; the consequent failure to view the ill, aged parent with any degree of objectivity; and, finally, the often unconscious anxieties about one's own mortality that can further alienate a caregiver from a dying parent (386). In other words, until a crisis forces a caregiver to surrender interpretations of the personal plot that positions her as the victim of her parent's past abuses, caregiving is felt to be a burden. On the other hand, caregivers who relinquish long-held grievances often discover that each period of life has what these researchers call "distinct tasks or psychological mini-crises that are expected and healthy aspects of growth" (390). As an additional benefit, adult caretakers who accomplish the task of reconciliation with their and their parents' pasts also have great hope for fulfilling relationships with their children when, in the years to come, they find themselves in need of that next generation's care.

Turning the sociological insights of contemporary gerontological research to fiction, we can see that a genuine transformation of the midlife daughter/aging mother plot would require not merely individual growth and maturity, but also vistas beyond most available fictive family tropes. Perhaps it should not be surprising that Dickens, who is habitually described as the leading Victorian novelist in celebrating (and skewering) the family, would also tend to interrogate and critique family life.[3] George Newlin, in fact, argues that the novelist actively and consistently resisted conventional family structure based on Newlin's count of 149 full orphans and 318 full or partial orphans in Dickens's novels (120). The experiences of older mothers and daughters lies outside the familiar family plots that gave shape to Victorian novels, which tend to ignore or marginalize midlife women and elderly women, with rare exceptions such as the aging spinsters and widows in Elizabeth Gaskell's *Cranford* (1853). For a typical young Victorian heroine like Florence Dombey to anticipate any sort of adulthood, much less a future that hints of happily ever after, fictions of family romance would require a more nuanced, capacious account of the life course, rather than ending with the marriage of youthful characters. In Dickens's case, as the world of the novel spreads its generational wings, new mother/daughter plots take flight even if the limits of Dickens's personal and historical vision clip those wings by the novel's end.

Dombey and Son's account of midlife daughters intriguingly anticipates the insights of these optimistic gerontologists: even very bitter, very angry, and very unwilling midlife daughters, such as Edith and Alice, find unanticipated, hard-won accomplishment in caring for their mothers once they forgive those mothers for real and imagined abuses. In Dickens's paired plots, the middle-aged daughters wrestle with feelings of being unloved, abused, exploited, and denied the simple pleasures of girlhood. Out of this youthful, sullen vengefulness, however, each character slowly makes her way toward the kind of maturity, acceptance, and generosity we all hope will come to us as gifts of midlife as each daughter learns to forgive her mother. Only then can the middle-aged daughter find fulfillment in simultaneously accepting herself as a daughter and mothering her own mother.

---

[3] See, for example, Catherine Waters's *Dickens and the Politics of the Family* (1997).

The melodramatic juxtaposition and moments of recognition that mark the final moments of both mother/daughter relationships envision such reconciliation, in a unique if only partial stitching together of the shredded social ties that have left Edith and Alice, these similar yet also deeply different middle-aged daughters, so desperately, furiously alienated from nearly everyone, yet still tied to their mothers.

While the individual scenes of importance in understanding the distinctive features of each mother/daughter relationship happen before and after the moment of the pairs' meeting, their strategic encounter provides the most crucial and revealing thematic and structural links uniting these characters. The importance of the scene is registered through a further doubling of text and image: the accompanying illustration by Hablot Browne (or "Phiz"), titled "A Chance Meeting," repeats and intensifies the force of the unexpected meeting (Fig. 4.1). In this uncanny confrontation, Alice voices her anger to Edith with shocking directness: "'What is it that you have to sell?' said Edith. . . . 'Only this,' returned the woman, holding out her wares, without looking at them. 'I sold myself long ago'" (Dickens 481). Stung by the implied accusation, Mrs. Brown pleads with Mrs. Skewton for sympathy as well as coins: "'She's my handsome and undutiful daughter. She gives me nothing but reproaches, my Lady, for all I have done for her. Look at her now, my Lady, how she turns upon her poor old mother with her looks'" (482). Stunned from her post-stroke haze by this startling reiteration of her own grievances, Mrs. Skewton doubles her coins and whimpers reassurance, even lecturing the silent Alice: "'I hope' addressing the daughter, 'that you'll show more gratitude and natural what's its name, and all the rest of it . . . for there never was a better mother than the good old creature's been to you'" (482). The mothers recognize themselves in one another as do the daughters, but at this point the daughters have yet to reconcile themselves to their respective mothers. Each accepts the care of her mother as an exhausting, inevitable, painful duty; neither has found much more than misery in her role as adult caretaker of a mother she may in some way love, but certainly also hates. The meeting of these four characters—the haggard, miserably failed, self-pitying old mothers for once placed at the center between their two proud, angry, yet curiously loyal middle-aged daughters—elevates the suppressed story of middle-aged daughter and dependent aged mother into an emblematic social script in the succinct melodramatic *tableau vivant* that Hablot Browne's etching makes it hard for us to forget. The scene most obviously works to introduce Mrs. Skewton and Edith to Mrs. Brown and Alice. However, it also self-consciously situates each pair as a mirror to the other in doubled, intensifying assertion of the thematic and formal importance

Figure 4.1. Hablot Browne's etching "A Chance Meeting" from *Dombey and Son*.

of the case that is building for fractured and alternative families that the novel ultimately pits against the suffocating effects of conventional family dynamics.

Turning to the individual pairs of mothers and daughters and their particular conflicts, we see that both Mrs. Brown and Mrs. Skewton are constructed through a range of associations that condemn them for being bad mothers and for failing to retreat before the desires of the middle-aged who seek to supplant older generations. An event outside the margins of the novel suggests how fascinated readers must have been with the terrifying exploiter of children, Mrs. Brown.[4] Even before the final installment of the novel appeared, Thomas Prochlus Taylor's play, *Dombey and Son; Good Mrs. Brown the Child Stealer* (sometimes with two acts, sometimes three, and often with fifteen tableaux based loosely on Browne's etchings) opened

---

[4] This fascination continues in the few recent critical studies that focus on Mrs. Brown. Michelle Mancini discusses Mrs. Brown's fusion of "the monstrous and infernal" with "the incapacitated, abject and needy" into an "agent of surveillance" who embodies Dickens's "fantasies and fears about observation and narration" (113–40).

at the Royal Strand Theatre in London on August 9, 1847.[5] The play was short-lived, but popular enough to be published in *G. Purkess' Penny Pictorial Plays* in 1848 (print editions also appear in 1858). Audiences' interest in Mrs. Brown probably emanated from the threats she embodied: as a thorough outcast whose chief allegiance—like Carker and Dombey himself—is to coin, Mrs. Brown barters stolen goods, secrets, and children with no remorse.

In the actual novel, the perversity of Mrs. Brown's maternity is established early on. We are introduced to her through her livelihood—kidnapping and robbing helpless and vulnerable children. When young, motherless Florence is separated from her maid in the chaos of London streets, she is briefly "adopted" by the brutally antimaternal Mrs. Brown, "a very ugly old woman, with red rims round her eyes, and a mouth that mumbled and chattered of itself when she was not speaking" (58). In addition to kidnapping Florence and stealing her clothes, Mrs. Brown also, and even more ominously, absconds with Florence's social identity by dressing the child in "a girl's dress quite worn out and very old; and the crushed remains of a bonnet that had probably been picked up from some ditch or dunghill" (60). Then in a mad scene worthy of Lear, Mrs. Brown is stopped short of violently pilfering Florence's hair by the paralyzing memories of her own lost daughter—"'If I hadn't once had a gal of my own—beyond seas now—that was proud of her hair . . . I'd have had every lock of it'" (60). Mrs. Brown's brutal treatment of Florence—in what Joss Marsh considers the key chapter in the novel as the scene of this daughter's defilement (408)—threatens us with the likelihood that the taint of the bad mother fatally dooms the daughter to become a social pariah as well as an emotional orphan. The moment graphically anticipates the emotional problem with which the plot must wrestle when that lost—in multiple senses of the word—daughter reappears. The extravagant grotesqueries of this "mother"—she is unrelentingly dirty, depraved, avaricious, brutal, violent, and witchlike in her periodic madness—forbid sympathy, much less redemption. The narrative encourages both our revulsion and a desire to see Mrs. Brown punished ruthlessly. This, then, is the mother whom the middle-aged Alice must claim.

The novel exploits, even as it inverts, the full resources of sentimental fiction when we first see mother and daughter together. To heighten readers' aversion to this terrible mother, the novel poisons the potentially soul-stirring scene of the mother/daughter reunion. We learn that after being

---

[5] The play is still available in the British Library, which holds a fascinating array of parodies, plays, and plagiarized short versions of the novel.

seduced and abandoned, Mrs. Brown's daughter Alice Marwood was convicted of theft and transported to the colonies. Alice's return seems equally motivated by her determination to destroy her seducer and her grudging sense of duty to her mother. Michelle Mancini argues that Mrs. Brown is seldom considered by critics and that when she is, her importance arises from her abduction of Florence or her role as Alice's mother, rather than as "someone who both has a story of her own and who learns, deploys, and manipulates the stories of others" (121). But in a perhaps too subtle distinction, I would argue that her connections to Florence and Alice constitute the real subject of the story. First the ersatz and then the actual mother/daughter relationship form that subject rather than either mother or daughter alone.

In the case of Mrs. Brown and Alice, the two characters struggle repeatedly for control of that mutually constituted story and its implications in a conflict that reinterprets maternal obligation on a social, even national scale. Mrs. Brown awaits Alice's arrival in a frightening, hysterical, animal state of pleasure and misery, "rocking herself to and fro with every frantic demonstration of which her vitality was capable" (409). The mother's only greeting for her "contemptuous" daughter is "a low moaning sound" of "inarticulate complainings" (410). Inevitably, that muttered complaint turns into demand, a demand expressive both of the mother's uncontrollable greed and of her insistence that Alice acknowledge her as a good mother. They debate their relationship in thoroughly Victorian terms as each raises the question of who owes *duty* to whom and of how one would exercise familial duty in the midst of poverty, deprivation, and utter collapse of any familial or social support. Alice adamantly resists her mother's interpretation of their story, as will Edith in an analogous scene with her equally insistent mother:

> "I don't know who began to harden me, if my own dear mother didn't.... Listen, Mother, to a word or two. If we understand each other now, we shall not fall out any more, perhaps. I went away a girl, and have come back a woman. I went away undutiful enough, and have come back no better, you may swear. But have you been very dutiful to me?" (410)

In shock and fury, her mother denies the claim of maternal duty: "'I!' cried the old woman. 'To my own gal! A mother dutiful to her own child!'" to which Alice coolly replies: "'I have heard some talk about duty first and last; but it has always been of my duty to other people. I have wondered now and then—to pass away the time—whether no one ever owed any duty to me'" (410–11). Alice is so traumatized by her mother's neglect of maternal duty, a failure exacerbated by the further evisceration of duty first by her gentleman seducer and then by a judge—in effect the legal system of the mother country itself fails her—that she is reduced to describing herself as a child in the third person. She forces her version of the past upon her mother, beginning the first of several versions of that history "in terrible derision of herself": "'There was a child called Alice Marwood . . .'" (411). Ultimately, the daughter couches her accusations against the now elderly mother as bitter memories of being "'born among poverty and neglect, and nursed in it,'" where "'[n]obody taught her, nobody stepped forward to help her, nobody cared for her,'" or alternately of being "'too well helped on, too much looked after'" once her mother discovered the value of her beauty (411). At this point in the shifting power structure of the mother/daughter relationship, the daughter's inability to escape their past temporarily resolves itself through the construction of a mutual enemy, the seducer both women can agree stole Alice's childhood and hence the villain they can mutually plot to punish.

In this phase of the mother/daughter plot, displacement of daughterly rage from the aged mother to the man who served as Mrs. Brown's sexually exploitive double leads Alice to a midlife truce with her mother, but not with their past. Though Carker has exploited her sexually and abetted her transportation and is therefore the object of her most intense rage, Alice's hostility to her mother, because more complex, is more corrosive. At the same time, Alice's third-person monologue moves from her own "ruin" (411) to the "'crowds of little wretches, boy and girl'" who face the same fate (412), thereby redefining maternal duty as the social obligation of the reader, of middle-class society, of the courts, and even of the country. These elaborated associations assert the epic proportions of failed maternity even as the novel castigates Victorian treatment of the poor. Yet this larger "maternal" failure also marks Alice's first steps toward forgiveness as she wearily calls a temporary truce:

> "There! I have done Mother. . . . Don't let you and I talk of being dutiful, whatever we do. Your childhood was like mine, I suppose. . . . I don't want to blame you, or to defend myself; why should I? That's all over, long ago. But I am a woman—not a girl, now—and you and I needn't make a show of our history, like the gentlemen in the Court. We know all about it, well enough." (412)

Here again, the language links maternal failure to social and legal failure, but because Alice is suppressing rather than addressing the anger she feels at her mother's past abuses, she falsifies a difference between familial and social "duty." The significance of this suppression becomes clear when Alice seems to turn into her mother, which would completely end any hope of her own redemption, much less that of her mother.

That dreaded fate—becoming the bad mother—threatens when Alice and her mother set aside their differences and indulge in mutual brutalization of a child. Young "Rob the Grinder" is a fawning, double-crossing weasel, but a child nonetheless. Mother and daughter torture Rob into revealing Carker's whereabouts after the manager's flight with Edith so that the enraged Mr. Dombey will carry out their vicarious revenge against Alice's seducer of old. In the scene, Mrs. Brown turns the tables on her daughter. Just as Alice has accused her of maternal neglect, she now accuses Alice of one of the greatest crimes against old age, the misreading of late life need as infantile dependency: "'You think I'm in my second childhood, I know!' croaked the old woman. 'That's the respect and duty that I get from my own gal, but I'm wiser than you take me for'" (606).[6] This second charge, like the first, resolves itself through mutual exogamous enmity. But as Alice urges her mother on: "'Well done, Mother. Tear him to pieces!'" (612), the daughter is tarred by the mother's brush. Alice degenerates into her mother—beating, badgering, and violently abusing a child for her own bitter ends. The brutally comic picture of Mrs. Brown extorting information, as mother and daughter ricochet between grotesque parodies of maternal tenderness and actual physical torture, confirms Alice's claims of her mother's cruelty and of the deeply damaging effects of that cruelty to the child who is now the grown daughter. However, the scene also pinions mother and daughter as doubles as well as antagonists in their generational struggle, thus illuminating yet another fundamental anxiety inhibiting progress in the mother/daughter plot—the dangers of a curiously hereditary identification pictured here as fatal repetition. Before Alice can escape this fate, she will have to face her other mirror, Edith, a second middle-aged daughter in a furious struggle with her mother over her and their futures. In that "chance meeting," each sees in the other what she might become if she remains trapped in a past of rage against victimization by her mother.

Only as she approaches her own death does Alice turn to her mother's story—the presumed story of a mother's failure to save her daughter from ruin. Implicitly asking Harriet Carker to look beyond the "red rims round her eyes, and a mouth that mumbled and chattered of itself when she was not speaking" (15), beyond Mrs. Brown's unexpected vanity, her wild

---

[6] For a rich discussion of the damaging impact of this metaphor, see Hockey and James's essay "Back to Our Futures: Imaging Second Childhood."

cries, mad laments, and uncertain temper, Alice compels her mother to tell Harriet the story of Mrs. Brown's own seduction and betrayal (690). Alice thus *shares* her conversion from embittered daughter clinging to youthful wrongs to a middle-aged daughter who in forgiving her mother has herself learned how to die. Alice explains with eloquent dignity:

> "I had heard so much, in my wrong-doing, of my neglected duty, that I took up with the belief that duty had not been done to me, and that as the seed was sown, the harvest grew. I somehow made it out that when ladies had bad homes and mothers, they went wrong in their way, too; but that their way was not so foul a one as mine, and they had need to bless God for it. That is all past. . . . You will not forget my mother? I forgive her, if I have any cause. I know that she forgives me, and is sorry in her heart. You will not forget her?" (691)

Seldom content with the pathetic when the bathetic tempts him, Dickens insistently marks this moment of the daughter's forgiveness by aligning her with Christian salvation even as she attempts to redeem her mother. Thus Alice dies with the Bible in her arms, saved by her capacity to forgive and rewarded with the rare moment of wisdom and maturity she savors as she connects her mother's story to her own and then forgives them both. In Mrs. Brown's case, the daughter is a Son—crucified by her mother and thus her mother's salvation—after all. Forgiven by the daughter, the sad, mad old woman loses that daughter only to have her resurrected in Harriet Carker. As the sister of the man who seduced Mrs. Brown's daughter, Harriet finds her own reconciliation with a cruel familial past when she adopts this aging, unregenerate, and pathetic elderly mother.

Our introduction to Mrs. Skewton and her daughter Edith similarly functions to cast the elderly mother in the flattening, distancing light of the grotesque in order to dramatize the distance the middle-aged daughter must go to reconcile with her mother and hence with herself. The closing lines of the sixteenth number of the serialized version of the novel explicitly link the two mothers and daughters, shifting narrative attention from the poverty-stricken pair to the pair dancing on the brink of middle-class financial disaster:

> Were this miserable mother, and this miserable daughter, only the reduction to their lowest grade, of certain social vices sometimes prevailing higher up? In this round world of many circles within circles, do we make a weary journey from the high grade to the low, to find at last that they lie close together, that the two extremes touch. . . . Allowing for great

difference of stuff and texture, was the pattern of this woof repeated among gentle blood at all?

Say, Edith Dombey! And Cleopatra, best of mothers, let us have your testimony. (417)

At this "high grade" of the social scale, Mrs. Skewton and her widowed daughter Edith haunt social settings where Mrs. Skewton uses her wiles to procure a husband for Edith and thereby to secure a ticket to wealth and social position for herself. Oddly analogous with, if far more polished and arrogant than, Alice, Edith lives in a state of barely suppressed fury, steeled to the bitter duty of buying a future for herself and her mother, yet clinging to her sense of honor by refusing any pretense that she feels love or pleasure at the prospect of marrying Mr. Dombey. While Alice submerges her anger at her mother in revenge on a third party, Edith first seems to be offered a much more fulfilling choice. She can escape her elderly mother by lovingly mothering her own new "daughter," Florence, to whom she is immediately drawn. However, Dombey makes clear that Florence will suffer if Edith shows the daughter tenderness even as she arrogantly defies her husband (and Florence's father). Thus, Edith's avenue of escape from her misery is cut off along with her hopes for maternity. One could argue that it is not Dombey nor Carker nor the bad mother (Mrs. Skewton) who sends Edith to her destruction, but aborted motherhood—first in the drowning of a son from Edith's previous marriage and then the even crueler, because utterly unnecessary, loss of her "daughter" and hence herself.

On the other hand, the novel goes to great lengths to tell the story, once again, not only of a mother and a daughter, but also of the history and character of their relationship. Mrs. Brown is driven by poverty to turn her daughter's beauty into a commodity, adding young Alice to the goods through which she might satisfy her greed as well as need; Mrs. Skewton's maternal failures arise from vanity. For years she lives in denial of her aging—a process that encompasses her social as well as familial role as "mother." Even after she submits to substituting Edith for herself as bait for male attention and the economic and social privileges of marriage, she ventriloquizes the daughter, using and usurping Edith for her own ends. Mrs. Skewton's maternity is thus stunted by her selfish desires. She clings to the privileged position of "the daughter," the character who commands center stage in the courtship plot. At the same time, she exploits her own daughter for the social rewards that accrue to young and beautiful heroines of Victorian fiction. At best, she plays at the fantasy that she and Edith are sisters rather than mother and daughter. At worst, she positions Edith as a sexual surrogate. She courts Edith's potential partners, flirting ferociously while shrewdly assessing tactics for her success. First she substitutes herself for her daughter and then she substitutes her daughter for herself. Ironically, both characters have aged past this role, a difficulty Mrs. Skewton circumvents in Edith's case by inventing tender emotions and delicate feelings that she attributes to her cold, steely daughter.

Whereas Mrs. Brown counters the losses of aging by perverting assumptions about maternity, quelling children to secure an income, Mrs. Skewton fends off poverty by subduing her physical self. For years, she freezes her aging body into what had popularly come to be seen as a timeless pose of that ageless seductress, Cleopatra. Adopting a famous Cleopatra "attitude" captured decades earlier by a painter who fancifully titled both portrait and girl "Cleopatra," Mrs. Skewton curiously embodies that ancient queen and her imagined vices. Dickens's initial notes make no reference to "Cleopatra," so that tag must have come to him late. In fact, Valier Gager speculates that Dickens initially intended to parody the neoclassical poses found in the Countess of Blessington's annual *Book of Beauty*. Several volumes between 1833–49 include flowery verses to young ladies by "a Septuagenarian" Mrs. Skewton's age, a suggestion obliquely supported by Hablot Browne's 1848 portrait of Mrs. Skewton in which a lady's magazine lies open to "La Mode" (Gager 204)[7] (Fig. 4.2).

In the years before Dickens began *Dombey and Son,* the ancient queen was increasingly on view in Britain and the Continent. Theater historian Margaret Lamb notes that nineteenth-century versions of Shakespeare's *Antony and Cleopatra* were either spectacles in which artillery and naval battles took precedence over actors—as in the 1813 Covent Garden production—or fusions of Shakespeare's play and John Dryden's *All for Love; or The World Well Lost* (1678), the tack taken by Dickens's close friend William Macready, in a short-lived 1838 Drury Lane production (Lamb 52). Lamb credits the 1813 play with establishing the "Cleopatra Pose," which came to dominate popular images of Cleopatra and which Dickens capitalizes on in the novel (58). A second theater historian, Lucy Hughes-Hallett, identifies colliding anachronisms in Victorian representations of Cleopatra. She is at once a Pharaonic Egyptian ruler; an Islamic,

---

[7] An 1848 illustration by Hablot Browne of "Miss Skewton" in the Cleopatra pose was published in a separate collection of illustrations that followed publication of the novel. A reproduction from Michael Steig's 1978 book *Dickens and Phiz* appears along with commentary on the Victorian Web at http://www.scholars.nus.edu.sg/victorian/art/illlustration/phiz/109.html. This Web site also reproduces a related illustration that appears in the novel, "Major Bagstock is delighted to have that opportunity," in which Mrs. Skewton attempts the Cleopatra pose in her wheeled chair when she encounters the major in the park.

Figure 4.2. Phiz (Halbot K. Browne) published a series of etchings based on the characters in *Dombey and Son* in 1848, including this portrait of Mrs. Skewton. Michael Steig discusses these etchings in chapter 4 of *Dickens and Phiz* (Bloomington: Indiana University Press, 1978). The chapter also appears on the Web at http://www.victorianweb.org/art/illustration/phiz/steig/4.html#plate64.

Orientalized prisoner of the harem (though she lived six hundred years before Muhammad's birth); and a domesticated queen, utterly dependent upon men, living in a contemporary European palace complete with Egyptian Revival decor (261).[8] (Perhaps this last gave rise to the often-repeated anecdote that a spectator of Sarah Bernhart's *much later* Cleopatra protested, "How unlike—how so unlike—the home life of our own dear Queen" [Hughes-Hallett 268]). In addition, Hughes-Hallett says that European stories, novels, and plays featuring Cleopatra in the 1820s through 1840s increasingly emphasized her sexual voraciousness, her decadent hungers, and her association with a civilization not merely old but extinct.

In England, Cleopatra's foreignness and her association with a dead culture and its monuments were highlighted in plays, paintings, and popular exhibitions, associations of special interest to critics such as Jeff Nunokawa and Suvendrini Perera who explore connections between the rise of capitalism and the marketing of empire to British citizens.[9] We cannot precisely know which of the many incarnations of the ancient queen Dickens encountered, but as an avid reader and frequent traveler to Europe, he must have absorbed at least some of these newly charged, newly fraught images of—in several senses—"old Egypt."

The contrast between Mrs. Skewton's age and social position as a widow, on one hand, and her dress and appearance, on the other, dominates her characterization:

> The discrepancy between Mrs. Skewton's fresh enthusiasm of words, and forlornly faded manner, was hardly less observable than that between her age, which was about seventy, and her dress, which would have been youthful for twenty-seven. Her attitude in the wheeled chair (which she never varied) was one in which she had been taken in a barouche, some fifty years before, by a then fashionable artist who had appended to his published sketch the name of Cleopatra: in consequence of a discovery made by the critics of the time, that it bore an exact resemblance to that Princess as she reclined on board her galley. Mrs. Skewton was a beauty then, and bucks threw wine-glasses over their heads by dozens in her honour. The beauty and the barouche had both passed away, but she still preserved the attitude, and for this reason expressly, maintained the wheeled chair and

---

[8] Francesa T. Roysters's *Becoming Cleopatra: The Shifting Image of an Icon* also offers a fine overview of cultural exploitations of Cleopatra, including a chapter on George Bernard Shaw's *Caesar and Cleopatra*.

[9] See Jeff Nunokawa, "For Your Eyes Only: Private Property and the Oriental Body in *Dombey and Son*" (1991) and Suvendrini Perera, "Wholesale, Retail, and for Exportation: Empire and the Family Business in *Dombey and Son*" (1990).

the butting page: there being nothing whatever, except the attitude, to prevent her from walking. (241–42)

The comic contrast between the faded gentility of a grasping mother who makes a spectacle of herself while pandering (echoing the character Panderus from stage versions of Cleopatra) escalates into vicious ridicule of an elderly woman who refuses to move from the center stage of youth to the wings where the elderly are told they must be content. This passage thus demonstrates the forged connection between the Victorian Englishwoman and the ancient Egyptian queen, on one hand, and the old/young tension, on the other.

Playfully tyrannical, lustfully flirtatious, willing prostitute of herself and panderer of her daughter, Mrs. Skewton, like an insect Cleopatra, is thus intent on creating an empire of her own. When the narrator wryly references Shakespeare in describing her inevitable pose—"Mrs. Skewton arranged, as Cleopatra, among the cushions of a sofa: very airily dressed: and certainly not resembling Shakespeare's Cleopatra, whom age could not wither" (245)—he exaggerates the comedy with an added flourish of dramatic irony. Not only may time "wither" this Cleopatra, but she is additionally "withered" in a different sense by the ministrations of her male servant, Withers. Mrs. Skewton's libido has not grown stale; it is she after all who longs for "all those yearnings, and gushings, and impulsive throbbings" (246), which she mimics in her empty flirtation with the equally grotesque Major Bagstock and pretends to detect in her daughter Edith's hostile tolerance of Mr. Dombey. Insinuating sex, exoticism, shrewdness, power, perfidy, betrayal, corruption, perverted maternity, mummification (as Robert Newsom has noted in *Charles Dickens Revisited* 101), and, above all, vast empires and great age, Cleopatra confronts us with the bitter losses that loom for an old woman without the financial security of a kingdom or a consort. Her only justification for manipulating her daughter into a miserable marriage, and it satisfies neither Edith nor the audience, is that the daughter is a sacrifice to Mrs. Skewton's longed-for economic empire. Like Carker the Manager, Mrs. Skewton succeeds by her careful management of more powerful figures than herself. Also, like Carker, she fancies that she can manage her powerful double—her daughter/sister Edith—into fulfillment of her own empire-building desires.

The figure of the old woman unwilling to sacrifice the pleasures of youth—from fashion to curls to flirtation to sex itself—draws frequent ridicule in Victorian periodicals as well as Victorian novels (sadly, a custom that also fails to grow stale). In 1863, in a *Cornhill Magazine* article, "Aids to Beauty," George Henry Lewes observes that "[t]he art of adorning the person is the earliest art acquired by the savage, and the last relinquished by reluctant old age," scorning men and women who indulge

> in the too common attempt to disguise age, and to dress old mutton like spring lamb. No one is deceived for more than a moment, and the reaction of disgust endures.... Old men and women, who would resist the irresistible *fact* of age, will never be brought to acknowledge the *beauty* of age; they want another beauty; they cling to the remembrance of departed charms. If the rouge-pot and the hair-dresser can help them to dead *simulacra* of those charms, they are welcomed; and although they keenly see through the like pretences in others, they cannot be argued out of the wisdom of employing such pretences themselves. (391; emphasis in original)

Mrs. Skewton understands far better than these fashion commentators what she stands to lose if she relinquishes her false youth and accepts her aged motherhood. Like the other elderly women who attend the Dombeys' first at-home and whom Dombey's middle-aged sister-in-law (from his first marriage) describes as "these indecent old frights with their backs and shoulders" (434), Mrs. Skewton has ample evidence that a visibly aging, postreproductive body means lost bargaining power, lost erotic pleasures, and lost economic salvation in the form of a husband and home. The price of no longer being "the daughter" drives the desperate woman into a refusal of aging and maternity alike.

The marriage contract, through which Mrs. Skewton secures her future by selling her daughter to Dombey, prompts Edith to initiate a weary, empty compact with her mother. The cold, contemptuous daughter declares a truce in the long battle of maternal ambition and filial pride in pity at the subjugation of this would-be queen. In an echo of the "reunion" scene in which Alice declares a temporary cease-fire in her ongoing war with Mrs. Brown, Edith briefly lashes out when Mrs. Skewton demands duty to a mother who has cared for her all these years:

> "Haven't you from a child—"
> "A child!" said Edith, looking at her, "when was I a child? What childhood did you ever leave to me? I was a woman—artful, designing, mercenary, laying snares for men—before I knew myself or you, or even understood the wretched aim of every new display I learnt." (333)

She compares herself to a "'slave in the market'" and a "'horse in a fair'" who, with her mother, has become "'almost notorious'" (333) even in the crass world of the marriage market. In Alice and Mrs. Brown's relationship, the novel locates one of the unconscious obstacles to a daughter's reconciliation with the mother: the fear of *becoming* the bad mother. Edith's protest zeros in on yet another obstacle, hinted at in Alice's accusations, the unforgivable loss of childhood and all it represents—innocence, maternal care and protection, safety, and time to progress through the life stages of youth—a loss that the robbed child recognizes only from an adult retrospective. As with Alice, we see justification for the daughter's rage in the emotional damage the daughter suffers in midlife. Edith's self-loathing is so profound that she fears contaminating the stepdaughter who could save her. Ultimately, she turns her rage so violently against herself that, like a suicide bomber, she destroys herself to wreak revenge on her enemy, Mr. Dombey, to whom her mother has sold her.

In Mrs. Skewton's death, social satire gives way to melodrama. Repeated strokes shake her from the Cleopatra pose and the fantasies of power—over time, over her daughter, and over "Society" as represented by Mr. Dombey's wealth—all of which make her such a miserable mother. Haunted by the crumbling tomb of youth she has built around herself—"the stone arm—part of a figure off some tomb, she says—is raised to strike her" (489), Mrs. Skewton stretches supplicating hands to Edith. She seeks gratitude for the bitter years of labor with which she has built what was to be Edith's palace but has become a prison, a bitter monument to a loveless, avaricious marriage. True to form, however, when Mrs. Skewton can least control her appearance, her environment, and her imagined suitors, her empire contracts. The only person she can tyrannize is her daughter.

Like Mrs. Brown, Mrs. Skewton whines at her daughter's distance; in the limited signs and speech of stroke victims, she demands filial duty: "she became hugely exacting in respect of Edith's affection and gratitude and attention to her; highly laudatory of herself as a most estimable parent; and very jealous of having any rival in Edith's regard" (445). As other characters retreat from her pathetic decrepitude, the mother attempts to master her daughter with the maternal gaze: "She would look at the beautiful face, in its marble stillness and severity, now with a kind of fearful admiration; now in a giggling foolish effort to move it to a smile; now with the capricious tears and jealous shakings of her head, as imagining herself neglected by it" (479). Initially, just as Edith resists Dombey's arrogant mastery through stoic defiance, she, like so many daughters, tries to pacify her mother with "mechanical attention and immoveable beauty" (480). In a final protest of Edith's failure to appreciate the economic empire she has captured on her and her daughter's behalf, Cleopatra protests: "'For I nursed you!'" (489) in imitation of her namesake's final words in Shakespeare's *Antony and Cleopatra*: "'Peace, peace! Dost thou not see my baby at my breast? That sucks the nurse asleep?'" (act 5). Implicitly, the allusion positions Edith as the viper, yet this viper represents long-resisted Death now welcomed and beloved. Earlier, the narrator has described the stricken "old woman in her finery leering and mincing at Death, and playing off her youthful tricks upon him as if he had been the Major" (444–45). In her very last moment Mrs. Skewton again turns her still animate desire to Death as "with her girlish laugh, and the skeleton of the Cleopatra manner" she "rises in her bed" (490), a horrifyingly appropriate courtesan soliciting a lover who will enfold decrepitude in an adoring if smothering embrace. Mrs. Skewton is reconciled to her great adversaries—daughter and Death—at last.

Between Cleopatra's closing line and final gesture, one of the most quietly moving moments of the novel takes place—a scene too easily eclipsed by Mrs. Skewton's awful "juvenility." We see Edith's rage, directed at her mother as well as herself, on the few occasions when Edith violently weeps, physically punishes herself, or verbally flays her mother. Anger against her mother surfaces in the bitterness with which Edith recalls her own premature aging, her lost childhood. Anger also motivates Edith's protectiveness of Florence, as when she forbids Mrs. Skewton to take charge of Florence while Dombey and Edith are away for their honeymoon: "'It is enough,' said Edith steadily, 'that we are what we are. I will have no youth and truth dragged down to my level. I will have no guileless nature undermined, corrupted, and perverted to amuse the leisure of a world of mothers'" (364). Eventually, however, Mrs. Skewton's sufferings precipitate at least a version of the "filial crisis" that Buckwalter and other gerontologists believe can lead to reconciliation. The contrast between the bitter accusations Edith levels at her mother in the scene above and Mrs. Skewton's death scene wrenches the mood from satire to sentiment. Edith gives her mother the greatest gift we *can* give one another as we face death—genuine compassion and forgiveness: "'Can you recollect the night before I married?.... I told you then that I forgave your part in it, and prayed God to forgive my own. I told you that the past was at end between us. I say so, again. Kiss me, Mother'" (490). Edith's compassion for her mother has as much potential to resurrect her from the midlife grave she is digging for herself as does her love for Florence.

The repetition of the two scenes in which Edith first mechanically tells her mother that she will forget the past—on the eve of her wedding—and this later allusion to that earlier moment signals Edith's progress from an exhausted attempt to silence maternal complaint to a genuine desire to give comfort. We see Edith kiss no one but the child Florence, whom she has come to love deeply, except in this scene. The momentary succor of being a mother teaches this middle-aged daughter compassion even in the midst of a life fenced in by shame, self-loathing, and vengefulness. In Edith's case, however, the reconciliation comes much too late to save her from the course on which her mother has set her. Cut off from mother and daughter alike, Edith throws herself into the destruction of "Dombey and Son" and almost welcomes the opportunity to do violence to herself in a hyperbolic enactment of the "training" she chastises her mother for both wrongly instilling and selfishly neglecting throughout her girlhood.

In *Dombey and Son,* two marginal, ferociously aged, hungry mothers frame "the Son who is a daughter after all" just as the long-dead grandfather, the original Dombey of the original Dombey and Son, frames Mr. Dombey and his domestic and capitalistic ambitions. The women's presence *replaces* the frame of sentimentality with genealogy, heredity, sexual abuse, paternal irresponsibility, and neglect, resettling narrow fantasies of the Victorian family in conditions that provoke critique.

Victorians increasingly framed family as an enclosed, exclusive, middle-class retreat from the world. The painful journey that leads these deeply wounded daughters to forgive their profoundly fallible mothers suggests that Dickens understood that compassion far exceeded conventional notions of filial *duty.* For good or ill, in the long run the novel uses the lessons of these relationships to argue for new filiations. Thus, *Dombey and Son* draws upon the traumas of midlife and late life to prepare readers for unprecedented cross-class, cross-generational "families" expansive enough to avoid obsessive, inverted, exploitive abuse and porous enough to include the orphaned, the widowed, the well, the ill, the poor, the rich, the falling as well as the rising, the young as well as the old. It should be no surprise that the novel ultimately embraces a range of characters with and without biological connections as a family. By the end of the novel, a unique family forms around the new mother, Florence, beneficiary of these many lessons in mother/daughter failures.

The most appealing couple in *Dombey and Son* is not Walter and Florence but Captain Cuttle and Sol Gills.[10] Captain Cuttle, in fact, takes a wedding vow in his own nautical fashion when Florence asks him to look after "Walter's uncle" in Walter's absence: "'with regard to old Sol Gills,' here the Captain became solemn, 'who I'll stand by, and not desert until death do us part, and when the stormy winds do blow, do blow, do blow'" (277). Joss Marsh very persuasively argues that *Dombey and Son* is driven by the "mechanism of displacement." Consequently, she explains, not only

---

[10] In "Change and Changeling in *Dombey and Son,*" Gerhard Joseph describes Mrs. Brown and Mrs. Skewton as "carefully paralleled bad biological mothers" set up to highlight the good nursing/mothering of characters like Polly Toodles just as he sees Sol Gills and Captain Cuttles as alternatives to a "bad biological father," that is, Dombey (190–91).

are characteristics displaced from one figure to another, but "a story which might develop or be uncovered about one character detaches itself, wanders, and becomes attached to another" (414). So it is with the two elderly mothers and their corresponding elderly bachelors. So it is with biological mothers and surrogate grandparents. Unlike mothers who desperately cling to visions of youth and their own youthful selves rather than supporting younger generations, particularly younger daughters, the bachelor couple Cuttle and Gills—assisted by their spinster companion Miss Tox—substitutes the fractious relations between daughters and mothers with a family built upon ontological and postsexual, almost postgendered, grandparenthood.

Not quite mothers or fathers and not in *fact* grandparents, these three characters mobilize the neglected emotional resources of grandparenthood. David Toise argues that from Florence's point of view "families are groups of people who 'act' like family; but of course, the very circularity of this formulation suggests that what defines family is a set of interpersonal exchanges which correspond to an abstract, representational concept of 'family' itself" (339). Toise credits Florence with founding such a family. However, I would argue that what Audrey Jaffe calls the "nonreproductive units" who "combine into a newly configured extended family" through Florence's wedding constitute the structural frame of this inclusive, cohesive community. Grandparenthood allows unusual flexibility (42). A grandparent or great aunt can shift among the roles of father, older sister or brother, friend, conscience, confidant, "second childhood," and mother and can even stand in for abstractions like home, history, or the past when necessary. Moving from the margins in the closing sections of the novel, their ultimate presence at its center marries genres, modes, and a richly diverse collection of characters into a communal family structured by social and affectional rather than solely biological relations. Moreover, this family displaces the middle generation—the generation that cannot seem to help abusing its daughters in this novel.

Grandparenthood possesses this flexibility in Victorian culture because grandparents have successfully passed the "great meridian of life." For many Victorians, the transition from youth to age was thought to be a precipitous fall from midlife into old age known as "the climacteric." This fall might leave the aged dashed on the rocks of madness. On the other hand, the more fortunate on the far side of the climacteric landed safely in a life newly devoted to moderation. For women, the climacteric was marked by the onset of menopause; for men the change was signaled by a decline in health, a withdrawal from work, or less aggressive behavior. Men and women alike who successfully navigated the dangerous waters of the climacteric often found themselves in surprisingly smooth seas with broad horizons of expectation when it came to gender roles. Historian Roe Sybylla's essay "Situating Menopause within the Strategies of Power" draws upon the work of leading Victorian medical practitioners to show that postmenopausal women were often thought to become more masculine, more independent (200–21). Doctor Edward Tilt even claimed women reached their "greatest mental vigor" after fifty-six (27). Similarly, freed from the demands of work, postclimacteric men were believed to develop heightened tenderness, sympathy, and attachment. With this presumed loss of sexual appetite, postclimacteric men and women were held to differ far less in their emotions and in their behavior than men and women in or clinging to youth and midlife.

Out of work, out of the sight lines of politics and social power, Captain Cuttle and Sol Gils serve the mother function far more successfully than the hungry, demonic mothers whose stories they displace. Welcoming all of the misfit, misplaced characters who survive the wreck of biological families, ambitious fathers, and demanding mothers, these ersatz grandparents create a home in which a motherless daughter has a chance to become the good mother. Perhaps the novel's end, with this family that can contain all manner of characters and relations among characters except that of the midlife daughter and the aging mother, is the novel's strongest statement about the tragic limitations even of momentary reconciliations between the abused daughter and her mother.

Works Cited

Anon. Review. "'The Book of Beauty,' edited by The Countess of Blessington." 8 vols. London, 1836. *Dublin Review* 2.3 (December 1836): 111–29.

Blenkner, M. (Margaret). "Social Work and Family Relationships in Later Life with Some Thought on Filial Maturity." In *Social Structure and the Family: Generational Relations*. Ed. E. Shanas and G. Streib. Englewood Cliffs: Prentice Hall, 1965. 46–59.

Dickens, Charles. *Dombey and Son* (1846–48). Rpt. Oxford: Oxford University Press, 1982.

Gager, Valier. *Shakespeare and Dickens: The Dynamics of Influence*. Cambridge: Cambridge University Press, 1996.

Hockey, Jenny, and Alison James. "Back to Our Futures: Imaging Second Childhood." In *Images of Aging: Cultural Representations of Later Life*. Ed. Mike Featherstone and Andrew Wernick. London: Routledge, 1995. 135–48.

Hughes-Hallett, Lucy. *Cleopatra: Histories, Dreams, and Distortions*. New York: Harper Perennial, 1990.

Jaffe, Audrey. *Vanishing Points: Dickens, Narrative, and the Subject of Omniscience*. Berkeley: University of California Press, 1991.

Joseph, Gerhard. "Change and Changeling in *Dombey and Son.*" *Dickens Studies Annual* 18 (1989): 179–95.

Lamb, Margaret. *Antony and Cleopatra on the English Stage.* London: Associate University Press, 1980.

Lewes, G. (George) H. (Henry). "Aids to Beauty: Real and Artificial." *Cornhill* 7 (March 1863): 391–400.

Mancini, Michelle. "Demons on the Rooftops, Gypsies in the Streets: The 'Secret Intelligence' of *Dombey and Son.*" *Dickens Studies Annual* 30 (2001): 113–40.

Marsh, Joss. "Good Mrs. Brown's Connections: Sexuality and Story-Telling in *Dealings With the Firm of Dombey and Son.*" *ELH* 58 (1991): 405–26.

Newlin, George. *Everyone in Dickens: A Taxonomy.* Vol. 3. Westport, CT: Greenwood Press, 1995.

Newsom, Robert. *Charles Dickens Revisited.* New York: Twayne Publishers, 2000.

Nunokawa, Jeff. "For Your Eyes Only: Private Property and the Oriental Body in *Dombey and Son.*" In *Macropolitics of Nineteenth-Century Literature: Nationalism, Exoticism, Imperialism.* Ed. Jonathan Arac and Harriet Ritvo. Philadelphia: University of Philadelphia Press, 1991. 138–58.

Perera, Suvendrini. "Wholesale, Retail, and for Exportation: Empire and the Family Business in *Dombey and Son.*" *Victorian Studies* 33.4 (Summer 1990): 603–20.

Royster, Francesa T. *Becoming Cleopatra: The Shifting Image of an Icon.* New York: Palgrave Macmillan, 2003.

Sherrell, Kathleen, Kathleen C. Buckwalter, and Darby Morhardt. "Negotiating Family Relationships: Dementia Care as a Midlife Developmental Task." *Families in Society: The Journal of Contemporary Human Services* 82.4 (2001): 383–92.

Steig, Michael. *Dickens and Phiz.* Bloomington: Indiana University Press, 1978.

Sybylla, Roe. "Situating Menopause within the Strategies of Power." In *Reinterpreting Menopause: Cultural and Philosophical Issues.* Ed. Paul Komesaroff, Philipa Rothfield, and Jeanne Daley. London: Routledge, 1997. 200–21.

Taylor, Thomas Prochlus. *Dombey and Son; Good Mrs. Brown the Child Stealer* (first performed at the Royal Strand Theatre, 1847). In *Purkess' Penny Pictorial Plays.* London: G. Purkess, 1848.

Tilt, Edward. *The Change of Life in Health and Disease.* London: John Churchill, 1870.

Toise, David W. "'As Good as Nowhere': Dickens's *Dombey and Son,* the Contingency of Value, and Theories of Domesticity." *Criticism* 41.3 (Summer 1999): 323–48.

Waters, Catherine. "Gender, Family, and Domestic Ideology." In *The Cambridge Companion to Charles Dickens.* Ed. John O. Jordan. Cambridge: Cambridge University Press, 2001. 120–35.

———. *Dickens and the Politics of the Family.* Cambridge: Cambridge University Press, 1997.

PART II

"Bad Mothers"

Caretaking, Class, and Maternal Violence

CHAPTER 5

Unforgiven

Drunken Mothers in Hesba Stretton's Religious Tract Society and Scottish Temperance League Fiction

Deborah Denenholz Morse

The most popular Religious Tract Society (RTS)[1] writer of children's fiction in the High Victorian period, the prolific Hesba Stretton,[2] often wrote of the desperate wanderings of outcasts in England's industrial cities of Manchester, Liverpool, and—most often—London. Stretton is known primarily as the advocate of poor urban children in both her life and her art. She was the friend of Dickens, and—in company with the great philanthropist Angela Burdett-Coutts and others—she campaigned in support of the London Society for the Prevention of Cruelty to Children.[3] In her urgent concern for England's children, whom she viewed as its most vulnerable citizens, Stretton constructed a corollary narrative to her stories of victimized children that focused upon negligent, often

---

[1] See Butts and Garrett, especially the introductory chapter by Fyfe, "A Short History of the Religious Tract Society," 13–35. For an excellent review of this recent book, see Sattaur.

[2] See Cutt's chapter "Hesba Stretton: Her Life and Legend" in her *Ministering Angels: A Study of Nineteenth-Century Evangelical Writing for Children* (Cutt 115–31) for the most thorough discussion of Stretton's life. See also Bratton, Demers (1991), Dickins, and Rickard. Rickard's article builds upon Cutt's portrayal of the activist, shrewd, intelligent Stretton as opposed to the saintly figure of the children's book writer enshrined in "legend." Rickard provides a fresh view of Stretton's toughness in negotiating with her publishers at the Religious Tract Society (RTS). See also Rickard's chapter on Stretton in Butts and Garrett, "'A Gifted Author'—Hesba Stretton and the Religious Tract Society," 104–15, in relation to Stretton's dealings with the RTS.

[3] See Hendrick 26.

drunken, and morally corrupt mothers. It is this cultural narrative of the oppressive drunken mother that I wish to examine.

Hesba Stretton, born Sarah Smith in Wellington, Shropshire, on July 27, 1832, was the third daughter of Benjamin Smith, a bookseller and stationer in the New Street who later became the first postmaster of Wellington, and of Anne Bakewell Smith, "a strict and notably intelligent Methodist."[4] "Hesba Stretton" is a name she adopted in 1858, with "Hesba" made up from the initials of her five siblings, while "Stretton" she took from the beloved town All Stretton, where her younger sister Anne had a house. She published her first story, "The Lucky Leg," at twenty-seven, in Dickens's *Household Words,* and thereafter became both a friend and a regular contributor to both *Household Words* and *All the Year Round.* By the end of the 1860s, Hesba Stretton became the most important writer for the Religious Tract Society, the highly successful publisher of Christian Evangelical works. The profits from RTS tracts, novels, children's stories, and magazines supported the Society's worldwide missionary work.[5] She never married, moving to Manchester in 1863, where she worked for a short time as a governess. It was in Manchester that Stretton heard the passionate sermons of George MacDonald, author and Congregationalist minister, and of William Gaskell, the minister of Cross Street Chapel, husband of the novelist Elizabeth Gaskell.[6] In Manchester Stretton witnessed the terrible conditions of street children that she documented in her best-selling novel *Pilgrim Street: A Manchester Tale* (1867). Soon afterward, Stretton and her younger sister Elizabeth, her lifelong companion, moved to London, where they eventually settled after extensive continental travel. Hesba Stretton died on October 8, 1911, and was eulogized in *Sunday at Home,* the evangelical magazine that in 1866 published her most famous novel, *Jessica's First Prayer.*[7]

Stretton wanted to make middle-class people aware of the dire state of England's poor urban children.[8] She was determined to call both her middle- and working-class readership to good works through an appeal to their Christian faith. She attacked Victorian social institutions and the hypocrisies of the moneyed classes—the prison system (*In Prison and Out*), the slum courts (*Pilgrim Street*), aristocratic owners of gin palaces (*Her Only Son*), and fashionable society churches (*Jessica's First Prayer*), and she called for protective legislation for children in prisons, in circuses, on the

---

[4] See Demers, "Sarah Smith."
[5] Again, see Rickard, "A Gifted Author."
[6] Ibid. 105–6.
[7] Again, see Demers, "Sarah Smith."
[8] See especially Cutt.

streets—and in the home. Stretton was instrumental in the establishment of the London Society for the Prevention of Cruelty to Children (LSPCC) in 1884; she was on its executive board for ten years, and she generously donated to the organization. Stretton also campaigned for the 1889 Act for the Prevention of Cruelty to Children, later known as the Children's Charter.[9] Stretton's portrayals of sottish mothers were a distinct feature of several of the cautionary tales she wrote for the evangelistic "publishing phenomenon" (Butts 7) that the Religious Tract Society had become by the 1860s and 1870s and for the Scottish Temperance League.[10]

In order to understand the force of Stretton's "drunken mother" narrative for both her middle-class and newly literate working-class readers of *Sunday at Home*[11] and other evangelical and temperance journals and novels, the context of the "drunken mother" narrative within the larger "child victim" narratives of Stretton and other Victorian novelists needs to be clarified. Although a number of the books I discuss were written for children or newly literate adults (*Jessica's First Prayer, Little Meg's Children, Lost Gip*), they were often read aloud in the family circle. Stretton was an early contributor to the "street arab" genre of fiction—as the recent *Norton Anthology of Children's Literatures* states, "use of the subject in children's

---

[9] Again, see especially Cutt and Rickard, "A Gifted Author," on Stretton's involvement in the child protection movement. Rickard writes specifically about Stretton's financial donations to the LSPCC on page 231 of "Living by the Pen." For information on the struggle to effect child protection laws, the Web site of the NSPPC is a good place to start: http://www.nspcc.org.uk/whatwedo/aboutthenspcc/historyofnspcc/historyofnspcc_wda33149.html. You can download their booklet, *The History of the NSPPC,* which details the heroes of this struggle: the Liverpool banker Thomas Agnew, who founded the Liverpool Society for the Prevention of Cruelty to Children in 1883, after a trip to New York during which he was impressed with New York's child protection society; the Reverend Benjamin Waugh, one of the first secretaries and the first director of the London Society for the Prevention of Cruelty to Children when Queen Victoria became its patron in 1889 and it was renamed the National Society for the Prevention of Cruelty to Children; the Reverend Edward Rudolf, the other inaugural secretary of the Society; and Lord Shaftesbury, inaugural president.

[10] The Scottish Temperance League was formed in 1844 in Falkirk for the purpose of "promoting the virtues of abstinence through associational culture" (Maver 159). Maver's groundbreaking study provides fascinating details about the lives of pioneer temperance campaigners like John Dunlop. See also Winskill 28. See http://gdl.cdlr.strath.ac.uk/airgli/airgli0128.htm, Glasgow University Digital Archive, for a less detailed history of the Scottish Temperance League.

[11] *Sunday at Home* was one of a number of "Sunday magazines." Others included *Good Words* (later *Sunday Magazine,* edited by Benjamin Waugh), *The Day of Rest,* and *Leisure Hour*. These magazines were intended primarily for Sunday family reading. Chris Baggs discusses the availability of these and other magazines to women not of the upper classes in his fascinating article describing public library reading in "ladies' reading rooms" (Baggs 2005).

books began only in the 1860's"[12]—and she did not elide the darker realities of slum life even when her primary reader was ostensibly a child. As Suzanne Rickard says of Stretton, "She managed to write about unmarried mothers, teenage prostitutes, abusive parents, exploitative employers, child death, drunkenness, homelessness, and other issues which were entirely sensational. Indeed, in other hands, the topics may have been almost controversial to treat in print. All the publicity given to Hesba's writing [by the RTS] stressed 'its purity of tone and high purpose.'"[13] Often citing parliamentary bluebooks as evidence, Stretton tells the stories of juvenile offenders (*In Prison and Out*), circus performers (*An Acrobat's Girlhood*), young factory workers (*David Lloyd's Last Will*),[14] drunkards' children (*Her Only Son, Jessica's Mother, Lost Gip*), child domestic workers (*Cassy*), and street waifs of every description (*Jessica's First Prayer, Pilgrim Street, A Thorny Path, Bede's Charity, Alone in London*). Some of Stretton's fictions make an overt connection between upper-class capitalist greed and lower-class misery—for instance, the aristocratic ownership of gin palaces that is criticized in the temperance novel *Her Only Son*. Stretton's focus is upon portraying the horrific circumstances of the poor, and most particularly, the suffering of the poorer classes' children. Her social critique works through eliciting sympathy for the innocent children caught in the web of abject poverty.[15]

In this concern for the child victim in her fiction, Stretton is in the mainstream of Victorian novelists, as Laura Berry argues in *The Child, the State, and the Victorian Novel:* "At an uncertain point in the nineteenth century, the welfare of the family, especially the state of the child, was intertwined with debates about the welfare of the state in England" (1). From Dickens's orphaned Oliver in *Oliver Twist* (1837–38) and Jo the Crossing Sweeper in *Bleak House* (1851–52) to Stretton's tales of suffering children in the 1860s and 1870s, the victimized child is a crucial feature in Victorian "social problem" novelists' critique of the English nation. In centering her

---

[12] See *The Norton Anthology of Children's Literatures: The Traditions in English* (Zipes 2005), 533. The Anthology includes excerpts from *Jessica's First Prayer.*

[13] Rickard, "A Gifted Author" 112.

[14] "No one can read [this writer's work] without being a wiser and better man or woman," declared the critic in the *Court Circular and Court News* (circa 1870), qtd. in Rickard, "A Gifted Author," 112. I personally could not stop reading this compelling, poignant novel that describes the hardships for England's textile factory workers during the American Civil War.

[15] See Berry, whose work is concerned with the increasing dominance of the narrative of the victimized child in nineteenth-century England: "This book examines the intense nineteenth-century fascination with victimized children to show how novels and reform writings authoritatively reorganize the ideas of self and society as narratives of childhood distress" (3).

"drunken mother" narratives on the most negligent of lower-class mothers, Stretton was performing cultural work that partly displaced middle-class responsibility and assuaged her middle-class readers' guilt for the child victim figures in these novels, as she differentiated her hardworking, pious, respectable working-class readers from these criminalized lower-class maternal figures. Simultaneously, Stretton called both her middle-class and working-class readership to action through Christian duty.

The "drunken lower-class mother" narrative is a polemical construction. This assertion is upheld by social histories of the second half of the nineteenth century, which consistently document the much greater adverse effect of paternal drinking upon poor children; fathers took the family's scant funds to the pub, away from the mother's allotment of money available for the children's food and clothing.[16] Stretton's narratives of the morally contaminating drunken mother are all the more powerfully memorable because Stretton in fact often depicts mothers of the poorer classes as admirable, self-sacrificing women who simply cannot cope with the relentless poverty that afflicts them (*Cassy, A Thorny Path, Bede's Charity*). As Nancy Cutt says of Stretton: "Twenty years before Charles Booth, she was pointing out that destitution did not necessarily result from idleness, extravagance, or vice, but was all too often the consequence of illness or lack of opportunity" (Cutt 133). Stretton's portrayals of strong if beleaguered poor mothers, based upon her own well-documented immersion in the East End, are confirmed by the remarkable work of historian Ellen Ross in *Love and Toil: Motherhood in Outcast London, 1870–1918,* in which the extreme self-starvation and the hard work of mothers in the poorest classes in London are examined.[17]

The drunken mother narrative is inescapably located in a complex Victorian gender ideology as well as in the social history of real mothers of the poor and "very poor" classes with whom Stretton was familiar. While scholarship has documented that mothers were sacred figures in middle-class Victorian gender ideology,[18] several important critical studies have also persuasively argued that middle-class women were not—in life or in

---

[16] Ellen Ross writes, "The poor man's drink was at the expense of his family's food and sometimes his own.... Wives' drinking could also, of course, be a drain on income, but arrests for drunkenness, pub watchers' figures for the proportions of women entering pubs, and family budgets show that married women spent much less on alcohol than their menfolk did" (Ross 43).

[17] For documentation of Stretton's involvement in the East End, see especially Rickard 1996. Ross writes of these poor mothers, "'I can't see them want' was the mothers' natural reply when well-wishing social workers urged them to eat more of the family food" (Ross 55).

[18] See especially Gorham, Kennard, Rees, Branca, Davidoff, and Vicinus.

literature—such angelic moral teachers.[19] However, from a middle-class perspective—and in the view of the lower classes emulating middle-class values—the dereliction of the mother was, if not the profaning of the sacred, then the subversion of the expected and conventional family moral structure. The mother was supposed to be the staunch moral center of the home sphere, the guardian of the domestic refuge from that fierce male sphere of business and politics. Middle-class anxieties about the lower-class family tended to center upon the mother, as Deborah Epstein Nord and Ginger Frost have pointed out.[20] From the historical record, Ross and others have demonstrated that the mothers of the poorest classes in Victorian England were the crucial factor in the family's physical, economic, and psychic success—and even survival.[21] If the mother was sober, thrifty, and ingenious, the family had much better odds of remaining intact and viable. A mother who went to the pub regularly was likely to bring her family down with her when she fell into drunkenness and squalor—or worse.

According to both middle-class ideology and working-class social history, then, the one East End mother who could not be tolerated or forgiven is the drunk, a figure Stretton presents many times over as the enemy to her children's welfare in a reiterative cautionary tale.[22] Even the mother

[19] See especially Langland, Shapiro, Newton, Auerbach, Vicinus, Thomson, and Barickman, MacDonald, and Stark.

[20] See Nord, *Walking the Victorian Streets: Women, Representation, and the City;* Frost in this volume. My thanks to Professor Frost, both for her own work and for reminding me of Nord's critique.

[21] Ross, *Love and Toil:* "In this era, without a reasonably competent adult woman or older daughter, households often 'broke up,' their members joining those of relatives or neighbors or entering the poor-law system with its cruel separation of spouses, parents, and children. . . . *Love and Toil* maintains that family survival was the mother's main charge among the large majority of London's population who were poor or working class. . . . To mother was to work for and organize household subsistence" (8–9). On middle-class observers in the slums of London: "The 'discovery' of the mother was part of the general middle-class recognition that the poor had their own distinct culture. Mothers and their domestic needs were in many ways the key to the order and pattern that the observers began to find in the noisy, bustling streets of the East End. As orchestrators of household survival and arbiters of neighborhood morality, mothers were the figures around whom the working-class culture had coalesced" (22–23).

[22] See especially Ross: "The work of a good wife was not exactly analogous to that of a good husband, for the woman had far less room for error. Sobriety, consistency, and at least some cleverness were built-in requirements for wives, and the absence of these qualities was much more likely to be noticed than their presence. After all, even the most drunken and neglectful husband usually had someone to take care of his home and children. Drinking (and therefore often heavy-pawning) wives were subject to literal battering by their husbands and to figurative battering by the poor-law, the COS, and other agencies. Mothers' heavy drinking and their concomitant neglect and mismanagement of their infants figure in many Old Bailey cases, for their dereliction had dire consequences for their families" (71).

who committed infanticide was in many respects sympathized with rather than wholly condemned. When Stretton focuses on drunken mothers, they inevitably die in order that their children can be freed to live middle-class lives. These mothers are beyond the pale; they cannot be rescued from their degradation, and they never undergo conversion experiences—an unusual narrative pattern in an explicitly Christian text. Indeed, they are not even named in her stories, so they become generic—they are not vouchsafed interiority or individuality. Looked at from the perspective of the "degeneration" debates of the late Victorian era, the drunken mother represents a kind of devolution of the mother figure, the embodiment of fears about the regression of the species as well as the degraded citizenry of the State.[23] Her fallenness from the pedestal of domestic goddess is nearly always associated with sexual fallenness as well: the drunken mother is associated with sexual impurity and prostitution, as in *Jessica's Mother,* where the mother has been an actress, a mistress, and eventually a prostitute. Finally, the drunken mother is linked to the mother who commits infanticide, as in *Lost Gip,* in which the neighbors whisper darkly that the lost little girl Gip has really been murdered by her drunken mother, frequenter of the corner gin palace.[24]

Lost Gip, which first appeared in 1873 in the Sunday magazine *The Day of Rest,* concerns the travails of Sandy, a young slum dweller whose drunken mother has lost his beautiful, dark little "gypsy" sister. Sandy lives in a filthy street in the East End, in a neighborhood where the gin palace is the center of activity, and "the door swings to and fro incessantly with the stream of men, women, and children passing in and out" (8). Sandy devotedly nurses his little sister Gip, who had been fed by his drunken mother

---

[23] See Maunder for insight into this argument on the connection between degeneracy fears and motherhood.

[24] See Ross: "Infanticide among the working classes had been the subject of a journalistic and official panic in the 1860's and early 1870's, stimulated in part by a few spectacular mass murders by 'baby farmers' and in part by two energetic and crusading medical men who served in succession as coroners for Central Middlesex, which included the heavily servant-keeping districts of St. Marylebone and Paddington.... Although single parents were apparently much more likely to try to kill their infants than married parents were, official interest in stamping out infanticide among the poor coalesced in the 1890's around the question of overlaying, or accidentally suffocating, babies sleeping in their parents' bed.... In the 1908 Children Act, however, a piece of legislation incorporating many of the themes of the previous decade's high-level discussions of infant welfare, a kind of criminal negligence theory of overlaying was adopted, and it became a penal offense if it happened after a parent had drunk alcohol" (187–89). See also Berry: "The mid-Victorian period saw the proliferation of a massive discourse about infanticide. Even in the absence of any persuasive evidence that infanticide was actually on the rise, reformers of all sorts wrote as if child murder were taking place not just daily, but hourly" (131).

"with more gin than milk." All the babies before Gip have died despite Sandy's care, but somehow, the brother/mother manages to keep his baby sister alive. Close narrative kin to Dickens's Jo the Crossing Sweeper in *Bleak House,* who is told to "move on" or he will be arrested, Sandy is told by the police to go about his business, but as he says to his toddler sister, "Where are I to go, Gip?"

Significantly, Sandy and Gip's mother is never given a name, and therefore seems to be intended as a kind of drunken lower-class Everywoman. In sharp contradiction to the middle-class ideal of the Angel in the House, she is always identified with the gin palace or spirit vault rather than the home, where she goes only to sleep off her last drunken bout. She begins Gip's initiation into the world of the gin palace early on in the little girl's life: "She swore at the child sometimes, but more often she took her inside, and poured the last drop or two of her glass of gin down Gip's throat . . ." (20).

Gip's mother not only teaches her little girl how to tipple—a role usually allotted in Victorian novels to dipsomaniac fathers, like Arthur Huntingdon in Anne Brontë's *The Tenant of Wildfell Hall*[25]—she also loses Gip when she is dead drunk. Sandy searches for his little sister for the rest of the story, a knight-errant on a Christian, brotherly quest. Only at the novel's close does he find his adored Gip at Miss Murray's Emigration Society for Children, based on Maria Rye's organization.[26] The polemics of Stretton's text argue for the middle class as caretakers to the urban poor's children.

Another strand of the narrative concerns a middle-class clergyman's family fallen upon hard times who nevertheless take Sandy in as a surrogate son. Their own crippled son, the Christ-like, doomed John Shafto, becomes the wandering boy's dear friend and serves as middle-class double to Sandy, who will ultimately take his place. Meanwhile, Sandy fears his drunken mother's return; it is his "secret dread, which haunted him day by day as he went to and fro about his work. . . . It was a great terror . . . whenever he had to pass the swinging doors of the gin-palace . . . a den of some ravenous beast of prey, lying in wait to devour him. . . . 'Lord,' he said often in his prayers, 'let mother be lost always, and never be found again; but please find little Gip for me soon!'" The child's prayers that

---

[25] Brontë: "So the little fellow came down every evening, in spite of his cross mamma, and learnt to tipple wine like papa, to swear like Mr. Hattersley, and to have his own way like a man, and sent mamma to the devil when she tried to prevent him" (chap. 39).

[26] See Cutt 150, and note 34; Diamond for the most thorough biography of this feminist philanthropist. Rye, a member of the "Langham Place" group, devoted her life to helping women and girls emigrate to Australia, South Africa, and New Zealand. After 1869 Rye focused upon the emigration of "gutter-children" to Canada.

the mother "be lost always" are chilling if wholly understandable—more terrible still if "lost" signifies the larger biblical meaning of "strayed from the path to salvation" or even "damned"; in this text, however, narrative sympathy is entirely on the side of the innocent child.

Despite Sandy's wish, like a ghost in a gothic tale or the predator in a nightmare, the "ravenous beast of prey" that is Sandy and Gip's drunken mother returns for a brief moment after Sandy finds his little sister. The children's mother wants to claim them so that Sandy can provide her again with drink money from his street work as a fuse-boy selling matches. Sandy can think only how "he could save little Gip and himself," but the mother suddenly dies before he must escape. There is no place for the conversion of the drunken lower-class mother in this narrative. Her death scene is juxtaposed to so many deaths of angelic middle-class mothers in Victorian fictions[27]: this drunken mother is dead among the tombstones in the churchyard, reduced to a frozen "figure," an "it" not only dematernalized but dehumanized: "they were quite close to the figure, and it did not move, though the wind ruffled the ragged shawl a little."

When the Shaftos emigrate to a farm in Canada, the drunken mother is left in the Old Country's earth. Sandy decides not to tell Gip about her mother—"don't let little Gip ever know!"—so the mother's existence is erased from the daughter's memory. Finally, in Canada Sandy and Gip live happily in a pastoral landscape, in "a loghouse of their own, within sound of the lapping of the waves of the Lake Huron"—in an Eden without the most fallen of Eves, the drunken mother.

Gip's dark skin and hair—"Gip" is short for "Gypsy"—complicate this narrative even further. If Gip is somehow the progeny of the nameless drunken mother and a foreign father, then she is twice Other, an impoverished little girl of mixed race. Significantly, dark Gip is about to be shipped out to Canada with lots of other poor children before she is rescued by Sandy and the Shafto family and emigrates with them. The children of the poor become exports, a "product" too costly to keep in England.[28] Reconstituted families occur in almost all of Stretton's fictions (as in many

---

[27] Peggotty relates Clara's death to David Copperfield: "'Let my dearest boy go with us to our resting-place,' she said, 'and tell him that his mother, when she lay here, blessed him not once, but a thousand times . . . she . . . gave me such a patient smile, the dear!—so beautiful!—'" Thereafter, David recalls the childish, loving, but irresponsible Clara as an angel-mother: "In her death she winged her way back to her calm untroubled youth, and cancelled all the rest" (chap. 7).

[28] Nancy Cutt argues that in *Lost Gip,* Stretton "adds to the temperance theme a plea for adoption of orphans, and drew flattering attention to the work of Maria Rye, who, like Miss Macpherson, Dr. Barnardo, William Quarrier, and others, worked to settle slum orphans in Canadian, Australian, or New Zealand homes" (150).

of Gaskell's and Dickens's works),[29] in which children and adults of different families end up as one new family united by Christ's love. In this instance, the difficulty is perhaps that Stretton—like Elizabeth Gaskell at the close of *Mary Barton,* when her working-class family is relocated to an Edenic rural Canada—cannot truly imagine a place in England where such an anomalous family could thrive and prosper.[30]

Jessica's First Prayer, Stretton's most famous and popular novel—a million and a half copies were sold in the years after its July 1866 publication in *Sunday at Home*—also features a terrifying drunken mother. Like Sandy's mother in *Lost Gip,* Jessica's mother does not have a name. She is an actress who has once apparently been very pretty and popular in the theater, but who is now a prostitute addicted to gin. She seems once to have been a gentleman's mistress; she claims that she "rode in my carriage once, man, I can tell you" (*Jessica's Mother* 80). Jessica's mother's story is, then, a version of the Victorian fallen woman narrative.

Therefore, Jessica's story is the tale of a fallen woman's child, a daughter saved by kindly middle-class men who are alternatives to those who exploit and pay her mother. Early on in the novel, Jessica runs from her violent mother to Daniel Standring, the chapel-keeper who has fed her from his coffee stall. She befriends not only Daniel but the chapel's minister and his two daughters. Ultimately, Jessica is adopted by Daniel, who "rented a little house for himself and his adopted daughter to dwell in . . . [he] was well pleased that there was nobody to interfere with his charge of Jessica" (54).

Jessica's mother's utter unworthiness is juxtaposed to the pathetic innocence and loving nature of Jessica herself. When the Methodist minister—who also does not have a name, in his case a marker of his representative position, not his character—offers Jessica some middle-class opportunities for education, churchgoing, and good, sturdy clothing, Jessica responds that her mother is "[o]ut on a spree . . . and she won't be home for a day or two. She'd not hearken to you, sir. There's the missionary came, and she pushed him down the ladder, till he was nearly killed. They used to call mother the Vixen at the theater, and nobody durst say a word to her" (38).

[29] Consider Gaskell's *Ruth,* in which the Reverend Thurston Benson and his sister Faith take in the fallen Ruth and her son Leonard, whom they continue to treat as a son after Ruth's death in a fever; "Libby Marsh's Three Eras," in which two lonely and bereaved women make a home together after the death of the boy they both love; or Dickens's *Bleak House,* in which John Jarndyce makes a home for Esther Summerson, Rick Carstone, Ada Clare, and Caddy Jellyby, to none of whom he is related by blood.

[30] A good essay could be written on Hesba Stretton's interpretations of the British Empire; for example, in *Bede's Charity,* a poor old country woman lost in the city views the West End parks as foreign lands.

The actors name Jessica's mother as the animal she is, although Stretton shows her to be worse than a "vixen" in being a mother who is unnatural. While Jessica's simple response to the Word of God draws Daniel and the minister's family to her aid, Jessica's mother abandons her when the child is seriously ill. Symbolically, Daniel finds Jessica in a stable, praying: "'Our Father,' said the little voice, 'please to send somebody to me, for Jesus Christ's sake. Amen.'" The earthly father, Daniel, responds to Jessica's prayer and becomes a good Christian thereafter, as well as a maternalized father figure.

The stability of Jessica's new middle-class life is still in danger from her drunken mother—who, it turns out, is still alive and now a street prostitute—a fact evident to adult readers of the novel. In *Jessica's Mother,* the sequel to *Jessica's First Prayer,* Jessica's drunken mother returns—like the drunken mother in *Lost Gip*—a ghost that will not be buried. She appears on Daniel's doorstep one night, "the figure of a person, which looked more like a heap of rags, crouching upon his door-sill. . . . The miserable creature before him shocked every sense of decency and propriety . . ." (75, 90). Even the innocent, loving Jessica herself cannot get her mother to reform. Daniel knows that "there was little hope . . . of a woman so enslaved by drunkenness being brought back again to religion and God" (97).

Yet Daniel does decide to emulate Christ. He provides for Jessica's mother although he abhors her and thinks she has "no more claim upon him than any other of the thousands of lost men and women who thronged the streets of London . . ." (100–101). When he sees her in those streets, Daniel follows her, and at last views her as "a strange dark figure on one of the great beams stretching over the river . . ." (112).[31] Daniel demonstrates both the courage of his Old Testament namesake and the self-sacrifice of the true Christian when he suffers mortal wounds trying to rescue Jessica's mother. However, in an iconographic fallen woman death, she drowns, a suicide.[32]

As narrative reward for his self-sacrifice, Daniel has a perfect Christian death, in stark contrast to the symbolic fallen woman's drowning of Jessica's mother. His death is depicted in a prolonged deathbed scene in which he is surrounded not only by Jessica, but by the fashionable chapel-goers for whom he has opened pews each Sunday. His death is an example of the "good death" that Gerhard Joseph and Herbert Tucker write of as one

---

[31] Again, this scene is reminiscent of *David Copperfield,* when the child Little Em'ly runs out on a "jagged timber" overlooking the sea at Yarmouth and nearly falls, which David recalls in retrospect, after the adult Emily has indeed become a fallen woman (chap. 3).

[32] See especially Auerbach for the iconographies of the drowned fallen woman in Victorian literature and painting.

of the "master narratives" of Victorian death.[33] The now recovered minister comes to Daniel's deathbed to pray with him, and he adopts Jessica as his own daughter when Daniel dies. The minister moves to the country, where he is "a man of calmer happiness than before" who preaches to a "simple congregation simple truths" (121). The city's fashionable chapel and well-to-do congregation are left behind. And Jessica the street urchin becomes a middle-class child in another reconstructed pastoral. As in *Lost Gip*, the taint of the urban drunken mother can only be purified, finally, within a middle-class home in an Edenic landscape.

This conclusion to the "drunken mother" narrative can be viewed as Stretton's call for middle-class responsibility through a sense of Christian duty: we are all a part of God's family. In stories that were read out loud by middle-class and working-class parents to their own children, this ending must have been reassuring. From another perspective, however, the drunken mother narrative seems to mask a fear of the unwashed, contaminating, possibly immoral poor that cannot be expressed through the figure of the innocent child victim. Concomitant with this fear is the paternalistic suspicion that without direct middle-class intervention in the poor family, the poor will not survive. In fact, what the poor needed above all was better wages, as historians of the nineteenth century have documented.[34] What the narrative of the drunken mother offers instead is a repository for blame and a fissure through which the lower-class family can be divided, with the uniting figure as the middle-class parent, in part symbolic of the State.

In order fully to contextualize the drunken mother narrative in Stretton's fiction, we can turn first to her plethora of lower-class mothers who are not drunks. Among these stories, the tales of the convicted thief Rachel Trevor in *The Storm of Life* (1876) and the beleaguered Hagar in *A Thorny Path* (1879)—who abandons her blind old father and little girl Dot when they all are starving—bear examination as counternarratives.[35] In *The Storm of Life,* the passionate Rachel Trevor begins her journey out of prison life with the chaplain's loving words—"Thou God seest me"—inscribed in his dying letter to her, as a talisman against evil, and in particular against the stealing that landed her in prison. After Rachel trudges through the snow to the workhouse to reclaim her child Rosy, the

---

[33] See Joseph and Tucker.
[34] See, for instance, Ross.
[35] *The Storm of Life* appeared in *Good Words* in 1876. It was published in a single volume by Henry S. King & Co. in 1876 and was also published in volume form by the RTS. *A Thorny Path* first appeared in *Sunday at Home* and was then published in a single volume by the RTS. See Rickard, "A Gifted Author" 115, and Cutt 208–10.

mother realizes the cost of her own crimes to her pretty child when her "merry laughing little darling" has become a reticent, "thin, long-armed girl of seven, with short clipped hair, and dull pale face. . . . This frightened-looking child had her face half hidden by an ugly green shade over her eyes, and she crept about carefully like one nearly blind." From that moment, Rachel heroically protects her beautiful little girl from her criminal father. Rachel becomes the ideal housekeeper of the small home she shares in London with an elderly couple who have taken her in and whose own daughter has died: "Never had the house been so clean, or his wife's room so spotlessly white. Never had there been so little money needed for housekeeping. Rachel baked and cooked, and washed and mended, as if the house were her own. It was her home." Rachel is identified with the respectable working classes who aspired to middle-class ideals of serene domesticity and "cleanliness as godliness." Significantly, Rachel, now an "angel in the house," is not only pure, but disseminates purity, making the wife's room "spotlessly white."

Rachel, in contrast to Stretton's drunken lower-class mothers, is portrayed as a heroic, self-sacrificing maternal figure. When her husband Trevor returns to London and accidentally meets up with Rachel, she separates herself from Rosy in order to protect her daughter from Trevor's plans to prostitute her: "It would be dangerous to let one of Trevor's comrades even see his little daughter." She refuses to steal for her husband and his cronies, and he punishes her by locking her in a garret to stitch for him.[36] Rachel's health is broken by her malnourishment and ill-treatment, but she survives her tormentor long enough to find her daughter once again and to die in her presence, a Christian deathbed scene that is witnessed not only by Rosy but by her surrogate father, the pastorally named Sylvanus, the worker who took Rachel and Rosy into his care in the wretched city. In this Christian death forbidden to the drunken lower-class mother, the former thief Rachel allies herself to her biblical namesake, Jacob's beloved wife, favored of the Lord. Stretton's Rachel calls upon the Lord as she dies: "'Father!' she cried, in a tone of amazement and of great joy. . . . The storm of life was ended for her, and already she was in the haven where she would be." Rachel—like Daniel in *Jessica's Mother*—is allowed a good, middle-class Victorian deathbed scene.

A Thorny Path begins with a shocking scene in which the recently widowed, destitute Hagar, carrying her new infant, abandons her blind old

---

[36] This dark Rapunzel-like Christian fairytale is inflected by Friedrich Engels's *Condition of the Working Classes* in England in 1844, in which starving, impoverished seamstresses sew for their lives. See also Morse 27–73.

father and her little girl Dot in Kensington Gardens: "The moment was come at last when despair had gained full possession of her."[37] Named for the biblical Hagar, mother of Ishmael, this poverty-stricken, desperate mother is immediately aggrandized in the Victorian reader's mind—as is Rachel—by her biblical namesake. This Victorian Hagar is also a beleaguered mother, also a victim of oppression by the patriarchy, as the biblical Hagar of Genesis, Abraham's concubine, suffered from the patriarch's judgment that she and her son Ishmael should be cast into the desert wilderness. Like the biblical Hagar, this Victorian mother, too, will ultimately find some peace.

Almost at once, Hagar repents of her deed, but when she returns to the spot in Kensington Gardens where she left the old man and the little girl, they are gone. Hagar is so distressed that she runs into the street, right under the wheels of a passing cab. Her baby dies, but Hagar is rescued by a kindly young man, the railway guard Abbott, who is in the cab that hits Hagar in the foggy evening, as he hurries to see his own devout mother before she dies that same evening. Abbott chooses to have Hagar's baby buried with his mother, signifying their union in the kingdom of heaven, and the equality of all children of God. Hagar tells Abbott that she has thought of drowning herself—but in this tale, as in others of women who are forlorn and even sexually fallen but not drunks, Hagar is saved from this fate. She is taken in by Abbott, who now owns his mother's beautiful, orderly house—again, as in *The Storm of Life,* associated with maternal purity. Eventually, Abbott and Hagar fall in love with each other, despite her tragic story of betrayal. Unlike the patriarch Abraham who cast out his son Ishmael, Abbott does not condemn Hagar and her child, but instead ultimately succeeds in finding the long-lost daughter. Thus Stretton revises the Old Testament, the ultimate patriarchal narrative.

The wandering Ishmael figure of the novel is a Dickensian street urchin who names himself Don after a dog he likes. Don's identification with a street dog is reminiscent of the scene in *Bleak House* in which the narrator comments upon Jo as having been taught less than the drover's dog.[38] This alignment indicates his cultural disposability, as Ivan Kreilkamp brilliantly

---

[37] See Ross: "A much larger group of 'bad' wives, far larger than that of drinkers, were women who had 'lost all hope,' as the saying went, women who, to use Beatrice Potter Webb's terms, were 'very dirty and untidy' or 'untidy, incapable, and careworn,' dragging themselves as best they could through their days and carrying out minimal domestic functions in a weary, depressed state. These symptoms could express a variety of underlying states: overwhelming fatigue, illness, depression, or rebellion" (71–72). Ross cites Potter Webb in her account book describing tenants in the Katharine Buildings, for which she was a rent collector from 1885 until 1889.

[38] Chap. 16, "Tom-All-Alone's":

argues in a recent essay (Kreilkamp). The abbreviated, nearly interchangeable names of these roaming street children—Dot and Don—suggest both their representativeness and their society's refusal to allow them to inherit their full humanity—much less a stake in the lawful inheritance of worldly goods that requires a surname. Stretton creates a figure embodying Christ's spiritual inheritance in the orphaned Don, who seems never to have had parents but is nevertheless a kind protector to little Dot.

The orphaned street arab Don is Stretton's example to the neglectful society that has cast these children out to wander. The most poignant section of the narrative is a long sequence in which the two children are alone in London while Don slaves as an errand-boy, sacrificing his health to provide for his charge. He ultimately dies of starvation: "Those who heard of Don felt it to be an infamy to the greatest and richest city in the world, a Christian city, that one of its children should famish in its streets" (chap. 19, "A Shameful Verdict").[39] The maternalized Don is buried in the grave with Abbott's mother and Hagar's baby: "He had no name that they could put upon the headstone; but they added a new inscription to that already upon it, one which would remind them of him whenever they came to the spot: 'He shall hunger no more, neither thirst any more; and God shall wipe away all tears from his eyes'" (chap. 19). The inscription

> A band of music comes and plays. Jo listens to it. So does a dog—a drover's dog, waiting for his master outside a butcher's shop, and evidently thinking about those sheep he has had upon his mind for some hours and is happily rid of. He seems perplexed respecting three or four, can't remember where he left them, looks up and down the street as half expecting to see them astray, suddenly pricks up his ears and remembers all about it. A thoroughly vagabond dog, accustomed to low company and public-houses; a terrific dog to sheep, ready at a whistle to scamper over their backs and tear out mouthfuls of their wool; but an educated, improved, developed dog who has been taught his duties and knows how to discharge them. He and Jo listen to the music, probably with much the same amount of animal satisfaction; likewise as to awakened association, aspiration, or regret, melancholy or joyful reference to things beyond the senses, they are probably upon a par. But, otherwise, how far above the human listener is the brute!
>
> Turn that dog's descendants wild, like Jo, and in a very few years they will so degenerate that they will lose even their bark—but not their bite.

[39] Ross: "Food was obviously also a matter of life or death, for starvation deaths continued to be a regular occurrence even in the kinder years after 1870." Ross states in her notes that "[c]ases of starvation deaths 'upon which a Coroner's Jury have Returned a Verdict of Death from Starvation, or Death Accelerated by Privation' were reported annually for the country and included in the Parliamentary Papers. London's local and metropolitan newspapers also gave ample details on many cases" (234).

from Revelation is the apocalyptic promise of the New Jerusalem, even for the least of London's creatures, a starved errand-boy with no given name. In the final lines of the novel, Don's sacrifice is, radically, likened to Christ's. And Hagar—the mother who has abandoned the child for whom the street waif Don perished—is content and well provided for in a Christian family of people who are united by Christ's love—and Don's sacrifice. Even a mother who abandons her blind father and small daughter can be redeemed, in Stretton's fictional world.

In order further to point up the characterization of the lower-class drunken mother as unredeemable, we can briefly examine two texts of the lower-class drunken father in which the drunken father not only lives, but is redeemed. This novel published by RTS directly appeals to Scottish working-class values. As Stan Crooke states in his review of William Knox's *Industrial Nation,* "Temperance was not a passing fad but a hallmark of working-class respectability." Knox points out that "[t]he Edinburgh Trades Council (ETC) met in a coffee bar from its inception until 1867 and then for the next twenty years, in a temperance hotel."[40] *Nelly's Dark Days* (1870), published by the Scottish Temperance League, is a harrowing story of a man of humble thatched-cottage country origins who has come to the city, been a successful, respectable skilled worker for a time, and then has taken to drink. Once an urban hero who saved a drowning match-girl, Rodney now locks his daughter out of the house on a bitter winter night; takes her beloved, scarlet-sashed doll to pawn for gin; and steals the violets from his wife's coffin in order to buy a dram. Finally, Nelly's clothes catch on fire as she is trying to cook for her drunken father, and in his state of inebriation, he can only watch her burn. Thinking that Nelly has died, when Rodney recovers his senses he goes to the river to drown himself, the narrative fate of Jessica's mother. Stretton's description of Rodney's tortured state of mind is dramatic:

> It was slow and weary work, creeping, creeping down to the river side. . . . He was drunk no longer. His mind was terribly clear. He knew distinctly what had happened, and what was about to happen to him if his strength would only take him down to the edge of yonder black water. (chap. 8)

But the drunken father's narrative is not the same tragedy as the drunken mother's. Rodney ends up unconscious, in delirium for weeks, and then in recovery, working on the docks and going to church again.

---

[40] See Crooke and Knox 73.

He decides that, in emulation of the Prodigal Son, he might be able to go home to both God and his rural mother. When Rodney returns to his childhood cottage, he recalls with Wordsworthian resonance the sweet purity and innocence of the time before he became a slave to gin: "Every step of the road was familiar and dear to him. Here were the nutbushes, where he and his brothers had come nutting in the autumn, when he was a boy. . . . Yonder was the bank where the violets grew thickest, and where he had been used to see the first-scented blossoms for Ellen, before they were married . . ." (chap. 13).[41]

In this state of remembered childhood innocence, Rodney finds not only his mother but Nelly, who has not died but is an invalid, scarred forever by the fire of her father's intemperance. Nelly lies on a couch, symbolically with a new doll to replace the one her father had stolen, and a cup of violets by her. Rodney's wife has died at Easter, and it is a year since her death. Nelly's cup of violets—linked to the stolen violets on Ellen's grave and the violets he once brought to her when they were courting—also signify a kind of Resurrection. Both Nelly and Rodney have come back from the brink of death. The book concludes on a hopeful note, with Rodney alone, reading his mother's old Bible: "My grace is sufficient for thee; for my strength is made perfect in weakness."

In *Her Only Son* (1887), also published by the Scottish Temperance League, the admirable countrywoman Joanna Fleming, aged sixty, has lived in the same thatched-roof stone country cottage for nearly forty years. The novel begins as she considers her decision to look after the newly motherless children of her beloved son, born in that same cottage, who has fled the country for city life in London. Born into a line of gardeners who have worked in the Squire's Hall Gardens for generations, "nigh on three hundred years" (chap. 1), John has become a quintessential urban working man, a cabdriver who owns his own cab, bought with Joanna's life savings. When Joanna leaves her country life and her beloved cottage, she says she is "plucking one's self up by the roots" (chap. 1).

The act of courage by the old rural mother is treated with great respect. Joanna possesses the middle-class virtues of cleanliness and orderliness: she packs a great chest with clothes and household linen, "white-scented sheets and cloths she had washed and laid in lavender weeks ago. Her own decent dresses and muslin caps, and black satin bonnet for churchgoing . . ." (chap. 2).

The city is a shock to Joanna. The value the narrative places on the purity of country life is embodied in her character, and her subjectivity is

---

[41] This is an example of what Patricia Demers analyzes as Stretton's romanticism in her insightful chapter "Mrs. Sherwood and Hesba Stretton."

valued by the narrative voice, who describes her confusion sympathetically: "Surely this was a foreign, outlandish country; not England. The England she knew was made up of fields and hedges, hills and little rivulets, with farmhouses and pretty cottages dotted about, and the sun or moon shedding a natural light over them all . . ." (chap. 2). The biggest shock by far awaits Joanna: her son's home. The first thing Joanna sees when she arrives at the ironically named 19 Gibraltar Court is the drunken men and women who have followed the cab from the spirit vaults. Her son John's home is one filthy room up a narrow staircase, in the attics.

The "industry, and thrift, and self-denial" that John associates with his mother help to transform the "miserable and filthy hole" that is her son's and grandchildren's home. But the London daughter-in-law, now dead, is remembered by John's kindly neighbor Mrs. Christie as the culprit, the bad influence for Joanna's son: "When a woman drinks like that, what can her husband do? He's bound to be drove to drink himself. . . . God help their children, I say!" (chap. 4). Mrs. Christie predicts that John's daughter Ally will be worse than her mother : "She's a little girl now, but in a two-three years she'll want money, and she'll get it" (chap. 4). The cultural narrative of the fallen woman in her most degraded form—the street prostitute—is thus again linked to the narrative of the drunken mother, as it was in *Jessica's Mother*.

The novel details Joanna's suffering because of her son's drunkenness. The power of the narrative lies in part in the portrayal of the drunkard's changing psychological state: "Slowly there grew in his clouded brain and besotted mind a feeling of resentment against his mother. He looked on her as a spy upon him, always treasuring up in her memory his sins against her and his children" (chap. 8). The son's drunken behavior culminates in his turning his mother out of the house on a cold February night. The most powerful section of the novel deals with Joanna's "sad pilgrimage" to find her old neighbor Mrs. Christie after she is pushed out the door by her son. As she becomes weaker and weaker, her thoughts about her past are portrayed: "There was a blear-eyed, hoarse-voiced, broken-down man somewhere, who called her mother, and turned her out of doors at night into the cruel cold. But that man could not be her dear child" (chap. 9). John Fleming finds his mother nearly frozen to death next to the Gibraltar Arms, this England's gin palace, in which he has spent all her money and his own.

Unlike the drunken mothers of *Lost Gip* and *Jessica's Mother,* John Fleming feels genuine remorse at the terrible pain he has caused: "It was all his doing; there was no one else to blame but himself" (chap. 10). With succor from the kindly vicar who runs Mission House, Joanna's son frees himself from his addiction to alcohol. At the close of the novel, the mother and son are together in their old country cottage again, raising her grandchildren together.

The drunken lower-class father is allowed, then, to live and to reform. However, there is an element of sorrowful responsibility that John always feels. He is not able to obtain his mother's forgiveness, for after her illness, she cannot remember her urban experience. Joanna is thus in a sense "purified" of her dark trials in London, while John continues to suffer for his past sins: "He feels again the bitter shame and degradation into which he once plunged, and dragged his children, and his mother down with him. They have forgotten; but he cannot forget" (chap. 12). The drunken working-class father's punishment is memory itself.

The social class of the drunken mother is the most crucial aspect that divides drunken mother narratives. In sharp contrast to the disposable mothers of *Lost Gip* and *Jessica's First Prayer/Jessica's Mother,* the middle-class mother, Sophy Chantrey, in *Brought Home* (1875)—published by the Scottish Temperance League—is not only treated with great sympathy but is allowed to keep her son Charlie. Morever, Sophy wins her struggle against alcoholism and is alive at the close of the novel to find pleasure in her freedom from addiction. She is not only redeemed at the end of the narrative, but she is also not haunted by her past behavior, as Rodney and John Fleming are. The middle-class mother eventually rejoices in her husband and son in England.

The focus in *Brought Home* is on the redemption of Sophy Chantrey and the rehabilitation of the spiritually and physically diseased middle-class mother. Sophy is the beloved wife of the incumbent of Upton Rectory in a "sleepy" market town about an hour's journey from London. The old Norman churchyard and death itself strongly pervade the novel's opening, as David Chantrey, rector of Upton, is so ill that he must leave Sophy for sunny Madeira to mend his broken health. Soon after this sober first scene, we see Sophy grieving over her dead baby's grave in the churchyard.

Stretton focuses for much of the story on the responsibility of the Christian community. Each person who should help Sophy reacts differently, and each is judged by the narrator for either attempting to rescue Sophy in her troubles or neglecting their duty. Among those who fail in their Christian duty, the foremost is the late archdeacon's widow, the rich, officious Mrs. Bolton, longtime arbiter of parish affairs and David Chantrey's aunt. Although Mrs. Bolton provides her nephew's wife with a comfortable home during his absence, the aunt declines to keep seven-year-old Charlie in her fashionable villa, and he is sent to boarding school. Thus Sophy is deprived of her maternal responsibilities. Mrs. Bolton also refuses to help

Sophy with her growing obsession with alcohol by forbidding spirits in her home, as the current rector, Mr. Warden, advises. Mr. Warden himself is presented as remiss in his Christian duty to his parishioner and to his friend David by not committing himself to helping Sophy with her drinking problem. This presentation of those persons who fail in their Christian duty to the falling sinner presents Sophy's problem as a concern of the entire Christian community. The result is that the reader sympathizes with Sophy and judges Mrs. Bolton and Mr. Warden instead.

Stretton provides a model Christian in the story as well, the saddler Ann Holland. She is an "elderly, old-fashioned woman [who] held firmly to all old-fashioned ways; knew her duty to God and her duty to her neighbour, as taught by the Church Catechism, and faithfully fulfilled them to the best of her power" (chap. 3). In a moving encounter between Ann and Sophy at the Chantrey baby's grave, Ann takes the initiative that her social "betters" will not assume, and she attempts to succor the troubled young clergyman's wife by telling her of her own alcoholic brother Richard. Eventually, Ann's brother dies from exposure during a drunken bout, and she decides to commit herself to helping Sophy by accompanying her to New Zealand, where both Ann and David Chantrey hope that Sophy will be able more readily to resist the lure of alcohol. The most admirable character in the story is sympathetic to Sophy despite her weakness—and the reader is urged to sympathy as well.

A number of narrative strategies serve to create sympathy and hope for the middle-class mother. Sophy's misery is documented in our access to her interiority: "There could be no harm, she thought, in taking just enough to deliver her from her very worst moments of depression . . ." (chap. 4). The reader sympathizes with the isolation and wretchedness that propels Sophy to drink, and then to drink in excess. One of the most powerful of these strategies is Stretton's portrayal of Sophy's struggle, shame, and love for her husband. Perhaps the most powerful of the scenes of their fight against Sophy's degradation is a fervent sermon that David preaches on the text, "Am I my brother's keeper?" At the close of this impassioned sermon, David sees his wife outstretched upon their baby's grave, drunk and asleep. Although this vision causes "a moment of unutterable shame and agony for him," he goes out to his "miserable wife" to take her home. When he is unable to lift her, he bursts into a passion of tears, after which his friends and parishioners help him to carry Sophy home, in an emblem of the need for community to save the erring sinner.

Another of the most effective of Stretton's narrative strategies in creating sympathy for the middle-class drunken mother is the love of her child, Charlie, who suddenly becomes a character in the story at this moment.

Charlie sees his fallen mother and says only: "My mother is ill, very ill. I saw her lying on baby's grave. Couldn't anything be done for her to make her well?" (chap. 10). The reader is encouraged to see with Charlie's innocent eyes that the besotted mother is more sick than sinful.

Perhaps the most memorable of Stretton's narrative strategies occurs on shipboard during the difficult crossing to the New Zealand missionary curacy David Chantrey has accepted in order to help his desperate wife. This strategy is to dramatize a scene that presents Sophy's heroic triumph over her desire for whiskey in the midst of a terrible storm during which her husband appears to be dying: "the strong, spirituous scent excited her." By the time the storm—and Sophy's symbolic psychic tempest—is over, David seems to be recovering strength, and Sophy herself has triumphed through prayer over her desperate desire for the brandy. As Sophy tells her husband, "God has made it safe for me" (chap. 17).

The middle-class drunken mother is allowed not only recuperation but eventual return to England. The recovery begun on shipboard continues in New Zealand. But unlike the emigration to Canada that closes *Lost Gip,* this colonial outpost is only a refuge for work and purification, not a final resting place. Eventually, David and Sophy are offered the possibility of returning home. Sophy's recovery from alcoholism is portrayed as complete when she is again the parish clergyman's wife at Upton Rectory, mother to her thriving son. In *Brought Home,* the alcohol-addicted mother is the heroine of a middle-class conversion narrative. She gets to erase her own narrative of shame by returning to the beginning of her story, and living it again, purified.

Thus the maternal ideal is salvaged in the middle-class narrative. The contrast between the narrative patterns describing the lower-class drunken mother's disgrace and erasure through death and the middle-class alcoholic mother's redemption seems to accomplish the cultural work of maintaining class distinctions and gender ideals while simultaneously—and in seeming contradiction—elevating the nearly Romantic, Dickensian innocent child of squalor into the middle classes under the general rubric of an equalizing Christian faith. There also seems to be an intermittent urge on Stretton's part to find a scapegoat for the dissolution of so many families of the urban poor, although she knew firsthand that even temperance-pledged mothers might find slum conditions impossible for their beleaguered families. Although Stretton has been called a "Christian Socialist," the trope of the drunken mother is a disturbing aspect of her generous and progressive fiction.

The child victim narrative is bolstered by the narrative of the gin-soaked mother who oppresses her own offspring. Stretton, one of the most vocal of children's rights advocates, upholds a child's right to a safe environment. Poor mothers who fail in other ways and lower-class drunken fathers are punished but not eliminated from Stretton's narratives, and they are represented as individuals capable of redemption. The concomitant sins of sexual fallenness and intemperance—no doubt actually often connected—suggest that symbolically, the willful contamination of the lower-class mother's body is the unforgivable sin. This covert fear of moral infection as well as bodily contamination by the poor may inform Stretton's representation. The lower-class drunken mother, a recurring figure in Stretton's Christian texts, is not granted Christian forgiveness. She is not only nameless and dead—she is unforgiven.

Works Cited

Auerbach, Nina. *Woman and the Demon: The Life of a Victorian Myth.* Cambridge: Harvard University Press, 1982.

Baggs, Chris. "'In the Separate Reading Room for Ladies Are Provided Those Publications Specially Interesting to Them': Ladies' Reading Rooms and British Public Libraries 1850–1914." *Victorian Periodicals Review* 38 (2005): 280–306.

Barickman, Richard, Susan MacDonald, and Myra Stark. *Corrupt Relations.* New York: Columbia University Press, 1982.

Berry, Laura. *The Child, the State, and the Victorian Novel.* Charlottesville and London: University Presses of Virginia, 1999.

Branca, Patricia. *Silent Sisterhood.* Pittsburgh: Carnegie Mellon University Press, 1975.

Bratton, Jacqueline S. *The Impact of Victorian Children's Fiction.* London: Croom Helm, 1981.

Butts, Dennis. "Introduction." In *From the Dairyman's Daughter to Worrals of the WAAF: The Religious Tract Society, Lutterworth Press and Children's Literature.* Ed. Dennis Butts and Pat Garrett. Cambridge: Lutterworth Press, 2006.

Crooke, Stan. Review of *Industrial Nation,* by William Knox. Fall 2000. http://archive.workersliberty.org/activity/fractions/scotland/history1.html.

Cutt, Margaret Nancy. *Ministering Angels: A Study of Nineteenth-Century Evangelical Writing for Children.* Broxbourne, England: Five Owls Press, 1979.

Davidoff, Leonore. *The Best Circles: Society Etiquette and the Season.* London: Croom Helm, 1973.

Demers, Patricia. "Smith, Sarah (1832–1911)." *Oxford Dictionary of National Biography.* Oxford: Oxford University Press, 2004. http://www.oxforddnb.com.proxy.wm.edu/view/article/36158.

———. "Mrs. Sherwood and Hesba Stretton: The Letter and the Spirit of Evangelical Writing of and for Children." In *Romanticism and Children's Literature in Nineteenth-Century England.* Ed. McGavran Jr. and James Holt. Athens: University of Georgia Press, 1991. 129–49.

Diamond, Marion. *Emigration and Empire: The Life of Maria S. Rye.* New York: Garland, 1999.

Dickins, Gordon. *An Illustrated Literary Guide to Shropshire.* Shrewsbury: Shropshire Libraries, 1987. http://www.3.shropshire-cc.gov.uk/strethes.htm.

Frost, Ginger. "Motherhood on Trial: Violence and Unwed Mothers in Victorian England." In this volume.
Glasgow University Digital Archive for the history of the Scottish Temperance League. http://gdl.cdlr.strath.ac.uk/airgli/airgli0128.htm.
Gorham, Deborah. *The Victorian Girl and the Feminine Ideal.* London: Croom Helm, 1982.
Hendrick, Harry. *Child Welfare: Historical Dimensions, Contemporary Debate.* Bristol: Policy Press, 2003.
Joseph, Gerhard, and Herbert Tucker. "Passing On: Death." In *A Companion to Victorian Literature and Culture.* London: Blackwell, 1999.
Kennard, Jean E. *Victims of Convention.* Hamden: Archon, 1978.
Knox, William. *Industrial Nation: Work, Culture, and Society in Scotland, 1800–Present.* Edinburgh: Edinburgh University Press, 1999.
Koven, Seth. *Slumming: Sexual and Social Politics in Victorian London.* Princeton: Princeton University Press, 2005.
Kreilkamp, Ivan. "Dying Like a Dog in Great Expectations." In *Victorian Animal Dreams: Representations of Animals in Literature and Culture.* Ed. Deborah Denenholz Morse and Martin A. Danahay. Aldershot, Hants: Ashgate 2007. 82–94.
Langland, Elizabeth. *Nobody's Angels: Middle-Class Women and Domestic Ideology in Victorian Culture.* Ithaca: Cornell University Press, 1995.
Maunder, Andrew. "*East Lynne* and the Spectre of Female Degeneracy." In *Victorian Crime, Madness, and Sensation.* Ed. Andrew Maunder and Grace Moore. Aldershot, Hants: Ashgate, 2004. 59–72.
Maver, Irene. "The Temperance Movement and the Urban Associational Ideal." In *Civil Society, Urban Places, and Associations, and Urban Places: Class, Nation, and Culture in Nineteenth-Century Europe.* Ed. B. M. A. DeVries, Boudien DeVries, and R. J. Morris. Aldershot, Hants: Ashgate, 2006.
Morse, Deborah Denenholz. "Stitching Repentance, Sewing Rebellion: Seamstresses and Fallen Women in Elizabeth Gaskell's Fiction." In *Keeping the Victorian House.* Ed. Vanessa Dickerson. Origins of Modernism Series. New York: Garland Press. 27–73.
Newton, Judith Lowder. *Women, Power, and Subversion: Social Strategies in British Fiction 1778–1860.* London: Methuen, 1985.
Nord, Deborah Epstein. *Walking the Victorian Streets: Women, Representation, and the City.* Ithaca: Cornell University Press, 1995.
Rees, Barbara. *The Victorian Lady.* London: Gordon & Cremonesi, 1977.
Rickard, Suzanne L. G. "A Gifted Author—Hesba Stretton and the Religious Tract Society." In *From the Dairyman's Daughter to Worrals of the WAAF: The Religious Tract Society, Lutterworth Press and Children's Literature.* Ed. Dennis Butts and Pat Garrett. Cambridge: Lutterworth Press, 2006. 104–15.
———. "'Living by the Pen': Hesba Stretton's Moral Earnings." *Women's History Review* 5 (1996): 219–38.
Ross, Ellen. *Love and Toil: Motherhood in Outcast London, 1870–1918.* New York and Oxford: Oxford University Press, 1993.
Sattaur, Jennifer. Review of *From the Dairyman's Daughter to Worrals of the WAAF: The Religious Tract Society, Lutterworth Press and Children's Literature,* edited by Dennis Butts and Pat Garrett. *Children's Literature Association Quarterly* 32.1 (2007): 76–78.
Shapiro, Ann R. *Unlikely Heroines: Nineteenth-Century American Women Writers and the Woman Question.* Westport, CT: Greenwood Press, 1987.

Stretton, Hesba. *Jessica's First Prayer* and *Jessica's Mother*. Chicago: W. B. Conkey & Co., n.d.
———. *The Storm of Life*. London: Religious Tract Society, n.d.
———. *A Thorny Path*. London: Religious Tract Society, n.d.
———. *Lost Gip*. London: Religious Tract Society, 1891.
———. *Her Only Son*. Glasgow: Scottish Temperance League, 1887.
———. *Brought Home*. Glasgow: Scottish Temperance League, 1875.
———. *Nelly's Dark Days*. Glasgow: Scottish Temperance League, 1870.
Thomson, Patricia. *The Victorian Heroine: A Changing Ideal, 1837–1873*. Oxford: Oxford University Press, 1956.
Vicinus, Martha, ed. *A Widening Sphere: Changing Roles of Victorian Women*. Bloomington: Indiana University Press, 1977.
———. *Suffer and Be Still: Women in the Victorian Age*. Bloomington: Indiana University Press, 1972.
Winskill, Peter Turner. *The Temperance Movement and Its Workers: A Record of Social, Moral, Religious, and Political Progress*. Vol. 3. London, Glasgow, Edinburgh, and Dublin: Blackie & Sons, 1892.
Zipes, Jack, gen. ed. *The Norton Anthology of Children's Literatures: The Traditions in English*. New York and London: W. W. Norton, 2005.

CHAPTER 6

Infant Doping and Middle-Class Motherhood

Opium Warnings and Charlotte Yonge's
The Daisy Chain

DARA ROSSMAN REGAIGNON

A wet nurse must never be allowed to dose her little charge with Godfrey's Cordial, with Dalby's Carminative, with Syrup of Poppies, or with medicine of any kind whatever. Let her thoroughly understand this; and let there be no mistake in the matter. Do not, for one moment, allow your baby's health to be tampered and trifled with. A baby's health is too precious to be doctored by an ignorant person.

—Pye Henry Chavasse, *Advice to Mothers on the Management of Their Offspring,* 8th ed. (1866)

Domestic fiction and domestic advice literature are arguably the two literary genres most closely identified with the middle classes, both in the Victorian period and in our own.[1] Because both genres are invested in not only imagining the domestic sphere but also in making it a supremely desirable space, these texts typically offer recurring, static spectacles of domesticity.[2] One of the characteristic tensions of these spectacles is that between the ideal of maternal caretaking and the assumption of paid child care; while middle-class women differentiated themselves from their aristocratic counterparts by being domestic creatures, they

---

[1] Armstrong's *Desire and Domestic Fiction* makes a classic argument for *why* this is; see also Leila S. May's critique of Armstrong. For considerations of the intersecting cultural work of novels and advice literature in the Victorian period, see Chase and Levenson, Cohen, and Langland.

[2] In *The Spectacle of Intimacy,* Karen Chase and Michael Levenson argue that while domestic scandals provided fodder for the public discussion (and hence normalization) of familial privacy, "even the complacency of self-delight participated in the spectacle" (12). Their focus is on how "Victorian private life came to know itself in the stress of popular sensation" (6). My interest lies not in what the Victorians recognized about themselves but in what they overlooked and marginalized.

differentiated themselves from those below by acting as ladies of leisure. We frequently find the fictional resolution of this tension in the epilogual tableau: David Copperfield's vision of his transcendent domestic felicity with Agnes, for example; or the pastoral calm of Dinah Morris and their small children greeting Adam Bede upon his return home from a long day of work. Charlotte Yonge (1823–1901) is typically more concerned with the messy quotidian details of middle-class life than either Dickens or Eliot, but she, too, assumes that her readers will register happy domestic scenes as idylls. Paid servants and other such interlopers are carefully omitted. The comfort and stasis such images promise—and which provide the basis of their ideological force—derive in part from their exclusion of the working hands that enable their clean and calm visions.

But while such domestic spectacles might offer closure in fiction, advice literature invokes such images in repetitive dialogue with the dangers they close off. The solutions of the middle-class family are thus always temporary; the servants who make the family's domestic idyll possible constantly intrude (to serve tea, to dust the table, to diaper the baby), requiring elaborate narratives that simultaneously justify and contain their presence. In this essay, I examine one category of such narratives: warnings that servants were giving middle-class babies opium to make them sleep. Such warnings do complex and messy work—work not unlike the messy work of child care itself. While on the surface they scare mothers back into the nursery—telling them that their presence or absence from that space has literally life-or-death consequences for their children—the ongoing assumption that middle-class families require paid child care suggests more ambivalence about the physical intimacy of mothering than at first appears. Yonge's *The Daisy Chain* (1853–55; 1856) offers what seems to be the only episode in Victorian fiction in which a middle-class infant dies from opium secretly given to her by her nanny. In a novel otherwise deeply invested in venerating the maternal, the episode surprisingly blames the baby's mother not only for relying on paid child care, but also for caring for the infant herself. Read alongside the opium warnings, it provides a useful lens through which to see not only the anxieties about mothering that paradoxically enabled the Victorians' idealization of the selfless, nurturing mother, but also how the generic conventions of advice literature help generate and maintain that ambivalent figure.

"The Poor Child's Nurse"

Physician-authored child-care manuals introduce warnings against the use of opiates at idiosyncratic and often unexpected moments—as an issue of the infant's diet; while discussing how often newborns cry; or, most logically, in a chapter on medicines.[3] The opiates take many forms, including alcohol-based preparations such as laudanum and the category of patent medicines known suggestively as "soothing syrups," such as Mrs. Winslow's Soothing Syrup, Godfrey's Cordial, and Street's Infant's Quietness. The variety of forms that opium takes, as well as its consistent appearance throughout these texts, does more than reflect how dependent Victorians of all classes were on the drug to medicate their minor and major ailments—although it does that, too. Opium's recurring presence in child-rearing advice literature also suggests that the drug operates in these texts as a narrative metaphor for children's vulnerability as both physical and social beings. Mortality rates remained high throughout the nineteenth century for children of all classes (Wohl 11). The possibility of sudden infant death haunts this literature: Thomas Bull opens the 1861 and later editions of his often-reprinted *Maternal Management of Children in Health and Disease* (first published in 1840) with the following grim statistic: "*One child in five dies within a year after birth, and one in three before the completion of the fifth year*" (1; emphasis in original; see also Barrett v). Both Bull and Thomas Barrett (whose *Advice on the Management of Children in Early Infancy* appeared in 1851) create a specific and disturbing nexus between opium, infancy, and death, asserting that roughly "three-fourths of all deaths that take place from opium occur in children under four years of age" (Barrett 68–69; see also Bull 1861, 160–61).

Mothers are carefully dissociated from this question. Manuals explicitly assume that their maternal readers would administer opium only under medical advice; "lazy," "ignorant," and "wily" servants (Bull 111; Chavasse 31; Barrett 67), however, cannot be trusted to use such discretion. This warning, from Bull's *Maternal Management,* is representative:

---

[3] See Chavasse 31; *Plain Observations* 19–20; and Bull 111, respectively. (References are to the 1840 edition of Bull's *Maternal Management* unless otherwise specified.) See also *Cassells' Household Guide* 11, and Barrett 66–71. I draw exclusively from child-rearing manuals by medical men that imagine a readership living in Britain for this essay. These texts differ in tone and content from those written by women, in that physician-authored manuals explicitly offer their "professional" expertise and are clearly invested in the project of professionalizing the medical field. (See Peterson, "Gentlemen and Medical Men" and *The Medical Profession in Mid-Victorian London,* and Poovey.) Opium rumors dot the advice literature written for Anglo-Indian audiences, as well. There, the most common form of opium seems to be simply an "opium pill," although the tone and content of the warnings are otherwise strikingly similar (see *Domestic Guide* 104, for example); in both cases, the clandestine administration of the drug symbolizes anxieties about the effective transmission of British middle-class identity in a context where parents are not the exclusive (or perhaps even the primary) early caretakers of their children. For a fuller discussion of these issues in nineteenth-century British India, see my "Accented English."

OPIATES

This class of medicine is often kept in the nursery, in the forms of laudanum, syrup of white poppies, Dalby's carminative, and Godfrey's cordial.

The object with which they are generally given is to allay pain by producing sleep; they are therefore, *remedies of great convenience to the nurse;* and I am sorry to be obliged to add, that, so exhibited, they are but *too often fatal to the little patient.* (110; emphasis in original)

Bull's guide was widely read and reprinted from the 1840s through the 1870s. Like its chief competitor, Pye Henry Chavasse's *Advice to a Mother* (first published in 1839, and in print through the twentieth century), *Maternal Management* is at great pains to elevate maternal care and to denigrate hired caretakers (nannies, nursemaids, nurses, wet nurses). Unlike the passage from Chavasse's *Advice to a Mother* that forms my opening epigraph, Bull's warning initially imagines a legitimate reason for giving a baby opium: the medicine "allay[s] pain." This sympathy for the caregiver (and this assumption of sympathy on her part) disappears, however, as we are assured that her only real concern is "convenience." Bull later extends this condemnation, pointing out parenthetically that opiates are "but too often administered by an indiscreet and lazy nurse, unknown by the parent" (111). The precise contours of the parent's ignorance are unclear here: while it might simply be that she does not realize that her child is being given opium, the phrasing also suggests that it is the nurse herself who is a stranger. This plays on more pervasive anxieties about servants, the intimate Others hired to live and work in middle-class homes. Bull's and Chavasse's warnings about the dangers of opium thus catastrophize the prevalent Victorian anxiety that you never *really* know your own servants.[4]

Opium warnings create a complex and unstable point at which class anxieties reinforce more physical fears for children's continued health. A narcotic is perhaps an ideal mechanism for this, since, as Barry Milligan points out, it was "literally ingested by British bodies . . . [and] had a reputation for altering the consciousness of its user" (30). Opium, in Bull's warning, produces not only physical illness (and death) but attendant psychological and social degeneration. After dismissing nannies who use patent medicines as lazy and selfish, Bull describes how opium poisoning presents medically:

---

[4] See Brian McCuskey's work on servants in the Victorian novel; in particular, "The Kitchen Police" and "Children below Stairs."

[B]y their continued and habitual use . . . a low, irritative, febrile state is produced, gradually followed by loss of flesh, the countenance becoming pallid, sallow, and sunken, the eyes red and swollen, and the expression stupid and heavy, and the powers of the constitution at last becoming completely undermined. Such an object is to be seen daily among the poorer classes,—the miniature of a sickly aged person: death soon follows here. (Bull 111)

In this list of symptoms the physical ("pale and sallow") soon gives way to the psychological ("stupid and heavy"), reflecting opium's power as a narcotic to work on both body and mind; but the psychological difference of the opium-addicted child quickly blurs into class identification: paleness, sallowness, and stupidity converge in this victim's resemblance to the "object . . . to be seen daily among the poorer classes." Opium makes middle-class children look like poor children; it replaces the chubby apple cheeks of middle-class childhood with the sallow pallor of their lower-class counterparts.

Milligan has traced the "Oriental" associations of opium in nineteenth-century culture, arguing that the drug was figured as "various forms of foreign invasion" (30). While the masculine and belletristic history he focuses on—including Coleridge, De Quincey, Wilkie Collins, Dickens, Conan Doyle, and Wilde—largely figures opium as a geographically foreign substance, the class emphasis we see in the advice literature and in *The Daisy Chain* is a competing and underexamined aspect of opium's place in the nineteenth-century imagination.[5] As Virginia Berridge argues in *Opium and the People,* the Victorians were much more concerned with working-class opium use as a national problem than with middle-class writers' (and others') reliance on the drug: for members of the middle classes, whose self-medication often shaded into recreational use and dependency, "opium was a simple part of life, neither exclusively medical nor entirely social" (Berridge 61) and was deemed an essentially personal problem. Opium *abuse* was apprehended as a specifically working-class issue (see Berridge 97), specifically in terms of two issues: the extent to which members of the working classes relied on opium as a lifelong medical crutch, and the frequency of opium overdoses leading to death. Although parliamentary reports did not fully acknowledge the extent to which the cost of medical care and the unsanitary conditions in which the poor lived made opium

---

[5] Anglo-Indian texts seize upon opium as a synecdoche for all the strangeness and danger of colonial life in the subcontinent, where the class anxieties of the English texts are further complicated by race.

use a necessary component of urban life, they did comment with some alarm on the extent to which regular opiate use seemed to begin in infancy and continue throughout adult life (Berridge 102 and passim; see also Chepaitis 36–40 and Wohl 34–36). The second discovery logically extends the first: opium was cheaply and plentifully available throughout England and Wales, at apothecaries, grocers, and other corner shops. According to Anthony S. Wohl, "In Manchester, according one account, five out of six working-class families used it habitually. One Manchester druggist admitted selling a half gallon of Godfrey's Cordial (the most popular mixture, it contained opium, treacle, water, and spices) and between five and six gallons of what was euphemistically called 'quietness' every week" (34). Its quality was essentially unregulated, it was cheaper than alcohol, and it suppressed the appetite—all of which contributed to a regular reliance on it by the poor.

We can see how this concern about overreliance on opium reinforced and extended negative stereotypes about working-class domestic life— more precisely, working-class maternity—in the cartoon from *Punch* in figure 6.1. In this cartoon, "The Poor Child's Nurse" seems to be the opium bottle on the small table in the center of the room. The untidy room, broken chair, and inadequate fire all reinforce the sense of neglect dramatized most pathetically by the baby leaning out of its cradle to sob inconsolably. Wohl contends that Victorian public health officials made a facile connection between "the extensive factory employment of female labour" (John Simon, qtd. Wohl 26) and infant mortality, including infant doping (23–27).[6] This use of maternal labor to explain the higher rates of infant mortality among the working classes reinforced the paranoid skepticism of working-class women's ability to properly care for middle-class infants promulgated by child-rearing manuals. Since doping infants was assumed to be a common practice of working (and hence working-class) mothers, it was easy—even logical—to assume that they would have every incentive to continue it when they were bound to their infant charges only by paid contract.[7]

---

[6] Wohl doesn't go into the details of the debate over the "effect of working wives on the health of their babies" (25), simply taking Victorian medical officers' conviction of the causal relationship as his topic. Berridge points out, however, that "most women with young babies did not go out to work" and that "most female operatives . . . tended to leave work after marriage" (101).

[7] In her PhD dissertation, "The Opium of the Children: Domestic Opium and Infant Drugging in Early Victorian England," Elia Vallone Chepaitis argues that "hired nurses . . . carried [the] child-care habits of the poor with them" (15). This was certainly the assumption and fear of the middle-class writers, although as Berridge points out, while "the practice [of infant doping among the working classes] was an undoubted reality, implicit in

THE POOR CHILD'S NURSE.

Figure 6.1. N. [William Newman], *Punch* 17 (1849): 193. From the collection of Special Collections & Archives, University of California Riverside Libraries, University of California, Riverside, CA.

But, as Bull's vision of the addicted infant suggests, the danger opium posed was not simply that of working-class child-rearing practices entering the bourgeois home. It was, more precisely, the danger that by entering the *bodies* of middle-class children, opium would transform them socially as well as physically. While these anxieties play out in contemporary

---

the campaign against it was class interest and a desire to re-mould popular culture into a more acceptable form" (97–98). In an 1869 article, "Babies by the Day" in *Chambers's Journal,* the anonymous author condemns the current state of "public nurseries," where "cries are quieted by something not so harmless as bread and butter"; he offers a idealistic vision of what such nurseries might become, if only they were used by "the wives of prosperous working-men" (148).

discussions of breastfeeding and wet nurses as well, opium provides particularly fertile ground for their expression since it is a substance that, once ingested, works on both body and mind. In *From Communion to Cannibalism,* Maggie Kilgour (following Derrida) argues that "the idea of incorporation . . . defends upon and enforces an absolute division between inside and outside; but in the act itself that opposition disappears, dissolving the structure that it appears to produce" (4). As a working-class substance, opium at once reinscribes the difference between the classes (through their child-rearing practices) and threatens to dissolve them utterly (when it is incorporated into middle-class bodies). As a narcotic—and therefore a substance that acts on both body and mind—opium justifies and even mandates an anxious assumption that ingestible substances can alter the psychology and social status of those who eat them. By relying on working-class persons to provide child care, the middle-class mother jeopardizes thus her family's class position both in the present and for the future generation; the specter of the pale and sallow infant, feebly gasping its life away, individualizes this social danger by going through a process of social devolution that ends in death.

By invoking this specter, child-rearing advice literature imagines the middle-class mother's presence as a kind of antiseptic barrier between her working-class nanny and the child she tends. But this antisepsis—and the idealization of maternal love and care that it relies on—are oddly compromised by the literature's ongoing assumption that its middle-class readers will employ monthly nurses, nursemaids, and nannies. While it's relatively unsurprising that these texts would include extensive instructions for wet nurses alongside their advocacy of maternal breastfeeding, given that there wasn't a good alternative to human breast milk until the very end of the century, it's more startling that many of the imagined questions Chavasse answers pertain to the employment of nursery staff,[8] or that in 1861 Bull includes extensive instructions not only on nursemaids (110–14), but also on how to manage the hierarchy of nursery staff (63). The books' resolute avoidance of the most obvious solution to infant doping follows this pattern: rather than suggesting that their readers *themselves* take on the "drudgery" (Chavasse 113) of routine infant care, they advise increased and more vigilant supervision. Bull, for example, concludes his chapter on opiates by warning mothers who live in "the manufacturing

---

[8] A telling example is the response to question 157, "*Have you any more hints to offer conducive to the well-doing of my child?*" Chavasse immediately responds, "You cannot be too particular in the choice of those who are in constant attendance upon him. Of course, you yourself must be his *head-nurse,* you only require some one to take the drudgery off your hands!" (113).

counties" that "it behoves [sic] [them] to be more than usually careful to whom they entrust their children" because of the prevalence of infant doping in those regions (1861, 164). The very danger that mandates a maternal presence in the nursery, then, also contains and limits it. While maternal supervision guards children against predatory caretakers, it seems that exclusive maternal care is also undesirable.

In his study of French child-rearing books from this period, Jacques Donzelot argues that this emphasis on maternal rather than hired care elevates maternal authority by making her the physician's representative. British advice books also create this bond, but it seems to be as much a way to contain maternal authority as to elevate it. They insist rigorously on their readers' youth and inexperience, imagining first-time mothers without recourse to friends or relations: Chavasse imagines readers about to "undertake the responsible management of children without previous instruction, or without forethought" (Chavasse 2); Bull characteristically catastrophizes this possibility, insisting "life itself [has] but too frequently fallen a sacrifice" to maternal ignorance (iv); and, as I've already noted, many texts routinely and iteratively invoke the fragility of child-life. Despite widespread idealization and veneration of the abstract maternal, Victorian child-rearing manuals thus reveal skepticism as to whether or not mothers are actually up to the challenge of keeping their children alive.

"If Preston killed her, I did!"

Near the end of *The Daisy Chain* occurs what I believe to be the only episode in Victorian fiction in which a middle-class infant is given a deadly overdose of a soothing syrup. The narrative work of this episode both echoes and extends that of the warnings I have discussed above; rather than simply *telling* mothers that their place is in the home, *The Daisy Chain* dramatizes the tragedy that ensues when middle-class women fail to supervise their nursery staffs. Preston—the young and inexperienced nurse who gives the baby Godfrey's Cordial—is left solely responsible for baby Leonora while Flora, her mother, pursues the ambitious and worldly life of an MP's wife. The episode therefore at first seems designed to summon Flora back into the nursery. By requiring her to maintain her quasi-professional work after the baby's death as a kind of penance, however, and by replacing Preston with the nameless "nurse" (Yonge 5 and passim) who tended Flora and her ten siblings from birth onward, the novel ultimately echoes the advice literature's assumption that maternal care is best left at something of a distance. This poses a striking contrast to the novel's extended mourning for the death of Flora's own mother in chapter 3; by interpolating a relatively brief incident of maternal failure into its dominant narrative of posthumous maternal perfection, I argue, *The Daisy Chain* lets us uncover its repressed discomfort with the maternal ideal it espouses.[9]

The Daisy Chain; or Aspirations, a Family Chronicle (as the novel's full title goes) is a sprawling domestic novel that follows the fortunes of the eleven children of the May family after their mother's death in a carriage accident. In following the family (the children range in age from six weeks to nineteen years at the opening of the novel) as they come of age, the novel focuses on the "aspirations" of several, testing and evaluating them through a matrix of self-interest and domestic-religious sacrifice. In particular, Yonge details the struggles of several of the older children: Flora, whose domestic and social skills make her dangerously self-satisfied; Norman, whose intellectual brilliance offers him a choice of highly visible careers as an MP, an Oxford don, or a poet; and Ethel, whose studious and undomestic bent is paired with a genuine religious faith. The novel details Norman's and Ethel's progress from temptation to selfless service: Norman discards brilliant public careers at home for missionary work in New Zealand; Ethel forsakes her classical studies for domestic responsibilities to her father and siblings and charitable work in a nearby hamlet. Flora's story provides a negative object lesson.

In explicit contrast to Ethel, Flora is naturally adept at the domestic skills of a middle-class woman. Her remarkable aptitude for the work of managing a household first appears in the novel's major moment of tragedy: the carriage accident that kills the children's mother, injures their doctor-father, and cripples the eldest sister, Margaret. While the other siblings are bewildered by grief, Flora rises to the occasion, providing a modicum of order and comfort to the distraught household. She quickly moves into the role of household manager: taking her mother's place in many necessary logistical matters, Flora orders the meals and directs the servants; she teaches letters and numbers to several of her young siblings; and she later assumes the social duties that fall to the female head of the family. Aware of her own skill—and how indispensable she has quickly become—

---

[9] This duality is a theme in Yonge criticism. In "The Two Worlds of Charlotte Yonge," David Brownell argues that her "picture of the family world makes clearer how the Victorian family could be at once sustaining and imprisoning for a child" (177). Catherine Sandbach-Dahlström points out that "Charlotte Yonge, as implied author, has access to patterns of thought and feeling that do not accord with the ideology that she sets out to preach" (107). Building on such insights, Talia Schaffer argues that this accounts for the complexity of any individual reader's response to her novels ("The Mysterious Magnum Bonum" 245).

Flora receives no check to a lifelong tendency toward unreflective self-satisfaction.

Once she marries a member of the local gentry, Flora's ambitions grow proportionately. Despite her husband's lack of intellect, she pushes him into standing for the local parliamentary seat and writes his campaign speech while still in bed after giving birth to Leonora, their first child. When they move to London at the beginning of the Season, she apparently weans the baby (who is then three months old), leaving her to the care of an inexperienced young nurse named Preston while she takes up the extensive social and charitable responsibilities of an MP's wife. Preston gives the baby Godfrey's Cordial to quiet her cries of protest at being "set aside" (506), and Leonora soon becomes addicted to the opiate. She dies of opium withdrawal soon after Flora, concerned that she seems lethargic and unwell, resumes direct care of her.

In the shock that follows Leonora's death, Flora tells her husband that if he is going to turn the nurse over to the legal authorities as a murderer, he should do the same for her: "[I]f Preston killed her, I did!" (507) she exclaims. Leonora's death seems to be a lesson in the dangers of the complacency that let Flora imagine that seeing her daughter at breakfast and late at night (after the baby was asleep) was sufficient maternal care. The narrative reinforces this interpretation, one that has been unproblematically accepted by critics. Jacqueline Banerjee argues that this episode is "partly engineered to recall . . . Flora to what Yonge considers her proper sphere—the nursery" (96). While I agree that Leonora's death does indeed "recall" Flora to "her proper sphere"—and, more importantly for Yonge, the proper considerations of faith and selfless service—conflating that social-domestic sphere with the architectural space of the nursery oversimplifies the relationship the novel establishes between middle-class mothering and physical child care. Leonora's death exposes Flora's perfect management for a sham; rather than supervising every aspect of her busy life, we see that she not only delegated what the novel considers her most important responsibilities to others, but also that she failed to supervise the execution of the delegated tasks.

Yonge's condemnation of Flora's absence gives straightforward narrative form to the advice literature's warnings: without the mother's watchful eye (and in part because her attention is elsewhere), the servant substitutes a narcotic for the loving care she has been hired to provide. This is the explicit focus of the retrospective description of how Leonora came to die:

> Poor little Leonora had been very fretful when Flora's many avocations had first caused her to be set aside, and Preston had had recourse to the remedy which, lulling her successfully, was applied with less moderation

and judgment than would have been shown by a more experienced person, till gradually the poor child became dependent on it for every hour of rest. When her mother, at last, became aware of her unsatisfactory condition, and spent her time in watching her, the nurse being prevented from continuing her drug, she was, of course, so miserable without it, that Preston had ventured on proposing it, to which [Flora] had replied with such displeasure sufficient to prevent her from declaring how much she had previously given. (506)

By drawing attention to Flora's "displeasure" upon hearing the mere name of the opiate, Yonge once again echoes the assumptions of authors such as Chavasse and Bull, drawing a stark line between middle- and working-class child-rearing practices, as well as between those of a hired nurse and even an insufficiently maternal mother. Flora is thus protected from one type of complicity in Leonora's death; although her "many avocations" create a vacuum that apparently only the addictive substance could fill, Flora understands the dangers—or at least the undesirability—of the drug.

But in the passage above, opium actually substitutes for the mother's care. More directly, it seems that for Leonora—as for many working-class babies—opium substitutes for the mother's *milk*. By associating Leonora's fretfulness with the moment when Flora "caused her to be set aside" (that is, weaned), Yonge threatens to collapse the distinction between drug and mother. Elia Vallone Chepaitis cites a pertinent story of a lace embroiderer in Nottingham recorded in the 1843 parliamentary report on "Children's Employment." Too poor to pay for child care, Mary Colton found that she could simply keep the baby with her if she dosed it regularly with Godfrey's Cordial; among lace workers, Chepaitis explains, "[i]nfants were often sedated and left across their working mothers' laps, but the women could not interrupt their work to give them milk. It took less time to drug the infant, and promptly continue work" (20). Wohl argues that stories such as this provided ample fodder for condemnations of maternal work as the root of widespread infant mortality. Such condemnations were ideologically weighted, informed by the middle-class commentators' beliefs that women were most appropriately based in the home rather than the factory (see Wohl 25–31). In such debates—as in Yonge's presentation of Leonora's care—Godfrey's Cordial and its ilk appear as the deadly inversion of the breast milk the children need to survive.[10]

---

[10] Early weaning was necessarily a dangerous moment in an infant's life, given the general ignorance about hygiene and the terrible sanitary conditions that existed. Further complicating the issue of infant feeding was the fact that "cow's milk . . . was perhaps the most widely adulterated good in Victorian Britain" (Wohl 21); even when it wasn't adulterated, it

These infants get *either* their mother's milk *or* Godfrey's Cordial—and, in the nurse's experience, it seems that the two substances do comparable work: both quiet otherwise fussy babies. This of course ultimately breaks down; Leonora's opium addiction is revealed by her physician-grandfather's diagnosis. Flora summons her father to London by expressing concern about the baby's "sleepiness" and "fretfulness," as well as a suspicious "look about the eyes" (Yonge 503). (Recall that Bull's list of symptoms included "a low, irritative, febrile state" and "red and swollen" eyes.) After a brief physical examination—which reveals other symptoms that contemporary readers would have registered as signs of opium exposure—he exclaims, "This is the effect of opium!" (504). A few moments later, his condemnation of both parents and nurse is even more devastating: "What have you all been doing? . . . I tell you this child has been destroyed with opium!" (504). This outburst is characteristic of Dr. May, but it also speaks a particularly surprised betrayal: Flora, the supremely competent domestic manager, has stumbled clumsily into the greatest domestic tragedy imaginable. Famous among her siblings for her "discretion and effectiveness" (269), her ability to anticipate and smooth away small obstacles with invisible interventions—that is, to provide perfect and nearly invisible supervision—Flora here is shown to have failed at the middle-class mother's most fundamental responsibility: to ensure the health and longevity of her children. Leonora died not because Flora herself wasn't in the nursery, but because she wasn't paying attention to what was going on in it.

Indeed, there's clearly little shared confidence between Flora and Preston, for the nursemaid is so frightened of her employer's expression of displeasure at the mention of Godfrey's Cordial that she never admits that she's given the baby the narcotic. The novel thus indicts Flora for surveillance that is judgmental as well as belated, but her rush to the sick baby's care exacerbates rather than exculpates her earlier crime. Flora's return to the nursery is the precipitating factor in the little girl's death: during the four or five months that Flora is busy with parliamentary blue books, charity work, and various social engagements, Leonora is addicted to opium but stable; Dr. May's diagnosis—"she is sinking *for want of* the drug"—suggests that Flora's refusal to let Preston continue the opium pushes Leonora's health over the edge. Opium therefore serves as the figure that elides

---

was frequently left uncovered and was typically "three or four days old before it reached the consumers" (Wohl 21). The first infant formula was introduced in 1867 by Liebig's (Nestlé and other companies soon followed), but these were quite expensive (Wohl 20). Advice manuals frequently offered infant food recipes; Chavasse's *Advice to Mothers* series modifies the recipe over the course of multiple editions, apparently bringing his recipe in line with advances in medical knowledge.

oppositions; this infant-doping episode in particular collapses the opposition between maternal presence and child death in the middle-class home. Flora's presence here is deadly. When she hysterically declares to her husband that "if Preston killed her, I did!" (507), she is right in more ways than she realizes or than the other characters admit: she killed Leonora by leaving her to a servant's care, but she also killed her by interfering in the work she'd earlier delegated.

The novel reinforces this interpretation through its treatment of Flora after Leonora's death and the birth of another daughter, named Margaret after her mother and aunt. Margaret is immediately given into the care of the nameless family nurse, and Flora considers having her husband withdraw from Parliament so that they can leave the "London life" that is "temptation and plague" to her as well as a "risk . . . for the baby, now and hereafter" (588). Ethel counsels her against such a step, and then their clergyman brother "show[s her] that, for George's sake, [she] must bear with [her] present life . . . and that the glare, and weariness, and being spoken well of, must be taken as punishment for having sought after these things" (591). The child-care structure for Margaret is thus identical to the one that resulted in Leonora's death; the particular nurse has changed, as does the mother's (apparent) mind-set.

The question that therefore emerges from *The Daisy Chain* is a version of the question of how to be a good mother. More particularly, it's a question of how to be a good mother at a time when infant mortality even among the middle classes was still common and when middle-class women were expected to at least *seem* to have little to do with the messy work of daily life—such as changing diapers. What do you do, when you can't be in the nursery or out of it? The novel's solution to this problem is one that only works in fiction: the ideal mother in this novel is the mother who dies in chapter 3. The association of Mrs. May with Heaven, as with saintly patience and all other feminine virtues, is used throughout the novel as a protective (but also stifling) influence over her children. The novel thus provides an illustration of Carolyn Dever's argument that the Victorian ideal of the selfless, nurturing, angelic mother could *only* be imagined in the absence of physical (or at least narrative) mothers (see xi and 7–8). Yonge idealizes Mrs. May—and, through her, maternity as a type—by converting her through death from a physical presence into a rhetorical effect that is underwritten by a religiously inflected nostalgia. One of the younger children mistakenly but tellingly refers to going to church as "going to mamma" (453), conflating the mother's grave with the more orthodox place of worship. Similarly, Dr. May confidently reminds a son about to leave home as a sailor that his mother "may be nearer to you everywhere, though you are far from us" (262).

This emotional identification allows Yonge to use Mrs. May as a kind of rhetorical principle of control. Because she is a flexible referent rather than an embodied character, the mother's desires become the language of appropriate choice among characters: what "mamma would say" blesses or condemns any potential project; it also authorizes or curtails habitual tendencies. An unfinished letter she leaves is crucial to this work. A letter to her sister in New Zealand, this document describes the three children with whom the novel is most concerned—Flora, Norman, and Ethel—in terms that identify their psychological strengths and weaknesses. Norman, the letter warns, "has never shown any tendency to conceit, but . . . has the love of being foremost, and pride in his superiority, caring for what he is compared with others, rather than what he is himself" (45). The mother fears that Flora "will find temptation in the being everywhere liked and sought after" (45), but notes that Ethel's "manifest defects" in domestic matters "have occasioned a discipline that is the best thing for her character in the end. They are faults that show themselves, and which one can tell how to deal with" (45). Yonge first presents the letter early in the novel, shortly after Mrs. May's death, and includes its full text for her readers. It thus simultaneously structures our interpretations of these characters and shapes their expectations for and interpretations of themselves.

By bearing out these early diagnoses, the novel at once obviates surprise and proves that mother does indeed know best. The letter provides content to the characters' invocations of Mrs. May throughout the novel—with that letter as the origin, the references to "mamma's" wishes or fears or standards carry meaning for readers that they otherwise would not. It operates in the novel as a kind of sacred text, providing personal insight that the characters take as deeply true as they do the Gospel. But of course the children have access to Mrs. May's posthumous letter only *because* she has died, and it therefore functions as a trace in the Derridean sense—in Spivak's formulation, "the mark of the absence of a presence, an always already absent present" (xvii). Mrs. May's letter carries the maternal word forward and transmutes maternal authority into the written word.

The version of Mrs. May that characters and readers abstract from the letter is, for example, what guides Norman away from worldly temptation and to a path—missionary work—that not only unifies spiritual and intellectual vocation but also gives him an erotic reward in the form of his marriage to Meta Rivers.[11] Early on, Norman reveals that he's internalized his mother's written criticism, deliriously reporting that in a dream she told him that "it was all ambition" (107); later, Ethel speculates that "the first

---

[11] Yonge's fervent interest in missionary work has been well documented; see Schaffer, "Taming the Tropics" for an analysis of *The Daisy Chain* in this context.

grief, coming at his age, and in the manner it did, checked and subdued his spirits.... But, perhaps, it is a good thing; dear mamma thought his talents would have been a greater temptation than they seem to be, subdued as he has been" (385). As Dever points out regarding Richardson's *Clarissa* (1748), the dead woman becomes "more powerful as an agent of discipline after her martyrdom than in life.... To appropriate Foucault's terms, 'a power relation' sustained 'independent of the person who exercises it' consolidates the monitory function of disembodied female virtue" (22). Here, we see not only that Mrs. May's word can be more influential once it has been separated from her body but also that her death itself has helped produce that effect. The peculiarly present absence of the ideal mother, then, appears possible only through her tragic death.[12]

The novel runs into difficulty, however, when it tries to imagine a living, embodied substitute for this ideal: Flora's attempt to "only be what [her] mother was" (362) is disastrous, and Margaret, the eldest sister, is crippled and ill from the carriage accident that kills Mrs. May. By the end of the novel, it is Ethel who fills many maternal functions: acting as companion to Dr. May, domestic manager, and teacher and confidante of the youngest siblings. But in venerating her brand of spiritual and auntly maternity, the novel minimizes her impact relative to that of a mother, by emphasizing the contingent nature of her relationships. In her interior monologue on the final pages of the novel, Ethel reflects:

> [H]er eyes had been opened to see that earthly homes may not endure, nor fill the heart. Her dear father might, indeed, claim her full-hearted devotion, but, to him, she was only one of many.... To love each [of her siblings] heartily, to do her utmost for each in turn, and to be grateful for their fondness, was her call; but never to count on their affection as her sole right and inalienable possession. (593)

Ethel immediately comforts herself: "What is that to me?... My course and aim are straight on, and He will direct my paths. I don't know that I shall be alone, and I shall have the memory—the Communion with them, if not their presence" (593–94). The loneliness of the earlier image is striking, however, and the comfort of "the memory—the Communion" seems

---

[12] Even before her death, Mrs. May's absence makes her presence all the more powerful. Her "gentle power" to quell "recklessness," "fidgeting," and "impertinence" (5–6) is framed by the knowledge that this is her first appearance downstairs since the youngest child's birth, six weeks earlier. When we reflect that this child is the eleventh Mrs. May has had in nineteen years, it becomes clear that she is often not physically at the center of family activities.

a weak one in a novel in which memory keeps loved ones alive in part through repeated expressions of deep and grief-stricken loss.

Ultimately, then, *The Daisy Chain* imagines that the best vehicle for a dead mother's influence is a maiden aunt, for it seems that only Ethel has finally internalized her mother's faith and values so well that she can be trusted to speak them to the next generation. She has, admittedly, paid a high price to get here: in addition to repeated lessons in controlling her unfeminine body, Ethel had to give up her scholarly pursuits when they competed too directly with her familial responsibilities, and has even had to put her philanthropic work behind the household demands. In "The Mysterious Magnum Bonum: Fighting to Read Charlotte Yonge," Talia Schaffer underscores "the way [Yonge's] characters initially fight the ideological vise that their author is inexorably closing upon them, and how they subsequently adjust to the cruel necessity of embracing this paradigm" (47). This process—the cruelty of the ideological vise but also the subsequent *embrace* of it—is perhaps best revealed in a small anecdote: shortly after Mrs. May's death, Ethel stops wearing the glasses her short-sighted eyes need because her mother "did not like [her] to use them" (54), despite Ethel's earlier insistence that without them she cannot "see twice the length of [her] own nose" (16). A child who will consign herself to the blind adherence to maternal dictates, then, can clearly be trusted as their vector.

The Daisy Chain thus both venerates and worries about the power of maternal influence. Even when that influence acts as a force for what the novel considers good—steering Norman away from worldly success and Ethel toward selfless service—*The Daisy Chain* marks how doing what mamma would want involves limitation and loss. Indeed, in a novel that equates church with the mother's grave it is perhaps unsurprising to find a blind faith that mother knows best. Flora's tragic story and punishment threaten to expose the impossibility that underwrites this fiction; if her crime is ultimately that of flawed supervision, the fault lies not in her lack of religious faith or her egoism, but in the fact that as a living woman she must either be in the nursery or out of it—she cannot, as her dead mother does, be both. And as a fertile, embodied mother herself, she cannot be the cipher for *her* mother's mothering.

It's perhaps surprising that a novel should prove less adept at keeping two oppositions in dialectic play than advice literature, but the requirements of novelistic closure ultimately force *The Daisy Chain* to choose. While the figure of the dead mother animates and controls the narrative, the novel's final replacement of mother with maiden aunt warns us not to place our faith in embodied maternal care. For all its sacralization of motherhood, then, *The Daisy Chain* gives us an oddly pessimistic view of living mothers. By contrast, the advice literature is better able to keep the two oppositions in dialectic play and therefore to offer readers a comforting vision of the possibilities of active mothering. Rather than presenting ideal maternity as deathly (or dead), advice literature collapses the poles between maternal absence and presence by imagining a maternal "presence" that relies both on the mother's physical absence and on evidence of her conscious and constant attention. The genre of the warning produces that focus and the resultant paranoid supervision. Warnings are "advice to beware a person or thing as being dangerous" (*OED* "Warning," def. 3). Unlike admonitions, which focus on the solution, warnings focus on the problem or danger; in doing so, however, they *imply* the solution. We can see this in common warnings such as "CAUTION: HOT" or "DANGER: FALLING ROCKS."

Rhetorical genre theory directs our attention not simply to the formal features of a text but to its rhetorical situation, which includes its social context.[13] Building in part on speech act theory, rhetorical genre theory encourages us to see genres as "typified rhetorical action[s]" (Miller 151), that is, patterned responses to recurring situations. It is not so much that genres are meaningless when removed from their rhetorical contexts, but that they invoke and even construct those contexts; as Anis Bawarshi puts it, "generic patternings dynamically respond to and construct recurrent rhetorical and social situations" (13). The warning thus responds to and constructs both the danger it speaks and the solution it implies. In the case of infant doping, this means that the warnings of the advice literature can keep opposed maternal mandates in constant, tense play with one another: there is no need to choose between them: "A wet nurse must never be allowed to dose her little charge. . . . Let her thoroughly understand this; and let there be no mistake in the matter" (Chavasse 31); "the danger . . . with which [the] use [of opiates] is fraught in the hands of a nurse should for ever exclude them from the list of domestic nursery medicines" (Bull 111). While Bull prescribes an interdiction, Chavasse recommends instructive supervision, but the iterative nature of the warning keeps both solutions temporary and partial. As a result, the mother doesn't need to die to achieve the intimate supervision they recommend; it is all she can ever achieve, as the disease, the servant, the drug all constantly recur, in different forms, throughout the life of the child and the text.

---

[13] For this summary, I'm drawing on the work of Amy J. Devitt, Carolyn R. Miller, and Anis S. Bawarshi.

Works Cited

Armstrong, Nancy. *Desire and Domestic Fiction: A Political History of the Novel.* New York: Oxford University Press, 1987.

"Babies by the Day." *Chambers's Journal of Popular Literature, Science, and Art* 271 (March 6, 1869): 145–48.

Banerjee, Jacqueline. *Through the Northern Gate: Childhood and Growing Up in British Fiction, 1719–1901.* New York: Peter Lang, 1997.

Barrett, Thomas. *Advice on the Management of Children in Early Infancy.* London: Whittaker and Co., n.d. [1851].

Bawarshi, Anis S. "Beyond Dichotomy: Toward a Theory of Divergence in Composition Studies." *Journal of Advanced Composition* 17.1 (1997): 69–82.

Berridge, Virginia. *Opium and the People: Opiate Use in Nineteenth-Century England.* New York: Free Association Books, 1999 (1981).

Brownell, David. "The Two Worlds of Charlotte Yonge." In *The Worlds of Victorian Fiction.* Ed. Jerome H. Buckley. Cambridge: Harvard University Press. 165–78.

Bull, Thomas. *The Maternal Management of Children in Health and Disease.* London: Longman and Co., 1861.

———. *The Maternal Management of Children in Health and Disease.* London: Longman and Co., 1840.

Cassell's Household Guide. New and rev. ed. London, n.d. [1880s]. *Victorian London.* Comp. Lee Jackson. July 17, 2003. www.victorianlondon.org/cassells/cassells-5.htm.

Chase, Karen, and Michael Levenson. *The Spectacle of Intimacy: A Public Life for the Victorian Family.* Princeton: Princeton University Press, 2000.

Chavasse, Pye Henry. *Advice to Mothers.* 8th ed. London: Longman and Co., 1866.

Chepaitis, Elia Vallone. "The Opium of the Children: Domestic Opium and Infant Drugging in Early Victorian England." PhD diss., University of Connecticut, 1985.

Cohen, Monica F. *Professional Domesticity in the Victorian Novel: Women, Work and Home.* New York: Cambridge University Press, 1998.

Derrida, Jacques. *Of Grammatology.* Trans. Gayatri Chakravorty Spivak. Baltimore: Johns Hopkins University Press, 1976.

Dever, Carolyn. *Death and the Mother from Dickens to Freud: Victorian Fiction and the Anxiety of Origins.* New York: Cambridge University Press, 1998.

Devitt, Amy J. "Generalizing about Genre." *College Composition and Communication* 44 (1993): 573–86.

A Domestic Guide to Mothers in India. 2nd ed., rev. Bombay: American Mission Press, 1848.

Donzelot, Jacques. *The Policing of Families.* Trans. Robert Hurley. With a foreword by Gilles Deleuze. New York: Pantheon, 1979.

Kilgour, Maggie. *From Communion to Cannibalism: An Anatomy of Metaphors of Incorporation.* Princeton: Princeton University Press, 1990.

Langland, Elizabeth. *Nobody's Angels: Middle-Class Women and Domestic Ideology in Victorian Culture.* Ithaca: Cornell University Press, 1995.

May, Leila Silvana. "The Strong-Arming of Desire: A Reconsideration of Nancy Armstrong's *Desire and Domestic Fiction.*" *English Literary History* 68 (2001): 267–85.

McCuskey, Brian. "The Kitchen Police: Servant Surveillance and Middle-Class Transgression." *Victorian Literature and Culture* 28 (2000): 359–75.

———. "Children below Stairs: Original Sin and Victorian Servants." *Australasian Victorian Studies Journal* 5 (1999): 96–105.
Miller, Carolyn R. "Genre as Social Action." *Quarterly Journal of Speech* 70 (1984): 151–67.
Milligan, Barry. *Pleasures and Pains: Opium and the Orient in Nineteenth-Century British Culture.* Charlottesville: University of Virginia Press, 1995.
N. [William Newman.] "The Poor Child's Nurse." *Punch* 17 (1849): 193.
Peterson, M. Jeanne. "Gentlemen and Medical Men: The Problems of Professional Recruitment." *Bulletin in the History of Medicine* 58.4 (1984): 457–73.
———. *The Medical Profession in Mid-Victorian London.* Berkeley: University of California Press, 1978.
Plain Observations on the Management of Children during the First Month. London: Underwood, 1828.
Poovey, Mary. "Scenes of Indelicate Character: The Medical Treatment of Victorian Women." In *Uneven Developments: The Ideological Work of Gender in Mid-Victorian Britain.* Chicago: Chicago University Press, 1988. 24–51.
Rossman, Dara Tomlin. "Accented English: Childcare in Nineteenth-Century Colonial Anglo-India." *Anglo-Saxónica* 2.12/13 (2000): 153–64.
Sandbach-Dahlström, Catherine. *Be Good Sweet Maid: Charlotte Yonge's Domestic Fiction: A Study in Dogmatic Purpose and Fictional Form.* Stockholm: Almqvist and Wiksell, 1984.
Schaffer, Talia. "Taming the Tropics: Charlotte Yonge Takes on Melanesia." *Victorian Studies* 47.2 (2005): 204–14.
———. "The Mysterious Magnum Bonum: Fighting to Read Charlotte Yonge." *Nineteenth-Century Literature* 55.2 (2000): 244–75.
Spivak, Gayatri Chakravorty. "Translator's Preface." In Derrida ix–lxxxviii.
Wohl, Anthony S. *Endangered Lives: Public Health in Victorian Britain.* Cambridge: Harvard University Press, 1983.
Yonge, Charlotte M. *The Daisy Chain; or, Aspirations, a Family Chronicle.* London, 1890 (1856).

CHAPTER 7

Motherhood on Trial

Violence and Unwed Mothers
in Victorian England

GINGER FROST

The veneration of motherhood in the Victorian period is a well-known cliché. But as many scholars have pointed out, this idealization was contingent on a number of factors. The mother as a loving, nurturing center of the home was far more difficult for the poor to attain than the well off. In fact, working-class mothers concerned the upper classes greatly throughout the century, from the agitation over married women working in factories in the 1840s to the investigation into working-class home life of the 1890s. By 1900, many reformers insisted that working-class mothers had the potential to be both saviors and destroyers of their homes. As Deborah Epstein Nord put it, such women were "all-powerful and, consequently, all to blame" when things went wrong (132). Though motherhood was complicated for all poor women, unmarried mothers had even more disadvantages. The mother of an illegitimate child had already transgressed Victorian ideals of womanliness through lack of chastity. Any further disorderliness on her part made her a serious problem.

Criminal cases have offered a way to analyze the state's response to the combination of unwed motherhood and violence. Many historians have studied infanticide cases and shown the complex maneuvers of the legal process in dealing with mothers who killed their newborn babies (Jackson; Ballinger 65–128; Higginbotham). In addition, feminist historians have demonstrated the misogyny inherent in the courts' treatment of violence against women. Men who murdered wives or cohabitees could use gender norms to mitigate the sentence or, if convicted of murder, successfully plead for mercy. Juries often believed an unfaithful or drunken wife was sufficient "provocation" to lessen a charge from murder to manslaughter, or even to give outright acquittal (Conley 68–95; Hammerton 34–67; Ross, *Love* 84–86). On the other hand, Martin Wiener has recently argued that judges became much less lenient with working-class male violence by the late Victorian period, a stance which offered more protection to working-class women. Indeed, historians agree that women had advantages as defendants, if not as victims. Most of women's murder indictments were for infanticide, and only 15 percent of these were prosecuted at all; those that made it to court rarely succeeded. For instance, Margaret Arnot has discovered that only three women were convicted in Sussex of murdering their children between 1840 and 1880; men who murdered children in this same period had higher rates of both conviction and execution (Wiener 123–69; Chadwick 289–315; Arnot 149–67). The complications of class and gender, then, could work both for and against working-class women, depending on circumstances.

Most historians have looked at violent women in the context of infanticide or spousal murder. As a contrast, this essay will concentrate on women who were accused of harming older children, either through neglect, desertion, or deliberate violence and who were also sexually nonconformist, that is, they lived in cohabiting relationships or had illegitimate children. With these circumstances, the courts had to adjudicate their cases knowing that the women were both unchaste and, apparently, failures as mothers. As a result, some judges and juries assumed that their disorderly lives proved that they were violent monsters who deserved no pity. This was especially the case with those trials that involved heavy alcohol abuse, insurance schemes, or neglect. On the other hand, some of these women passed the character test of the court despite their unchastity; thus, they received mercy, usually because they appealed to stereotypes of the irrational, neurotic woman. The difference between these two possible reactions depended on many factors, including the woman's tendency to drink, the state of her home, and her relationship with her mate. Nevertheless, the most crucial aspect in the character test was motherhood. The appeal to the ennobling experience of motherhood could be successful in defending even an unwed mother, though she had to be careful using a rhetoric that glorified a traditional, legal family.

The larger data base for the study comes from a collection of 265 violent incidents within cohabiting families and unwed mothers culled from the *Yorkshire Gazette, Lancaster Guardian,* and *London Times* between 1850 and 1905. The vast majority of these (93 percent) involved the working class; only 7 percent had even one partner in the lower middle or middle classes, so I will limit my analysis to working-class mothers. In addition, only fifty-six of these cases involved accusations of violence or neglect of mothers against their older children (most were violence between the adult partners or infanticides). Obviously, these incidents were a tiny fraction of those prosecuted—much less committed—in the fifty-year period. But this group can begin an investigation into the connections between unwed motherhood, violence, and the criminal courts.

As many historians have discovered, women who committed violent acts, drank, cursed, or fought back when their mates became violent did not receive much sympathy from the Victorian courts. Thus, a woman who committed violence against her children or failed to care for them properly was highly suspect to judges and juries. Though most Victorians pitied women who committed infanticide, they were less indulgent to women who killed or injured older children. Women who killed newborns could excuse themselves as being mentally unstable, due to having just given birth; some doctors even saw breast-feeding as having a deleterious effect on women's brains. In addition, infanticide was difficult to prove, since the prosecution had to show that the child had been born alive, and juries were also often aware of the mental anguish of women who gave birth to illegitimate babies in secret and tried to hide their shame, so jurors took the merciful step of convicting of "concealment of birth" rather than murder. But women who had successfully gotten through the danger period had less obvious excuses for violating their most sacred duties, and older children had obviously been born alive. These cases, then, did not get the same automatic sympathy. In general, the courts approached these cases in one of two ways. First, they could stigmatize the mother as a monster or fiend who had "unsexed" herself through rampant sexuality, drunkenness, and violence. Second, they could assume, as in infanticide cases, that the mother had gone insane; surely any woman who would kill her children had to be pathologically ill. The choice that the juries, judges, and newspaper editors made depended on the circumstances of the case and the woman's respectability.

These factors played out in two major sets of cases, one of which was accusations of neglect. Toward the end of the nineteenth century, middle-class "child-savers" formed associations to rescue children from inadequate or cruel parents. The most prominent of these organizations was the National Society for the Prevention of Cruelty to Children (NSPCC), founded in 1884. According to George Behlmer, neglect cases made up 38.5 percent of the NSPCC's prosecutions between 1888 and 1889, and a whopping 89 percent by 1913–14. Behlmer argues that NSPCC leaders found it easier to berate parents for poor care rather than deal with horrific violence, which seemed inexplicable (Behlmer 108; see also 104–28). For whatever reason, the organization prosecuted numerous cases that confronted the difficulties of working-class motherhood in the most direct way. Eleanor Hannah Frost, tried in 1902 for neglecting Edith Greener, a child of six, was a case in point. Frost lived with Antony Greener, who was tried with her, and the two between them had nine children (at least one in common). Edith was Antony's child with his first wife. Jane Dadmon, a neighbor, testified that the child came back from school eighteen months before in good health, but in the last four months had sickened. Dadmon stated, "I told Frost lots of times the child wanted medical attendance . . . she said that the child was more artful than ill. . . ." Dadmon also claimed that Edith had to live in the attic and that she did not get as much food as the other children. Dadmon wrote to the NSPCC twice about Edith, once before and once after her death (*R. v. Frost and Greener,* PCOM, 1101).

The NSPCC inspector stated that when he first visited the house, Frost substituted her daughter Kate for Edith to satisfy him as to her treatment of her stepdaughter. On the second visit, after Edith's death, Frost admitted the deception, but insisted that Edith had consumption and she had done all she could: "[O]n Monday I took her downstairs to the kitchen and nursed her . . . I sent my husband for Dr. Hook, but she died before he got here. . . .[S]he was not neglected, and she had the same food as we had. . . ." Charles Ross, the inspector, reported that the "bed and bedding where she slept were filthily dirty, and covered with vermin. . . ." Greener, when he arrived at the house, emphasized that Edith "has been consumptive from birth . . . I did not call in a doctor because I knew it was no use. . . ." The doctor who examined Edith's body said she died of "emaciation," and he added, "its hair was dirty and verminous, there were flea bites on its body. . . ." He pointed out that Frost had gotten medical attention herself recently, so the couple could afford doctors (quotes from PCOM, 1103–4).

The prosecution witnesses had painted a picture of a slovenly, selfish, and indifferent set of parents, but most of the focus was on Frost. As the mother, she had the responsibility for the welfare of the children and her home; furthermore, authorities were always suspicious of stepmothers. Frost's defense barrister did his best for her, getting most of the witnesses to agree that almost all poor houses had vermin and that Frost had a heavy mothering burden, having nine children (Dadmon, her main accuser, had only one). In addition, the doctor stated that the child had no sign of starvation, but was just ill, and that the other eight children were fine. He also admitted that better care would not have saved the child's life. Basically, Edith died of tuberculosis, hastened by the poor conditions of her home.

Thus, Frost's defense centered on her difficulties as a poor mother: "[S]he had nine children to look after . . . two of the sons were grown up, but all were at home. . . ." She denied starving Edith or locking her in the attic. She also pointed out that the doctor had come to help her with her last confinement, but not for other health problems, so she had not spoiled herself while depriving the girl (PCOM 1104).

Though fairly skillful, Frost's defense did her little good. Justice Jelf refuted her defense barrister's contention that there was a difference between "neglect" and "wilful neglect," and the jury found both parents guilty, but "the male prisoner to a lesser degree." Jelf agreed with this differentiation between the parents with his sentencing. He complained, "When she herself was ill the female prisoner took care that she had a doctor and every comfort. It was shocking that a woman should undertake the duties of a mother to a child and neglect the child as she had done." In contrast, Jelf asked if there was a way to punish Greener without causing him to lose his job, though the prosecution said his employers had already fired him. Jelf then sentenced Greener to a month at hard labor, and Frost to four months (*Times,* October 31).

Neither parent in the case came out well, but Frost took most of the blame. Greener, after all, was away from home working most of the time, trying to support the family. Frost, in contrast, oversaw a vermin-invested home and filthy children. She lied to the NSPCC inspector, and she had apparently ill-treated a sick child. Despite a spirited defense, she seemed a stereotypically cruel stepmother. This characterization might have been accurate, but the evidence also admitted of a different interpretation. Frost's actions may have been the result of exhaustion and illness by a woman trying to rear nine children on inadequate pay, especially as she had apparently had a child not long before. Frost did not get any sympathy in her postpartum difficulties, perhaps because she was not really the mother of the girl in the case. She was a "wicked stepmother," as well as being an example of working-class pathology. She lived with a man not her husband and had selfishly bought medical attention for herself, but not for Edith. She did not fit the "self-sacrificing angel" ideal for Victorian mothers.

Frost's experience was a good example of the court's uneasiness with working-class motherhood in general. The conditions of her family of eleven pointed up uncomfortable truths about the living conditions of the poor, especially the lack of decent housing. Rather than admit that poverty was a factor, the jury and judge blamed the mother for the vermin, lack of food, and slowness to summon medical help. In fact, the testimony about the dirtiness of the house took up as much space as the medical report.

Jelf even insisted that "the prisoners had ample means to provide for the child," though Greener was a brewer's storeman, hardly a well-paid job (*Times,* October 31). Frost had lied to the NSPCC, but this may have been the result of working-class mistrust of the "cruelty man" rather than guilt, and Greener's attitude that the doctor "would be no use" seemed more like fatalism than deliberate cruelty.

The tendency to blame the mother more than the father showed up in many cruelty cases. Of course, at times, this was because the father was unavailable. Mary Ann Payne was charged at the Lambeth Police Court with "grossly neglecting" her three children, "[t]he fruit of the prisoner's improper intercourse with a married man. . . ." Her neighbors testified to her poor treatment of the children; she locked them up in the house "for days and nights together, while she herself was in the publichouse [*sic*] wallowing in drunkenness and dissipation." The disgusted magistrates took the children to the workhouse and gave Payne four months in prison with hard labor. The equally neglectful father of the children, however, received no punishment at all (*R. v. Payne*). Quite often, the problems of illegitimate children were vastly compounded by the lack of a breadwinner, but the Victorian poor law system, even after some midcentury reforms, offered only limited help to unwed mothers (Shanley 91). Again, rather than dealing with structural inequalities, the courts punished the failing mother.

When the father was present, both parents got some blame; yet, as with Frost, the mother's punishment was often more severe. For example, in 1895, Sarah Ann Simpson and her cohabitee, John Holt, were both charged with neglecting her three children. Simpson was a potter, and Holt was a carter, and they had insured all of the children, which roused the suspicions of the NSPCC. The NSPCC inspector visited in February 1895 and cautioned them "on account of the filthy condition in which their children were found." In September, the officer returned and found the two older children, aged thirteen and nine, "in a shocking state of filth, their bodies and clothes infested with vermin." The youngest, who was four, was dead, apparently from diarrhea, weighing only fifteen pounds at his death. The Recorder was so disgusted with the apparently mercenary motives of the couple that he claimed, "A worse case of neglect it was impossible to imagine. . . ." Yet he differentiated between the two; Simpson got fifteen months' hard labor, while Holt was sentenced to nine (*R. v. Simpson and Holt*). In this case, the mother was a working potter, but she still had responsibility for the home.

Once a mother had been found guilty, she was all the more likely to be convicted from subsequent accusations. In the 1890s, Elizabeth Morrison lived with William Bell, who was a laborer for a builder in Lancaster. They had two children, one over two years old and the other four months. They got into trouble one weekend when Bell got paid and the two "went on a spree." When Morrison got too drunk to care for the older child, Bell tried to leave his daughter at the police station and then at a shelter. Alerted by these actions, the police went to China-lane, where Morrison was sitting, drunk, breast-feeding the baby. The police told them to go to the workhouse, and they did so, only to meet investigators from the NSPCC. Again, the description of the children centered on their dirtiness. The older child "was found to be so dirty that it looked like a little negress, and it was covered with vermin." The doctor admitted that the child was not starving, but insisted she was "very flabby and unhealthy and had several sores on its face and legs." Morrison indignantly insisted that she had gone to three doctors with her daughter, and Bell defended himself vigorously against the charge that he was a "tramp." The bench dismissed the cruelty case, and Bell went free. Morrison, on the other hand, was detained for drunkenness, something of which she had been convicted nineteen times before. She went to Lancaster castle for two months. Her infant went to the workhouse, and the NSPCC persuaded the magistrates to let them put the older child in a Roman Catholic home, despite Bell's protests (*R. v. Bell and Morrison*). In this case, both parents were drunk, but only the mother went to jail, in part because of her previous offenses, but probably also in part because of her maternal failures.

Interestingly, the exception to this tendency to hold the mother most responsible was if the father had failed to provide, especially if the family did not have shelter. Providing was so crucial to respectable masculinity and fatherhood that the mother could not be blamed as much for domestic problems if the father had failed in this duty. In this way, cruelty cases point up the importance of idealization of both fatherhood and motherhood in these trials, though in different ways. In a case in 1885 in Stockton, Margaret Dover had to answer for her two sons, John Henry and William Scott, who were begging in the streets. She explained that "she had seven children and one ill in bed. The man she lived with, but to whom she was not married, was out of work, and she was obliged to send the children out to beg." The police superintendent testified that "the man was drinking all Saturday night and Sunday, and could keep the children out of the street if he would." Since the drunken father was the main problem, the magistrates dismissed the case on Dover's assurance that she would not let the boys beg again (*R. v. Dover*).

An even clearer example happened in Lancaster in 1900. John Howard, a hawker, faced charges of cruelty to his two sons, John, thirteen, and

Downes, eight. Inspector Miller of the NSPCC targeted Howard, since he found the boys "asleep on a rubbish heap that was full of rats." Though Howard was living with a woman (who had an infant with him), she was not charged. The authorities were appalled that the family slept out of doors with no shelter, and they blamed the father for not providing a home. Interestingly, in this case, the dirtiness of the children and the fact that they were "practically naked" and "covered with vermin" was a problem for the negligent father, not their stepmother. Howard went to prison for two months at hard labor and the boys went to the workhouse, but the record is silent on the fate of Howard's lover and her baby. Most likely, they went to the workhouse, too (*R. v. Howard*). In any event, the fact that the father did not provide was the key piece of evidence. Obviously, a mother could not keep a house clean when it did not exist, so the seemingly feckless father took the blame.

In short, neglect cases delineate the expectations for both parents. A father's duties were more limited than a mother's. He had to provide a home, work steadily, and avoid excessive drinking (even an occasional "spree," like Bell's, might lead to trouble). On the other hand, a mother had to keep the house clean, nurture and feed all children, and rid her house and children of vermin. She was also the main caretaker and should sacrifice her own health for her children. In addition, the authorities assumed that mothers should provide food, despite their poverty or lack of steady breadwinners, demonstrating a point other historians have made— that these mothers had great responsibility, but relatively little power (Ross 27–55). The courts were not even sympathetic to a woman who worked to help provide, like Simpson, showing the great ambivalence of the Victorian middle class toward working mothers. Victorian authorities assumed a successful mother stayed home; any mother who left her children for hours every day failed in her duty, even if she was trying to earn enough money to buy food. (This assumption was behind much of the panic about women's factory work as early as the 1840s as well.) Yet the pay in many men's jobs was often not sufficient to support large families. Rather than confront such economic realities, the courts blamed the working mother.

Nevertheless, if the father did not provide, the mother got less of the censure for the poor state of her family. In other words, a father's duties were more limited, but still crucial. Indeed, most of the fathers in these cases got some jail time, just not as much as the mothers. This conclusion indicates that Victorian judges and juries regarded the successful father as one who provided, but also one who was ultimately in charge of the family. The middle-class ideal of a father as a benevolent patriarch who took an active role in rearing his children was unattainable for most working-class men, though many could have been more involved had they spent less time at the pub. Still, the courts expected fathers both to provide a home and to oversee its activities in a supervisory way. The separate social lives of working-class men and women seemed unnatural to many middle-class Victorians, who emphasized domesticity as part of masculinity and strong marriages (Tosh 79–101; Gillis 231–59).

As Behlmer argued, neglect cases were less of a challenge to Victorian ideals of "natural" parental behavior than cruelty, since it was more passive. Women who deliberately harmed their children transgressed the most deeply held Victorian views of mothers as nurturing and giving, and thus provoked more extreme reactions. In most of the violence cases, the judge, jury, and newspapers took one of two tacks. The first, and more popular, route was to assume that mothers who killed their children were insane; their behavior was so shocking that they must not be responsible for their actions. These assumptions received support from many doctors who argued that women were always on the verge of "hysteria" and "brain storms," due to their reproductive systems (Showalter 121–44; Chadwick 289–301; Smith 143–60). On the other hand, a second response was deeply negative, a more extreme version of the reaction in neglect cases. Sexually unchaste women who had committed violence were part of a pathological working-class culture that included sexual incontinence, alcoholism, and brutality. Such women were not only barely female, but barely human, as in the case of baby farmers, who received virulent condemnation from press and public (Knelman 145–80; Rose 93–107).

The appeal to insanity was less common outside of infanticide cases than within them, though some women mirrored the former enough to qualify, as the case of Mary M'Neil demonstrates. M'Neil, a servant, lived in London in 1855 as the mistress of her former master, a man named James Williams. By the age of twenty-five, she had three sons with her lover: George, four; Charles, almost three; and Edwin, a baby of four months. Williams appears to have stopped visiting Mary after Edwin's birth, though she was not poverty-stricken, acting as a landlady for the rental property in which she lived. Early in the morning of December 1, 1855, Charles Pickering, who rented the upstairs set of rooms, found her cash box sitting on the stairs. This was so unusual that he went to M'Neil's set of rooms and knocked on the door. When she replied only "What have I done?" he came into her room and found both George and Edwin dead, their throats cut. Summoned by Pickering, a police constable went into the room and found M'Neil standing by the fire. He asked her if she had killed her children and she said, "I did. Oh, my poor children!" (*R. v. M'Neil, Times,* December 1).

M'Neil appeared to have no motive for her violence, so the police investigation centered on her mental state from the start. Pickering and his wife, Eleanor, told the constable that she had been behaving oddly since Edwin's birth; she was depressed and "troublesome." Both Pickerings told the police that Mary constantly complained about her poverty, though she had plenty to eat, and about the dirt of the house, though it was clean enough. At the trial, the couple continued to stress her mental problems, and they were aided by the police officers and doctors. Pickering told the court that Mary was "extremely unhappy, and extremely bad at times . . . on one Sunday morning I offered to take the little boy for a walk with my own little boy—she said he could not go, because he had nothing to put on. . . . I took him out; and his clothes were very nice indeed, as nice as any gentleman's child need appear in." Eleanor Pickering testified that M'Neil had "milk fever" since the birth of her youngest child. In fact, Charles, the middle child, had been sent to the country after M'Neil had threatened to drop him over the stair bannister. Constable Thompson also explained that Mary was "rocking and muttering" when he found her before the fire. Two doctors, J. R. Gibson and George Amsden, further testified that in their opinion she was insane when she committed the act. Though judges were notoriously unimpressed with insanity defenses, Baron Martin did not dispute this interpretation. He gave only a short summation, and the jury found her not guilty by reason of insanity (PCOM).

To the modern reader, M'Neil probably had severe postpartum depression, compounded by the fact that her lover had left her. The dynamics of the investigation of her case, and her trial, read much like infanticide cases, with the emphasis on her instability due to having recently had a child. Doctors assumed that women who were menstruating, pregnant, or nursing were naturally unstable, and women could use these assumptions to gain mercy. George Amsden, the doctor who delivered Edwin, testified that M'Neil had "exhausted herself by nursing the child, and by so doing brought on a state of great nervous depression." He had seen her on September 23, and she was "under extreme excitement, so much so that I ordered persons to attend to her" (PCOM). Thus, M'Neil became unhinged precisely because she was trying to be a good mother. Because of this testimony, the judge and the jury pitied her, ignoring her unchastity and violence. Ironically, in some ways, the fact that a woman was a mother of illegitimate children helped her in these trials, since Victorians could readily believe that the horror of her situation, and her fears of abandonment, could tip her into criminal insanity.

Historians have long noted the sympathy that women who committed infanticide elicited, but M'Neil had killed a four-year-old along with her baby and had attempted to kill the two-year-old a few months before. Nor was her case unique. Margaret Sutton killed her two daughters, Jane and Annie, who were four and two years old, in 1860 in Bradford. She cut their throats and then her own, though she lingered for several days before dying. When her cohabitee, John Gowland, an attorney's clerk, returned to the house, he found the girls dead and Sutton lying between them with her own throat bleeding. Gowland ran for the police, who were immediately suspicious of him, not of Sutton, and took him into custody. She had to absolve him of all blame from her deathbed before the police would release him. Her reason was apparently jealousy; again, fear of abandonment with small children led to a desperate act. Even after Sutton was charged with the murder, the newspapers continued to refer to her as "the poor woman" while attacking Gowland. The two had a marriage certificate, but both admitted that it was not valid; in addition, when Gowland was searched, the police found "papers upon him of a grossly obscene character, showing him to be a filthy fellow." The magistrate, in disgust, wanted to keep Gowland in custody on a charge of perjury or forgery. The magistrates' and newspapers' obsession with Gowland instead of Sutton was another indication of their sympathy with a desperate "fallen" woman. The jury at her inquest mercifully found that she had committed murder and suicide while "temporarily insane" rather than felo de se so she could be buried with her children (*R. v. Sutton, Lancaster Guardian;* see also Bailey 65–77).

Similarly, in 1885, Isabella Hewson confessed to hanging her three-year-old son to the police in Hull. When charged with the murder, she claimed that she had done it because "she did not wish to see him turned out on the street." The newspaper account does not give her any occupation, nor does it mention the father of her child, and a single woman had a great deal of trouble supporting a child alone. Though she was apparently rational when she confessed, the newspaper reporters, the judge, and the jury all agreed that she had lost her mind by the time of the trial. She struggled against examination by the doctors, crying out "'my child,' 'my child,' imploring those round her to fetch her boy." When she was committed to trial, "she struggled fiercely, creating another painful scene." Because of Hewson's wild behavior in court, the coroner's jury did not have to consider whether her poverty was a rational motive for murder. Instead, the jury decided that she was "not competent to plead," and she went to the asylum (*R. v. Hewson*). In all these cases, the mothers had a legitimate reason to be worried about their futures; either the father of their children was losing interest or he had already gone. The court ignored the failure of the fathers to do their duty, yet evaded punishing the mothers by declaring them insane.

Though many murdering mothers appeared unfit to plead, others failed to make this case. These women showed the second tack of judges and juries to violent mothers—that of fierce condemnation. These women combined the worst of both of the previous types of trials, for they committed deadly violence while living in situations that showed them to be unrespectable and unwomanly. Like baby farmers, they had gone against the "natural" maternal instincts of their gender. A mother who drank, was sexually active outside of marriage, and also behaved violently was the ultimate "monster mother." The case that sums up the negative possibilities for violent women was that of Annie Lawrence, who committed both adultery and violence during her short life. Lawrence had left her husband, Stephen, in 1864 and lived with Walter Highams, who had left his wife some years before. Lawrence had a son, Jeremiah, with her husband, and gave birth to Highams's child in 1865. Highams worked as a market gardener. They had lived together two years when Lawrence discovered that Highams had two children with a woman in a neighboring town. Lawrence was furious at this defection, and the relationship deteriorated rapidly. On the morning of April 19, Lawrence attacked Highams with a billhook, badly injuring him. When the police arrived, they found Highams bleeding in the yard and Jeremiah, aged four, dead inside the house from similar wounds. Lawrence insisted that Highams had killed Jeremiah, and she had attacked Highams in response; Highams blamed Lawrence for both attacks. The police arrested Lawrence (*R. v. Lawrence*).

The inquest and trial of Lawrence turned particularly on character tests for both parties in their roles as parents. Because Lawrence had accused Highams of attacking Jeremiah, much of the trial consisted of Highams asserting his paternal success and vilifying Lawrence, while Lawrence tried to prove that Highams was abusive and she was a loving mother. Indeed, one of the first things Lawrence told the police was that "[n]o one can say I ever used my children but in a kind manner" (*Tonbridge Wells Standard,* April 20, 1866). Lawrence insisted that Highams resented Jeremiah, her child with her husband. At the magistrate's court, she demanded that Highams admit to letting Jeremiah get wet and dirty and then saying, "That young devil won't sit still nowhere" as an explanation. Higham's response led to the following exchange:

> WITNESS—I did not say such a thing. You should not talk like that, gal. You know I never said any such thing. I never said a word to the child like that....
>
> PRISONER—Did he not cry out for some of the porter I had?

WITNESS—I did not notice. He always had what he wanted; and when he asked for it, he always had it. You know that yourself.

PRISONER—Didn't you say, "He is crying for everything he sees—he don't [sic] want anything?"

WITNESS—He had everything he wished. (*Tonbridge Wells Standard,* April 20, 1866)

As that testimony indicated, Highams vigorously defended himself as a stepfather: "I was always giving him pennies or something. . . . I used to take him in my arms and buy him things." At the police court hearing, he admitted that Lawrence was good to her son, so he was baffled by her attack. By the time of the inquest, though, he had changed his story and painted her as an "unnatural" mother: "She used to 'hide' the child. . . . She used to behave cruelly towards the child. She would not give it the food it required sometimes." Not only did she use corporal punishment, then, but she starved her son; according to Highams, Lawrence had failed as a mother even before she became violent. In addition, Maria Taylor, a neighbor, testified that Lawrence had been gone the week before to London, where she was investigating Highams's other family. In doing so, she had left her nine-month-old baby in the care of Highams, another dereliction of maternal duties (*Tonbridge Wells Standard,* April 20; December 21).

After he gave evidence of her failures as a mother, Highams also emphasized her sexual incontinence and bad temper, despite his own less than stellar record. He claimed that Lawrence had approached him and "said she did not like her husband, and that she should leave him and live with me." He added that she got in a fistfight with his "other" woman, who had come to tell Lawrence that she was pregnant by Highams. The witnesses in the trial also stressed Lawrence's "unwomanly" behavior, especially her unchastity. Joseph Hollands, Highams's business partner, insisted that Lawrence was violently jealous and complained to him about Highams's behavior. Hollands unsympathetically told her "not to make herself unhappy, and that if she had kept at home with her husband she would not care where Highams went." Another neighbor, Edmund Cavey, saw part of the attack, and his description masculinized Lawrence; he "saw the prisoner 'pummelling' the man's head against the wall. . . . The woman appeared to be quite the master of the man. . . ." In his earlier deposition, he had said, "It appeared to me that the man had not the strength to resist her." Several neighbors also gave depositions that stressed Lawrence's bad language, including multiple uses of "bugger" (*Tonbridge Wells Standard,* December 21, 1866, 3; ASSI 36/12). All these witnesses built up a version of Lawrence as an uncontrolled virago.

Lawrence, as the defendant, could not testify on her own behalf, so Highams's version of events predominated, but her defense barrister, Mr. Ribton, did his best. He argued that the evidence supported Highams as the murderer as much as it did Lawrence. He also "strongly animadverted on the unfaithful and exasperating conduct of Highams towards the prisoner in first inducing her to leave her husband to satiate his depravity, and then throwing her off for the illicit amours of another concubine." In addition, to overcome the negative view of Lawrence, Ribton appealed to the "universal" ideal of motherhood: "[A] woman would save her child's life even at the price of her own. The affection of woman for her offspring was not the growth of habit or the product of civilizations but it existed in the rudest age, in the wildest clime, and in the most untutored breast . . ." (*Times,* December 22).

These tactics did not erase the terrible impression of Lawrence; indeed, appealing to the ideal of motherhood may have backfired. Lawrence's temper, desertion of her husband, and violence made it difficult for the judge and the jury to believe she could also be a loving mother. Baron Channell told the jury that they should "deal with facts, and not with impressions." He also spent much time pointing out "the expressions made use of by the prisoner," which, in his opinion, showed premeditation. The jury took three hours, but found her guilty of murder, and Lawrence went to the gallows in January 1867. Before her death, she confessed to the murder, at least according to the newspaper, but her confession was strangely limited. She said she was "frenzy-mad" and could not remember doing the crime. She claimed that she thought Highams had been to see his other woman the night before the crime, thus indicating that she could have pled the kind of provocation that often got a manslaughter verdict for men (*Tonbridge Wells Standard,* December 21, 1866; *Maidstone Telegraph,* January 12, 1867). But these qualifications came too late to save her life.

Lawrence did appear to be guilty, and her failure to get mercy—or even much sympathy—was based in part on the fact that she had killed her son, rather than her faithless lover. But she had also not been able to dispute the characterization of her as violent, bad-tempered, sexually promiscuous, indifferent to her children, and the physical "master" of her lover. She was an "unsexed" woman, then, and not entitled to chivalry or mercy. Highams was no angel himself, a man who was highly promiscuous and had little interest in supporting his children with his other mistress. But his neighbors and the court excused his sexual sins, and his behavior did not automatically mean that he was not a successful stepfather. After all, he did provide for his primary family. Serjeant Parry, the prosecuting barrister, admitted that Highams was "a bad character," but he added that it was unlikely from his "general demeanour and conduct towards the deceased" that he had committed murder. On the other hand, Lawrence, though she was Jeremiah's natural mother, was different (*Tonbridge Wells Standard*, December 21, 1866). Women had some advantages in violence cases, but when they fell outside the acceptable excuses for incontinence, they could pay the ultimate price.

Clearly, unwed mothers who appeared in violence and neglect cases provoked complex reactions from the courts. In many ways, these cases give further support to historians who point out that late Victorian and Edwardian authorities made increasingly difficult demands of parents without giving them the economic wherewithal to achieve these goals (Ross, "Mothers," 53–63; Behlmer 230–71; Davin 199–217). Fathers should be the sole breadwinners, despite low pay, so that mothers could stay home and care for children. Mothers somehow should make sure that all children had enough food, even if the provision was low, and they should also keep homes clean and children free of vermin, despite the lack of decent housing or indoor plumbing. In short, the middle class's increasing insistence that mothers have close relationships with each individual child clashed with the reality of most working-class women's lives (Ross, "Mothers" 53).

Most notably, the Victorian obsession with dirt and filth comes through clearly in the neglect cases. As scholars have shown, middle-class writers associated dirtiness with sexual impurity, disease, and general moral laxity (Stallybrass and White 131). Indeed, an unchaste woman was already "filthy" in the moral sense, so more inclined to produce defective children. Though men like John Gowland were "filthy fellows," most of the concern was with children, the next generation, and so the onus fell more on mothers. Unwashed children covered with vermin were the ultimate sign of degeneration. As William Cohen puts it, "People are denounced as filthy when they are felt to be unassimilably other . . ." (Cohen and Johnson ix). Unless the parents could claim insanity, their dirty homes and children set them beyond the respectable pale. In particular, the middle classes used dirt's connection to disease to intervene directly into the family lives of the poor; such filth, after all, could lead to a contagion—physically or morally. The government increasingly regulated poor families in the Edwardian period, in part because they could rationalize invading family privacy for sanitary reasons (Cohen and Johnson xxiv).

Yet working-class women were more concerned with avoiding starvation than with cleanliness. In poor families, non-life-threatening conditions (such as filthiness, small sores, or nits) were not high priorities. Because of low resources, the poor consulted doctors only in dire emergencies. Working-class mothers had to think about the good of all of their children;

focusing too many resources on one child might mean hunger and misery for the others. This prioritization came to be seen as cruelty and neglect by the more fortunate middle class, who did not have to make such hard choices. The courts and the NSPCC reflected these values, equating dirt with general working-class pathology. But to the mothers' way of thinking, muddy clothes and the occasional nit were unimportant compared to providing food and shelter. This dilemma pointed up that the interests of mothers and children, or even brothers and sisters, sometimes diverged, a troubling notion to Victorian authorities. Those caught up in the criminal justice system were the ones whose needs had diverged the most, but they were on the same spectrum as the poor parents around them. Of course, at times horrific neglect and violence did happen, and the courts did well to protect children in such situations. But jailing parents for neglect without also providing economic reforms meant that the state dodged the most difficult and challenging aspects of a large problem.

All the same, though the state's anxiety about the working-class family hurt mothers, these disadvantages were partially mitigated by the court's insistence on proper masculinity as well as femininity. The courts demanded that fathers take their roles seriously—at least if they had not absconded. Highams had to defend himself against Lawrence's accusations in order to make his charges stick, and the fathers in neglect cases were also convicted and served time, if not as much as the mothers. Indeed, violent fathers could not plead a tendency to neurosis or insanity as mothers could, and so received mercy less often. Thus, though one cannot draw too many conclusions on these limited cases, a working hypothesis might be that mothers suffered more in neglect cases, but fathers got harsher sentences in assault, manslaughter, and murder trials. Failing as a mother was a serious sin for any working-class woman, but the role of fathers added another contingent factor in determining the fate of "murdering mothers." Sadly, these mothers got support only because the courts were willing to stigmatize both parents in the working-class home rather than dealing with the structural problems that beset poor families.

Works Cited

LIST OF CASES CITED

R. v. Bell and Morrison. *Lancaster Gazette,* May 25, 1895, 2; June 1, 1895, 2; June 8, 1985, 3.

R. v. Dover. *Yorkshire Gazette,* February 17, 1885, 3.

R. v. Frost and Greener. National Archives, Old Bailey Sessions Papers, PCOM 1/154, 1101–1105; *Times,* October 17, 1902, 2; October 31, 1902, 2.

R. v. Hewson. Yorkshire Gazette, May 30, 1885, 11; June 20, 1885, 9; July 25, 1885, 6.

R. v. Howard. Lancaster Guardian, July 14, 1900, 8.

R. v. Lawrence. National Archives, Home County Depositions, ASSI 36/12; *Tonbridge Wells Standard,* April 20, 1866, 2–3; July 27, 1866, 3; December 21, 1866, 3; *Maidstone Telegraph,* January 12, 1867, 2; *Times,* December 22, 1866, 8.

R. v. M'Neil. PCOM 1/70, 293–96; *Times,* December 1, 1855, 9; January 10, 1856, 9; *Yorkshire Gazette,* December 8, 1855, 12.

R. v. Payne. Times, March 24, 1854, 11.

R. v. Simpson and Holt. Yorkshire Gazette, October 19, 1895, 5.

R. v. Sutton. Lancaster Guardian, October 27, 1860, 2; *Times,* October 23, 1860, 3; October 24, 1860, 12; November 5, 1860, 5.

Secondary Sources Cited

Arnot, Margaret. "The Murder of Thomas Sandles: Meanings of a Mid-Nineteenth-Century Infanticide." In *Infanticide: Historical Perspectives on Child Murder and Concealment, 1550–2000.* Ed. Mark Jackson. Aldershot, Hants: Ashgate, 2002. 149–67.

Bailey, Victor. *This Rash Act: Suicide across the Life Cycle in the Victorian City.* Stanford: Stanford University Press, 1998.

Ballinger, Anette. *Dead Woman Walking: Executed Women in England and Wales, 1900–1955.* Aldershot, Hants: Ashgate, 2000.

Behlmer, George. *Friends of the Family: The English Home and Its Guardians, 1850–1940.* Stanford: Stanford University Press, 1998.

Chadwick, Roger. *Bureaucratic Mercy: The Home Office and the Treatment of Capital Cases in Victorian Britain.* New York: Garland Publishing, 1992.

Cohen, William A., and Ryan Johnson, eds. *Filth: Dirt, Disgust, and Modern Life.* Minneapolis: University of Minnesota Press, 2005.

Conley, Carolyn. *The Unwritten Law: Criminal Justice in Kent.* Oxford: Oxford University Press, 1991.

Davin, Anna. *Growing Up Poor: Home, School and Street in London, 1870–1914.* London: Rivers Oram Press, 1996.

Gillis, John. *For Better, For Worse: British Marriages, 1600 to the Present.* Oxford: Oxford University Press, 1985.

Hammerton, A. James. *Cruelty and Companionship: Conflict in Nineteenth-Century Married Life.* New York: Routledge, 1992.

Higginbotham, Ann. "'Sin of the Age': Infanticide and Illegitimacy in Victorian London." *Victorian Studies* 32 (1989): 319–37.

Jackson, Mark, ed. *Infanticide: Historical Perspectives on Child Murder and Concealment, 1550–2000.* Aldershot, Hants: Ashgate, 2002.

Knelman, Judith. *Twisting in the Wind: The Murderess and the English Press.* Toronto: University of Toronto Press, 1998.

Nord, Deborah Epstein. *Walking the Victorian Streets: Women, Representation, and the City.* Ithaca: Cornell University Press, 1995.

Rose, Lionel. *Massacre of the Innocents: Infanticide in Great Britain, 1800–1939.* London: Routledge and Kegan Paul, 1986.

Ross, Ellen. *Love and Toil: Motherhood in Outcast London, 1870–1918.* Oxford: Oxford University Press, 1993.

———. "Mothers and the State in Britain, 1904–1914." In *The European Experience of Declining Fertility, 1850–1970: The Quiet Revolution*. Ed. John Gillis, Louise Tilly, and David Levine. Oxford: Blackwell, 1992. 48–65.

Shanley, Mary Lyndon. *Feminism, Marriage and the Law in Victorian England*. Princeton: Princeton University Press, 1989.

Showalter, Elaine. *The Female Malady: Women, Madness, and English Culture, 1830–1980*. New York: Penguin Books, 1985.

Smith, Roger. *Trial by Medicine: Insanity and Responsibility in Victorian Trials*. Edinburgh: Edinburgh University Press, 1981.

Stallybrass, Peter, and Allon White. *The Politics and Poetics of Transgression*. Ithaca: Cornell University Press, 1986.

Tosh, John. *A Man's Place: Masculinity and the Middle-Class Home in Victorian England*. New Haven: Yale University Press, 1999.

Wiener, Martin. *Men of Blood: Violence, Manliness, and Criminal Justice in Victorian England*. Cambridge: Cambridge University Press, 2004.

CHAPTER 8

A Murdering Mother

Frances Knorr

LUCY SUSSEX

At the beginning of the twentieth century, the city of Melbourne in Victoria, Australia, had its own version of Madame Tussaud's Chamber of Horrors. Kreitmayer's Waxworks contained such sensational artifacts as the Klatscheige (Scold's Bridle) and the Stocks, as well as a gruesome array of wax murderers. *Kreitmayer's Waxworks Exhibition Catalogue* (c. 1903) gives us a detailed listing of the cheap thrills on display. No. 142 in the catalogue was Frances Knorr, who was "found guilty of having murdered two infants on or about 11 April 1893, and buried the bodies in a garden. She was executed 15 January 1894" (14).

Frances Knorr was a mother of two daughters, one by her husband, and another conceived when he was in jail. This fact alone would have put her outside the Victorian category of "good woman," without her having committed murder—in a monstrous inversion of the motherhood ideal, of two babies. They were not her children, but infants for whom she was caring in a private, lethal crèche. She is most commonly described as a baby-farmer, a term referring to women who took over the care of infants for a fee. The babies were illegitimate, often born to single mothers who could not afford to stop working, nor to lose their "reputation," as Knorr had.

Until the twentieth century and the scientific development of milk formula, separating a child from its mother was to risk its health and life. In official orphanages, the mortality rate was high. With baby farming, the situation was worse: frequently there was a tacit agreement that, in handing over a child, a mother was paying for her baby's quiet disposal.

Baby-farming cases occurred throughout the nineteenth century, and it was Knorr's fate that in the 1890s they were being aggressively prosecuted. Thus she became a notorious woman, the worst of mothers, and a murderer whose image adorned a Chamber of Horrors.

Kreitmayer's Waxworks no longer exists, but an approximation of its Chamber of Horrors can be found at the Old Melbourne Gaol museum, with its collection of death masks, taken from the freshly hanged. Here can be found the death mask of Frances Knorr, one of two women displayed, the other being the demented poisoner Martha Needle (also listed in the Kreitmayer's catalogue). Until the 1990s, also exhibited was Knorr's skull, together with that of Needle and the murderer Frederick Deeming (also in the Waxworks catalogue), explanatory plaques positioning the trio as examples of a major twentieth-century bogey, the serial killer.

This Melbourne Gaol reading was rendered dubious by misinformation in its labeling: Knorr was confused with Needle, and called "Martha." It might seem pedantic to note the error, but it is not isolated: errors pervade the Knorr literature to varying degrees. It is predictable that mistakes would be found in pulp treatments of the case, such as James Holledge's *Australia's Wickedest Women,* whose very 1960s cover represents female evil by a beehived redhead doing a striptease for several James Bond lookalikes. Yet mistakes occur in serious studies. To cite just one instance: Michael Cannon's *The Woman as Murderer* (1994) again conflates Knorr and Needle by applying an *Age* editorial of December 4, 1893 (126), specifically on Knorr, to Needle, who was hanged in October 1894.

Where fact can be doubted, so can interpretation. Even in the 1890s, as this essay will show, the received image of Knorr as monstrous mother was by no means universally accepted. A contextual reexamination of the Knorr case creates further ambiguity, even confusion. The monster image slips out of focus, blurs. Judging Knorr becomes by no means simple.

Knorr's Contexts

Can we term Knorr a victim? Some would automatically say no. The most potent image in Christian iconography, Christ on the cross apart, is the babe in the manger, adored by mother Mary. The inverse of this image, the subsequent "Massacre of the Innocents," is less commonly depicted; but the phrase recurs in nineteenth-century discussions of infanticide. Such "massacres" were not an isolated, historic, biblical instance but relatively common throughout the period. This article will concentrate on Knorr's Australian, colonial context, but as Benjamin Disraeli commented in his novel *Sybil:* "Infanticide is practised as extensively and legally in England, as it is on the banks of the Ganges; a circumstance which apparently has not yet engaged the attention of the Society for the Propagation of the Gospel in Foreign Parts" (book II, 131).

Colonial discourse on female infanticide in India elided the many small skeletons found, in some cases, literally in the imperialists' water closets. The corpses of infants were also unearthed in back gardens (as in the Knorr case), dredged from rivers, or simply stumbled across in public places. To glance, as I have, at the death registers of late-nineteenth-century Australia is to note an extraordinary proportion of anonymous corpses under the age of one. With a regularity approaching monotony, newspapers covered these cases, usually allotting only a paragraph to them, unless the details were particularly sensational.

Frances Knorr lived in two countries, England and colonial Australia, and in both infanticide was rife—for the latter, Judith Allen estimates that the murder rate of the newborn was fifty-five times that of adults (*Sex & Secrets* 31). It could hardly be anything but, given the unholy conjunction of medicine, public morality, and economics then prevalent. The lack of reliable, easily affordable contraception and safe abortion created a gross oversupply of babies that, when born out of wedlock or to poor families, were vulnerable. Allen argues that many child deaths in New South Wales, accepted at inquest as accidental, were nothing of the kind: the "accidents" included overlaying, when a mother rolled on her child during sleep and smothered it; "sudden delivery," which meant giving birth over a lavatory or chamber pot and somehow drowning the infant or fracturing its skull in the process; and improper feeding ("Octavius Beale Re-considered" 116). All of the above appear frequently in inquest reports, and indicate infanticide functioned as a form of last-ditch, postnatal contraception.

Legally, infanticide could be a hanging offense. However, as Allen's inquest evidence shows, there was a difference between legal principle and practice, a willingness on the part of authorities to give the benefit of the doubt. Infant mortality was still high, and inquests often could not determine cause of death. For instance, in 1893, out of nearly four hundred coroner's inquests in Victoria, 101 were on infants; of these only 32 returned findings of infanticide (Laster, "Frances Knorr" 155). Reluctance to admit the degree to which women were killing babies may have been a mitigating factor here, as well as an uneasy if guarded recognition of sexual inequalities.

Of Australian defendants indicted in infanticide cases, Allen has found that 85 percent were unmarried women (*Sex & Secrets* 31). This figure is not surprising, given that the position of the unwed mother was particularly invidious. It was well-nigh economically impossible for her to keep the child, even if she wanted a little "badge of shame" marking her as a "fallen woman." Such was suicide, especially for domestic servants, working women who were dependent on their good names for employment. Who would hold the baby? In Melbourne there were some private charitable agencies, such as the Maternity Aid Society (founded 1883) and the Victorian Infant Asylum (1877). In addition, Donella Jaggs notes that de facto adoption was practiced informally or by "statutory or voluntary agencies which dealt with destitute children," like the government Department for Neglected Children (119). However, the supply of care was quite unequal to the demand, particularly since Melbourne lacked an official foundling hospital. The most common options of the unwed mother were abandonment (called baby-dropping), infanticide, or baby farming.

Some baby-farmers were incompetent, being poor women, without training in nursing. Others found it all too profitable to cut costs and neglect the child. The high fees charged by child minders (10 shillings a week, plus deposit, was the usual rate in 1893–94) meant that the parent, who, if a servant, was lucky to earn that same amount per week, could not keep up the payments and work honestly. In such cases the unpaid minders often withdrew care or actively ensured the infant's convenient death.

By the 1890s the colonial Australian governments had reluctantly begun to regulate the trade, requiring all baby farms to be registered and any deaths subject to inquest. Yet abuses were still common: in 1892, the year prior to Knorr's trial, Sydney baby-farmers John and Sarah Makin were found guilty of murdering a dozen infants and burying them in their various rented backyards. The case was fresh in recent memory when, in Melbourne, similar "massacre" evidence emerged.

The Crime and Its Reportage

The scene of the crime was Brunswick, an inner suburb of a city gripped by depression. The *Age* of September 6, 1893, reported:

> The locality is a very quiet one, and the vacant houses which crowd the vicinity, with their broken windows, ragged fences, defaced "To Let" boards and general appearance of dropping to pieces, make it seem a peculiarly suitable locality for the perpetuation of dark deeds of the class now brought to light. (5)

If the above sounds like a passage from a detective novel, it should be remembered that contemporaneously Sherlock Holmes stories were being penned by Conan Doyle for the *Strand* magazine. More locally, Fergus Hume's 1886 novel *The Mystery of a Hansom Cab,* set in Melbourne but a worldwide best seller, begins with a fictional murder report from the *Argus,* the other major morning newspaper in Melbourne. However, it should be noted that the emergent tropes of the detective genre tended not to be applied to the subject matter of baby killing. Despite the frequency of infanticide reports in colonial newspapers, the crime is largely absent from contemporary detective fiction. Pioneering woman crime writer Mary Fortune, who wrote under the pseudonym W. W. for the *Australian Journal* from 1865 to 1910, was unusual in writing about the subject thrice—but that was out of a total of over five hundred stories.

The colonies' newspapers competed for circulation-boosting information on the case. It unfolded in their pages like a thriller, one in which they had no qualms about prejudging the accused as guilty, and even a monster. The *Argus* of September 5, 1893, reported:

> Added to the long list of child murders on the records of the City Morgue is one which was discovered by Mr Clay, a commercial traveller, who has recently taken up his residence in Moreland-road, Brunswick. He was digging in the garden, when he came cross the body of a child. . . . [T]he state of decomposition indicated that the child had been buried for about three months. . . . An examination of the body clearly showed that its death had undoubtedly been caused by violence, and that murder had been committed. The skull was fractured, in fact almost broken to pieces. Other injuries were also visible on the body, which was perfectly nude. (5)

The *Argus* was premature here, as the inquest established this baby girl had died of causes unknown. The "injuries" had been caused by the police's picks and shovels. The report then went on to detail how a woman occupying the house prior to Clay had borrowed a neighbor's spade, shortly before removing to another Brunswick address:

> This woman, while occupying the house in Davis-street, came under the notice of the police in connection with a baby-farming case, and soon afterwards she most mysteriously disappeared from the district. Since her removal she has been most anxiously required by the police, owing to her connection with nearly all the recent cases of trafficking in babies which have been reported in *The Argus* [but discovering] the woman's identity, owing to her innumerable *aliases,* has almost become an impossibility.

One infant had been found, scarcely grounds for stating the wanted woman was single-handedly responsible for the baby traffic of Melbourne.

Already the public was being prepared for a "holocaust of infants"—to use the September 6 *Age*'s phrase—sacrificed à la Makin (5). When the police arrived at Davis Street carrying spades, a crowd collected, sitting on the fence or watching from carts, as the back garden was given a good dig. This time the tally was two tiny corpses.

Both the *Argus* and the *Age*, by September 6, were able to report more about the suspect, Frances Knorr alias and neé Minnie Thwaites. A house agent had found her "respectability to be beyond question," but her evenings "were given to conviviality with friends . . . marked by a free use of intoxicants." She had stolen away from Davis Street "in a manner which of itself was sufficient to excite suspicion," leaving unpaid rent. Furthermore, she and her husband were stated to be jailbirds. It was certainly clear from the witnesses quoted that Knorr was involved in the baby trade, but murder was not proved. Nonetheless, the *Age*, from which the aforementioned is taken, referred to her as "a female Herod" and a "wholesale butcher" (5). Somewhat hopefully, the paper further suggested that the missing woman would excel the Makins, victim-wise.

The September 6 *Argus* was less judgmental. It even contradicted the *Age*, by stating that Knorr was of "temperate habits," also noting that an inquest on a child who had died after leaving Knorr's care "came out all right," because death was from natural causes (5). Both papers quoted a police description: "Aged 32 [she was actually 24]; height, 5 feet 3 or four inches; stout build, sallow complexion, brown hair, heavy lower jaw, usually wears a black dress, black jacket trimmed with astrachan [*sic*] and a black gem hat."

Of the Davis Street bodies, one had also died of causes unknown, but the other revealed evidence of foul play, shocking the editorial writer of the *Argus* (September 1).

> To many people the most impressive and horrifying incident in the baby-farming tragedy just now being explored is the discovery . . . of a bit of string tightly knotted round the neck of infant "No. 2" and as effective for strangling purposes as the *roomal* of any Thug. (9)

To return to the *Argus* editorial of September 6:

> The loop of that fatal bit of string was narrowed to the circumference of a half-crown piece, and so careless were the unknown fingers that drew it tight, or so habituated to the infernal operation, that the cruel noose was left knotted round the tender little throat when the tiny body was buried. . . . If that miniature and tragical noose were exhibited thousands would rush to gaze at it. Mothers would weep at it and men would swear.

The editor then—almost obsessively—harps on India again: "But the whole story draws aside for a moment the curtain which hides a chamber of cruelty black as the Subada Khotee at Cawnpore, where the butchers of NANA SAHIB slew such a multitude of English women and children, and the healthy imagination does not willingly cross its dreadful threshold."

The editorial continues, with nods at Makin and the English Society for the Prevention of Cruelty to Children, before concluding:

> It is clear that in too many cases even the sweet wine of a mother's love can ferment into the gall of a cruelty hideous enough to satisfy even the ferocity of NANA SAHIB's sepoys at Cawnpore. The "straying cherub" we call a child who "strays" into a baby-farmer's den somehow evokes a worse cruelty than anything which inhabits a tiger's den. Behind the baby-farmer and her—or his—victims stands the baby-farmer's employers; who do not commit murder with their own hands, but hire it. And the whole group forms a sort of human fresco, which the grim and cruel irony of SWIFT might delight to place high on the facade of the great Temple of Modern Civilisation.

The message was clear: baby farming was an embarrassment to a culture priding itself on "higher" civilization, as is indicated by the allusions to the Black Hole of Calcutta and Jonathan Swift's "A Modest Proposal." However, the *Argus* did not go as far as a contemporary cartoon showing "Baby Farming—The Real Murderer": Mrs. Grundy, that icon of Victorian respectability, throwing a naked infant to a crocodile (repr. in Laster, "Frances Knorr" 159).

Meanwhile the case continued sensationally: Knorr and her husband, Rudolf, were detained in Sydney. The *Argus* again: "The arrest ... was one of those lucky incidents which import elements of romance into the dry detail of police duty" (September 7, 5). The use of the words "romance" and "police" is a clear reference to the *roman policier,* a genre originated by the French writer Émile Gaboriau, which might be regarded as the original police procedural novels. Fergus Hume cited them as inspiration for *The Mystery of a Hansom Cab*. The narrative of Knorr thus resembled briefly, thanks to a coincidence, the narratives of fiction: a Sydney constable who had previously dealt with Knorr recognized her when visiting a boardinghouse and, when he heard shortly afterward that she was wanted again, simply returned and arrested her.

The account states:

> Thwaites had been on the wanted list of the Sydney police in times past.

Prior to 1888 she was a prominent figure in Sydney, being rendered conspicuous by constantly wearing a long ulster [which] did not conceal an extremely well-proportioned figure. She left after serving a term of imprisonment for misappropriating a sewing machine.

The first visit of the constable might have caused Knorr to flee, but she was restricted by the fact of her motherhood. When arrested, she had recently given birth to her second baby, Reita Daisy. This reportage for the first time identified Knorr as a mother, a category that had almost sacred status in the Victorian era. However, Knorr as mother was rendered ambiguous by her crime. She was alleged to have committed infanticide while pregnant herself with Reita Daisy and with her firstborn Gladys in tow. The dead children were other people's, but as several witnesses asserted, Knorr was passionately devoted to her own children and very fond of others.

Also ambiguous was Knorr's class. She married and consorted with petty crooks, worked as a domestic, and had what were commonly regarded as working-class morals: the September 9 *Age* gleefully reported that her husband, Rudolph, disputed the paternity of her new baby (5). Yet, two days earlier the same paper noted that she had put adoption advertisements in the paper, in which she claimed to be a "lady" and was "said to be well-connected . . . the daughter of a hat manufacturer in King's Road, Chelsea" in London (5). If this background was true, to have come from a good bourgeois home would have made her even more of a "terrible woman," as the *Herald* of January 15, 1894, described her (5). Others used stronger language: in the words of investigating detective John Nixon, Knorr was of "very loose habits, immoral character and hardened nature" (Report, VPRS series 264, file 22).

In newspaper illustrations Knorr was also mutable, with all her portraits different. Two sketches were run in the *Weekly Times* of January 20, 1894 (21), as evidence of how Knorr had changed during the course of her trial. Interestingly the second of these, of Knorr in her prison uniform, has a photographic counterpart. They significantly differ: in the drawing Knorr has been made to look lined and haggard, while the original photograph is serene. In toto, she appears ordinary, even nondescript—in sharp contrast to the stereotypical evil baby-killer represented in a *Bulletin* caricature of November 1892. This cartoon appeared at the height of the Makin case, and shows the baby-farmer as a witch, or crone, complete with missing teeth and warty nose (repr. in Palmer 1170).

The witch may have been the stereotype, but by the close of Knorr's trial, a different, even pitiable image had emerged. To begin with, Knorr was less of a baby-farmer, with a household of neglected and dying infants, than what was known as a baby-sweater: a broker of infants, the intermediary between the parent and the actual caretaker, usually a needy woman. Such was profitable for Knorr—she would pocket the substantial difference between the parent's deposit and what was paid the minder. Very often the latter would find no money, after the initial payment, forthcoming; she would indignantly return the child, not always easy since Knorr frequently moved house. Testimony revealed that Knorr received a continual stream of apparently interchangeable babies, passing them on from one carer to another. Her business was disorganized—from the evidence it seems she barely kept track of these transactions, let alone which child was which. Far more than the three dead babies passed through her hands, but though every property she had rented was dug over, no more bodies were found. The court never made sense of it and even Knorr appeared confused.

Moreover, her baby farming was the direct result of poverty and misfortune. The life of Frances Knorr was almost too much of a moral tale to be true, for it followed the narrative trajectory of a Harlot's Progress: initial fall, petty crime, prostitution (which was how her common-law relationship with another man while her husband was in jail would have been regarded by the middle-class jurors), and finally murder.

I have not been able to verify the truth of Knorr's early life, nor when it entered the public record, but the following is gospel in nearly all accounts. Like the subject of an evangelical tract, she was a willful and passionate girl: when she returned home after a failed elopement with a soldier, her god-fearing family first sent her to the local house for fallen women, then packed her off to Australia, that useful dumping ground for English misfits. On arrival in Sydney in 1887, she apparently had little money, for within a month she was arrested for larceny. Two more petty charges followed and a year's jail. She appeared to be going straight when she married Rudolph Knorr, but it was his eighteen-month sentence for theft that forced her into the baby trade. She had Gladys to care for, no means of support, and though the September 8 *Age* sneered that she found baby farming "more congenial" (6) than other work, her testimony, as recorded in the Trial Transcript, was simply that she could not make a living otherwise. At the time of the murders, her relationship with a shady young man called Ted Thompson, a fishmonger, had broken down, leaving her pregnant again and destitute.

The following comes from the transcript of evidence and is Knorr's account of what happened the night of the first baby's death. The scene is a rented room with a double bed in it, in which slept the pregnant Knorr; her daughter Gladys, eleven months; and a baby-farmed illegitimate infant, known as the child Crichton, who was less than a month old:

> I slept very well until about 2 o'clock when they woke up for a drink. I had a foot warmer [for heating milk] and when I got up and got the bottles rinsed out I found the milk was turned completely thick, quite sour, and it was impossible to give it to either of the children. I had no barley in the house and could not make barley water. I tried a little bread beaten up in hot water to make a sop. The two children continued screaming until morning and about a quarter to four the child Crichton died. It went black in the face and was working all over. I got vinegar and applied it to the head and put it on the lips but it never came to. It died from convulsions and not from any ill treatment on my part. I swear that I did everything in my power to resuscitate it. . . . I thought of going to the police first but got frightened. Then I thought "I will bury it." (Transcript *R. v. Knorr,* VPRS Series 264, File 22)

Either the baby died of natural causes—an autopsy failed to establish the cause of death—or else Knorr, at the end of her tether, killed it. Had she been simply tried for this case alone, infanticide could not have been proven. Therefore, the prosecution admitted similar fact evidence, namely, the other two bodies, which included the child found with its murder weapon. Still, the case against her was circumstantial until Ted Thompson produced a letter, written to him by Knorr. It provided instructions for manufacturing defense evidence:

> She must say she answered an advertisement for a kind person to look after a baby. We meet on a Monday and I arranged to give her the child on the next evening (send her address to me), and she can say I brought the child to her house on the 11th April, Tuesday, and she kept it a little over three weeks, and she wrote to me saying that her husband would not let her keep it any longer, and she wrote to 25 Davis St, Bruns and I fetched it. . . . Now that is all she will have to say and that will clear me. (*Australian Law Times,* XV, 1894, 445)

Knorr would claim Thompson suggested she write the letter after the inquest at the City Morgue, where Thompson had, suspiciously, been permitted by the Crown Prosecutor to have "interviews" with Knorr (*Age,* November 29, 6). Was he part of a police entrapment? It seems incredible that this piece of evidence, so useful to the prosecution, should be spontaneously generated.

The December 1 *Argus* (7) reported that Thompson admitted in court that he had obtained a baby from a Mrs. Brett early that year and passed it on to Knorr. Its fate is unknown. Such evidence should have been sufficient to charge him with being an accessory, as was Rudolph Knorr. Yet

Thompson was never charged. Knorr claimed he told her: "Don't mention about the Brett case [in the letter], because I have seen Detective Nixon, and been down to Brett's, and that is all squared. Nixon is a customer of mine, and will believe me where he would not believe you" (*Argus,* December 1, 7). What was Thompson selling to Nixon? It seems an extraordinary coincidence that a detective investigating the Knorr case should happen to buy fish from the chief prosecution witness. Rather more likely was that Thompson was a "fizzgig," selling information to the police. The use of informers by Melbourne detectives was endemic, as was revealed in evidence given to a Royal Commission of 1881–83. The commission heard that an informer had conspired with detectives to entrap a man they wanted behind bars to the extent of setting up a bank robbery. Detectives would go to great lengths to protect their sources, even condoning felonies by fizzgigs: in one instance of art theft, a suspect threatened to implicate his accomplice, who was an alleged informer, and the charges were dropped. Nixon was involved in both cases; small wonder he was one of three detectives found "untrustworthy" although he kept his job (Lahey 154, 264–65). In the second half of the letter, Knorr addressed Thompson intimately, and from it she emerges as muddled, incoherent, and truly sad:

> [obliterated] really think for one moment I will live with my husband again, no never Ted, I know you will forgive me for the past and let bygones be bygones, I would never go home to my parents again. Even if my father wanted me to go. I have my two little ones to look after and if I am spared to take care of them I will. I do wish you could see my dear baby Ted if I am parted from you I have your living image.... (*Australian Law Times,* 1894, 445)

Knorr's pathetic faith in Thompson is showed by her concluding the letter with a request for him to collect some hat feathers she was having cleaned, so that she should be smart in court. When found guilty, she sobbed hysterically and cried: "God help your sins, Ted." Before being bustled out of the court, she added: "God help my poor mother! God help my poor baby!" "Altogether," the December 2 *Argus* reported, for once understating the case, "it was a most painful scene" (10).

That Knorr was sentenced to death for infanticide was highly unusual. As stated earlier, the rates for indictment of women following inquests on babies were low; lower still were convictions, and when they occurred, the sentence usually was commuted—although John Makin was executed, his wife, Sarah, got fourteen years' hard labor, for instance. The *Age,* which had earlier represented Knorr as unredeemedly wicked, did not swerve from its stance:

> We are asked by the spurious humanitarianism of the day to feel some thrill of pity for the stricken monster who left the dock on Friday crying, "Oh, my poor babies" . . . this is a very false and jarring note of philanthropy. If there is anything to distinguish the woman Knorr from the crowd of child murderers who have gone before, it is her utter abandonment in depravity. (December 4, 1894, 2)

Yet women and men were disturbed by the severity of Knorr's sentence: they marched, appealed, and petitioned against the capital punishment, recognizing the crime was motivated by poverty rather than by immorality. However, the strongest protest was made by William Walker, the colony's hangman. In perhaps the most dramatic event of the case, this man, who had earlier hanged Deeming with no qualms, but who was now unbalanced by alcoholism, an unhappy marriage, and his neighbor's hostility to a woman's execution, cut his throat.

Knorr never knew of his death, but the speed and fervency of her conversion to religion, once all avenues of appeal had been exhausted, indicates that she was now as mentally unstable as Walker, if she had not been so all along. Representing Knorr as mad rather than bad is an alternative view that appeared even before her death, with Rudolph Knorr seeking clemency for his wife on the grounds that Frances was an epileptic and given to irrational behavior. Laster has also argued that she was disturbed ("Frances Knorr" 151). While reading Knorr for insanity has some credence, it should not obscure the desperate economics behind her actions. She was alone, thousands of miles from an unforgiving family, and with children to support.

Rudolph had been encouraging Frances to confess, but she, probably wary after her letter to Thompson, did nothing initially. In early 1894, Rudolph passed a document to the jail governor, in which Frances denied responsibility for her crimes but implicated another person, charging him with three more infanticides. Almost certainly this individual was Thompson, although Knorr had associated with another man, a racetrack spieler, whom police could not trace. As she could not supply any details of the deaths beyond what had been published in newspapers, the confession was discounted as fantasy. Then came Knorr's violent attack of repentance, manifested in strident hymn singing and yet another confession. Only the gist of this document and its postscript were released. In it, she confessed to smothering the first two babies, though still denying any involvement with the strangled child. Because of the different modus operandi, and the fact that the murder weapon was buried with the infant, this claim may well be true. Smothering a child, though abominable, lacks the sadistic violence of strangulation. "A man's crime," commented crime writer Kerry Greenwood to me, "hanging a baby like hanging a puppy."

The confession's postscript, as reported in the January 6 *Argus,* read:

> As I feel that I have not expressed myself clearly, I now desire to state that upon the two charges known in evidence as No. 1 and 2 babies I confess to be guilty.
>
> Placed as I am now, within a few hours of my death, I express a strong desire that this statement be made public, with the hope that my fate will not only be a warning for others, but also act as a deterrent to those who are perhaps carrying on the same practice. (5)

Laster describes this last wish as "manufactured" ("Arbitrary Chivalry" 175). The complete text, reportedly in Knorr's autograph, is currently missing from her Victorian Public Record Office file. However, to judge from the postscript alone, I concur with Laster. The formal, even legal, language of this extract, so unlike the expressions used in her letter and her reported speech, suggests words were being put into Frances's mouth or that she was even taking dictation. But she was probably past caring about anything except the manner of her dying. Here, contemporary narrative apparently influenced the life, for Knorr's ending was pure theater, the final scene of a Victorian melodrama or the pious tracts supplied by her prison visitors. She arguably thus exerted some control over her representation, confounding all expectations that she would have hysterics or have to be dragged to the gallows. The following is drawn from the January 20 *Weekly Times,* which provided the best coverage of the execution.

On the morning of her execution, the strains of "Abide with Me" and "Safe in the Arms of Jesus" were heard coming from the condemned cell. When Knorr emerged, in brown prison dress, she looked composed and walked steadily to the scaffold. When asked if she had anything to say, she replied: "Yes; the Lord is with me. I do not have fear what men may do with me, for I have peace, perfect peace." Her skirt was drawn tight around her ankles with a cord, weird chivalry intended to prevent any immodesty during the hanging. Then the noose was placed around her neck and Knorr positioned on the trapdoor. Next moment she, to use a phrase of the time, stepped into eternity. Death was instantaneous. While Knorr's small weighty body dangled for the required amount of time before being cut down, the prison matron went into a hysterical faint, sobbing and moaning. The Chief Warder commented on Knorr: "No mistake, she was plucky, she was as brave as Ned Kelly" (21), the iconic Australian outlaw. Such was high praise—something of which there had been little in Knorr's life.

To conclude this representation of the very complex (though possibly a bit simple) Frances Knorr, I want to return to the Melbourne Gaol again. Following a revamp of the exhibition, the skulls are no longer displayed. Knorr's death mask does remain on view, together with her prison photograph, and an account of the crime that expresses more sympathy for her case. It states: "Jobs were scarce, there was no state welfare and it was difficult to avoid being involved in petty crime"—let alone the major crime of infanticide.

Knorr's Babies

Gladys Knorr last saw her mother two days before the execution. The January 20 *Weekly Times* described the scene: "[T]he sight of the mother clinging to the baby was particularly painful. . . . She heaped kisses on the poor little mite, and prayed that she should never know" her mother was hanged (21). There is no mention of any contact with Reita Daisy, the baby born shortly before her mother's arrest. The following paragraph appeared in the January 4 *Argus:*

> The Case of Mrs Knorr
> The Infant Before the City Court
>
> The infant Reita Daisy Knorr, which had been frequently before the City Police Court as a neglected child, was formally handed over to the custody of the department for neglected children. The child was born at Sydney shortly before Mrs Knorr was arrested on the charge of child murder (for which she is now under sentence of death). Since her arrival in Victoria the child has been in the custody of the police. An order was made by the Bench at the City Police Court for its commitment to the department for neglected children. (7)

This item appears, significantly, immediately above a report on an inquest into the death of May Kennedy, a baby-farmed child. Nobody was committed for trial in this case, although it is highly suspicious that the infant died soon after the child-care money ran out, from improper nourishment. The juxtaposition, which is ironic and also unpleasant, implies that Knorr's judicial murder was no deterrent.

However, Reita Daisy Knorr did not share Kennedy's fate, although her putative father (Thompson) disowned her. As she was in police custody, the authorities were thus responsible for her welfare. Reita Daisy was fostered out from October 25, 1893, and in 1898 was formally adopted by her carers. The final entry on her file in the *Children's Register of State Wards* is as follows: "No information having reference to this child's parentage is to be given, as the adopting parents have been promised that such shall not on any account be disclosed" (v. 15, 298). Renamed Doris May Gladstone, she likely lived and died with no knowledge of her notorious mother.

Postscript:
A Modern Knorr Relative's Reaction

At the May 4, 2007, launch of the book *Meaner Than Fiction,* a study of legal injustices, I met Kathy Laster, now CEO of the Victorian Law Foundation, whose work on Knorr is cited in this article. We discussed the case, and she said:

"Did you hear what happened at the Public Record Office? Someone screamed out loud."

"A Knorr descendant?" I asked.

"No, a Thwaites, researching the family history. They'd never heard about Frances Knorr before."

"They screamed from horror?"

"No, the surprise—at having such a famous and well-documented relative."

Works Cited

Allen, Judith. *Sex & Secrets: Crimes involving Australian Women since 1880.* Melbourne: Oxford University Press, 1990.

———. "Octavius Beale Re-considered: Infanticide, Baby-farming and Abortion in NSW 1880–1939." In *What Rough Beast? The State and Social Order in Australian History.* Ed. Sydney Labour History Group. Sydney: George Allen & Unwin, 1982. 111–29.

Cameron, Lindy, ed. *Meaner Than Fiction.* Rowville: Five Mile, 2007.

Cannon, Michael. *The Woman as Murderer.* Mornington, VIC: Today's Australia Publishing Company, 1994.

Children's Registers of State Wards in the Colony of Victoria. Old Series (Admissions): 1864– 1899. Blackburn: Australian Institute of Genealogical Studies, 1995.

Disraeli, Benjamin. *Sybil.* 1845. Ed. Thom Braun. London: Penguin, 1980.

Fortune, Mary. *The Detectives' Album.* Shelburne, ON: Battered Silicon, 2003.

Holledge, James. *Australia's Wickedest Women.* Sydney: Horwitz, 1963.

Hume, Fergus. *The Mystery of a Hansom Cab.* Melbourne: Kemp & Boyce, 1886.

Jaggs, Donella. *Neglected and Criminal: Foundations of Child Welfare Legislation in Victoria*. Melbourne: Phillip Institute of Technology, 1986.

Kreitmayer's Waxworks Exhibition Catalogue. Melbourne, c. 1903.

Lahey, John. *Damn You, John Christie!* Melbourne: State Library of Victoria, 1993.

Laster, Kathy. "Arbitrary Chivalry: Women and Capital Punishment in Victoria, 1842–1967." In *A Nation of Rogues? Crime, Law and Capital Punishment in Colonial Australia*. Ed. David Phillips and Susanne Davies. Melbourne: Melbourne University Press, 1994. 166–88.

———. "Frances Knorr: 'She Killed Babies, Didn't She?'" In *Double Time: Women in Victoria—150 Years*. Ed. Marilyn Lake and Farley Kelly. Melbourne: Penguin, 1985. 148–55.

Nixon, John. Report. Victorian Public Records Office, series 264, file 22.

Palmer, Andrew. "Digging up the Dirt on Makin." *Law Institute Journal* (December 1993): 1170–72.

Sussex, Lucy. "Portrait of a Murderer." In *On Murder*. Ed. Kerry Greenwood. Melbourne: Black, Inc., 2000.

Victorian Public Records Office, series 264, file 22.

PART III

Maternity and Difference

Nation, Race, and Empire

CHAPTER 9

"My Own Dear Sons"

Discursive Maternity and Proper
British Bodies in *Wonderful Adventures of
Mrs. Seacole in Many Lands*

DEIRDRE H. MCMAHON

In the spring of 1854 the fifty-year-old freeborn black Jamaican and self-professed doctress Mary Seacole first heard of the British engagement in the Crimea; by the following winter Seacole had traveled from the Caribbean to Balaclava to become, in her words, "doctress, nurse and 'mother'" to the British soldiers.[1] Underscored by her insistent claim that "unless I am allowed to tell the story of my life in my own way, I cannot tell it at all," Seacole's 1857 autobiography presented a challenge to Victorian England: the empire, she obliquely argues, not only includes me, it needs me (147). Her challenge, of course, lies in her skin color. By declaring a British, and at times an English identity, Seacole defies the supposed link between British superiority and Anglo-Saxon stock. In a deft manipulation of prevailing discourses of domesticity, Seacole's self-inscription in *Wonderful Adventures of Mrs. Seacole in Many Lands* legitimizes this black dispossessed widow as a mother to the British soldiers in the Crimea. Seacole literally writes her way into the fabric of Englishness; moreover, her specific strategies of self-representation undermine one of the primary

---

[1] Mary Seacole, *Wonderful Adventures of Mrs. Seacole in Many Lands* (New York: Oxford University Press, 1988), 124. Originally published in 1857. Further references to this edition will be made parenthetically in the text.

foundations of British imperialism and British identity: the sanctity and stability of British motherhood.

For Victorians, the Crimean conflict was without doubt an imperial war. Allied British, French, and Ottoman forces spent only two years repelling Russian expansion into the Balkans (March 1854 to March 1856), but this relatively quick conflict was potholed with logistical faults and military blunders. Though provisions were supposed to be stockpiled in the Turkish city of Scutari, more than two hundred miles across the Black Sea, for the first year British troops in the Crimea lacked the most basic of supplies, including food, clothes, and even lint for bandages. There were very few wagons to transport the wounded and fewer surgeons to tend the injured. Cholera swept the camps. Reports of insufficient food, poor medical care, and incompetent leadership haunted the families and friends of the 21,000 British soldiers who died there, especially as three-quarters of the men had died from disease.[2]

> It has become painfully evident that the medical arrangements for the army in the East have been most inadequate, both as regards the provision against cholera and epidemic disease, and the attendance upon the wounded in battle.... [W]e greatly fear that, however brilliant the courage and glorious the achievements of our soldiers, it will have to be recorded as a reproach against the administrative authorities and the leaders of the expedition that inadequate provision had been made for the care of the sick and wounded. (*Lancet,* October 21, 1854)

It quickly became clear that the high death rate was as much the result of mismanagement as of battle, and that in battle the soldiers were gaining precious little ground. In effect, the imperial father figures of the British military and Parliament seemed to have failed, a failure captured for the first time in graphic daily newspaper accounts from the front.

> As to the town [Balaclava] itself, words cannot describe its filth, its horrors, its hospitals, its burials.... The dead, laid out as they died, were lying side by side with the living; and the latter presented a spectacle past all imagining. The commonest accessories of a hospital were wanting; there was not the least attention paid to decency or cleanliness; the stench is appalling; ... and, for all I could observe, these men died without the least effort being

---

[2] British mortality figures for the war vary from 21,000 to 40,000, but even the most conservative sources estimate that only 3,000 to 5,000 British soldiers died directly from wounds received in battle. The rest died of disease, malnutrition, medical neglect or mistreatment, or lack of basic medical supplies. See the *Times,* October 12, 1854.

made to save them. There they laid just as they were gently let down upon the ground by the poor fellows, their comrades, who brought them on their backs from the camps with the greatest tenderness, but who are not allowed to remain with them. The sick appeared to be tended by the sick, and the dying by the dying. (Russell 154)

British enthusiasm for the war was tempered not just by the loss of British soldiers, whose casualties might be expected to follow from battle, but by the possibility that soldiers could "die without the least effort being made to save them."

Into this chaotic landscape stepped Mary Seacole, determined to volunteer her services to the British imperial war effort. Seacole traveled to London in the autumn of 1854 to petition for inclusion in Florence Nightingale's newly formed nursing corps, yet despite a great deal of medical experience, especially in treating the cholera that was decimating British troops, she was told there was no vacancy. Her skin color precluded her work at the newly established British Hospital. Instead of returning to Jamaica, Seacole booked transit to the Crimea to set up her own medical and mercantile establishment in Kadikoi, an outpost near Balaclava that was much closer to the front than Nightingale's hospital in Scutari. Seacole's aptly named "British Hotel" offered British soldiers reasonably priced food, a comfortable meeting place, and Seacole's expert medical care, as well as access to whatever necessities "from an anchor down to a needle" that the British chain of command was unable to procure (114). There she diagnosed, operated on, and oversaw the recuperation or burial of many "poor lads," some of whom bore "names familiar to all England" (126–27).

Seacole's participation as a voluntary member of the British military machine in the Crimea unsettles what may appear to be a commonplace nineteenth-century equation of war (and imperialism) with masculine endeavor; similarly, her postwar life in London suggests that the phenomenon of the colonial "return" to the metropole, most often identified as an early- to mid-twentieth-century practice, was already under way during the Victorian period. Though her very presence in these sites highlights the instability of clear racial and gender boundaries, it is through the act of authorship that Seacole makes manifest the ideological contradictions under which she lived and produced her text.

Written after her return to London, during a period in which Seacole faced ill health and financial ruin (in no small part because she had destroyed her stock at the sudden end of the war rather than trade with Russians), *Wonderful Adventures of Mrs. Seacole in Many Lands* attempts to capitalize on the sympathy and fascination extended to those who had served in the Crimea. Seacole's autobiography was a popular success, going through two printings within twelve months, a publication record which gestures, if only loosely, toward a measure of ideological affinity between author and audience. But the narrative authority established by conventions of autobiography—she was there, she saw the battles, she helped the soldiers—is complicated by Seacole's race and sex. She is a woman, a "Creole" woman, traveling alone, fraternizing with British soldiers and profiting from war (1). To deflect any potential charges of illicit or parasitic behavior, Seacole both mediates and cements her authority through reference to the domestic, particularly the maternal. *Wonderful Adventures* presents Seacole as a "Crimean heroine," British to the bone in her enthusiasm not only for Britain's cause in the Crimea, but also for the care of the young British men whom she calls her "sons" (76, 127). Seacole justifies her position on the battlefield by framing her "adventures" as womanly duty. According to Seacole, the British war effort needs women, because "only women know how to soothe and bless" the desperately wounded (75). Thus Seacole reports that as soon as she heard of the war, her greatest wish was to use her medical skills, garnered from her own mother and from the Jamaican medical tradition, in service to Great Britain: "[W]hat delight should I not experience if I could be useful to my own 'sons,' suffering for a cause it was so glorious to fight and bleed for!" (75–76).

Seacole presents herself as English by choice, and by her own authority, as if her work in the Crimea were the proof rather than the cause of her essential Britishness (and as if Britishness by definition would accommodate multiple claims of identity, offering a kind of continuum on which to inscribe oneself). On this imperial continuum, Seacole implicitly argues, Englishness stands not just as a model, but as an attainable goal for the British colonial. Recent criticism has tended to ignore the radical import of Seacole's self-fashioning, focusing instead on her apparent complicity with discourses of empire; readers at the time, however, seem to have been remarkably receptive to Seacole's acts of self-definition.[3] Her reception

---

[3] Sandra Pouchet Paquet claims that *Wonderful Adventures* "reflects an enthusiastic acceptance of colonialism in the aftermath of slavery" (651), so much so that her memoirs "project [Seacole] as the lackey of male privilege and Empire" (655). According to Paquet, Seacole is saved from "unmediated parasitism" only by her sustained interest in medicine and travel (655). Amy Robinson describes Seacole's assertion of Britishness as an "offensive affiliation" (554). William L. Andrews sees Seacole's Britishness as a doomed venture, concluding his introduction to the Oxford edition of *Wonderful Adventures* by questioning if Seacole saw the "pathetic irony" of her "condition as a black woman trying assiduously to make a respectable place for herself in the Western scheme of things" (xxxiv).

thus suggests a significant level of malleability in midcentury conceptions of race, nation, empire, and appropriate gender roles.

Domesticity at War: Race and the Narration of Britishness

In his insightful analysis of imperial femininity, Simon Gikandi argues that Seacole "can only be recognized as an English national by unconditionally espousing the imperial cause." According to Gikandi, Seacole positions herself as English by combining a fervent and unconditional imperialism with "an archetypal mid-nineteenth-century trope" identified by Raymond Williams as "the new bourgeois ethic of self-making and self-help" (132). Though the ideals of diligence, industry, and self-denial that would later inform Samuel Smiles's 1859 *Self-Help* certainly wind their way through the pages of *Wonderful Adventures,* Seacole's investment in *narrative* control acts as the primary means by which she claims her English identity. Anticipating the rhetorical weapons others may use against her, Seacole preemptively introduces whatever may leave her marginal (be it her colonial origins, her skin color, her family history, her ambition, or her bankruptcy) in such a way as to insist upon a sense of solidarity with her readership. Seacole's strategy of turning a potential weakness into a strength is especially evident in her negotiations of race and racial identity. For Seacole, race both is and is not somatic; is and is not a matter of biological inheritance; and most importantly, both is and is not possible to be dismissed, redefined, or transformed. On the first page of her autobiography Seacole explains, "I am a Creole, and have good Scotch blood coursing in my veins." She continues: "My father was a soldier, of an old Scotch family," thus positioning herself within a more conventionally (white) British rather than colonial lineage (1), yet though she occasionally lays claim to Scottish stereotypes of thrift or temper, she never mentions her father again. Neatly raising and then avoiding issues of racial ambiguity, intermarriage, and miscegenation, Seacole's self-description depends upon the presence and erasure of a white father who literally embodies her claim to Britishness, but whose influence is so absolutely undescribed that he seems more like a necessary precondition of her narrative legitimacy than an active component of it.

The very ambiguity of the term "Creole" allows Seacole a range of racial self-representation, as do her varied terms of self-portraiture. She explains she is "only a little brown" (4), or "yellow" (78), but also describes herself as "dusky" or "a few shades duskier," comparing herself implicitly to a standard of white womanhood (4). However, while her range of racial self-representation is phrased with deliberate ambiguity, Seacole also affirms her allegiance to an African diasporic identity:

> [I]f I have a little prejudice against our cousins across the Atlantic—and I do confess to a little—it is not unreasonable. I have a few shades of deeper brown upon my skin which shows me related—and I am proud of the relationship—to those poor mortals whom you once held enslaved, and whose bodies America still owns. And having this bond, and knowing what slavery is; having seen with my eyes and heard with my ears proof positive enough of its horrors—let others affect to doubt them if they will—is it surprising that I should be somewhat impatient of the airs of superiority which many Americans have endeavored to assume over me? (14)

Although framed as a criticism of American assumptions of white hegemony, this passage contains Seacole's sole reference to Britain's own history of slavery and, by extension, colonialism. Here she allows a moment of anger to seep into her otherwise conciliatory text. Instead of continuing to align herself with her British audience (as she does when referring to Americans as "our cousins across the Atlantic"), Seacole not only proclaims her pride at being of African descent but also turns a critical eye on Britain's own history in the slave trade. (Her shift in pronouns alone, from "*our* cousins" to "those . . . whom *you* once held enslaved," speaks to a fissure that Seacole chooses not to efface.) Indeed, her barbed insistence that she "knows what slavery is . . . let others affect to doubt [its horrors] if they will" suggests her rage and disdain for any apologists, be they American or British. In its defensive frame of pride in her African ancestry, this passage demonstrates Seacole's awareness that her contemporaries might stress her racial difference at the expense of her patriotism and medical expertise.

Seacole's paradoxical self-inscription—acknowledging a decidedly non-British identity that her autobiography diligently works against—depends upon the radical instability of race in nineteenth-century British culture.[4] It is exactly because "race" could refer to an ethnic, chromatic, religious, continental, national, class, or sexual taxonomy that racial distinctions proffered a valuable means of political exclusion in which the norm of British subjecthood remained the province of white, upper- or middle-class Englishmen. However, *Wonderful Adventures* shows that

---

[4] Many scholars have noted the indeterminacy of the term "race" in nineteenth-century British culture. See McClintock's discussion of the "antinomies of race" (52–56). See also Bolt and Stepan.

British racial instability could be employed, as in the case of Mary Seacole, to include those whom it would usually marginalize. In fact, the bulk of *Wonderful Adventures* partakes in a narrative trajectory that executes subtle shifts in Seacole's self-representation toward an ever more overt affiliation with a British, indeed, with an English, identity. The act of authorship alone enables Seacole to produce and protect a range of permeable subject positions, aligning her at once with Caribbean, African, and English identities, which she negotiates through reference to Britishness, itself a contested category, and motherhood, which is at once naturalized and exposed as a cultural construct.

Narrative control, "telling the story of [her] life in [her] own way," allows Seacole to navigate the rocky waters of self-definition, but *Wonderful Adventures* is troubled by gaps, omissions, and moments of explicit unease which disrupt both the text and the connection with the British public that Seacole labors to construct. In this way, *Wonderful Adventures* not only works within and reproduces the abiding ideologies that inform Seacole's act of authorship, it also exposes the jagged edges, or, as Mary Poovey would say, the "unevenness" of competing ideological imperatives. By attending to the warring signifying effects within *Wonderful Adventures,* and to the warring cultural work Seacole's autobiography performs, it is possible to chart how sustaining logics of race and gender in Victorian England could be manipulated to articulate identities that imperialism would seem to deny out of hand. Rather than launching a large-scale critique of the racial and gender ideologies that seek to curtail blacks from authorship or women from travel, medicine, or war, Seacole simply inserts her experiences into existing discourses of patriotism and proper femininity. In doing so, she radically refigures domesticity so that it includes exactly that which it conventionally denies: profit, travel, medical training, professional recognition, and black British subjectivity.

Though domesticity's power as an ideological construct is strong enough to legitimize, at least on a surface level, Seacole's decidedly unconventional life story, significant gaps in the text point to tensions in existing discourses of race and femininity. Seacole's self-representation as a woman called to aid "[her] fellow countrymen" transforms the "womanly art of healing" into an overt mercantile scheme, one that is charted clearly in her text, but given no credit as a motivation for her "motherhood" (75, 89). Seacole repeatedly emphasizes and attempts to legitimize her presence in Kadikoi as that of merchant and doctor. She does this without mention of the many inadequacies in British leadership; one of the striking omissions in Seacole's text is the absence of descriptions of military mismanagement. Rather than accuse British authorities of incompetence, Seacole invokes the highly gendered rhetoric of separate spheres to justify her refusal to comment on anything but her own establishment: "Mismanagement and privation there might have been, but my business was to make things right in my sphere, and whatever confusion and disorder existed elsewhere, comfort and order were always to be found at Spring Hill" (113). Her phrasing suggests a boundary Seacole refused to cross—as a woman and as a loyal supporter of the British army she would not criticize (and did not need to criticize) military authorities. Of course, correspondents like Thomas Chenery and W. H. Russell had already exposed severe inadequacies in the structure of the British army, and the reading public was well acquainted with its failures. In contrast, Seacole embraces silence, a code of conduct with dual cultural resonance as a mainstay of both military decorum and patriarchal custom.

In the context of the terrible anxieties raised by British military blunders, the "comfort and order" of the material goods Seacole supplies, though vital to the well-being of British soldiers, fade in comparison with the ideological work performed by her bold assertion that, at least in her enclave in Spring Hill and in her meager but pointedly named "British Hotel," proper British conduct was maintained in the midst of the chaos of war. Government officials may have refused her help, and in doing so refused to acknowledge her talents, training, and the "naturalness" (78) of a mother's offer to tend to her sons (or of a subject's desire to support her nation), but in merging maternal care with patriotism as a higher moral order, Seacole insists that her call to "serve" transcended their racism: Britain needed her help, even if the authorities were blinded by their prejudice, and she was determined to give it (76, 80).

In direct contradiction to the prevailing stereotype of the drunken, incompetent nurse, Seacole presents herself as a trained and dedicated doctress, cloaked in maternal care and discipline. She explains that she not only supplied British soldiers with meat, tea, coffee, linens, medicines, fruit, wine, and doctoring at the British Hotel, but also enforced a strict code of behavior at her establishment: "neither permit[ting] drunkenness among the men nor gambling among the officers" (145). Far from scrambling in the dirt, without morale or effective leadership, as other reports suggested, the soldiers at the British Hotel admirably withstood hardship, in part because Mother Seacole demanded that they do so. In shameless paralepsis, *Wonderful Adventures* makes clear that the soldiers received the support they needed not from official channels, but from Seacole herself. By cooking, procuring supplies, dispensing medicine, stitching wounds, and acting as an amanuensis for men too ill to write, Seacole was able to provide what she terms "home comforts" and "little home tokens" desperately needed on the front (185). But though she incorporates frequent mention of her medical skills and business acumen, these accomplishments are subsumed into a framework of womanly duty.

> [A]lthough I did not hesitate to charge [a sick soldier] with the value of the necessities I took him, he was thankful enough to be able to *purchase* them.... Don't you think, reader, if you were lying, ... thousands of miles from mother, wife or sister, ... and thinking regretfully of that English home where nothing that could minister to your great need would be left untried—don't you think you would welcome the familiar figure of a stout lady[?] ... I tell you, reader, I have seen many a bold fellow's eyes moisten at such a season, when a woman's voice and a woman's care have brought to their minds recollections of those happy English homes which some of them never saw again. (125–27; emphasis in original)

Seacole addresses her readers as if in direct response to any number of tacit accusations, all of which can be forestalled through a single strategy. Though she rather baldly mentions that "she did not hesitate to charge" the soldier for food and medicine, her identity here is not that of a merchant engaged in a business transaction. Instead, she positions herself as a figure of womanly care, and moreover, as a reminder of the homes and families these men had left behind.

Framing her narrative through the rubrics of sentimentality, the bread, breakfasts, and conviviality of the British Hotel are suggestive of domestic ritual, of a quotidian interest in food and friendship that remains in marked contrast to the war just beyond the hotel's walls. With constant disjuncture in her descriptions of the Crimea, vacillating between the utter devastation caused by the conflict and the men's own heart-warming camaraderie, Seacole invokes both the emotional needs of the troops and the cultural construction of "home" as sacred space, as the very reason for which nations go to war. In doing so, she is able not merely to align herself with the women left in England, but literally to embody English femininity and to stand as a symbol of the home, hearth, and empire for which England was supposedly fighting. Consider her descriptions of dying soldiers, comforted by the "touch of a woman's hand":

> [B]ending over a poor fellow whose senses had quite gone, and, I fear, would never return to him in this world, he took me for his wife, and calling me "Mary, Mary," many times, asked me how he got home so quickly, and why he did not see the children; and said he was sure he should soon get better now. Poor fellow! I could not undeceive him. I think the fancy

happily caused by the touch of a woman's hand soothed his dying hour; for I do not fancy he could have lived to reach Scutari. I never knew it for certain, but I always felt certain that he would never wake from that dream of home in this world. (99)

Here Seacole's medical skills are not as important as her sex: standing in for his "Mary," her very presence prompts the dying soldier's "dream of home in this world." This "fancy," Seacole implies, eased the man's passage from this world to the next. Obviously, such a description offers reassurance and solace not to the troops, but to Seacole's readership. Beneath *Wonderful Adventures* is the promise that the men in the Crimea thought constantly of their homes and loved ones; that they behaved in ways fitting for representatives of the Crown; and, moreover, that at least some soldiers died peacefully, if only under the delusion that they had been reunited with their families.

Sentimentality buoys Seacole's descriptions of the soldiers and their day-to-day lives on the front. She would comfort the wounded awaiting transport to Scutari, for example, with a taste of lemonade and simple sponge cake, because "they all liked the cake, poor fellows, better than anything else: perhaps because it tasted of 'home'" (101). In direct address, she explains further to her "gentle reader" that she endeavored to bring the soldiers "a taste of home" on rice pudding day, adding that if her readers had traveled to the British Hotel during the war, they, too, might well have shared some rice pudding, or have "stumbled upon something curried, or upon a good Irish stew, nice and hot, with plenty of onions and potatoes, or upon some capital meat pies" (138, 140), fare in contrast with most descriptions of provisions in the camps. References to home—to London, to England, and especially to the families the soldiers had left behind—run consistently throughout Seacole's descriptions of life (and death) in the British camp. Like World War I, the Siege of Sebastopol required extensive trenches, and those guarding the trenches at night often suffered sneak attacks and sniper fire. Seacole explains it was "very usual" for young officers ordered to the trenches to stop by the British Hotel to "shake me by the hand at parting, and sometimes . . . say: 'You see, Mrs. Seacole, I can't say good-bye to the dear ones at home, so I'll bid you good-bye for them. Perhaps you'll see them some day, and if the Russians should knock me over, mother, just tell them I thought of them all, will you?'" (152).

Such passages succeed in painting a piteous scene (and in positioning Seacole as symbol of home and maternal care) only if they pull at the readers' heartstrings. The scene's first layer of sentimentality lies in the recognition, shared by Seacole and the soldiers, that each good-bye could be a final farewell, but the sense of loss and tragedy is further heightened for the readers of *Wonderful Adventures* by the certain knowledge that so many of the British soldiers serving in the Crimea indeed did not return "to the dear ones at home." Seacole acts as witness, participant, and chronicler, documenting the war with an eye for British heroism; significantly, it is her words as much as her actions, her descriptions of care and affection for the soldiers, that engender affective bonds between author and audience. Seacole's life story becomes a tale of British imperial virtue made manifest by the mourning, pride, and patriotism she and her readers share.

To summarize the work of Nancy Armstrong, Jane Tompkins, and others, sentimental literature engenders its affective response by evoking a set of shared symbols and values, but far from being merely a reaffirmation of community standards, the visceral reactions engendered by the text open the possibility of an active refashioning of value structures—of what can and must be valued as well as how it should be valued. To rephrase, using Jane Tompkins's terms, sentimental literature is always already a "political enterprise, halfway between sermon and social theory" (126). The pathos of the battlefield shadows the second half of Seacole's autobiography, but the psychological, physical, and financial costs of war consistently remain subordinated to the narrative of maternal care on which so much of the affective response to *Wonderful Adventures* depends. In this context, Seacole's imperial zeal and descriptions of dying soldiers function in tandem to support her larger goal of reconstituting the British family, with herself at its center. Throughout Seacole's text, however, the urgency of her repetitions, her near constant references to her role as caregiver, and her frequent nostalgic gestures toward "those happy English homes" suggest authorial anxiety; her autobiography must not only provide a marketable record of her experiences as a traveler, merchant, and doctor, but also create a valid space for Mary Seacole in the London to which she had returned. In the words of Simon Gikandi, "writing *Wonderful Adventures* is [Seacole's] ultimate attempt to claim her Englishness" (127). She succeeds at claiming Britishness, even Englishness, but at great cost. Her attempt is fraught, I argue, because the rubrics on which her text relies—patriotism, domesticity, proper femininity, and, most specifically, motherhood—simultaneously secure and undermine her ability to inscribe herself as a subject within Victorian culture.

Seacole's dependence on the rhetoric of maternity emblematizes the double-edged sword with which she asserts her authorship. Consider her analogy of war with childhood illness: "I used to think [battle] was like having a large family of children ill with fever, and dreading to hear which one had passed away in the night" (152). By framing her narrative in the language of maternal care, Seacole creates a power differential favoring herself as doctor/mother and infantilizing the (implicitly white) male British soldiers whom she calls her "boys" (153) and "sons" (152). But the role of mother is not necessarily liberatory, and is especially problematic for women deemed racial others. It could certainly be argued that the success of Seacole's autobiography was due at least in part to her audience's comfort with the *Mami*/mammy figure of the Caribbean and American South. While this may well be true, Seacole differs from the stereotype of the mammy (the faithful black female—often slave—retainer, nurse, and mother substitute) in her control of her own narrative and in her insistence that she was an entrepreneur, a talented "doctress," and a hotelier *paid* for her efforts and recognized for her abilities. Herein lies the rub: in order to legitimize her presence and activities in the Crimea, Seacole cannot rely merely on her roles as patriot, merchant, or physician—these roles *must* be mediated through reference to maternity and domesticity. But should Seacole situate herself solely within the realm of domesticity, she runs the risk that her race and colonial background will position her in the Caribbean and American tradition of the dispossessed, subservient mammy, rather than as an English mother or as a British subject integral to the empire.

Discursive Maternity

In light of Seacole's repeated claim to the profession of "doctress," the critical trend to see Seacole as a self-appointed mammy reduces her actions and narrative to a subject position she does not fit.[5] Rather than situating (and limiting) Seacole within the role of mammy or substitute white mother, I think it useful to pause for a moment and consider the repercussions of her claim to maternity. As critics as varied as Adrienne Rich, Dorothy Dinnerstein, and Sara Ruddick have shown, motherhood, even in its strictest sense, functions as an *institution* as well as a biological phenomenon, and as such motherhood serves inherently political functions. This occurs on at least three levels. First, there is a long tradition in which women are given value through their reproductive capacity. Second, children are born not only into families, but also into preexisting positions within dominant power structures of race, gender, and class. To a significant extent, women's

---

[5] Amy Robinson describes Seacole as "always already a derivative of the 'real' white mother" (547). Simon Gikandi gives a more nuanced reading of *Wonderful Adventures*, but does not question that Seacole is mimicking motherhood; "for these lonely soldiers, she is 'Mami'—the surrogate mother" (140).

reproductive labor participates in the long-term maintenance of social institutions—including but not limited to class hierarchies, normative gender roles, the concentration of wealth though inheritance, and nationalism itself. Finally, as many feminist theorists have noted, motherhood as an *institution* regularly takes precedence over the *experience* of having or raising a child, often with disciplinary consequences for actual women. The supposedly timeless (i.e., "natural") maternal ideals of tenderness, self-sacrifice, and "instinct" rather than intellect, as well as the expectation that the mother holds primary responsibility for her offspring's safety, well-being, and growth, confer iconic status upon women as guardians of culture and tradition as well as of children. These same ideals, however, validate a very conservative and repressive vision of both women and the family—at its most extreme, mothers are seen as conduits of the social order rather than as citizens in their own right. Legal theorist Martha Fineman explains: "Motherhood has always been, and continues to be, a colonized concept—an event physically practiced and experienced by women but occupied, defined and given content and value by the core concepts of patriarchal ideology" (217).

To this investigation of motherhood as a socially constructed, ideologically laden phenomenon with significant semiotic play, I would extend the arguments of theorists like Hortense Spillers, Jennifer DeVere Brody, and Laura Doyle to insist that the compulsion to naturalize motherhood, to simplify motherhood as a resolutely gendered but apolitical experience, to deny the ideological underpinnings of what constitutes maternity itself, much less what constitutes a "good" or "bad" mother, conceals the extent to which women are positioned as sites of racial anxieties for the culture at large. Indeed, it is exactly because race is usually portrayed as "natural," biological inheritance, thus as necessarily mediated through the female body, that race and sex stand as mutually constitutive categories, *requiring* each other but producing a dizzying variation in their dynamics. Women's bodies are deemed unruly, and subject to scrutiny and control, due to the fact that their reproductive capacity both continues and threatens hierarchies of race, class, and sex. The implicit threat of reproduction—men cannot reproduce without women, but for any particular child, men do not have the certain knowledge of paternity that women perforce have of maternity—means that anxieties about race are always also anxieties about sex, female autonomy, and the control of female bodies and desires. In this way, the mother figure in particular serves not only as a point of access to cultural and racial identity, but also as an end limit of transparent sexuality. Controlling, marking, limiting, or celebrating certain maternal bodies serves to support (or proscribe) individual women's sexual activity;

policing individual women, however, functions simultaneously to inscribe value upon the children produced, thus reinforcing the political viability and cultural reproduction of various groups. As Laura Doyle forcefully argues, the mother acts as a "cultural vehicle for fixing, ranking, and subduing groups and bodies" (4).

In its anxieties about station, birthright, and race, Victorian society recognized the ideological effects of motherhood and reproduction, though this recognition typically remained cloaked behind the idealization of mothers and maternity. Indeed, for many midcentury Victorians maternity was invested with sociopolitical importance: "On the maternal bosom the mind of nations reposes; their manners, prejudices, and virtues,—in a word, the civilization of the human race all depend upon maternal influence" (Martin 47). Here civilization itself rests on mothers' rather than on fathers' shoulders, a worldview which makes Seacole's claim to maternity, or to be more precise, her self-representation as a mother to British soldiers, effectively an assertion of her own status not only as a standard bearer of British virtue, but also (and more implicitly) as a model of the "civilized," domesticated colonial subject. Put another way, this passage suggests that "maternal influence" works to "civilize" children and nations, as if traditions and mores are transmitted along with breast milk (a dangerous claim, but one entrenched in nineteenth-century notions of the family). In contrast, Seacole's rhetoric of maternity suggests that in the Victorian imagination unruly or transgressive female bodies can be made intelligible, even commendable, through reference to a very powerful ideal of femininity that understands women as the sites as well as the conduits of material and cultural reproduction. Of course, not just any form of maternity will do. At issue is not reproduction per se, but the replication and care of dominant discourses that validate or make vulnerable subjects under their sway. For in fact, the idealization of maternity is invested in the reproduction of ideology rather than children—safeguarding norms and ideas, including the boundaries of identity.

At once discursive and material, the nexus of woman/culture/nation is consistently centered on the female body, so much so that control of women's bodies (in nineteenth-century debates about women's legal status, education, employment, and access to the professions) was portrayed as a matter of public concern, just as knowledge about a woman's body (what she *really* is in terms of class, race, religion, or morality; with whom she has or has not had intercourse) implied knowledge about her offspring. It is significant, then, that *Wonderful Adventures* works to erase Seacole's sexuality. Her autobiography goes to great lengths to establish Seacole as an older, properly circumspect, and certainly *nonprocreative* woman. With the specter of miscegenation haunting the pages of her text, Mother Seacole invests herself in a decidedly discursive maternity, one that need not trouble her readers' sexual mores (or anxieties about racial identity). Maternity, or rather the invocation of maternity, *redefines* Seacole's body, transgressive though she was in skin color, place of origin, occupation, and location; through her rendition of near-idyllic domestic order in the Crimea, her sexual body dissolves into a sanitized narrative in which a mother struggles to maintain a safe home for her sons.

Paradoxically, discursive maternity desexualizes Seacole even while emphasizing her femaleness, lending respectability to her presence among the many men with whom she constructs long-standing, intimate, but discursive bonds of kinship. As her body is effaced through text, the threat of her racial ambiguity fades, or rather, the racial threat of her body's reproductive capacity fades. This is no small point, especially when considering Seacole's near silence on the extent to which British slavery is implicated not only in the region in which she spent the first fifty years of her life, but in the imperial history she seeks to support. Motherhood and slavery, it seems, cannot coexist, at least not in a British autobiography. As Hortense Spillers cogently argues, maternity functions with particular signifying power in slave societies: while fatherhood may be contested, motherhood is most often known, and should the mother be a slave in the Americas, the child usually inherits her legal status. Thus in the reproductive politics of slavery, motherhood is dangerous, with the act of birth conferring *illegitimacy* and disenfranchisement on one's children, and with children functioning as collateral for their parents' goodwill.

In telling contrast, Seacole attempts to legitimize both herself and the imperial project by creating a discursive space in which she can be mother to British *soldiers,* and hence a vital component in the propagation and maintenance of Britain's imperial power. In an inversion of conventional patterns of inheritance and identity, the Britishness of her soldier-sons lends a significant measure of legitimacy to Seacole as British herself. Seizing maternity grants Seacole one of the highest powers afforded women, a form of acceptable agency that naturalizes her work in the public sphere as a necessary outgrowth of her need to protect and nurture those dependent upon her. The benefits of discursive maternity allow Mother Seacole to be autonomous and unmarried without censure; indeed, her autonomy depends upon sexual probity, as her body's dual threats of sex and skin color remain constrained by the collective fiction of her motherhood. In this way, discursive maternity functions as an ideological fail-safe, as an office without material basis that works if and only if there is a public recognition of its constructedness. In Seacole's case, however, discursive maternity was based on the ugly material facts of war. Tending the bodies of men who were dying so far from home, Seacole's maternity exceeded its discursive limitations by operating on a literally somatic level: her efforts saved British lives. To some extent, then, Seacole's rhetoric of motherhood, complete with affection, grief, and patriotism, gained a level of authenticity that belied its constructed status. Seacole's successful renegotiation of identity, her self-inscription not only as a British mother, but as a British mother to soldier-sons, exposes just how constructed even the most "natural" web of relations (the family) can be.

Strikingly, the London popular press seemed to accept Seacole's claim to maternity and Britishness, even Englishness. Journals ranging from *Punch* to the *Illustrated London News* to the illustrious *Times* gave column space to her bankruptcy and urged readers to send subscriptions to the fund established in her name. According to the May 30, 1857, edition of *Punch,* for example, both "the honour of the British army and the generosity of the British public" will be "disgraced" if sufficient funds are not raised for the "genuine English" Seacole (221). As a British—and at times an English—mother, Seacole can rally the "troops" at home, calling in *Wonderful Adventures* for her postwar readers to continue to endorse the conventional imperial ideology that Britain acts as a mighty civilizing force, spreading its good values across the globe. Not coincidentally, they can show their fervor for empire by donating to the subscription in honor of her own good work. The success of her autobiography (and thus the likelihood that she would rise out of debt) depended on the Victorian public's willingness to embrace the vision of imperial domesticity (a form of global politics humanized) she provides. The implications are far-reaching: imperial ideology is thus *reproduced* through the body (her actions, the intimate yet asexual contact and care she gave the soldiers) and the text (including the somatic charge gained from its rhetoric of motherhood) of this black colonial woman writing about her work on the battlefield. What *Wonderful Adventures of Mrs. Seacole in Many Lands* offers, then, is a vision of empire that explicitly connects English, Irish, and Scottish homes with battles abroad, and moreover, a vision that not only includes women at the forefront of imperial effort, but also suggests a new litmus test for Britishness: cultural reproduction.

This new framework for Britishness is only possible though Seacole's careful manipulation of her historical and cultural circumstances, a manipulation which affects both the structure and content of *Wonderful Adventures*. Though freeborn herself, Mary Seacole gained maturity in a Caribbean still dominated by slavery. In a telling omission, save for the passing remark quoted earlier, Seacole describes neither England's nor Jamaica's participation in the slave trade, despite the fact that during much of her adulthood black slaves constituted 78 percent of Jamaica's population, whereas only 13 percent of the total population were free people of color such as herself.[6] Distinctions of color, class, education, and civil rights—the colonial inheritance of slavery—similarly remain unremarked, though turmoil over the property rights of "coloured creoles" such as herself would lead to the Morant Bay Massacre only eight years after the writing of *Wonderful Adventures*.[7] Even details of her personal life are conspicuously absent from her autobiography. As if to position herself as always already British, untainted by the violence of self-inscription, *Wonderful Adventures* excises almost all mention of Seacole's friendships or family. Seacole glosses over discussion of her roots in Jamaica, and in the space of a single paragraph she meets, marries, nurses, and buries Mr. Seacole, who had been "very delicate" (5). Thus she establishes her credentials as a respectable widow, a woman who could be a legitimate mother, while also declaring her freedom to travel the globe. "Mother Seacole" cannot legitimate her claim to be a constitutive member of the British family if she recognizes that the British Empire has historically excluded and exploited people of color. Thus her autobiography enacts a dual revision of history: her own colonial past is given short shrift even as the British imperium is whitewashed into a narrative without slavery or systemic racial prejudice.

"My own dear sons": Enlarging the Family Circle

After Sebastopol fell on September 12, 1855, the Allies considered themselves the victors in the conflict and soon began negotiations for an armistice with Russia. Seacole admits a bifurcated response to the prospect of peace. On the one hand, the cessation of conflict signaled a victory for the British, albeit a limited one.[8] For Seacole, however, the war's end meant

---

[6] Seacole does not mention even the quickly suppressed Jamaican slave insurrections of December 1831 and January 1832, instead reserving her criticism for the "Yankee" institution of American slavery (11, 14, 51–53, 58). For Jamaican population statistics, see Bleby and Semmel.

[7] The Morant Bay Rebellion began in October 1865 with agitation over the civil rights of black and "coloured creole" men. A month later, four hundred black Jamaicans were dead, including free "coloured creole" citizens like George W. Gordon, landowner, minister, and member of Jamaica's legislature, who, although he never participated in the riots, was arrested, court-martialed, convicted, and hanged for leading the insurrection. See Semmel.

[8] British troops had not given a good showing on the Redan, the site of the last major battle heading to the fall of Sebastopol, so much so that French troops took the lead in

the dismantling of all she had built: the closing of her store guaranteed bankruptcy; regimental redistribution would send her sons to the far corners of the empire; and, perhaps most importantly, peace negated her position as "doctress, nurse and mother" to the troops. Her ambivalence about the end of the war is evident in her declaration that "I was very glad to hear of peace, also, although it must have been apparent to everyone that it would cause our [the British Hotel's] ruin" (189). Far from being celebratory, her tone here is rather pensive, deflecting onto others the knowledge that peace would be another form of destruction for her.

Taken in aggregate with her repeated identifications with Englishness cited above, Seacole's final chapter suggests a level of anxiety not limited to her dire financial situation, though, as Barbara Weiss argues, bankruptcy carried considerable emotional freight for Victorians. Indeed, the sharp increase in mentions of "home," "friends," and "the comrades left behind" (found on almost every page of the final chapter) indicates incongruity: the seat of war is home to Mother Seacole and every step toward England is a step closer to the dissolution of her "family" (and perhaps of her Englishness). She explains:

> [A]ll this going home seemed strange and somewhat sad, and sometimes I felt that I could not sympathise with the glad faces and happy hearts of those who were looking forward to the delights of home.... Now and then we would see a lounger with a blank face, taking no interest in the bustle of departure, and with him I acknowledged to have more fellow-feeling than with the others, for he, as well as I, clearly had no home to go to. (192)

Seacole fails to mention Jamaica or her sister who lived in Kingston, as if her efforts on the front precluded any possibility of colonial return. Her future, it seems, lies in England, perhaps because her service to the British war effort had brought her such happiness and contentment. Peace, on the other hand, is unsettling and "somewhat sad." This passage seeks to frame the end of the Crimean War under a new rubric of sentimentality, one that aligns Seacole with the rootless veteran even while emphasizing her vulnerability as a woman in the process of losing her home and vocation. Seacole's twofold bid for sympathy as a servant of the crown and as an older woman in need of its protection acts as the last in a long chain of figurative strategies that have enabled her to stand at once as soldier, mother, creole, merchant, doctress, and Englishwoman. The final pages of her text hint

---

capturing the Russian stronghold, a blow to British pride. No major battles occurred after the fall of Sebastopol; the peace treaty was signed on March 30, 1856.

at her recognition that her efforts might have been in vain, that England might reject her as quickly as the War Office had done before.

Seacole's blunt revelation that she has no home to go to after the war works to reaffirm the British Hotel as her true home, a site of cultural plasticity in which the financial and filial obligations incurred by the British soldiers she tended, some of whom failed to pay her as a result of their own losses during the war, could be transferred onto the shoulders of her readers. Implicit in her discussion of her uncertain circumstances is the reminder that any lack of recognition of her maternal status on England's part would not only reduce her to penury, but would dishonor the Crimean military family she had willed and narrated into existence. Thus, building from the bonds of sympathy she earlier had forged between author and audience, Seacole rhetorically enlarges her familial circle from the troops stationed in the Crimea to the extended family of her readers. Surely they, having read her *Wonderful Adventures,* will recognize her efforts and her Englishness; surely they will give her a measure of support (not charity), just as she had supported England in her hour of need. This radically refigured and mutually sustaining vision of the British family is contingent upon Seacole's discursive maternity. England and the British Empire must return her affection and loyalty, if only because the logic of domesticity and familial bonds demands that response: it would be "unnatural" for the British to turn their backs on Seacole now.

What *Wonderful Adventures* offers, then, is an inside (and carefully verified) look at the Crimean War, one that focuses less on battle than on British strength and gallantry, even in the face of death. Seacole's readers see her as a British heroine, but also, and more importantly, they see their sons as heroes and Seacole's "British Hotel" as a small piece of England. In this way, Seacole creates what Ian Baucom, borrowing a term from French philosopher Pierre Nora, calls a "lieu de mémoire." Baucom argues that certain places are invested—even enshrined—in our personal or national consciousness. These places, "textual, monumental or topographic," stand for a "need to stop time," and function as rallying points for a collective identity (19). Seacole's intervention into national discourses about the Crimea "stops time," carving out a secure space that contradicts reports of British failure and suffering. To the British public, hungry for stories of the war but horrified by the newspaper reports they had read, *Wonderful Adventures* furnishes a kinder, gentler account of the Crimea in which war functions as a backdrop to a narrative of domestic and imperial success. In her narrative, and only through her narrative, the "British Hotel" remains a safe harbor for the still-mourned "boys" lost in the war. There, in the pages of her text, British soldiers are tended by their "Mother," given food and proper care, and are helped back to England, if only in the form of their letters.

In effect, Seacole transforms domesticity and maternal care into commodities that she sold to the British soldiers; similarly, her autobiography transforms and commodifies her experiences into narrative, which she sold to the British public. Seacole, faced with return to the inflexible racial hierarchies of London (where she was not seen as a doctress and where she had difficulty finding employment), responds by narrating a frontline account in which she is accepted as a guardian of British values away from home. Seacole doesn't attempt to deconstruct the national and racial politics of the Crimean War. Instead, she celebrates her participation in the British imperial project in the Near East. But by successfully aligning herself with the mothers waiting in England, even as her text reveals the discursive props, entrepreneurial outlines, and shaky narrative walls of its vision of domesticity, Seacole quietly calls into question the ways motherhood (and the motherland) are constructed. As far as Seacole is concerned, her sons who died at Balaclava were no more British than she. British identity, her autobiography hints, is not "natural" or fixed: its origins lie in the stories one tells oneself, in the ideologies one embraces, not in lineage, skin color, or place of birth. That the reception of her autobiography was so enthusiastic, especially within the cultural milieu whose standards of inclusion it implicitly challenges, suggests a hitherto unrecognized flexibility in popular definitions of Britishness. Despite her celebrity, however, Seacole's quick erasure from the historical record suggests the extent and power of normative standards of nineteenth-century British citizenship. If Seacole's autobiography managed to effect an exception to these standards, it was a temporary one. As the generation who mourned the Crimea faded away, so did the dark-skinned Seacole's heroic status. She became expendable, while the pale, chaste figure of Florence Nightingale retained her purchase on British history.

Works Cited

Andrews, William L. "Introduction." In *Wonderful Adventures of Mrs. Seacole in Many Lands*. By Mary Seacole. New York: Oxford University Press, 1988. xxvii–xxxiv.

Armstrong, Nancy. *Desire and Domestic Fiction: A Political History of the Novel*. New York: Oxford University Press, 1987.

Baucom, Ian. *Out of Place: Englishness, Empire and the Locations of Identity*. Princeton: Princeton University Press, 1999.

Bleby, Henry. *Death Struggles of Slavery*. London: Hamilton, Adams and Co., 1853.

Bolt, Christine. *Victorian Attitudes to Race*. London: Routledge, 1971.

Brody, Jennifer DeVere. *Impossible Purities: Blackness, Femininity and Victorian Culture.* Durham: Duke University Press, 1998.

Dinnerstein, Dorothy. *The Mermaid and the Minotaur: Sexual Arrangements and Human Malaise.* New York: Harper and Row, 1976.

Doyle, Laura. *Bordering on the Body: The Racial Matrix of Modern Fiction and Culture.* Oxford: Oxford University Press, 1994.

Fineman, Martha A. "Images of Mothers in Poverty Discourse." In *Mothers in Law: Feminist Theory and the Regulation of Motherhood.* Ed. Martha Albertson Fineman and Isabel Karpin. New York: Columbia University Press, 1995. 205–23.

Gikandi, Simon. *Maps of Englishness: Writing Identity in the Culture of Colonialism.* New York: Columbia University Press, 1996.

Martin, Louis Aimé. *The Education of Mothers of Families, or, The Civilization of Mankind by Women.* Trans. Edwin Lee. London: Whittaker and Co., 1842; Philadelphia: Lea and Blanchard, 1843.

McClintock, Anne. *Imperial Leather: Race, Gender and Sexuality in the Colonial Contest.* New York: Routledge, 1995.

Paquet, Sandra Pouchet. "The Enigma of Arrival: The Wonderful Adventures of Mrs. Seacole in Many Lands." *African American Review* 26.4 (1992): 651–63.

Poovey, Mary. *Uneven Developments: The Ideological Work of Gender in Mid-Victorian England.* Chicago: University of Chicago Press, 1988.

Rich, Adrienne. *Of Woman Born: Motherhood as Experience and Institution.* New York: Norton, 1976.

Robinson, Amy. "Authority and Public Display of Identity: Wonderful Adventures of Mary Seacole in Many Lands." *Feminist Studies* 20.3 (1994): 537–58.

Ruddick, Sara. *Maternal Thinking: Toward a Politics of Peace.* Boston: Beacon, 1989.

Russell, William Howard. *Russell's Dispatches from the Crimea, 1854–1856.* Ed. Nicolas Bentley. New York: Hilland Wang, 1967.

Seacole, Mary. *Wonderful Adventures of Mrs. Seacole in Many Lands.* New York: Oxford University Press, 1988.

Semmel, Bernard. *Jamaican Blood and Victorian Conscience.* Boston: Houghton Mifflin, 1963.

Spillers, Hortense. "Mama's Baby, Papa's Maybe: An American Grammar Book." *Diacritics* 4.17 (Summer 1987): 65–81.

Stepan, Nancy. *The Idea of Race in Science: Great Britain 1800–1960.* London: Macmillan, 1982.

Tompkins, Jane. *Sensational Designs: The Cultural Work of American Fiction 1790–1860.* New York: Oxford University Press, 1985.

Williams, Raymond. *Marxism and Literature.* New York: Oxford University Press, 1977.

CHAPTER 10

Conceiving the Nation

Visions and Versions of Colonial Prenatality

DEIRDRE OSBORNE

> It behoves every wife the instant she knows she is about to become a mother, to set the house of her health into as perfect order as it is in her power to do.
> —Mrs. Annie Ellis, *The Australian Baby: A Handbook for Mothers* (1902)

> ... [E]verything concerning women has one solution: it is named pregnancy.
> —Friedrich Nietzsche, *Thus Spake Zarathustra* (1883)

In the context of late-nineteenth-century Australian colonization, women's maternity provides a crucial but overlooked dimension in both contemporary Victorian and retrospective historiography and literary studies.[1] British and American scholarship over the past twenty years has extensively investigated anxieties regarding degeneration, imperialism, and the ideology of motherhood that circulated at the source of empire in Britain. However, the feedback or alternatives effected by the colonial experience have yet to be integrated wholesale into accounts of women's history and literature. Intra- and intercolonial interactions (politically and culturally) often provided more reformist or radical possibilities for women's emancipation and full citizenship than those at the imperial metropolitan center.[2]

---

[1] Motherhood is foregrounded as a contributing feature of Australian nation building in the work of four Australian revisionist feminist historians, Grimshaw, Lake, McGrath, and Quartly's *Creating a Nation*. They open their volume with an (unsubstantiated) anecdote about a birthing indigenous mother, thus memorably employing a literary approach in order to establish the context of their historical retrieval.

[2] Vida Goldstein and Catherine H. Spence are two examples of influential white Australian women who positioned their pro-suffrage drives within a global arena, advising English

As Elleke Boehmer notes, "With few exceptions postcolonial theories of colonial power and anti-colonial resistance have privileged the relationship of European self and other; of colonizer and colonized" (1).[3] Many imperialist paradigms were reworked in the unique conditions provided by the colonized spaces to reveal both nuanced and oppositional relationships. The basis for imperial roles—man as provider and woman as domesticater—was affected by the impossibility of faithfully replaying the exported imperial family model in a colonial landscape. Australia's geography and climate frequently demanded such reconfigurations. From the strain on imperial values, a space emerged wherein feminine and masculine roles altered, a space that is articulated in particular literary and polemical representations of rural (bush) women's motherhood.[4]

Women's maternity and motherhood consolidate the acquired territories in colonization. Contemporary instruction manuals for girls, wives, and mothers of the period might suggest a colonial replication of the British imperial project,[5] yet the representation of motherhood in some contemporary colonial fiction points to a reworking of the "female metaphor" (Hein 458) due to the specific adaptations the colonial context engendered.[6]

---

and South African movements that were some decades behind the Antipodes in achieving the vote for women. Spence also lectured on suffrage throughout the United States and Canada (*Australian Woman's Sphere* [April 1901]), and John Docker identifies the extent to which Australian women's journalism and conference attendance reveals active contributions to a worldwide exchange (4–6).

[3] Elleke Boehmer addresses the interactions of colonized people through placing peripheries at the center in relation to India, South Africa, and Ireland.

[4] Sue Rowley has argued that images of women as mothers in bush mythology "are almost invariably represented in the home" as, from the 1890s, "[i]ncreasingly, it became difficult to represent women within nationalist mythologies except as mothers" (76). While my focus does not address Australian nationalism, I do aim to highlight resistances and alternatives to this relentless maternal domestic anchoring in Barbara Baynton's short story "A Dreamer."

[5] Australian didactic texts include Mrs. Annie Everett Ellis's *The Australian Baby,* and the Old Housekeeper's *Australian Housewives' Manual* and *Men and How to Manage Them.*

[6] As Susan Stanford Friedman has elaborated, the childbirth metaphor has served the artistic needs of both women and men in terms of articulating human procreativity. This insinuates an equivalent valuing of creativity and (pro)creativity which, throughout Western literary history, has not been the case. At every turn, woman is debilitated or devalued by her birthing capacity in relation to her creative powers while man's creative powers are celebrated in the form of literary *couvades,* what Günter Grass has termed the "headbirth." A uniquely female experience is appropriated linguistically so that it becomes indicative of aspects of male sociocultural identity—according to sex-gender power relations which privilege men. Following on from Friedman, Hein identifies how women have been confined (in their childbirth capability) to a noncreative procreation: "Ironically, the language of procreation, commonly used to describe the activity of the artist, has been used in a manner that excludes women from that activity. Insemination, fertilisation, conception, gestation, incubation, pregnancy, parturition—all parts of the birth process—are invoked to denote

Furthermore, this fiction might be viewed as resisting the imperial models of womanhood as it articulates female autonomy within the socially codified anonymity and silencing ascribed to women's maternity—what Julia Kristeva, from a twentieth-century vantage point, describes in this way:

> Silence weighs heavily none the less on the corporeal and psychological suffering of childbirth and especially the self-sacrifice involved in becoming anonymous in order to pass on the social norm. . . . A suffering lined with jubilation—ambivalence of masochism—on account of which a woman, rather refractory to perversion, in fact allows herself a coded, fundamental, perverse behaviour, ultimate guarantee of society, without which society will not reproduce. (183)

The anonymity to which she refers is that of the birthing female—conduit for the perpetuation of the species—her offspring accorded a specific and viable social identity after birth, in relation to men. Of course Kristeva, as a late-twentieth-century mother, theorizes maternity and childbirth in "Stabat Mater" from a revisionary position within the academy, whereas late-nineteenth-century women's representations were inscribed within a marginal discourse of pregnancy.

In Victorian women's fiction, pregnancy is a rare topic[7] because of the protocols of modesty to which respectable women were expected to adhere and, if treated at all, is referred to euphemistically or to further reveal aspects of a male protagonist. The focus on maternity resides in the

---

an activity that is also theologised as the paradigmatic male act of will" (458) This has had implications upon the processing of women's maternity in relation to nation building. The appropriation of reproductive metaphors for the imperial and colonizing enterprises reveals the literal falsity and inadequacy of their application when reviewed in terms of the childbirth (female) metaphor for creativity.

[7] Occasionally, in Victorian women's life writing (diary entries and letters), articulations about experiences of pregnancy and childbirth can be found. For an Australian example, see *The Diaries of Ethel Turner* (author of the children's classic *Seven Little Australians* [1894]) where Turner first acknowledges her pregnancy as "Felt queer all the morning and had to lie down" (July 9, 1897) and her labor as "I was seventeen hours ill; the last eight being exquisite agony. Pain will always be a matter of comparison now; I believe I should be able to smile over a trifling matter like having a limb sawn slowly off. They used a 2 oz. bottle of chloroform on me but it scarcely had any effect. I was never quite unconscious a moment. . . . They owned that I had a very bad time being so small" (February 7, 1898). Diarist and explorer Emily Caroline Creaghe was just twenty-two when she arrived with her husband, Harry, in the Northern Territory in 1883 as part of a six-month exploration party. Having just suffered the death of her first son, she was pregnant for most of the trip—undertaken on horseback—a fact her diary omits except for one allusion of "feeling squeamish" frequently on the return trip (James 57, Cadzow 233n21).

outcome—the child—who confirms the mother's social status—"fallen" if she bears her child out of wedlock, or respectable if she fulfills the socially expected result of a marriage and her biological destiny. Dale Spender in her study of women's writing and experience affirms the textual marginality of maternity in general:

> Given the number of novels in which childbirth is of central significance it is staggering to find that the event itself is virtually invisible. Women labour between the lines, children are born outside the pages, and rare even is the record of women's response to such a momentous occasion. Fear, pain, post natal depression—anger? Little can be learned about these aspects of women's relationship to childbirth from women's fiction. (115)

Furthermore, the transmission of childbirth knowledge has been predominantly oral, depending upon intergenerational hearsay, advice, and myth. As a topic beyond the firsthand experience of men, its problematic elaboration has affected the treatment of maternity in the male-dominated "public/ published realm" (Spender 115). Therefore, it is important to offer critical attention to literary representations of prenatality. Two short stories, by white indigenous Australian women writers, offer this rare opportunity. "A Cross Line" in *Keynotes* (1893) by George Egerton and "A Dreamer" in *Bush Studies* (1902) by Barbara Baynton[8] use pregnant protagonists to illustrate the uneasy relationship between expected and enacted maternal roles. Ambivalence and anxiety regarding pregnancy traverses both their respective European and Antipodean settings, yet the differing narrative treatments reveal the conservative maternal role to which Egerton's heroine subscribes compared to her colonial counterpart, Baynton (although

---

[8] George Egerton was born Mary Chavelita Dunne in Melbourne, Australia, in 1859. Jennifer Plastow writes that she "grew up travelling around the world" (Todd 209). She traveled with Henry Higginson, a violent and alcoholic bigamist, and eloped to Norway in 1887, where he died in 1889. Egerton remained in Norway studying the works of Strindberg, Ibsen, and Bjornson, meeting Knut Hamsun, whose novel *Hunger* she translated after returning to London in 1890. Moving to Ireland with her husband George Egerton Clairmonte in 1891, her first collection of short stories, *Keynotes* (London: E. Matthews and J. Lane, 1893), was published, followed by *Discords* (London: J. Lane, 1894). Her son was born in 1895 and her marriage ended. She married Reginald Golding Bright and, as Charlotte Rich notes, "after her marriage to Bright, she turned to writing plays, which were likewise unsuccessful" (Rich 134n1). Egerton died in Sussex in 1945. Barbara Baynton was born in 1857 (but claimed it was 1862), married three times, and died as Lady Headley in 1929, dividing her time between Britain and Australia from 1904. She began writing in the 1890s. In 1896 her first story was published in the *Bulletin,* and upon visiting London during 1902–3 her collection of short stories, *Bush Studies* (London: Duckworth, 1902), was published.

as Harris notes, "[I]t was she [Egerton] who was viewed with the greatest animosity by the keepers of conventional morality and the guardians of traditional literary decorum" [1968, 31]).⁹

Egerton's tale represents women as caught in a masquerade of role-playing which stifles their instincts and essential womanhood to produce—what she later terms, in the same collection—"a struggle between instinctive truths and cultivated lies" ("Now Spring Has Come," *Keynotes* 40).¹⁰ The narrative is focalized through a married woman in the first stages of pregnancy. Daydreaming on a riverbank one summer afternoon, she is interrupted by a passing man who seeks her advice on the best place to fish, an exchange that implies their attraction. This adulterous impulse leads to the woman's scrutiny of her husband and to musing over the compromises women must make in marriage despite "the eternal wildness, the untamed primitive savage temperament that lurks in the mildest, best woman" ("A Cross Line" 11). Later in her career, Egerton stated that her project as a writer had been to render experience from a uniquely female perspective: "I realised that in literature, everything had been done better by man than woman could hope to emulate. There was only one small plot left for her to tell: the *terra incognita* of herself, as she knew herself to be, not as man liked to imagine her" (Gawsworth 59). Egerton renders these internal states of female consciousness in "A Cross Line," which, daringly for the 1890s, articulates sexual passion and its outcomes in both women and men. Egerton allows her heroine a fantasy life that becomes increasingly associated with primitivism and eroticism in order to ratify her sexuality just as her maternity promises to curtail it. The heroine imagines herself first as Cleopatra, then in Arabia astride "a swift steed" (19), and finally as a demonic dancer who goads her male audience to frenzy. These fantasies are set against her domestic situation, her stolid husband, and her

---

⁹ It should be remembered that black Australian women's maternity and motherhood operate at tragic counterpoint to any narratives of memoir and fiction generated by white settler women such as Baynton and Egerton. Black indigenous mothers were systematically disempowered with little recourse to justice. Grimshaw, McGrath, Lake, and Quartly briefly address the decimated black indigenous population in terms of a decrease in black women's maternity. They attribute the significant decrease in black women's motherhood to the fact that, from the 1830s, it became increasingly difficult for black men to find black wives (in a culture where polygamy was common) and that black women's cohabitation with white men lessened the number of available wives. In addition, "The differential impact of diseases and application of food taboos that affected women's protein intake, along with the stresses of pregnancy and childbirth, contributed to the low numbers of women giving birth" (Grimshaw and Evans 142).

¹⁰ Iveta Jusova argues convincingly that "Egerton's interest in Nietzsche's notion of the reassertion of the body and senses often sets her model of women's behaviour directly against the traditional restrictive ideal" (42).

eventual choice to remain with him rather than escape with her would-be lover. Her narrative acknowledges how material and social realities shape women's lives and deny them access to a power which she posits as witchery: "Deep in through ages of convention this primeval trait burns, an untameable quantity that may be concealed but is never eradicated by culture—the keynote of woman's witchcraft and woman's strength" (22). Martha Vicinus notes, "Throughout her work, the highest compliment Egerton could give a woman was to declare her a witch, in the sense of being bewitching" (Vicinus x)—a radical reclamation. Conversely, Iveta Jusova argues that Egerton's allusions to ancient and oriental cultures fix her literature within patriarchal cultural forms, for "places where women could express their drives and desires freely are the same imagined places where Victorians typically situated their desires and fantasies. . . . [They] were familiar images in nineteenth-century English culture, although they were usually marginalized and vilified" (Jusova, *New Woman* 62).

In contrast, Baynton's story, "A Dreamer," explores maternal rather than sexual instincts through a lone pregnant woman's struggle in stormy weather to be reunited with her mother. Like Egerton's heroine, she is nameless—evoking Kristeva's maternal anonymity—yet the minutiae of perceptions around which both writers construct their narratives dissolves any Everywoman generalization. Internal states of consciousness are accessed through the characters' detailed and particular experiences. In the opening of her story, Baynton's protagonist disembarks a train where "[p]assengers from far up-country towns have importance from their rarity" (Baynton 46). The woman is returning to where she was raised, to visit her long-neglected mother—the reasons for the neglect are not specified. Her mother's home is in an isolated hollow on the banks of a river—some distance on foot—which the pregnant woman walks. The stormy conditions have swelled the river, and the wind and rain create difficulties for the woman in orientating herself in a place she once knew well. This strangeness of landscape mirrors the woman's anticipation of her maternity, her own changing form. As she battles to cross the flooded river and is almost swept away, the surety of a reunion with her mother inspires her and drives her on. The story has no male characters apart from the station porter and references to the central character's absent husband. Her nostalgia for her own childhood as she anticipates seeing her mother again is devoid of any father. The maternal power of the text resides not only in the clearly self-sufficient, female-only bush family, but also in the act of will on the part of the protagonist to reconnect with her mother as she herself is becoming one. In late-nineteenth-century terms, the woman's active and physical endeavors in dangerous conditions defy the passivity ascribed to pregnant women. However, the story is ultimately a tragedy. She arrives too late—her mother is dead—attended by women who are strangers to the protagonist.

When read alongside contemporary maternity discourses, these short stories also reveal how representing maternity exposes the constraints of genre, not only in their choice of subject matter—by centralizing an obvious outcome of female sexual functioning—but also by highlighting the limitations of linear realist and naturalist narrative forms. Both writers use the short story form (to which late-nineteenth-century women writers contributed innovatively)[11] as a means of feminizing fiction writing, and their narratives anticipate subsequent modernist techniques. Their stylistic and thematic differences reveal the contrasts between writing from imperial and colonial contexts, and the effect this contrast has upon the potential scope for rendering women's experiences in an imaginary located beyond patriarchal culture.

Pregnancy and childbirth still remained the one area of which men could have no firsthand knowledge. However, the increased interventions of male-dominated social institutions claiming authority and expertise ensured that pregnancy became increasingly scrutinized and supervised in both Britain and Australia. Men dominated representations of both nation building and maternity. At the source of empire, the ideological function of the male-authored imperial mother responded to a falling birth rate, disastrous performance by troops in the Boer War,[12] and increasing infant mortality in poor social sectors.[13] Anna Davin's groundbreaking essay "Imperialism and Motherhood" identifies motherhood as a crucial aspect of both the iconography and practice of empire maintenance in the late nineteenth and early twentieth centuries. The mother was ascribed a responsibility for imperial race-rearing. While the entrapment of biology

---

[11] Investigations into the late-nineteenth-century short story form in relation to Egerton include Wendell Harris, Ann Heilmann, Iveta Jusova, Rosie Miles, and Charlotte Rich.

[12] See Arnold White: "In Manchester district 11,000 men offered themselves for war service between the outbreak of hostilities in October 1899 and July 1900. Of this number 8000 were found to be physically unfit to carry a rifle and stand the fatigues of discipline" (102–3). Sir John Frederick Maurice in "Where to Get Men" and "National Health: A Soldier's Study" highlights the two most common grounds for rejection of potential army recruits (bad teeth and flat feet) as attributable to an inadequate supply of milk during infancy and the ignorance of mothers in caring for their babies. Late-twentieth-century women historians Carol Dyhouse, Jane Lewis, and Pat Thane have comprehensively addressed how this dilemma created patterns of social control based upon maternal supervision.

[13] See *Maternity: Letters from Working Women,* edited by Margaret Llewelyn Davies. This collection testifies to the experiences of working-class motherhood in the last decade of the nineteenth century.

was insurmountable for women, the circumstances in which maternity was fulfilled differed greatly according to class. The malnourishment of working-class manhood was attributed to working-class women's "mal" mothering and as working-class women needed improving in their mothering skills, middle-class women were deemed ideally able to undertake an imperial mission to tutor them. By the end of the century, all women appear to have been telescoped into the role of mother. This became a dominant paradigm for women, whether as biological mothers giving birth and rearing children, as sisters vigilant over the moral purity of their brothers, or as social workers and welfare instructors.[14] Thus, the future of the empire became the responsibility of women via motherhood, and they were urged to excel in this capacity. A range of medical and didactic texts, produced by both women and men, sought to prescribe optimal mothering practices,[15] addressing a middle-class audience at a time when concerns about working-class motherhood were being implemented in interventionist social policy.[16] Medically trained and untrained women writers produced extensively in this genre in the late nineteenth century—whether or not they had actually experienced childbirth themselves.[17] As

---

[14] By 1909, Sir John Seelby had coined the term "Army of mothers" and in 1912 Dr. Caleb Saleeby referred to "virgin mothers" (*Woman and Womanhood*), acknowledging the network of unmarried, childless women who operated as social health missioners and maternal supervisors.

[15] A range of these include: *Maidenhood and Motherhood* by Mrs. Robert Stephenson (1887), *Woman in Health and Sickness: or What She Ought to Know for the Exigencies of Daily Life* by Robert Bell, MD (1889), *Motherhood: A Book for Every Woman* by Dr. Alice Ker (1891), *A Woman's Words to Women* by Dr. Mary Scharlieb (1895), *Educate Our Mothers or Wise Motherhood* by Mrs. Hannah Pearsall Smith (1896), *The Power of Womanhood; or, Mothers and Sons* by Ellice Hopkins (1899), *Motherhood* by Charles J. Gleeson, MD (1901), and *Feminology: A Guide for Womankind, Giving in Detail Instructions as to Motherhood, Maidenhood, and the Nursery* by Dr. Florence Dressler (1903).

[16] These texts presuppose, for the most part, that all women require educating in maternity and that working-class motherhood threatens to be the most inadequate sector in this respect. They fashion motherhood into a specialization for women under the ideological guise that this is to be their foremost contribution to empire maintenance. Intriguingly, they frequently downplay the crucial function of girls in the continuation of the male-centered empire (except as producers of sons) in their advocacy of the ideal—an indefatigable, thrifty, energetic, and devoted motherhood—one which many of the recipients of the advice would have found to have been at odds with actual mothering experiences.

[17] This customarily positioned nineteenth-century women's maternity in relation to the male-dominated medical profession whether or not the doctors happened to be women. Practical handbooks from the *fin-de-siècle* period (which were generally produced by medical experts) tend to approach pregnancy and childbirth as potentially a diseased state or as an anatomical description. One example, *A Handbook for Mothers: Being Simple Hints to Women on the Management of Their Health during Pregnancy and Confinement* (1893) by Jane H. Walker, MD, devotes only 13 pages (out of 199) to labor and childbirth.

didactic manuals have long instructed women in submissiveness, this manifestation was a means to ensure that women perform as strongly and creditably as possible within their narrow role as mother. The colonial context also registered anxieties regarding its Anglo-Saxon population. As the British Inter-Departmental Committee on Physical Deterioration (1903) ascertained, the causes "which led to the rejection of so many recruits for the army on the grounds of physical disability" (Nicholls 75), the New South Wales Royal Commission on the Decline of the Birth-Rate (1903) in Australia grew out of concerns regarding a decrease in the white population.[18] A constituent of the colonizing enterprise, motherhood crucially legitimized invaders' claims to invaded territories. A nation of white people was literally created (and imported) while the black indigenous population was concurrently decimated through genocide and miscegenation.[19]

However, the Australian colonial context produced intricacies of population growth and decline that were vastly different than those in Britain, derived as they were from a legacy of genocidal settlement policies as well as franchised white female citizenry, beneficiaries of reformist political agendas.[20] As black mothers were discouraged from producing and raising their families through the policies of miscegenation and dispersal introduced from the early twentieth century, white women were scrutinized for restricting their pregnancies. Sue Rowley charts how pregnancy and childbirth increasingly became the State's responsibility: "Over the decade of the 1890s, women's practices of birth control and family limitation became *public* knowledge, and men began to formulate a role for themselves in controlling reproduction" (89). As Neville Hicks notes, the Royal Commission's report concluded that "the cause or causes of the Decline of the Birth rate must be a force or forces over which the people themselves have control" (21).

The Australian press did not directly connect female fertility with a perceived demise in population growth. Nor was the mother represented

---

[18] For accounts of the population debate, see Bain Attwood, C. L. Bacchi, Mary Cawte, Colin Forster, and Neville Hicks.

[19] Henry Reynolds and David Day have sought to estimate the actual decimation of the black indigenous population as a result of colonization. Highlighting the catastrophic reduction in numbers, Day writes, "It was estimated that there were just 60,000 Aborigines remaining in Australia by 1888. The estimates of the Aboriginal population in 1788 vary from 300,000 ... to the more recent estimates of between 750,000 and 1,500,000.... By 1860, some 4,000 pastoralists with their 20 million sheep had occupied 400 million hectares of inland Australia" (130).

[20] Australian women gained the vote decades before their British and American counterparts. For a contemporary account of the political context, see William Pember Reeves.

unilaterally as a site of blame as she was in Britain. The *Sydney Morning Herald* identified drought conditions and compulsory unionism as the primary reasons for nonimmigration from Europe (hence affecting population growth), rather than women's lack of reproduction or inadequate child rearing. Letters from readers to various mainstream newspapers voiced concerns over emigration from the state of New South Wales as emanating from the government's favorable bias toward workers rather than women's reluctance to subscribe to maternity.[21] Just as late-nineteenth-century Australian white women took the lead with contraception and pregnancy termination in marriage, they exercised their political and employment rights. In an era of reformist politics, paid working women were present in vast numbers in the Australian state machinery of health, education, municipal authorities, and public service so that the reproduction of the State did not merely entail choosing marriage as it had earlier in the century.[22] The differing approaches of the Australian political state toward its population produced manipulations of women and children that contrasted to the British system.

While similarities *are* identifiable in concerns expressed over urban public health and infant mortality rates in fledgling Australian coastal cities, the example of the white settler rural mother—central to Baynton's short story—offers a unique strand to the fabric of women's history at this time. Baynton's literary representation of experiences outside the cultural mainstream entered the slipstream of white pioneer women's resilience and contemporary motherhood discourse. With their portrayals of a pregnant woman, Baynton's "A Dreamer" and Egerton's "A Cross Line" explore this relatively occluded dimension—a woman's approaching maternity, at a time when the connection between articulations of nationhood and motherhood proved intimate.

---

[21] The range of correspondence on this subject may be sampled in the following newspapers: *Sydney Morning Herald,* March 21, 1903, 10C, July 24, 4B, July 29, 9G, July 30, 8C; *Daily Telegraph,* March 28, 1903, 8E, June 17, 10D, June 18, 3G, June 19, 8D, June 25, 3G, June 27, 11F, June 30, 8D, July 2, 6C, July 7, 3E, July 8, 9D, July 11, 13D, July 14, 8C, July 15, 5B, July 31, 3A, July 27, 5F, July 29, 6C and 9G, July 30, 7C; and the *Evening News,* March 18, 1903, 4A, July 16, 4A, July 23, 4A, July 31, 4A, and August 3, 4A.

[22] See Alistair Davidson and Luke Trainor. Edna Ryan has drawn attention to the multitudes of women workers who were excluded from official statistics as they were engaged in "invisible work" such as prostitution and also home industries: child minding, and fostering of children for which the government paid relatively well. She notes that "[b]etween 1891 and 1901 'only 6,000 men moved to Sydney as against 17,000 women.' . . . This had the effect upon the service sector of the workforce which increased in size without the wages bill to employers increasing to the same extent" (262).

"A Cross Line" and "A Dreamer"

Although they were born and raised in Australia, Baynton and Egerton spent the majority of their adult lives in England and Europe, were often first published in London, and received acclaim for their work there. Susan Sheridan has noted how Australian colonial women writers such as Ada Cambridge, Rosa Praed, and "Tasma"—contemporaries of both Egerton and Baynton—faced an oft-repeated charge that they "wrote for an English audience" as they were published by houses like Heineman and were included on the circulation lists of Mudie's and other libraries (Sheridan 51). Even contemporary critics have perceived an imperial-centered derivativeness. Attributing this to economics, John Scheckter refers to the "subsidiary nature of much colonial publishing," which led many authors to write for "English and imperial markets, rather than for local Australian audiences; not wanting to appear unsophisticated or provincial, such writers tended to adopt a detached, touristic, and often ironic viewpoint based upon English models and English values" (20). Egerton and Baynton's two stories undo Scheckter's claims. The alternative writing strategies these women writers employ reveal an attempt to access subject matter and themes beyond that which can be articulated in the realist mode, and in ways not necessarily registered or sustained in contemporary novels.

Innovations that emerged from colonial marginality were in tension with the imperial halter that was placed around the necks of many British-based writers. Baynton's story is necessarily articulated using the recognizable cultural forms and expected content for a woman writer available to her in the late nineteenth century. Yet in rendering a woman's relationship to her unborn child, the Australian bush context and its challenge to imperial domestic roles serves Baynton well, so that she represents what is a traditionally hidden and essentialized dimension of women's experience more radically than in Egerton's European setting. In representing this relationship, Baynton's text offers an example of female sexual functioning that dismantles the dominance of masculinist cultural agendas in which female identity is signified solely by a woman's relation to a man. Baynton's heroine's instinctive desires and sexual power are transferred to the bond with her mother and unborn child, producing a spiritual and imaginative continuum which excludes the male presence. In contrast, Egerton's narrative figures the pregnant woman only in relation to men, whether as potential lover or actual father of her unborn child, figuring female sexuality as dependent upon a heterosexual completion as a couple, even after conception. Although alluding to the protagonist's pregnancy, Egerton scripts a conservative outcome in the family triad of mother-father-child as the heroine suppresses her desires after she realizes she is pregnant.

Both short stories present nameless pregnant women who do not actually give birth within the scope of the narrative and whose state creates a yearning for their own (dead) mothers.[23] They disengage their heroines from the generalizing ideology of motherhood to focus upon personal desire, individual experience, and their relation to their approaching maternity. The women are, however, denied the inheritance of and access to their mothers' knowledge of childbirth. While the female protagonist's consciousness is central to both narratives, Egerton's use of asterisks to fragment her text creates elliptical points, gaps in her narrative and in the female and male characters' understandings of each other. Her use of parentheses, reminiscent of stage directions in plays, underscores her instruction to the reader as to how the interactions are to be read.

"Do not I understand you a little?"
"You do not misunderstand me."
"That is something."
"It is much!"
"Is it? (searching her face). It is not one grain of sand in the desert that stretches between you and me, and you are as impenetrable as the sphinx at the end of it. This (passionately) is my moment, and what have you given me?" (25)

The economy of detail and lack of orientation tempt the reader to work through a maze of minimal clues like an eavesdropper upon a conversation, encouraging an unconscious scrutiny of how one reads, the tools that are used, to forge a satisfactory relationship with a text and make it meaningful. While Egerton's episodic narrative technique might defy the ordering imposition of realist linearity, it creates a logical progression in its own terms. As only the reader and the protagonist are privy to the compromise the author creates, the fragmentation produces a bond rather than distance between them. As shall be demonstrated, this indeterminacy between the actual female and male speakers contrasts with the communion Baynton's heroine achieves through exclusively female-female (daughter-mother) identification. Egerton's woman's impending maternity forces her to accept crossed lines of communication with her husband—"he looks uneasily at

---

[23] Egerton's mother died when she was sixteen, eighteen years before she wrote "A Cross Line." As a result, Rich notes that "she played the role of stepmother to a large number of younger siblings" (123).

her, but doesn't know what to do" (32)—compared to her potential lover, whose vision of their life together excites "the freedom, the freshness, the vague danger, the unknown that has a witchery for me, ay, for every woman!" (27). Her fantasy of taking power and running away with him is unrealized.

Although Egerton may be "positing inherent erotic and/or maternal desires and female identity grounded in sexuality," as Kate McCullogh suggests (206), the woman's desires are curtailed by the limitations of her material reality—a wife and hence financially dependent upon her husband. Egerton sets her protagonist's unexpected pregnancy against her sexual desire rather than incorporating maternity as an aspect of female sexuality. McCullogh attributes this complex tension as emanating from "the outsider's critique of dominant British gender codes" which she supports with reference to Egerton's own multinational and multicultural life experiences (207). Indeed, Egerton's "outsider" experience of living in Norway and settling in England has been well documented; yet the fact that she was born and raised in Australia remains primarily unregistered. Eurocentric literary criticism does not engage with this greater dimension of Egerton's personal migration pattern, one which embraces experience of being a colonized *and* gendered subject. Although Jusova argues in detail that Egerton—as daughter of a Welsh woman and an Irish man—defies an imperial identity,[24] she ignores her initially colonial one.

While Egerton uses the situation of her protagonist to probe the constraints around the subversive potential of female sexual identity, her pregnant woman is uneasy with her condition. McCullough suggests that Egerton depicts maternal desire as the most authentic, natural state for a woman; that this is a valorizing representation which incorporates a concurrent sense of self-loss. However, Egerton has set textual parameters of conflicting inner desires and external compromise. As a writer she falls short of the potential of her project to redefine womanhood; to create a viable Everywoman as a motif to which male social-shaping has no direct access. Later she reflected upon her aims and disingenuously claimed, "[O]ne is bound to look at life through the eyes of one's sex, to toe the limitations imposed on one by its individual psychological functions. I came

---

[24] Jusova argues that "her mother being from Wales, her father a rebellious, bohemian, and penniless Irishman with scorn for conventional English tastes and values, and herself born in Australia, where the relations between Irish and English populations were particularly vexed—served to problematize any simple sympathetic identification with English bourgeois interests and conventional sensibilities" ("George Egerton," 28), to deliver a somewhat simplistic glossing over of the demographic, national, and cultural affiliations that comprised Egerton's native context.

too soon.... I would unlock a closed door with a key of my own fashioning. I did. My imitators forged theirs to a different end" (Gawsworth 58).

In contrast to Egerton's heroine, Baynton's nameless, pregnant protagonist experiences desire for the motherhood that her own mother has already experienced in a matrilinear narrative. "A Dreamer" portrays a female subjectivity that reaches beyond realist narrative conventions to render an experience culturally coded as unknowable—a woman's anticipation of childbirth—and articulates her relationship to her own mother and the unborn child she carries. The title evokes the realm of unconscious yearning activated in the heroine, simultaneously suggesting the impossible wish of reexperiencing the all-powerful maternal presence of infancy that she herself now provides her own unborn child. In doing so, Baynton reworks a number of literary conventions which characterize late-Victorian women's writing through the imagery, activity, subject matter, and context she renders. It is clear, both literally and literarily, that the challenge to the domestic desideratum posed by the Eurocentric New Woman figure already had a practical and circumspect working model of resistance in the Australian Bush Woman. Conditions endured by women in isolated locales challenged the idea that women should not undertake manual work, irrespective of social position. Contrary to advice offered in *The Australian Baby* (1902) by Mrs. Annie Everett Ellis—that the prenatal woman should "[g]ive up her more feverish pleasures" (12)—Baynton's solitary pregnant woman battles unaided through a stormy night, in an isolated bush landscape, to cross a flooded river to visit her mother whom she has neglected. The boundaries between incorporeal and tangible, reality and imagination are continually blurred as the woman attempts to negotiate the countryside of her girlhood, which is now unfamiliar.

The power and agency of maternal protection is recorded in the woman's pysche as she struggles through the storm of the antagonistically personified landscape. A cacophony of maternal voices protectively surrounds her. First, "From the branch of a tree overhead she heard a watchful mother-bird's warning call" (46), followed by "'Bless, pardon, protect and guide, strengthen and comfort!' Her mother's prayer" (48), and "Then a sweet dream-voice whispered 'Little woman!'"(50). Baynton narrates the daughter as *actively* identifying with her mother through her own impending motherhood as she faces near death in the flooded river. Resisting the essentializing alignment of women with nature, Baynton's protagonist exerts her defiant will against the climatic, geographical hindrances and the supposed encumbrance of her own pregnant body. This heroine challenges notions of conventional female passivity and private domesticity that prevailed in didactic texts and acceptable models of

Victorian femininity. Baynton's story also portrays a female subjectivity that transcends patriarchal imperatives—that of a woman's relationship to her own mother, intensified because of her own unborn child. Baynton's story activates Egerton's *"terra incognita* of herself." Frost might argue that "[t]he images convey feeling without analysing it. This is a difficulty with the story as a whole. Too many questions are left unanswered" (63). Yet to focus primarily upon conventional literary standards is to disable the rare perspective the story offers. Gaps or fault lines that gesture toward marginalized stories frequently represent distinctive female experience—areas of the narrative that evoke rather than explain.

As Baynton's pregnant woman defies nature, Egerton conversely consolidates the link of women to nature. Birth in this story is transcribed in terms of animals' parallel experience. Nature functions as tutor to humans in birth and nurture, demonstrated in a hen and its chicks, which stir the husband's paternal feelings. His delight in the newborn chicks contrasts with the revulsion the woman feels.

> "Aren't they beauties (enthusiastically)? This one is just out" showing her how it is curled in the shell, with its paddles flattened and its bill breaking through the chip, and the slimy feathers sticking to its violet skin.
>
> She expresses an exclamation of disgust, and looks at his fresh-tinted skin instead. He is covering the basket, hen, and all. (9)

His first response to her nausea is, "'What is it' (anxiously)? '[I]f you were a mare I'd know what to do for you. Have a nip of whisky?'" (8). Concealing the graphic reality of the chicks' birth from the woman evokes Victorian social mores, which discouraged women's knowledge of their own physical functioning. Unlike Baynton's heroine, whose "elated body quivered" (47), Egerton's protagonist displays no sense of elation at her pregnancy. Her impending motherhood in fact creates a desire for escape from all maternal markers. As an overt and tangible outcome of female sexuality, pregnancy is not celebrated but acquiesced to. This attitude undermines Martha Vicinus's assertion that "Egerton was never interested in guilt or punishment; rather, her works celebrate the potential in women, not the possibly debilitating consequences of living the life of a New Woman in an old world" (Vicinus ix).

Baynton, in contrast to Egerton, removes her character from the contexts of class and gender roles so that the woman is left with one truth—that she will be a mother and she has a mother. However, fused with this indubitable prospect of mothering-motherhood-nurture is an incipient threat to this sense of continuity in neglect—death—motherlessness. The precariousness and arbitrariness of the outside world operates at counterpoint to this inner certainty as the heroine negotiates once-familiar surroundings.

> Once she had known every hand at the station. The porter knew everyone in the district. This traveller was a stranger to him.
>
> If her letter had been received, someone would have been waiting with a buggy. [S]he saw nothing [p]erhaps the porter had a message! [H]e was locking the office door, but paused as though expecting her to speak. [S]he hastily left him. (45–46)

Baynton loads up the signs of impending loss. The woman in particular notices the funeral parlor workers: "They work late tonight, she thought, and, remembering their gruesome task, hesitated, half-minded to ask these night workers, for whom they laboured. Was it someone she had known?" (46). The ownerless dog with whom she shares a feeling of kinship and the "watchful mother-bird's warning call" (46) all serve to underscore the isolation of the woman and herald her ultimate orphaning.

The woman's relationship with the forces of nature, encompassed by the bush landscape, is uneasy. She keeps losing her bearings and then remembering them. Her memory is fallible and the landmarks illuminated by the lightning, questionable. "Still it was the home of her girlhood, and she knew every inch of the way. [S]he went on, then paused. Was she on the right track? . . . [W]hen she should have been careful in her choice, she had been absorbed. . . . [I]f this was the right way, the wheel-ruts would show. . . . [S]he believed, she hoped, she prayed, that she was right" (47–48). This uncertainty parallels her initially divided loyalties. She is torn between consideration of her husband and child and her urgent quest to reach her mother in such adverse weather. However, the quest for reunion with her mother surpasses all. "What mattered the lonely darkness when it led to mother! [H]er mouth grew tender, as she thought of her husband she loved, and of their child. Must she dare! She thought of the grey-haired mother [T]his dwarfed every tie that had parted them" (49). The communion the woman seeks privileges an intergenerational continuum between women as being of paramount importance over the husband-wife bond. Baynton's aesthetic is unambiguously matrilineal.

"A Cross Line" infuses the pregnant woman's sexual power in her fantasy of unobtainable and objectified femme fatale figures: Cleopatra and a Salome-like figure who "bounds forward and dances, bends her lissom waist, and curves her slender arms, and gives to the soul of each man what he craves, be it good or evil" (21). In contrast, "A Dreamer" portrays ecstasy and reverence in the anticipation of reaffirming daughterhood and motherhood. Baynton employs extreme language to denote the excitement of the woman's pregnancy and her anticipated reunion. The daughter worships her mother at the time when her own body is becoming one.

> "Daughter!"
> "Mother!"
> She could feel loving arms around her, and a mother's sacred kisses. She thrilled, and in her impatience ran. [T]hen the child near her heart stirred for the first time. The instincts of motherhood awakened in her. Her elated body quivered. (46–47)

Baynton places the anticipated reunion in the realm of the sacred, which in turn introduces the reader to the woman's pregnancy and shifts the parameters of expectation about what her body should and should not do. The impetus for her character's desperate actions almost surpasses the means that Baynton has—as a late-Victorian female writer—to narrate them. To render this mother-child bond across two generations, she evokes other areas of heightened human emotion: religious experience and facing one's own mortality. The heroine's ambivalent relationship with the elements further severs the late-nineteenth-century ideological shackling of women to biological essentialism. The storm simultaneously aids and impedes her in her quest: "An angled line of lightning illuminated everything, but the violence of the thunder distracted her" (47). The wind carries her forward yet takes her breath away. This dynamic causes her to doubt her instincts in negotiating her route, and there are terrors in the tempest. "Malignantly the wind fought her, driving her back, or snapping the brittle stems from her skinned hands. The water was knee-deep now, and every step more hazardous" (49). To defy the inclement weather and dangers of the flooded river, she draws totally upon the inspiration derived from the transcendental identification with her mother. Her physical endeavors serve as her penance for her prior neglect of her mother—"There was atonement in these difficulties and dangers. . . . [L]ong ago she should have come to her old mother and, her heart gave a bound of savage rapture in thus giving the sweat of her body for the sin of her soul" (49).

The personification of nature and the geography throughout, and the woman's personal battle against the storm, blur the boundaries between human and natural world so that there is overwhelmingly a sense of *will,* a quality more generally associated with masculinity.[25] As the heroine faces death, it is her mother's voice whispering "Little woman" that refocuses

---

[25] See Hein.

her and enables her to reach the other side of the river. Yet she arrives too late. Her mother is already dead: "The daughter parted the curtains, and the light fell on the face of the sleeper who would dream no dreams that night" (53). Because mother and daughter are not reunited, their spiritual bond remains an idealization, a fantasy of matrilineality. The cultural occlusion of the mother-daughter bond is greater than the individual project written against it.

Like Egerton, Baynton produced her text at a time when motherhood and maternity were key issues for women reformers and constituted an area of anxiety. Motherhood as most desirable endpoint for a woman's destiny was concurrently challenged by the late-nineteenth-century exceptions to this role—evident in aspects of the New Woman figure and the suffrage and socialist movements. Baynton's pregnant woman *is* fulfilling her natural biologically prescribed role as conservative discourse would deem most appropriate, yet she is not behaving as convention and medical and didactic texts would have advocated. Mrs. Ellis declares that "[i]t behoves every wife the instant she knows she is about to become a mother, to set the house of her health into as perfect order as it is in her power to do" (9). The pregnant woman in Mrs. Ellis's text must aim to keep herself continually placid, serene, and trustful, for fear of passing on negative characteristics through a concept of heredity that is channeled into prenatal maternal behavior and attitudes. Baynton subverts the notion of delicacy, modesty, and passivity ascribed to pregnant women. There is no sense that the woman's pregnant body hinders her. Further, while the storm unequivocally hampers her journey, her primary concern is shown not to be that of potentially losing her child but rather that loss of her own life will prevent her reunion with her mother. The references to her mother evoke the self-sufficient bush woman who copes with all tasks, an adaptive feminine subjectivity and a common motif in *fin-de-siècle* Australian literature. There is no male presence in Baynton's narrative except for the porter at the train station and the mention of the pregnant woman's husband. The woman recalls her childhood only in terms of her mother planting trees along the riverbank, fixing overflowing tanks, and diverting water during floods for the drier months—a skill which the woman herself has acquired.

> Why had not mother diverted the spout to the other tank!
> Something indefinite held her. Her mind went back to the many times long ago when she had kept alive the light while mother fixed the spout to save the water that the summer months made precious. . . . After she had seen mother, she would come out and fix it. . . . (52)

Egerton's heroine by contrast is still in the throes of morning sickness, "stopped every moment by a feeling of faintness" (30). Her pregnancy is morbidly oppressive to her: "And what a sickening pain she has; an odd pain. . . . Supposing she were to die. . . . Strange how things come to life . . . she buries her face in her hands and sits so long a time" (33). She is suffocated by the diminished identity that her motherhood will offer her while she yearns for "the freedom, the freshness, the vague danger, the unknown that has a witchery for me, ay, for every woman!" (27).

Egerton's story opens with a contrast between female and male modes of perception. The protagonist is daydreaming and evoking imaginary interior worlds that transport her beyond her immediate surroundings. Her first perception of the stranger (who becomes her potential lover) is aural as he disturbs her reverie. "It seems profane, indelicate, to bring this slangy, vulgar tune, and with it the mental picture of footlight flare and fantastic dance into the lovely freshness of this perfect spring day . . . why, it is like the entrance of a half-tipsy vagabond player . . .—the picture is blurred" (1–2). Egerton's omniscient narration is impressionistically rendered from the outset, and here she makes the first of many references to the woman's active fantasizing as a means of transporting her from a mundane actuality. "Her mind is nothing if not picturesque; her busy brain, with all its capabilities choked by a thousand vagrant fantasies, is always producing pictures and finding associations between the most unlikely objects" (1). Egerton employs the technique of direct speech without indicating who says what, thus making the reader a witness to an oral exchange, which she punctuates with free indirect narration and impressions focalized through either character.

> A pause. His quick glance has noted the thick wedding ring on her slim brown hand, and the flash of a diamond in its keeper. A lady decidedly. Fast? perhaps. Original? undoubtedly. Worth knowing? rather. . . .
>
> "Trout run big here?" (what odd eyes the woman has, kind of magnetic.)
>
> "No, seldom over a pound, but they are very game."
>
> "Rare good sport isn't it, whipping a stream? . . . "
>
> She smiles assentingly. And yet what the devil is she amused at he queries mentally. (5)

As a potential disruption to her marriage, the man disturbs the clarity of her wifely identity by activating her desire for freedom. The domesticity she finally chooses because she is pregnant refocuses her fantasizing energies onto preparing baby clothes and expelling the marker of her sexual power, the potential lover. Egerton conveys the agitated isolation this produces—"oh, she wants some one so badly to soothe her"—which results in a yearning for the impossible, "[t]he little mother who is twenty years under the daisies" (52). Her pregnancy evokes death and isolation, not only that of her mother but also the death of her individual self and her desires. This is distinct from the kind of isolation that the colonial prenatal mother faces in Baynton's text, which clearly derives from her trek in the bush where her pregnancy is incidental to her overall mission.

Egerton's impressionistic technique seems to have failed to sustain a whole body of work, to render viable alternatives to a patriarchal cultural repertoire. In the opinion of Elaine Showalter, Egerton and other radical women writers of the *fin-de-siècle* "have not fared well with posterity" (194). Egerton's career was brief and Showalter feels that "her lack of growth seems perversely deliberate" (124) as, "In the end, she could not please anyone" (215). A. A. Phillips similarly described the "lack of bulk" of Barbara Baynton's fiction (Baynton 30). Egerton anchored her work in female subjectivity. Although she contributed to the short story genre in ways that anticipate modernist introspection and incompleteness, her creativity seems to have been curtailed as she curtails the desires of her heroine in "A Cross Line." Having supported herself through writing after achieving success in the 1890s, she lived until 1945 without ever replicating her *fin-de-siècle* fame with the reading public.

Until the late twentieth century, women rarely wrote explicitly about pregnancy in fiction. The textual enigma of childbirth points to its existence beyond the cultural forms available to late-Victorian and early-Edwardian colonial women. Records of childbirth are at best rare and euphemistic or metaphorical. Modesty, the crucial signifier of Victorian femininity, inhibited the widespread articulation of such material. Written accounts primarily resided in journal entries, advice manuals, and letters—the traditional areas of women's writing that have fallen outside the generic boundaries of the conventional canon. Fictional renderings of pregnancy and childbirth are ambiguous and understated, never overtly represented. Childbirth itself does not occur within these narratives, and what to expect from the actual birth process is absent in both fiction and polemic. The focus is upon its result—the physical separation of the mother and child and the context of socialization, the family.

Woman's primary role as mother not only supports and advances imperial and colonial enterprises, but also is habitually underacclaimed and omitted from the concept of history making. The devaluing of the female creative metaphor, childbirth, to *re*production and not production within a patriarchal ordering, has consistently prevented the articulation and recognition of women's integral contribution, except to serve an ideological function. The persistent anchoring of women to biological inevitability meant that their contribution to late-nineteenth-century social and national development was limited. Although childbirth was a key dimension in establishing a white settler colony, its importance was devalued—maternity was simply something that women were born to and did not actively forge—whereas men built nations and made history through feats of conquest, agriculture, industrialization, and economics. In male-dominated discourse, women are represented as merely following the natural course their physiology dictates. Men, by contrast, create by overcoming the impossible (indigenous resistance or geographical hardship), their creativity emanating from an exertion of will. Through imposing form upon inchoate matter—discovering territories or building a nation—men achieve transcendence while women fulfill their natural function.

Maternity clearly requires alternative acts of enunciation when it is easily converted into male-dominated discourse. For this reason, these short stories represent an intriguing exception to the norm. As both demonstrate, "literary textual articulations" (Boehmer 23) of maternal experience can indeed rework conventional narrative forms or expose the limitations in rendering a female-only experience such as pregnancy. Baynton's text aspires to a sublimation of the mother-to-be that is beyond Egerton's representation, despite the latter's association with narrative innovations in representing *fin-de-siècle* women's psyche and sexuality. In contrast, Egerton's pregnant protagonist, oppressed and constrained by her condition, does not fulfill Egerton's own thesis that woman should map the terra incognita of herself. As a writer, Egerton sought to redefine womanhood as a hitherto uncharted subjectivity that male writers could not access. However, in her writing, her character's independence becomes curtailed into an unwelcomed and conventional domesticity.

Displaced from both imperial center and its replication in the colonial metropolis, Australian rural mothers negotiated vastly different circumstances socioeconomically and geographically to their British counterparts. Although attempts were made to maintain urban protocols, the link to the feminine civilizing role was frequently tenuous and necessarily reworked to ensure survival. Pioneer women survived in isolated and often dangerous climatic conditions. Baynton's literary representation acknowledges a version of this actuality—albeit dramatically rendered in gothic overtones. Women's daily realities and the ideologies transmitted in didactic texts produces an interface at which fictional renderings such as "A Dreamer" became possible. In portraying a pregnant woman's struggle with the forces of nature, and her willed transcendence to achieve a mother-daughter reunion against all physical and climatic odds, Baynton places her heroine in an Australian sublime in matrilineal terms. As Hein argues, the exertion of will to actively shape one's surroundings is customarily represented as a male-dominated experience, both in terms of social power and creativity. A final discouraging note is struck, however, for while the female characters resist the constraints of socially prescribed feminine behavior, the illusory quality evoked by the title "A Dreamer" and the woman's compromise in "A Cross Line" dilute their liberating potential.

Two short stories, of course, constitute only a sample of the power of the peripheral—women's writing, colonial women's writing—and its modes of self-invention within the context of the late empire. In noting the sociohistoric circumstances of late-nineteenth-century Australian women, Grimshaw and Evans suggest that the merit in reviewing certain women writers resides in the fact that "at specific moments, they did diverge from prevailing codes in ways that are worth noting." Moreover, these women "offered fragmentary alternative readings that contested spaces of the dominant colonial" (81) and, in Egerton's case, the imperial center. In differing degrees, Egerton's and Baynton's fiction exemplifies such divergences and underscores the significant ways in which maternity is an intrinsic constituent to any conceptualizing of the imperial-colonial enterprise. Through focusing upon women writers' articulations of pregnancy, preparations for maternity and responses to the prenatal mother-child bond, these stories acknowledge and restore a key aspect of white settler women's participation in Australian colonization to feminist literary history.

Works Cited

Attwood, Bain. "Aborigines and Academic Historians: Some Recent Encounters." *Australian Historical Studies* 94 (April 1990): 123–35.

Austin, A. G., ed. *The Webbs' Australian Diary* (1898). London, Bath: Sir Isaac Pitman, 1965.

Bacchi, C. L. "The Nature-Nurture Debate in Australia, 1900–1914." *Historical Studies* 19.75 (October 1998): 199–212.

Baynton, Barbara. "A Dreamer." In *Bush Studies*. Intro. A. A. Phillips. Melbourne: Angus and Robertson, 1902; repr. 1965. 45–53.

Boehmer, Elleke. *Empire, the National, and the Postcolonial (1890–1920): Resistance in Interaction.* Oxford: Oxford University Press, 2002.

Bolton, Geoffrey. *Spoils and Spoilers: Australians Make Their Environment 1788–1980.* Sydney: George Allen and Unwin, 1981.

Cadzow, Allison. "Footnoting: Landscape, Space and Writing in the Exploration Diary of Caroline Creaghe." *Southerly* 56.4 (Summer 1996): 219–33.

Cawte, Mary. "Craniometry and Eugenics in Australia: R. J. A. Berry and the Quest for Social Efficiency." *Historical Studies* 22.86 (April 1986): 35–51.

Coghlan, Timothy. *The Decline in the Birth-Rate of New South Wales and Other Phenomena of Childbirth*. Sydney: Government Printer, 1903.

———. *Childbirth in New South Wales. A Study in Statistics*. Sydney: Government Printer, 1900.

Cognard-Black, Jennifer, and Elizabeth MacLeod Walls, eds. *Kindred Hearts: Letters on Writing by British and American Women Authors, 1865–1935*. Iowa City: University of Iowa Press, 2006.

Davidson, Alistair. *The Invisible State: The Formation of the Australian State 1788–1901*. Cambridge: Cambridge University Press, 1991.

Davies, Margaret Llewelyn. *Maternity: Letters from Working Women*. London: G. Bell and Sons, 1915.

Davin, Anna. "Imperialism and Motherhood." *History Workshop Journal* 5.6 (1978): 9–65.

Day, David. *Claiming a Continent: A History of Australia*. Melbourne: Angus and Robertson, 1996.

Diaries of Ethel Turner. Ed. Philippa Poole. Sidney: Ure Smith, 1979.

Docker, John. *The Nervous Nineties*. Melbourne: Oxford University Press, 1991.

Dyhouse, Carol. *No Distinction of Sex? Women in British Universities, 1870–1939*. London: UCL Press, 1995.

———. *Feminism and the Family in England 1880–1939*. Oxford: Basil Blackwell, 1989.

———. *Girls Growing Up in Late Victorian and Edwardian England*. London: Routledge & Kegan Paul, 1981.

———. "Social Darwinistic Ideas and the Development of Women's Education in England 1880–1920." *History of Education* 5.1 (1976): 41–58.

Egerton, George. "A Cross Line." In *Keynote and Discords*. Intro. Martha Vicinus. London: Virago Press, 1983. 1–36.

———. "A Keynote to *Keynotes*." In *Ten Contemporaries: Notes toward Their Definitive Bibliography*. Ed. John Gawsworth. London: E. Benn, 1932. 58–60.

———. *Discords*. London: J. Lane, 1894.

———. *Keynotes*. E. Matthews and J. Lane, 1893.

Ellis, Mrs. Annie Everett. *The Australian Baby: A Handbook for Mothers*. London: Ward, Lock and Co., 1902.

Forster, Colin. "Aspects of Australian Fertility, 1861–1901." *Australian Economic History Review* 14.2 (September 1974): 105–22.

Friedman, Susan Stanford. "Creativity and the Childbirth Metaphor: Gender Difference in Literary Discourse." *Feminist Studies* 13 (1987): 49–82.

Frost, Lucy. "Barbara Baynton: An Affinity with Pain." In *Who Is She?* Ed. Shirley Walker. St. Lucia: University of Queensland Press, 1983. 56–70.

Gawsworth, John [Terence Armstrong]. *Ten Contemporaries: Notes toward Their Definitive Biography*. London: Joiner and Steele, 1933.

Grimshaw, Patricia, and Julie Evans. "Colonial Women on Intercultural Frontiers: Rosa Campbell Praed, Mary Bundock and Katie Langloh Parker." *Australian Historical Studies* 27.106 (April 1996): 79–95.

Grimshaw, P., M. Lake, J. McGrath, and M. Quartly. *Creating a Nation*. Melbourne: Penguin Books, 1994.

Hackforth-Jones, Penny. *Barbara Baynton between Two Worlds: A Biography*. Melbourne: Penguin Books, 1989.

Harris, Wendall V. "Egerton: Forgotten Realist." *The Victorian Newsletter* 33 (Spring 1968): 31–35.

———. *British Short Fiction in the Nineteenth Century: A Literary and Bibliographic Guide*. Detroit: Wayne State University Press, 1979.

Heilmann, Ann. *New Woman Fiction: Women Writing First-Wave Feminism*. London: Macmillan Press, 2000.

———. "Egerton: Forgotten Realist." *Victorian Newsletter* 33 (Spring 1968): 31–35.

Hein, Hilde. "The Role of Feminist Aesthetics in Feminist Theory." In *Feminism and Tradition in Aesthetics*. Ed. Peg Brand and Caroline Korsmeyer. University Park: Pennsylvania State University Press, 1995. 448–63.

Hicks, Neville. *"This Sin and Scandal": Australia's Population Debate 1891–1911*. Canberra: Australian National University Press, 1978.

James, Barbara. *No Man's Land: Women of the Northern Territory*. Melbourne: Collins Publishers, 1989.

Jusova, Iveta. *The New Woman and the Empire*. Columbus: The Ohio State University Press, 2005.

———. "George Egerton and the Project of British Colonialism." *Tulsa Studies in Women's Literature* 19 (2000): 27–55.

Kristeva, Julia. "Stabat Mater." In *The Kristeva Reader*. Ed. Toril Moi. New York: Columbia University Press, 1986. 160–86.

Lewis, Jane, ed. *Women and Social Action in Victorian and Edwardian England*. Aldershot: Edward Elgar, 1991.

———, ed. *Labour and Love: Women's Experience of Home and Family, 1850–1940*. Oxford: Basil Blackwell, 1986.

———. *Women in England 1870–1950: Sexual Divisions and Social Change*. Brighton: Wheatsheaf, 1984.

Magarey, Susan. "Sexual Labour: Australia 1880–1910." *Debutante Nation: Feminist Contests in the 1890s*. Ed. Magarey, Rowley and Sheridan. St. Leonards: Allen and Unwin, 1993. 91–99.

Maurice, Sir John Frederick ("Miles"). "National Health: A Soldier's Study." *Contemporary Review* 82 (January 1903): 41–56.

———. "Where to Get Men." *Contemporary Review* 81 (January 1902). 78–86.

McCullough, Kate. "Mapping the 'Terra Incognita' of Woman: George Egerton's *Keynotes* (1893) and New Woman Fiction." In *The New Nineteenth Century Feminist Readings of Underread Victorian Fiction*. Ed. Barbara L. Harman and Susan Myer. New York and London: Garland Publishing, 1996. 205–33.

Miles, Rosie. "George Egerton, Bitextuality and Cultural (Re)Production in the 1890s." *Women's Writing* 3 (1996): 243–59.

Nicholls, W. A. "Feeding of Public Elementary School Schildren—How Far an Educational Function?" In *Rearing an Imperial Race*. Ed. Charles H. Hecht. London: St. Catherine's Press, 1913. 75–90.

Old Housekeeper. *Men and How to Manage Them: A Book for Australian Wives and Mothers* Melbourne: Massina and Co., 1885.

———. *Australian Housewives' Manual* (1883). In *Freedom Bound I: Documents on Women in Colonial Australia*. Ed. M. Quartly, S. Janson, and P. Grimshaw. St. Leonards: Allen and Unwin, 1995. 119–22.

Phillips, A. A. "Barbara Baynton's Stories." In Baynton, *Bush Studies*, 27–42.

Reeves, William Pember. *State Experiments in Australia and New Zealand*. Vols. 1–2. London: Grant Richards, 1902.

Reynolds, Henry. *Dispossession: Black Australians and White Invaders*. St. Leonards: Allen and Unwin, 1989.

———. *Aborigines and Settlers: The Australian Experience 1788–1939*. Melbourne: Cassell, 1972.

Rich, Charlotte. "Reconsidering *The Awakening:* The Literary Sisterhood of Kate Chopin and George Egerton." *Southern Quarterly: A Journal of the Arts* 41.3 (Spring 2003): 121–36.

Rowley, Sue. "Inside the Deserted Hut: The Representation of Motherhood in Bush Mythology." *Westerly* 4 (December 1989): 76–96.

Ryan, Edna. "Women in Production in Australia." In *Australian Women: New Feminist Perspective*. Ed. Norma Grieve and Ailsa Burns. Melbourne: Oxford University Press, 1986. 258–72.

Saleeby, Caleb. *Woman and Womanhood: The Search for Principles*. London: William Heinemann, 1912.

Scheckter, John. *The Australian Novel 1830–1980: A Thematic Introduction*. Studies of World Literature in English Series. New York: Peter Lang Publishing, 1998.

Sheridan, Susan. "'Temper, Romantic; Bias, Offensively Feminine': Australian Women Writers and Literary Nationalism." In *A Double Colonization: Colonial and Post-Colonial Women's Writing*. Ed. Kirsten Holst Petersen and Anna Rutherford. London and Sydney: Dangaroo Press, 1986. 50–68.

Showalter, Elaine. *A Literature of Their Own: British Women Novelists from Brontë to Lessing*. Princeton: Princeton University Press, 1957.

Shuttleworth, Sally. "Demonic Mothers: Ideologies of Bourgeois Motherhood in the Mid-Victorian Era." In *Re-writing the Victorians: Theory, History, and the Politics of Gender*. Ed. Linda M. Shires. New York and London: Routledge, 1992. 31–51.

Spender, Dale. *The Writing or the Sex*. New York: Teachers College Press, 1989.

Thane, Pat, ed. *Foundations of the Welfare State*. London: Longman, 1982.

———. *The Origins of British Social Policy*. London: Croom Helm, 1978.

———. "Women and the Poor Law." *History Workshop Journal* 5, no. 6 (Autumn 1978): 29–51.

Thane, Pat, ed., with Gisela Bok. *Maternity and Gender Policies: Women and the Rise of the European Welfare States 1880s–1950s*. London: Routledge, 1991.

Todd, Janet. *British Women Writers: A Critical Reference*. New York: Continuum, 1989.

Trainor, Luke. *British Imperialism and Australian Nationalism: Manipulation, Conflict and Compromise in the Late-Nineteenth Century*. Cambridge: Cambridge University Press, 1994.

Vicinus, Martha. "Introduction." In *Keynotes* by George Egerton. London: Virago Modern Classics, 1983; repr. 1995. vii–xix.

Walker, Jane H. *A Handbook for Mothers: Being Simple Hints to Women on the Management of Their Health during Pregnancy and Confinement*. London: Longmans, Green and Co., 1893.

White, Arnold. *Efficiency and Empire*. London: Methuen and Co., 1901.

White, Terence de Vere, ed. *A Leaf from the Yellow Book: The Correspondence of George Egerton*. London: Richards Press, 1958.

CHAPTER 11

Orphan Stories and Maternal Legacies in Charlotte Brontë

MARY JEAN CORBETT*

Possessed by "Titan visions" (362) of "the first woman," "heaven-born," from whose "vast" heart "gushed the well-spring of the blood of nations" (360), Shirley Keeldar communes with her "mighty and mystical parent" (362) simply by lingering in the churchyard on a "warm summer evening": "She is taking me to her bosom," she tells Caroline Helstone, "and showing me her heart" (361). "Dreaming, too, in her way" (361), Caroline embodies her more modest "filial hopes" in "a gentle human form . . . unknown, unloved, but not unlonged-for" (362). Shirley's Eve—strong, daring, and vital mother of all living things—is an "undying, mighty being" (361) besides whom any human mother would appear small; when such a mother does materialize, she is much as Caroline pictured her. And although Agnes Pryor is no Titan, she is still more than adequate to her daughter's deepest wishes and speaks the sort of revivifying words Caroline had fantasized she might hear: "All the love you have needed, and not tasted, from infancy, I have saved for you carefully. Come! it shall cherish you now" (362).

The mother's miraculous return in *Shirley* (1849) restores her daughter to health by giving Caroline the reason to live that she has sorely lacked.

---

* My thanks to John Plotz and Leah Price for occasioning the longer essay from which this material is drawn, to Kelly Hager for supporting its development, and to Deborah Denenholz Morse for improving it by her insight and intelligence.

Yet when we situate that return in the context of the two younger women's distinct imaginings of maternal presence as creative power and sustaining love, Mrs. Pryor's representation of her unnecessarily prolonged absence from her daughter's life emphasizes by contrast her own failures. Having escaped an abusive husband, she indicts herself for a lack of "moral courage": "It is that which has made me an unnatural parent—which has kept me apart from my child during the ten years which have elapsed since my husband's death left me at liberty to claim her: it was that which first unnerved my arms and permitted the infant I might have retained a while longer to be snatched prematurely from their embrace" (492). Unlike Helen Huntingdon of *The Tenant of Wildfell Hall* (1848), who removes her son from his father's house without legal sanction in order to ensure his physical and moral safety, Agnes Helstone abandons her child to a fate she feels no ability to alter: "I let you go as a babe, because you were pretty, and I feared your loveliness; deeming it the stamp of perversity" (492). Once freed from "the yoke of the fine gentleman," she cannot "dare to encounter his still finer and more fairy-like representative" (492), for Caroline has inherited from her father "a certain manner as well as certain features," modified only by a gentle tone that he, too, could assume, but that, "when the world was not by to listen," would give way to "sounds to inspire insanity" (491). "A form so straight and fine, I argued, must conceal a mind warped and cruel," so that with "a strange, unmotherly resolve" (492), Agnes left her daughter in her brother-in-law's care even though she might have sought to take custody of Caroline immediately after her husband's death. Only now, in the novel's present, does she reverse her judgment that her child was not her own, having discovered herself "to be the parent of my child's mind" and deemed that "it belongs to me: it is my property—my *right*" (486; emphasis in original).

Like many actual nineteenth-century mothers, the fictional Agnes Helstone would not have had legal control of her child's person in the face of statutes that assigned to fathers alone the "right" to filial "property." Moreover, we can assume that, as a poor governess at the time of her marriage, Agnes would have had no access to the financial and familial resources that might have enabled her, like Helen Huntingdon, to hide herself and her daughter under the shelter of a brother's protection. Yet by her own account, she relinquished the baby girl she "might have retained a while longer" and failed "to claim her" as soon as she could for reasons over and above these legal and material impediments. Agnes has so internalized her own powerlessness that she disavows any share in her child, wrongly reasoning from the "air of native elegance" (493) she sees in Caroline's portrait that a child who displays all "the delicacy of an aristocratic flower" (492) would, like her father, turn out to "conceal a mind warped and cruel" and so, perhaps, would turn against her: "I thought perhaps you were all his . . . I find it is *not* so" (486; emphasis in original).

Recognizing her own "right" to and "property" in her adult daughter is, in effect, a matter of Mrs. Pryor finally being able to see *herself* in her child; to learn that Caroline has not inherited all from her father; to acknowledge her own share as "the parent of my child's mind," even if her actual, practical experience of parenting Caroline has been radically limited. "Unnatural" and "unmotherly" though it may have been for Agnes not to cling to her child for as long as she was able, or not to return to her as quickly as she could, her narrative suggests that ideological conceptions of the natural and the maternal—or the vision of the two as one that Shirley's Titan Eve instantiates—exist at some great distance from the experience of ordinary mothers. Their subjection to husbands, their limited means of support, and perhaps their own legacies of daughterly disinheritance may conspire to make mothers—even loving mothers—unable to understand themselves as having anything to bequeath to their daughters. What Agnes above all seems to fear, however, is that Caroline, in being her father's daughter, would reject, despise, and torment her in unnatural and unfilial fashion.

In Mrs. Pryor's story, Charlotte Brontë revises and expands a plot that had been foundational to her earlier writing, not just by resurrecting the mother on whose absence so many of her narratives were founded, but also by giving her a voice that expresses a variegated view of maternal powerlessness. In general, however, most of Brontë's writing from the juvenilia forward takes the parentless child as its focus rather than honing in on the perspective of the parent, shaped in part by generic models that foreground what Carolyn Dever has identified as "the *structural* advantages of maternal loss" for "Victorian melancholic fictions" (22). Heavily inflected by their literary and mythic antecedents, the multiple and various orphan stories that Brontë frames for her characters put those generic patterns to new uses in the narratives that unfold from them.[1] Many of Brontë's works participate in what Deborah Epstein Nord calls "a larger novelistic tradition of foundling or bastard plots, in which the hero of indeterminate or questionable origins discovers himself to be the (usually illegitimate) child of a well-born or aristocratic parent" (191). Thus in one of her early stories, "The Foundling" (1833), the protagonist eventually learns that he is the son of the Duke of York; he marries a noblewoman and inherits his rightful

---

[1] For discussions of the foundling plot in Brontë's fiction, see Clarke and Adams. Useful studies of the orphan plot include Howe and Peters.

position in an entirely conventional rendering of that paradigm. What's distinctive about the plot of the restored mother in *Shirley,* by contrast, is that the change in the gender of its key characters—mother and daughter rather than father and son—coincides with a change in the terms of what the child inherits and the parent regains: Caroline reunites with a mother decidedly not aristocratic, belatedly accessing love and nurture rather than fortune and status, while her mother discovers a spiritual rather than a material heir, and in doing so is enabled to identify and articulate a legacy of her own.

In the fairy tale that is *Jane Eyre* (1847), in which the mother stays dead but the father metaphorically lives on in the different forms of patriarchal inheritance, the orphan heroine need not choose between mutually exclusive alternatives: Jane gets both her rightful position and loving nurturance from two new families by novel's end. I will argue in what follows that it is primarily by successfully negotiating the structures that keep mothers dead and disempowered that Jane improves her fortunes. To establish a fuller context for images of maternal powerlessness and disinheritance in *Jane Eyre,* I juxtapose it with other orphan stories from the Brontë juvenilia, and specifically those that represent instances of cross-racial adoption in which a boy or girl, son or daughter, rebels against the imperial/patriarchal power structure with very mixed results, creating a series of cautionary tales for motherless children. In the juvenilia as in the adult fiction, orphans and adoptees clarify and criticize the racialized lines along which familial membership is drawn, in being differentiated from some families and affiliated with others. Gender, too, plays a critical role in determining the kind of access to racial and class privilege that adoptive and biological sons or daughters possess. But what most distinguishes Jane Eyre and, to a lesser extent, Lucy Snowe from their African antecedents is that despite a lack of power, these English heroines develop the means to tell their own stories, and thus rewrite the experience of being marginal to the family in ways that support the feminist critical contention that the mother's absence underpins the daughter's ability to shape her own path.[2] Although Brontë does create at least one dying African mother who articulates an anti-imperial legacy for her son and his adopted daughter, who aims to take up his mission, colonized adoptees are given much less access to narrative voice. Even if, as Susan Meyer suggests, the adoptees of the juvenilia both engage Brontë's imaginative sympathies and enact her recognition of the class and gender limits on her own privilege,[3] they are, in some sense, also

---

[2] Among a whole host of critical studies that consider motherlessness as a potentially enabling narrative structure, see especially Rich, Hirsch, Homans, and Dever.

[3] This, in brief, is the argument of Meyer's chapter on Charlotte Brontë's juvenilia (29–59).

colonized by Brontë's ability to appropriate other worlds for her fictional empire. That African orphans and adoptees are also identified as (or with) characters of color means that they enter into imperial families on even less advantaged terms than their European counterparts.

By juxtaposing figures from the juvenilia and the adult fiction, I aim to demonstrate nonetheless some important continuities in these orphan stories. Jane's own quest for kin, we should remember, moves her from one adoptive family to another, from a house in which, like Heathcliff, she had experienced herself as degraded almost to the status of a servant to a dwelling where she gains the power to make a family of her own and to confer that power on her paternal kin. Exposing the limits of blood relation, *Jane Eyre* pays particular attention to how differences between maternal and paternal lines of descent shape the contours of the orphan's plot by its juxtaposition of the mother's relations, the Reeds, and the father's relations, the Rivers. These symmetrical families of first cousins differ in almost every respect; moreover, in carefully distinguishing between those who do or do not "feel like" family, Brontë plays on two salient meanings of the term "affinity"—a natural "inclination or attraction" on the one hand, which Jane feels for the Rivers family, and a "relationship by marriage" on the other (*OED*), the customary obligations of which the Reeds do not honor. That Rivers and Reeds are differently and quite pointedly racialized also registers the experiences of exclusion and inclusion that Jane endures and enjoys, as a motherless daughter who eventually receives her patriarchal reward.

I.

The "really doleful" (22) ballad that Bessie sings to Jane Eyre laments the exile of the friendless orphan even as it allegorizes every Christian soul's journey to an eternal end. Propelled on its road "so far and so lonely" by the "hard-hearted" men who have denied it earthly sanctuary, the "weary" body makes its way across a "moonless and dreary" landscape; though the track is rugged, the cloudless, starry skies signify God's merciful "protection" (22). He will "take to His bosom the poor orphan child" should it stumble or stray from the path: "Of shelter and kindred despoiled" in this world, every orphan has a dwelling and a family in the next, for "Heaven is a home" and "God is a friend" (23). By learning to direct her thoughts upward on her own "dreary" journeys, Jane regains "shelter and kindred" in this world after leaving Gateshead, where she has felt herself "an uncongenial alien" (17) to her mother's brother's wife and children and rebelled against their authority. The ballad thus shapes the orphan's path by teaching her to read it as both an immediate paradigm of her experience and a figurative emblem for each individual's spiritual pilgrimage, initiating what Penny Boumelha terms "the providential theme" of the novel, "the story dispensed and directed by Our Father" (69). Every orphan, like every Christian, has a father (but no mother) in heaven with a mansion of many rooms; only the fortunate few find that sanctuary here below.

The Christian allegory thus effaces maternal origins in directing the soul's return to its true paternal home; whatever Jane's status in this world, her father in heaven provides an authoritative parentage and a consoling vision. But in another "doleful" song by Brontë, drawn from the massive collection of the siblings' juvenilia, "a dying woman's moan" that sounds "like a requiem for the dead" ("African" 6, 4) becomes the medium for shaping the orphan's story, entrusting her son not to heavenly refuge, but to earthly vengeance. In "The African Queen's Lament" (1833), the eponymous speaker interprets each natural sound—the "wild moan" of the palm trees, the "faint mingled cries" of the river—as "a sign, a warning token" (4) of a desired future in which her child will avenge his loss of shelter and kindred by his own hand rather than being solaced by any god's love. Widow of the murdered leader of the Ashantee forces defeated by the Twelves at the Battle of Coomassie, the mother implores her sleeping son to hear the "sound of prophecy / Which speaks of bloody recompense" (6) and enjoins him, once he reaches manhood, to "swift and bright as wand'ring star / Go piling heaps of dead" (5). Adopted by Brontë's fictive Duke of Wellington, "from whom he experienced as much care and tenderness as if he had been that monarch's son instead of his slave" ("Green Dwarf" 178), Quashia Quamina aims to live out the destiny his mother plans for him: "notwithstanding the care with which he had been treated by his conquerors"—most immediately, the duke and the rest of his adoptive family—"he retained against them, as if by instinct, the most deeply rooted and inveterate hatred" (179). Seeking to even the score for the double loss of a familial home and national autonomy, he raises an unsuccessful native rebellion against domestic/colonial authority and is executed by order of his foster brother Zamorna, biological son of the duke who had "nourished [Quashia] on his own hearth . . . with almost parental tenderness" (180).

Reading these two orphan stories together, we can see how Bessie's ballad suppresses particular elements—the race, gender, and origins of the orphaned adoptee among them—in order to achieve a universalizing tenor. Jane may enact this narrative because it belongs to no one in particular; and she may successfully revise it through her own experiences, needs, and desires because it belongs to everyone (or at least to every Christian) in general. Although Jane moves throughout the novel from one mother figure to another, each of them impresses her with a version of this same story: she is never without a heavenly father who counts her among his many children. The avenging mother of "The African Queen's Lament," by contrast, speaks from and about a specific experience of violence and destruction that both produces the orphan *as* orphan and foreordains him to carry on his dead father's legacy to fulfill her wish that he will his "father's mind [and] form, / His kingly soul inherit" (5); she creates her son in his father's image, to be sure, but it is her mournful rage that gives "form" to the father he will never know. While Jane makes earthly homes and finds congenial kindred by subduing the anger she feels as "an interloper" (17) at Gateshead, enacting a script of submission to the divine father, Quashia ultimately acts out a comparable rage, transmitted through his mother, in an effort to destroy the adoptive family that constitutes his oppression. He stages rebellion from within the very structures of imperial domination that aim to allay his "inveterate hatred" with the parental "care and tenderness" that forge his "gilded fetters" ("Green Dwarf" 178). Though he heard his mother's injunction to rebel as a child, when "he could not understand it" ("African" 3), Quashia "as if by instinct" internalizes the particular message of resistance, very different from Bessie's ballad, that the queen's voice conveys. If Jane's way is made smooth in part by her ability to identify and embrace an alternative narrative to the one that Gateshead writes for her, then Quashia remains wholly within his dead mother's paradigm; inciting rebellion among the Ashantees against the colonizers, who seek to produce the adoptee through "education and the upbringing in an Angrian court ... as *colonised* subject" (Azim 126; emphasis in original), her story, which becomes his, figures adoption as itself a colonizing enterprise.

Jane expresses her resistance to the unloving authority of the Reeds with unbridled resentment, which enables both her aunt and Brocklehurst to damn her as a heathen, a rebel, and a liar, and Quashia Quamina's hostility similarly functions for his adoptive family as a sign of a perverted nature that leads him to betray his benefactors. From the perspective of those who adopt him, the central motif of Quashia Quamina's story and the keynote of his character is treachery: "his mother's last advice will not, I imagine, be entirely lost upon him," the Duke of Wellington predicts, and "he may give our nation trouble yet" ("African" 3). "His disposition was bold, irritable, active, daring," and "at the age of seventeen" he had already "kindled in these wild savages a spirit of slumbering discontent and roused them to make an effort for regaining that independence as a nation which they had lost" ("Green Dwarf" 179). Although "A Leaf from an Unopened

Volume" (1834) portrays Quashia according to the conventions of noble savagery—as "a man in whose person all the virtues of savage life were so nobly united, even though it cannot be denied that he possessed likewise many of its concomitant vices" (326)—the overwhelming tenor of his representation in the juvenilia is as "the young viper," "deeply treacherous" ("Green Dwarf" 179), who foments rebellion in the service of his mother's dream of revenge against those who rescued and raised him. In the clash of perspectives that constitutes the Gateshead section of *Jane Eyre*, Brontë directs readerly sympathies toward the narrating Jane, but the particulars of Quashia's interior life are left opaque; it is only by virtue of "his mother's last advice" that we have access to an alternative story that counters the altogether negative representation of the adoptive child as an enemy within.

Still more obliquely, Quashia's "treachery" functions as part of a larger dynamic within the juvenilia that registers a series of tensions among the creole colonizers: the African adoptee figures one aspect of the rivalry between men that constitutes a recurring thematic in the representation of the family/empire, which also figures in different forms, as I will examine below, in the adult fiction. For Brontë and her erstwhile collaborator/competitor Branwell do not limit revengeful motives to Quashia alone, since Alexander Percy (later referred to as Northangerland) also figures as an internal enemy to Wellington's son Zamorna (also known as the Emperor Adrian). Their political opposition notwithstanding, Percy and Zamorna are inextricably intertwined through the marriages they arrange and contract for themselves or others, in which both daughters and sons function as instruments for consolidating power. For example, when Mary Percy marries Zamorna, Percy becomes grandfather to their many children; subsequently, Zamorna's eldest legitimate son by a previous wife marries another of Percy's daughters, not only further extending the web of familial relationships between these two leading men, but also intensifying their competition. In "The Green Dwarf" (1833), Percy betrays imperial interests by warning Quashia of Zamorna's plan to attack the rebels under cover of darkness. And when Zamorna's army catches up with the African forces the next day, Quashia declares that "freedom would this night have received her death-stab from the hand of the White Tyrant" (Zamorna) "had not a traitor" (Percy) "arisen in the camp of oppression" (188), albeit Percy's intervention only delays the rebels' imminent defeat. As Firdous Azim observes, the "fear of danger from outside (the unexplored and unsubdued natives) and from within (internal dissension, rivalries and corruption) . . . do not remain so schematically marked off from each other" (119); nor do treachery and loyalty break down neatly along racial lines.

The betrayals that both adoptive brother and father-in-law perform in "The Green Dwarf" take shape in "the camp of oppression," with their seeking to undermine the power of the Wellington line from within. The charges of treachery that cling to Quashia are thus made in turn against the other major rival to Zamorna's power, who, like the adoptee (albeit for different reasons), cannot be said to be wholly outside the parameters of the imperial family. Viewed in this light, relations by marriage and relations by adoption both mark the boundaries and threaten the security of the familial/colonial state.

As an orphan who turns on those who adopt/oppress him, Quashia clearly anticipates Heathcliff (a more successful plotter) as well as the young Jane, who attributes her vision of John Reed as "like a murderer... like a slave-driver... like the Roman emperors" to her reading of "Goldsmith's History of Rome" (11) rather than to her own creator's earlier creation of a "White Tyrant." And like those two other adoptees, Quashia also comes to function as an adoptive parent, bequeathing a legacy to his child that echoes his mother's wishes for him, although the gendered and racialized differences between father and daughter issue in decidedly different outcomes. Put to death by the Emperor Adrian at the very opening of "A Leaf" for his resistance to white rule, Quashia leaves behind a motherless daughter who seeks to avenge his death. Zorayda's narrative adheres to foundling conventions more closely than does Quashia's: while Quashia had retained the memory of his mother's injunction to revenge, Zorayda does not even know the story of her own birth, which is unfolded in the action of "A Leaf," and identifies entirely with her adoptive context.[4] Her mother leaves her nothing but a ring, which will subsequently provide evidence of her ancestry, while her allegiance to her African parent and her ultimate restoration to the care of her "true" father situate her as a counter within two competing patriarchal plots. Although Quashia's fate, as Azim has argued (132–36), is far more fatally fixed from the outset than Zorayda's, the specifics of her plot reveal a particularly feminine version of the orphan story in which the politics of racial identification and membership play a pivotal role.

If Quashia represents a sexual threat to white male prerogative both in Brontë's "Roe Head Journal" (ca. 1836) and at the outset of the novella *Caroline Vernon* (1839),[5] then Zorayda figures as a sexual object for white

---

[4] Although Plasa writes that "Zorayda believes herself to be the mixed-race child of a liaison between Quamina and a white woman" (6), I do not see any evidence in the text to support this idea, as Zorayda never refers in any way to her birth mother.

[5] For a reading of the eruption of Quashia into the "Roe Head Journal" passage, see Meyer 41–47. In a letter inserted near the beginning of *Caroline Vernon,* Quashia lays claim to

men. Her advent at court provides a further occasion for the extant rivalry between the emperor's twin sons, aptly named Alexander and Adrian after their grandfather and father, respectively. As twins, Alexander declares, "[O]ur affection ought to be the stronger, but that circumstance, instead of generating an increase of love, has caused a greater degree of aversion" ("Leaf" 342): and it is this inexplicable "aversion" between what are arguably the closest of kin (comparable to the undermotivated antagonism of the Crimsworth brothers in *The Professor* [1857]) that affords the mainspring of Alexander's plot to kidnap Zorayda from under Adrian's nose and make her his own. Zorayda initially figures herself, however, as unavailable to either brother. She resists assimilation into the court, at which she arrives incognito just after Quashia's execution with the secret intent of retaliating for it; the primary site of her resistance lies not on the battlefield, but in the boudoir, as she repudiates the possibility of marrying into the colonial élite. Adrian proposes a marriage "to which [she] will never consent," representing her birth as "an impossible barrier to our union" ("Leaf" 343) and betraying what Carl Plasa calls "an anxious sense of racial mixing as profane" (11): "Never, never shall the blood of my race mingle with that of yours, Lord Adrian! It would *not* mingle! Dissensions and hatred of the deepest dye, the dissensions of near kindred, would be the result of such an unhallowed union" ("Leaf" 343–44). Blood that "would *not* mingle"—literal and metaphorical sign of an impassable, "impossible" gulf between African girl and creole colonizer—metonymically links up in this passage with "dissensions" among "near kindred," such as the rivalry of the twins and the enmity of their father and grandfather. Although Zorayda suggests that any effort to cross the racial "barrier" would create divisions within the family, the broader framework of the juvenilia makes it clear that rivalrous antagonisms already divide the extended family that constitutes the empire. With Zorayda's refusing a marriage she casts as potentially miscegenous and thus a source of conflict, the narrative simultaneously gestures toward the extant differences that pit members of the royal family against one another even though they are presumably of one blood.

Having voiced the minoritized perspective of resistance to imperial oppression, both in her secret revenge plan and her overt resistance to marriage, Zorayda is ultimately restored by a twist of the plot to her birth family. "Abducted by savages" (365) along with her mother, now revealed to be the daughter of an Angrian noble who "died shortly after her capture,"

---

this young ward of Zamorna, who will subsequently become her guardian's mistress (*Five Novelettes* 282–84).

"the infant was adopted by Quamina for his own daughter" (375), an act that reverses the circumstances of his own adoption. The white child is taken in by the Africans, but unlike the black child who rebelled against the imperial adoptive family, Zorayda is assimilated into the Ashantees' culture and identifies with their cause. She learns her own history only after she has tried and failed to become "the avenger of the unjustly slain," announcing herself as "Quamina's daughter" (371) before the assembled court as she plunges a knife into Zamorna's chest; ironically, however, in aiming explicitly to avenge her adoptive father's fate, she unwittingly acts out the rivalrous wishes of her as yet unknown grandfather, too. For Zorayda turns out to be the noble Northangerland's granddaughter—the child of a son he never acknowledged owing to his expressed "aversion to male offspring" (377)—and thus related by blood to Adrian, Alexander, and much of the rest of the imperial family. Meeting the unharmed emperor's assertion that "Quamina was not your father" with "a glance of mingled surprise and indignation," she becomes "abashed and bewildered" at the revelation that "it is to a white man you owe existence; such a form was never the daughter of darkness" (372): "weeping and ashamed, she was led by her father and grandfather out of the imperial presence" (373). Her "true" parentage thus lies not with Quashia and the Africans, but with the white tyrants, which establishes her place as a marriageable daughter within the white community.

At a stroke, the assertion of the adoptee's "real" paternity, which confers on her a privileged majority status, blots out the racial identity she had been adopted into and which she had adopted for herself. With Zorayda stunned into silence and seemingly overcome by remorse, within three weeks' time, her marriage to "Prince Adrian was celebrated over all Adrianopolis in a style of regal magnificence suited to the rank of the high contracting parties" (377): her adoptive identity is thus put at an even further remove once she is transferred from father to husband. In the resolution of her story, then, the discovery of her "true" lineage obliterates Zorayda's "false" adoptive identity and the racialized identification with Africans that it has enabled, making her already a part of the imperial family whose internal ties her cousin-marriage will further consolidate, even if such a marriage does not resolve that family's tensions. She is transformed from a resistant African daughter, honoring the legacy of both Quashia and his mother, to a submissive colonial wife whose place within the royal community dictates her obedience to "father and grandfather." Within the tale, who Zorayda is and how she functions within the framework of whiteness, to which Brontë insistently calls attention, thus wholly depend on who her birth parents are, with particular emphasis on her paternal descent. Even her attempt on the life of the emperor can be excused, undertaken as it was on the basis of a misconception as to where her familial/racial loyalties should lie.

Reclaimed by the white tyrants, Zorayda is also repudiated by the black rebels. The architect of the revenge plot on the emperor's life, Shungaron, calls her his "last hope" for vengeance against Adrian the Magnificent, but professes not to be surprised that Zorayda does not succeed in her effort: "The royal blood of Quamina did not really flow through her veins and how could constancy or courage be expected from the daughter of a white man? . . . [I]n the hour of trial the pale alien has failed and been forgiven" (375). Unlike Quashia, represented as always at some critical distance from his adoptive context, Zorayda's self-identification as "daughter of darkness" is so complete that she never grasps her adoptive status as a "pale alien" until the emperor makes his announcement; once that racial reclassification is accomplished, we hear almost nothing more from or about her. On both sides of the struggle, then, Zorayda's biological inheritance trumps the identifications her upbringing has created; she crosses the "impossible barrier" between native African and creole colonizer not through marriage, but by a plot twist that severs her ties to Quashia and the legacy of resistance he imbibes from his dying mother. Restored to her "true" fathers and revealed to be "really" white, she becomes yet another instrument of forging relationships within the extended imperial family, married off as a Percy granddaughter to a Wellington son to bridge that gulf between two rivalrous male lines within the white kingdom. Only in the muting of Zorayda's response to her change in status, fortune, and racial privilege do we hear a faint critique of the cost of the foundling's return.

II.

To become some man's daughter, some man's wife, might appear to constitute the apex of the female orphan's plot, but this is not always so in Brontë's adult fiction. "[J]ust listen to the difference of our positions," Ginevra Fanshawe says to Lucy Snowe "in an expostulatory tone." Accomplished and admired, "I am the daughter of a gentleman of family, and though my father is not rich, I have expectations from an uncle"; lacking either looks or lovers, "[Y]ou are nobody's daughter . . . you have no relations" (*Villette* 179). The obscurity of Lucy's origins—or, to put it more precisely, the origins she deliberately obscures—may deny her access to Ginevra's fantasy of feminine fulfillment, but being "nobody's daughter" also keeps Lucy clear of the patriarchal loop exemplified in Zorayda's narrative: "[T]his very privation is also a kind of freedom," Boumelha argues, "for it seems to place Lucy irretrievably outside the determining structures of class, family and patrilineage" (119).[6] When, for example, Mrs. Bretton receives a disturbing letter in the first chapter of *Villette,* Lucy "thought at first that it was from home, and trembled, expecting I knew not what disastrous communication" (6). As it turns out, the letter is indeed "from Home," declaring the break-up of his establishment—which follows closely on the death of his wife, "a giddy, careless woman, who had neglected her child, and disappointed and disheartened her husband" (7)—and announcing Paulina's impending arrival. "This little girl . . . had recently lost her mother; though indeed, Mrs. Bretton ere long subjoined, the loss was not so great as might at first appear" (7): to lose a mother who has been no good woman is something on the order of a fortunate fall, comparable to Rochester's "transplant[ing]" the orphaned Adèle Varens from "the slime and mud of Paris" to "the wholesome soil of an English country garden" (*Jane Eyre* 151). Polly's subsequent devotion to father and future husband ("a bond to both, an influence over each" [*Villette* 546]) effaces all signs of her mother's unsettled past and its potential influence on the daughter's career. This motherless child is and always will be some man's daughter, some man's wife, in no small part because such a mother within the patriarchal economy can only be well lost.

While the fortuitous return of *Shirley*'s Mrs. Pryor recalls the fairy-tale foundling plot, Jane Eyre's mother and father, like Lucy Snowe's, stay dead. Instead, what lives in *Jane Eyre* are inter- and intrafamilial conflicts and antagonisms of the sort dramatized in the juvenilia, stripped of their high-life trappings and transposed to a middling sphere in an ambiguously realist fiction, with many (though not all) of their racialized overtones displaced onto the Bertha/Rochester plot. If, as everyone notices, *Jane Eyre* begins with one set of cousins and cannot conclude until it finds another, it is less often observed that cousinship in Jane's generation is overwritten by the in-law rivalries and jealousies of the earlier one, aversions and antagonisms among those who should, normatively, be affinal "friends" or "kin." As in the juvenilia, these conflicts and rivalries, which shape relationships between women as well as men, have fractured the families that Jane enters into, first as a young child at Gateshead, then as an adult woman at Moor House. Dividing Jane's mixed inheritance along maternal and paternal lines, the novel takes some pains to represent the tensions

---

[6] Elsewhere in her excellent monograph, Boumelha usefully locates the drama of the male orphan in *The Professor* in relation to the narratives of homeless girls and women that Brontë usually creates, arguing that his story deploys "tropes of plot victimage more commonly associated with female protagonists" (47).

between and within what I will call first and second family—that is, one's family of origin, whether biological or adoptive, and one's family by marriage—as a critical factor in Jane's history that shapes her narrative possibilities, fleshing out the universalizing orphan story of Bessie's ballad with quotidian detail. Over its course, Jane's narrative is gradually peopled with dead relatives—particularly male ones—whose living intentions make the seemingly singular plot a multifarious set of intersecting familial enmities and animosities, recalling and refiguring the intrigues of the Angrian court even as they also reposition Jane (like yet also unlike Zorayda) squarely within the father's camp.

What Jane retains instead of her forgotten parents is another figure she cannot remember and whose former existence has secured for her only an insecure and uncertain place:

> I could not remember him; but I knew that he was my own uncle—my mother's brother—that he had taken me when a parentless infant to his house; and that in his last moments he had required a promise of Mrs. Reed that she would rear and maintain me as one of her own children. Mrs. Reed probably considered she had kept this promise; and so she had, I dare say, as well as her nature would permit her: but how could she really like an interloper not of her race, and unconnected with her, after her husband's death, by any tie? It must have been most irksome to find herself bound by a hard-wrung pledge to stand in the stead of a parent to a strange child she could not love, and to see an uncongenial alien permanently intruded on her own family group. (16–17)

Uncle Reed's early death deprives Jane of the surrogate father in whose goodness she continues to trust long after his demise: "I doubted not—had never doubted—that if Mr. Reed had been alive he would have treated me kindly" (17), which is to say "as one of [his] own children." Mrs. Reed, however, appears to abjure the putative claims of kinship in relation to her husband's niece and her sister-in-law's child; from her point of view, Jane's uncle's death cancels any bonds of obligation between his second family, which she now heads, and his first family, to which he maintained fraternal ties. Although Mrs. Reed describes herself more than once as Jane's "friend" (38, 42), to young Jane she remains, at best, "my uncle's wife" (74) and, at worst, "no relation of mine" (38). Indeed, the "uncongenial alien," "an interloper not of her [aunt's] race," represents herself as a stranger within the "family group" and finds "an inexpressible relief, a soothing conviction of protection and security," in the presence of other strangers "not belonging to Gateshead, and not related to Mrs. Reed" (19).

The "insuperable and rooted aversion" (27) between them is (or becomes) mutual.

Aunt Reed and Jane each identify the other as "alien" or "not kin," a motif that suggests a broader change in the contours of family membership as Brontë traces them. Juxtaposed to the assertion of friendship, the trope of "the stranger"—here deployed not only to exclude the unrelated from the family circle, but also appropriated by Jane to represent her experience of exclusion—indicates the difference between familial intimates and others. At an earlier moment in the history of English kinship, siblings-in-law had been "the closest of relatives" (Trumbach 413) in light of the mutual obligations and connections that pertain among these "friends": how, then, does this aunt come to see this niece—daughter to her sister-in-law, and thus a portion of her husband's flesh and blood—as not part of her own family? Ruth Perry's analysis of "the great disinheritance" that deprived eighteenth-century women of access to work and property, with immense consequences for the shape of domestic fiction, demonstrates how a shift "in the definition of what constituted the primary kin group" (2) from consanguineal relations to conjugal ones "privileged the limited nuclear family of spouses with their immature children over the laterally defined kin group including the siblings of spouses (uncles and aunts) and the offspring of those siblings (cousins)" (31). Like some latter-day variant of John Dashwood, who regards his stepmother and her daughters "with as much kindness as he could feel towards any body beyond himself, his wife, and their child" (*Sense* 5), Aunt Reed pares down her "friends and family" to exclude those who fall outside the narrowly nuclear borders of her immediate circle (a decision she might well have come to regret once she discovered that Jane would be heir to her paternal uncle's fortune). While familial connection in Austen's era was not exclusively or even predominantly a matter of blood and biology, Brontë operates within a framework in which the fact of Jane's being related to her Reed cousins only on her mother's side—and thus more tenuously connected to them—makes it possible for Mrs. Reed to understand her niece-by-marriage as no kin to her.[7]

If Mrs. Reed limits the scope of her relations to just her conjugal family, then Jane also implicitly accepts that definition: even the way in which she phrases her complaint suggests that she thinks it not entirely unreasonable for Mrs. Reed, "bound by a hard-wrung pledge" exacted by a dying man, to "not really like" his sister's orphan child. Most importantly, when Jane herself adopts the terminology of "alien" and "interloper" to gloss the dif-

---

[7] See Corbett for an extended analysis of kin relations in Austen's fiction.

ference between a relation by blood and one by marriage, she more or less posits that the absence of consanguinity, rather than the presence of affinity, governs her lack of family feeling for Aunt Reed and Aunt Reed's parallel attitude toward her. Even though Jane might say just as truly of her Reed cousins what she later tells her Rivers cousins—that "half our blood on each side flows from the same source" (405)—she significantly underplays what she shares with John, Georgiana, and Eliza, opting instead to represent herself as unrelated not just to her aunt-by-marriage, but also to her cousins-german.

Jane and her author infamously heighten the rhetoric of exclusion from the family by representing the separation between the two "lines" in racial terms. Although the text eventually discloses that Jane's patriarchal legacy itself derives from colonial oppression, Brontë invokes the metaphorics of slavery to represent the Reeds' treatment of Jane: casting the child as a slave means characterizing mother and son as slaveholders, as contaminated as the West Indian planter class by its position of power over subjugated peoples. Through this strategic disavowal and displacement of the contaminating effect of slavery on those who enslave others, Jane further distances herself from her affinal relations on the mother's side, representing the "impossible barrier" between them in terms that clearly echo the racializing discourses of the juvenilia, and thereby dramatizing her lack of affinity for the Reeds. If, from the Reed perspective, Jane the adoptee, like Quashia, figures as a sort of enemy within, then the Reeds represent for Jane the enslaved orphan's naturalized fate of dispossession.

Departing from the juvenilia, however, Brontë does give a genealogy to Aunt Reed's "aversion" to her husband's sister's daughter, representing it as motivated by a rivalry that also suggests broader cultural changes within family formation. While Jane represents her circumstances at Gateshead as a matter of being excluded from the "family group" as "an interloper" to whom her uncle's wife has no blood tie—a relative by marriage of another "race" or lineage for whom the Reeds feel no affinity—Mrs. Reed sees Jane as the living avatar of her husband's dead sister, who stood between her and her husband and with whom she competed for his attention. When the niece asks her dying aunt why she wishes Jane Eyre dead, Mrs. Reed situates her animosity toward Jane within a longer familial history: "I had a dislike to her mother always; for she was my husband's only sister, and a great favourite with him . . . when news came of her death, he wept like a simpleton" (243) and had his sister's child brought to his house. The wife's envy of her sister-in-law's status as "favourite" is not slaked by her death, but rather finds a new object in Jane. The orphan also freshly occasions Mrs. Reed's jealousy in relation to her own children: while she "hated [the baby] the first time I set my eyes on it . . . Reed pitied it; and he used to nurse it and notice it as if it had been his own: more, indeed, than he ever noticed his own at that age" (243). Once perceived by Mrs. Reed to usurp her children's rightful primacy in their father's affections, Jane bears the brunt of her aunt's displaced feelings of exclusion: Mrs. Reed cuts Jane out of the "family group," we may speculate, because she has experienced herself as cut out from the first-family tie between brother and sister that her husband did not fully relinquish upon marriage. By withholding John Eyre's offer of adoption, Aunt Reed exacts her "revenge" (251): "[F]or you to be adopted by your uncle and placed in a state of ease and comfort was what I could not endure" (251) because "I disliked you too fixedly and thoroughly ever to lend a hand in lifting you to prosperity" (250). But that antagonism has an earlier origin in her rivalry with another "favourite," such that Aunt Reed punishes Jane as the living proxy of the dead mother.

III.

In the final analysis, Aunt Reed's "revenge" against her sister-in-law only defers access to the "ease and comfort" she aims to deny her niece altogether: even though she never enters his presence, Jane comes to inherit her uncle's estate by a circuitous route. Significantly, the absent uncle is a rich relation on the father's rather than the mother's side who has gotten on in the world at the expense of his own relations: and it is the disposition of the "colonial possession and wealth" accumulated by this childless man that will "restore [Jane] to the family of origin" (Azim 177). There is no such possibility of accession to fortune through the mother: already disowned by her parents for marrying a poor clergyman, Jane's mother leaves "nothing to bequeath" (*Jane Eyre* 250) her daughter in material terms except the short-lived protection of her brother's care. When Aunt Reed claims that she "would as soon have been charged with a pauper brat out of a work-house" (243), she expresses in the very starkest terms the extent of Jane's maternal disinheritance.

That Jane inherits wealth and kin on the father's side, however, has been subordinated even in those interpretations of the novel that emphasize the importance of Jane's finding a new family. Maurianne Adams, for example, has argued that in moving from Gateshead to Lowood to Thornfield to Moor House, Jane Eyre "supplants bad foster-families with good" (172), emphasizing the narrative fact that "prior to establishing a family by marriage" with Rochester at Ferndean, "she regains and reunites a family of origin" (173) at Marsh End. By contrast with the claim that Jane's "rediscovery of her female cousins remains only a minor event, firmly relegated to the background of the novel" (Kucich 112–13), Adams suggests that it "prepares for the marital resolution with Rochester, in which affinity, monetary inheritance, social status and mutual interdependence are of a piece" (169). Accepting Adams's reading, in closing I want to inquire more specifically into why Brontë identifies Jane's true or good "family of origin" with her paternal relatives, and why it matters that she inherits kin and fortune from an Eyre rather than a Reed.

The short answer, as Perry's work suggests,[8] is that mothers are themselves symbolically dispossessed and disowned by marriage (as Jane's mother actually was) so that to be a girl child without parents or portion in the home of "rich, maternal relations" (399) is quite literally to be, as Ginevra Fanshawe would say, "nobody's daughter." A closer look at the circumstances of the Rivers of Moor House, who also suffer a reversal through a failure of maternal kin, further confirms the point. The origins of the siblings' loss of fortune, like Jane's loss of family, lie in the unresolved conflicts and patrilineal bias of the generation that preceded them. Diana tells the story of how her maternal uncle (i.e., Jane's father's brother) led his sister's husband to ruin:

> " . . . we have never seen him or known him. He was my mother's brother. My father and he quarreled long ago. It was by his advice that my father risked most of his property in the speculation that ruined him. Mutual recriminations passed between them. . . . [I]t appears he realised a fortune of twenty thousand pounds. He was never married, and had no near kindred but ourselves, and one other person, not more closely related than we. My father always cherished the idea that he would atone for his error, by leaving his possessions to us: that letter informs us that he has bequeathed every penny to the other relation. . . ." (376–77)

Although he is the figure within the extended Rivers family who stands in a parallel place to Uncle Reed, this "mother's brother" does not take a protective role toward either his sister or her children. Financial ruin entails a family falling-out, and while the father of the Rivers children clearly believed that recompense was due them for what he had lost by

---

[8] Perry (38–76) provides an extended analysis of what she calls "the great disinheritance" of daughters owing to changing economic circumstances in the eighteenth century that concentrated transmissible wealth in the hands of eldest sons. Although her study concludes with Austen, the narrative patterns of family and kin formation that she traces are, I would suggest, still very much present in nineteenth-century fiction.

"speculation," those "mutual recriminations" over a deal gone bad would presumably have played some part in Uncle John's making his brother's child his sole heir. More broadly, however, leaving his fortune to Jane Eyre alone indicates Uncle John's commitment to the male line: although Diana describes her as yet unknown cousin "as not more closely related than we" to their common uncle, that Jane is a brother's daughter while Diana, Mary, and St. John are only a sister's children makes a crucial difference. Here again, although in another key, differences in the treatment of affinal relations—and specifically those on the mother's side—expose the asymmetries in gendered privilege, leaving that sister's children with nothing while endowing a brother's child with ample means.

Ultimately placed in a position where she can compensate the disregarded Rivers siblings by making the amends their mother's brother would not, Jane undoes the fate of disinheritance that her own mother had endured and symbolically repairs the broken link between a brother and a sister. In doing so, Brontë also suggests that Jane's kinship with her Rivers cousins is effected from the outset by their as yet unknown consanguinity. Her effort to make things right follows in part from her established friendship with Diana and Mary Rivers: initially glimpsing them through the windows at Moor House, she reports that "I had nowhere seen such faces as theirs: and yet, as I gazed on them, I seemed intimate with every lineament" (350). With each of them alive to "the pleasure arising from perfect congeniality of tastes, sentiments, and principles" (368), "our natures dovetailed: mutual affection—of the strongest kind—was the result" (369). Here what Jane certainly casts as a natural "inclination or attraction"—an affinity arising from a certain sameness—precedes the discovery of biological relationship, so that Jane may subsequently remark that even "when I knew them but as mere strangers, they had inspired me with genuine affection and admiration" (405). Such "congeniality" may also lend credence to Jane's much earlier assertion that "sympathies" exist "between far-distant, long-absent, wholly estranged relatives"; but the force of that claim itself rests on the fact of biological likeness, in that what is said to promote "sympathies" between the otherwise alienated is "the unity of the source to which each traces his origin" (231). The discovery, then, that "half our blood on each side flows from the same source" retroactively goes to show why Jane, Mary, and Diana get on so well together from the outset, even if, as I have already indicated, shared blood does nothing to unite Jane, Georgiana, and Eliza. If the initial affinity among these cousins is in some sense predicated on their common biological inheritance, then it also makes the sharing of the monetary inheritance a critical element of the "integration of blood and kinship ties" (Adams 169) that paves the way for all three women to marry and for their brother to embark on his Christianizing mission in India. And while the dark Reeds do not prosper or propagate themselves, and St. John dies in bringing light to the dark places of the earth, the lustrous Rivers sisters no doubt become mothers who people their conjugal homes with happy children, as does Jane herself.

These mothers of the next generation, then, will presumably not share the fate of their own mothers, or that of the other Brontëan mothers considered here: the dying African mother who motivates her son's resistance; Zorayda's Angrian mother, whose very lack of a name suggests the incompleteness of her daughter's maternal legacy; and even Mrs. Pryor, restored to her child, but not without some lingering anxiety as to her proper share in her daughter's portion. As Boumelha has observed of Jane Eyre, Brontë's daughters exist largely within "the patriarchal determinations of kinship and inheritance" (64) so that they may be restored to a quintessentially feminine place as some man's daughter, some man's wife—a place that is, however, implicitly marked out for white women alone, whose relations to their father's kin constitute a critical element in their narrative fortunes. For if I have made clear that Jane's story can only begin to end once her creator has afforded her the narrative means to repair and reconcile the gendered inequities of maternal disinheritance, then I hope also to have illustrated that the patriarchal and imperial interests in which this motherless daughter is implicated and from which she profits both privilege and problematize the ties of blood.

Works Cited

Adams, Maurianne. "Family Disintegration and Creative Reintegration: The Case of Charlotte Brontë and *Jane Eyre*." In *The Victorian Family: Structure and Stresses*. Ed. Anthony S. Wohl. New York: St. Martin's Press, 1978. 148–79.

Austen, Jane. *Sense and Sensibility*. 1811. Ed. James Kinsley. Oxford and New York: Oxford University Press, 1990.

Azim, Firdous. *The Colonial Rise of the Novel*. London: Routledge, 1993.

Boumelha, Penny. *Charlotte Brontë*. Bloomington: Indiana University Press, 1990.

Brontë, Anne. *The Tenant of Wildfell Hall*. 1848. Ed. Herbert Rosengarten. Oxford and New York: Oxford University Press, 1992.

Brontë, Charlotte. *An Edition of The Early Writings of Charlotte Brontë*. Vol. 2, pt. 1. Ed. Christine Alexander. Oxford: Published for the Shakespeare Head Press by Basil Blackwell, 1991.

———. "The African Queen's Lament." In *Early Writings*. 3–6.

———. *Caroline Vernon*. In *Five Novelettes*. Ed. Winifred Gérin. London: Folio Press, 1971.

———. "The Foundling." In *Early Writings*. 43–125.

———. "The Green Dwarf." In *Early Writings*. 127–206.
———. *Jane Eyre*. 1847. Ed. Margaret Smith. Oxford: Oxford University Press, 1993.
———. "A Leaf from an Unopened Volume." In *Early Writings*. 321–78.
———. *The Professor*. 1857. Ed. Margaret Smith and Herbert Rosengarten. New York: Oxford University Press, 1987.
———. *Shirley: A Tale*. 1849. Ed. Herbert Rosengarten and Margaret Smith. Oxford: Clarendon Press, 1979.
———. *Villette*. 1853. Ed. Margaret Smith and Herbert Rosengarten. Oxford: Oxford University Press, 1990.
Clarke, Micael M. "Brontë's *Jane Eyre* and the Grimms' Cinderella." *Studies in English Literature* 40 (2000): 695–710.
Corbett, Mary Jean. "'Cousins in Love &c.' in Jane Austen." *Tulsa Studies in Women's Literature* 23 (2004): 237–59.
Dever, Carolyn. *Death and the Mother from Dickens to Freud: Victorian Fiction and the Anxiety of Origins*. Cambridge: Cambridge University Press, 1998.
Hirsch, Marianne. *The Mother/Daughter Plot: Narrative, Psychoanalysis, Feminism*. Bloomington and Indianapolis: Indiana University Press, 1989.
Homans, Margaret. *Bearing the Word: Language and Female Experience in Nineteenth-Century Women's Writing*. Chicago and London: University of Chicago Press, 1986.
Howe, Patricia. "Fontane's 'Ellernklipp' and the Theme of Adoption." *Modern Language Review* 79 (1984): 114–30.
Kucich, John. *Repression in Victorian Fiction: Charlotte Brontë, George Eliot, and Charles Dickens*. Berkeley: University of California Press, 1987.
Meyer, Susan. *Imperialism at Home: Race and Victorian Women's Fiction*. Ithaca: Cornell University Press, 1996.
Nord, Deborah Epstein. "'Marks of Race': Gypsy Figures and Eccentric Femininity in Nineteenth-Century Women's Writing." *Victorian Studies* 41 (1998): 189–210.
Perry, Ruth. *Novel Relations: The Transformation of Kinship in English Literature and Culture, 1748–1818*. Cambridge: Cambridge University Press, 2004.
Peters, Laura. *Orphan Texts: Victorian Orphans, Culture and Empire*. Manchester and New York: Manchester University Press, 2000.
Plasa, Carl. *Charlotte Brontë*. Houndmills: Palgrave Macmillan, 2004.
Rich, Adrienne. "Jane Eyre: The Temptations of a Motherless Woman." In *On Lies, Secrets, and Silence: Selected Prose, 1966–1978*. New York: W. W. Norton & Company, 1979. 89–106.
Trumbach, Randolph. *Sex and the Gender Revolution*. Volume 1, *Heterosexuality and the Third Gender in Enlightenment London*. Chicago and London: University of Chicago Press, 1998.

CHAPTER 12

Distance Mothering and the "Cradle Lands"

Imperial Motherhood and
Lady Duff Gordon's *Letters from Egypt*

CARA MURRAY

In 1862 Lucie Duff Gordon left her husband, children, and home in England and headed for Egypt to recuperate from tuberculosis. For the next seven years, until her death in Cairo at age forty-seven, she wrote letters to her family in which she narrates her experiences in Egypt and offers motherly advice to her two youngest children; in effect, she conducts her mothering from a distance of 3,800 miles. In her letters Duff Gordon takes pains to represent herself to her family as a good mother to the Egyptians among whom she lives. To this end, she creates an Egyptian "family" which consists over time of an Egyptian servant named Omar, whom she affectionately calls her "son"; two European women domestic servants; and seven young slave "children." Her mothering practices, I argue, offer a liberal critique of British imperialism, aimed at using maternal methods to improve upon it.

In the 1990s critics began to reconsider the roles that women played in imperial enterprises. Whereas the imperial practices of nineteenth-century women travelers to Egypt, such as Harriet Martineau, Florence Nightingale, and Amelia Ann Blanford Edwards have since been documented, Duff Gordon's relation to imperialism remains underexplored.[1] This may

---

[1] See Jill Matus for a discussion of the ways in which Florence Nightingale and Harriet Martineau are implicated in colonialism. See Billie Melman for a broader discussion of the relations between gender and imperialism in the nineteenth century in the Middle East. See

be because the liberal Duff Gordon was one of the strongest critics of British arrogance abroad in her day, and she persistently contradicted European claims that Arabs were lazy, unclean, and uncivilized. Faiza Shereen captures the refreshingly critical aspect of Duff Gordon's work in her article in the *Dictionary of National Biography:* "A hundred years before Edward W. Said, Chinua Achebe, and Frantz Fanon, Duff Gordon was observing and recording some of the most pernicious aspects of European orientalism—and questioning some of the most dearly held views of her time" (162).

Still it is important to consider Duff Gordon's relation to imperialism, especially since she makes the subject of how to better rule the colonies a theme of her work. Throughout her letters she attempts to controvert strategies of colonial rule that depend upon the use of crude force, such as those held by her contemporary in Egypt, the British explorer of the Nile, Samuel White Baker, who had asserted in his 1866 work, *Albert N'yanza,* that the Egyptians were "brutes" who should be conquered by the British (280). In contrast, Duff Gordon shows that Egyptians need not be conquered, just cared for. Duff Gordon's representation of herself as a good mother to her Egyptian family offers a counterpractice to what she perceived to be the prevailing practice of the day, what she called "rule by the stick." In place of heavy-handed paternal rule, she offers the ideal of the domesticating woman—who will care for the native with a woman's touch, and who will replace the ideology of the stick with the subtlety of maternal manipulation.

Duff Gordon focuses her maternal goodwill on her household servants and slaves, whom she considers her family. It was not uncommon for Europeans living abroad to imagine familial and affective ties with their native household servants. Ann Laura Stoler demonstrates through a series of interviews with Dutch colonials about their home life in Indonesia during the colonial period that many nostalgically referred to the Indonesian domestic servants who worked for them as "family." None of the domestic workers whom she interviewed, however, shared their bosses' affection. Many of them could not even recall their employers' names; they did, however, remember in detail the dull chores and hard work that they performed in the Dutch households. Stoler's interviews reveal just what the word "family" can mask in the colonial setting.

Duff Gordon's representation of her Egyptian household not only provides us with a rare glimpse of a Victorian family at work but also articu-

---

James Buzard for early statement of the case against seeing nineteenth-century women as just innocent bystanders of imperialism.

lates the relation between the workings of the household and the colonial enterprise. Anne McClintock shows how during the nineteenth century, as the number of female domestic servants in England swelled to become the second-largest labor category, the recognition of the economic value of domestic labor became socially taboo, resulting in the erasure of the female domestic worker from the field of representation.[2] She links the denial of the value of women's domestic labor in the industrial metropolis to the devaluation of colonized labor which happened in the same period (138). Further, she argues that because the economic value of women's domestic labor in the metropolis could not be recognized, female domestic servants "were frequently depicted in the iconography of degeneration—as 'plagues,' 'black races,' and 'primitives'" (42). In other words, because the female domestic servant imperiled the "natural" separation between private home and public market by carrying the "whiff of the market" into the drawing room, she was often represented as black (McClintock 164–65). Thus, her affinity with the undervalued colonized laborer was marked. McClintock's insights into the racialization of women's domestic work in England help us to understand Duff Gordon's peculiar construction of her family of workers in Egypt, for as we shall see, Duff Gordon takes great pains to remove all of the female European laborers from her household and to replace them with an all-male group of African "maids" who are feminized by the work that they do. In constructing her ideal family as a group of male workers, she frees herself from the taboo of representing female domestic labor. The result is that she makes the hidden work of the Victorian family visible at the same time that she invites one to see domestic work in relation to colonial labor.

Duff Gordon's construction of her Egyptian family does more than just reveal the erasure of the female domestic laborer. She displays a home which is distinguished by all sorts of erasures and disruptions of the "natural" order. Within her roomy apartment above the Temple of Luxor where she resides for the majority of her seven-year stay, for example, a woman directs and supervises the labor of men; European servants work alongside Africans; female Christian maids flirt with male Muslim "maids"; an aristocrat shares daily meals with a servant; and feisty European domestic workers disobey their liberal British master. The multiple modifiers that each actor within her household actually demands—"upper-class white British woman," "young male African slave," or "poor female German domestic worker," for instance—suggest intersections between categories often dealt with as disparate. By shaping this diverse group of people into

---

[2] See Anne McClintock, who writes that by 1851, 40 percent of wage-earning women were domestic servants and that female domestic workers were the largest labor category apart from agriculture (85).

a "family," a process which involves inclusions as well as exclusions, Duff Gordon offers insights into the interworkings of race, class, gender, and religion in the colonial household.

This is to say that the relation of mothering to colonialism is complex and should not be too narrowly mapped. Limiting motherhood to its reproductive work, for instance, Melissa Lee Miller writes that mothering for the colonial woman becomes a way in which she could "simultaneously enact previously held beliefs and teachings specific to women and seek to create, or recreate the Other in the British/parental image" (230). One problem with such an argument is that it presumes that the British/parental image is a known entity and as such easily reproduced. By contrast, Stoler argues that the colonizer/colonized is a "historically shifting pair of social categories" (13); inclusion in or exclusion from these categories "required regulation of the sexual, conjugal, and domestic life of both European colonials and their subjects" (43). By setting herself up as a mother of an Egyptian family, Duff Gordon was well poised to regulate the domestic lives within. Simultaneously, she monitored the lives of her British children from afar. Using Stoler's insights into the constructed nature of the colonizer/colonized, I argue that the mother's work under colonialism was not simply to reproduce the colony in the image of the colonizer, but to help to construct the colonizer/colonized through her vigilance toward the family.

The centrality of the mother to Egypt's modernization has been posited by Lisa Pollard, who argues that both the British colonialists and the Egyptian nationalists relied upon her work to reform the nation. The British justified the establishment of Egypt as a protectorate in 1882 by denigrating the Egyptian household. Elite Egyptian men were unfit to rule, British politicians reasoned, because of their backward domestic habits, polygamy being one of the most frequently cited. In order to fix the problem, the British advocated for the education of women. These educated women would become the mothers who would raise a well-behaved elite cadre of rulers. In the meantime, the British would mother the Egyptians until their leaders were ready to govern. The Egyptian nationalists similarly made the mother central to their reeducation plan; for them, the mother was the most able to nurture the new nation by reeducating its sons. Pollard, however, only considers elite mothers and sons. This relationship looks different when it is the nation's working poor who are being mothered; neither the colonialists nor the nationalists ever expected them to govern.[3] Duff Gordon exposes how the mother shaped Egypt's laboring poor.

---

[3] Evelyn Baring Cromer, for example, considered the fellaheen, who made up 90 percent of Egyptian society, to exist outside of the class structure altogether. He argued in *Modern Egypt* that they, like animals, could never be expected to rule.

Duff Gordon demonstrates to her English family that she is a good mother by representing herself as successfully mothering her Egyptian family. Her letters revolve around the relationship that she has with her Arab servant, Omar, who appears in just about every letter. Duff Gordon constructs a story in which she is a doting mother to an affectionate son. Although Omar nurses her around the clock, Duff Gordon pointedly shows her family how well she takes care of him—feeding him, clothing him, traveling with him, and even attempting to provide for him financially in the event of her death; indeed, she makes it appear as if she is indispensable to him. She demonstrates a mother's love for him, claiming, "He is everything to me." He, in turn, claims that she is "the mother he found in the world" (361).

In addition to Omar, Duff Gordon welcomes seven slaves into her family throughout her seven-year stay, often referring to them as her little boys.[4] She depicts them happily at play, but more often than not, she shows them hard at work, ironing, cooking, and cleaning. Duff Gordon makes a point of never beating them, demonstrating how well children will work if properly treated.[5] Duff Gordon slowly rids her home of all female influence, shedding her female slaves and her European domestic workers so that in its final and ideal form her household consists of one woman in charge of a gaggle of boys. She shows how through tender care her all-male family becomes an efficient work unit that eagerly picks up the slack, not only doing more work, but doing the work of women when she fires her female laborers and hires no replacements.

Duff Gordon pits the productivity of her newly created family against her own idle one, suggesting at every turn that her British children have something to learn from her Egyptian ones. We must understand her biological family in relation to her chosen one not only because her British children are encouraged to learn from her Egyptian ones, but also because it is only through the former that the latter become visible at all. Therefore, I will first consider Duff Gordon's mothering of her youngest biological children, Urania (Rainie) and Maurice, and then turn to a discussion of her Egyptian family. Duff Gordon had one grown daughter, Janet Ross, whom I will not discuss, for she was already married and living in Alexandria at the time that Duff Gordon began writing.

---

[4] Of the seven slaves who live with her throughout her seven-year stay, only two are female, Zeyneb and a slave whom she never names. Neither of them, however, stays with her for long, for she dismisses them soon after acquiring them.

[5] Duff Gordon does mention one beating, which she treats as her motherly duty: "I was forced to flog Mabrook yesterday for smoking on the sly" (278). Mabrook was flogged for smoking, a cultural offense, she explains, for smoking by young boys is considered rude in Egypt.

I. Distance Mothering

1. Mother and Daughter: Rainie's Moral Lessons

Duff Gordon's letters have two audiences. Written for her family, whom she was aware she might never see again, they obtain a level of intimacy uncommon to the travel narrative genre. But they are also written for the general public. Prior to moving to Egypt, Duff Gordon lived for just under a year in South Africa with her maid Sally. When it was clear that the weather there was not improving her health, they returned home, and at her doctor's behest, moved to Egypt. The letters that she wrote to her family from South Africa were published in 1864, only two years after she arrived in Egypt, suggesting that Duff Gordon recognized the value of her Egyptian letters for a wider audience than her immediate family. In 1865 her Egyptian letters, edited by her mother, Sarah Austin, were published. Indeed, the publication of all of Duff Gordon's letters was mediated by her family. Her eldest daughter, Janet Ross, republished her mother's Egyptian letters in 1875 to include those written in the last four years of her life to which Ross added a memoir of her mother. In 1969, her great-grandson, Gordon Waterfield, published a reedited version of those letters, adding to the front matter a drawing of an unnamed but suspiciously Duff Gordon-like woman cradling a baby while feeding it from a saucer. Such familial involvement in the packaging of all of the extant editions of Duff Gordon's letters promises to keep her status as a mother at the forefront of her reader's attention. Even those outside of the family stressed Duff Gordon's "motherly" attributes, as did George Meredith when he wrote in his introduction to her letters that she benefited the Egyptians most by "giving these quivering creatures of the baked land proof that a Christian Englishwoman could be companionable, tender, and beneficently motherly with them, despite the reputed insurmountable barriers of alien race and relation" (xx).

Because Duff Gordon writes letters to her children and writes about them in her letters to her mother, husband, and grown daughter, her children have a regular place in her text. Whereas with her youngest daughter, Rainie, who was just four when Duff Gordon left for Egypt, she takes on the tone of a loving schoolteacher offering moral lessons that will guide her child through life, with Maurice, her son who was thirteen when she departed, she adapts an urgent and interventionist attitude, attempting to correct what she believes are poor educational decisions made by his father, Sir Alexander Duff Gordon. Duff Gordon conducts her letters to Rainie as lessons; for instance, when Rainie is learning to write she begins her letter by writing her own address in Arabic letters, explaining to her that "[i]t is very difficult to learn them, and I think the little Arab boys, who sit in the courtyard of the Mosque, as the Church is called, with their slates must have harder work with their A B C than you have" (217). Although she is reputedly teaching her daughter a lesson about Arabic culture, she cannot refrain from inculcating industriousness by comparing Rainie to the Arab boys who work harder than she.

But at the core of Duff Gordon's lessons is the creation of a liberal justification of empire through motherly acts of beneficence. She made her home the center of such acts of kindness, and the acquisition and treatment of household labor a favorite example. Portrayals of domestic slavery in the colonies were even rarer than depictions of domestic labor in the industrial metropolis.[6] Duff Gordon, however, searching for a way to relate to her own children, reveals much about the practice of slavery in British households long after it had been abolished in England and in the colonies. She writes to Rainie about her acquisition of a young boy named Khayr:

> A poor man, a traveller, was very ill and died in my house, and his black slave, a boy bigger than Maurice, is here still. He is called Khayr, but his name in his own village far away in the middle of Africa was Faragella. He was stolen by Turkish soldiers and can only speak a little Arabic yet. (219)

Only through her letter to Rainie does the history of Khayr creep into her account at all. Indeed, her desire to exhibit her mothering skills to her children necessitates the inclusion of her child slaves into her story.

All of Duff Gordon's household laborers are depicted as children, irrespective of their age. Duff Gordon often tells her biological children that her slaves are just like them, only differing in that they are painted brown or black. Nevertheless, she makes it clear to her own children where they stand. In a letter to Rainie about Khayr, Duff Gordon writes, "When I heard you had been reading *Robinson Crusoe,* I wished to send him to you to be your Man Friday, when you play at Desert Islands" (219). Thus, she draws an affinity between the two families based upon ownership of labor through the imaginary transfer of Khayr between households.

Duff Gordon never depicts herself as actively participating in the slave trade. Like the rest of her slaves, Khayr arrives at her doorstep through somebody else's misfortune or misdoing. And also like her other slaves,

---

[6] It is true that British antislavery tracts describing the conscripted labor used by the French or Turks to build such projects as the Suez Canal, irrigation works, cotton infrastructure, and sugar factories are common; however, descriptions of domestic slavery are hard to come by.

Khayr begs her to keep him. She represents the purchase of Khayr as his desire rather than her own. Avoiding words that would intimate a financial transaction, such as "buy" or "purchase," she instead uses familial words such as "inherit" or "adopt," creating the illusion that it is her moral imperative to take in slaves. In Khayr's case, this morality is simple enough for her seven-year-old daughter to grasp:

> Khayr is black as ink and very ugly and his teeth were filed to sharp points like a dog's when he was little in his own country, but he is a very good boy and I like him and shall be very sorry when he goes to his master who is a little boy of eight or nine and whom he means to take great care of and to work for, if his father has left him no money. But if his little master's family sell him he wants me to buy him very much. (219)

The inclusion of Khayr's story reveals how Duff Gordon teaches her daughter to accept not only her own reasons for keeping slaves, but also the British justification for their imminent rule in Egypt, for Khayr's story has imperial parallels. It is important to remember that Egypt would soon come under British rule after England invaded Alexandria in 1882. By telling Khayr's story, Duff Gordon provides a familiar context for other tales that she relates, such as the one of two sheiks who, outraged by Turkish rule, "begged me to communicate to the Queen of England that they would join her troops if she would invade Egypt" (245). Duff Gordon teaches Ranie that just as Khayr, stolen from his home by Turkish soldiers, desires to be restored a home by a kindly British woman, Egyptians, whose land has been invaded by the Turks, call out for their home to be restored by a kindly British queen. Thus, she not only provides a moral justification for a British invasion, but also a precedent for it in her own family.

2. MOTHER AND SON: MAURICE'S SEX EDUCATION

Duff Gordon devotes twice as much space to her son as she does to her daughter. Yet she spares no space on Maurice until she receives word that he is "idle" (334). After this she concentrates on wresting the responsibility for Maurice's education from his father, eventually persuading him to send Maurice to Egypt for nine months during the last year and a half of her life. The fact that she felt compelled to bring him to Egypt demonstrates the major difference between the education of her daughter and son. While Duff Gordon was content to mind Rainie by post, she needed to educate Maurice in the flesh. To understand Duff Gordon's urgent request for her son's presence, we can turn to Ann Laura Stoler, who writes that "what is striking when we look to identify the contours and composition of any particular colonial community is the extent to which control over sexuality and reproduction was at the core of defining colonial privilege and its boundaries" (39). In other words, colonial privilege was actively defined through the control of sexuality rather than passively granted based upon one's race or nationality. I argue that Duff Gordon brings Maurice to Egypt in order to take control of his sexual education and by doing so initiates his colonial career.

Duff Gordon frequently complains to her husband that her son has become idle under his watch. By labeling Maurice with a term often reserved for the colonized and used to justify their subjection, Duff Gordon challenges Maurice's presumed authority over them. Likewise, her accusations threaten to keep him from performing his duties in his family, for she reprimands him for his laziness by telling him that he is currently "unfit" to resume care for her in the event of her husband's death. Duff Gordon sees Maurice's idleness manifesting itself as hedonism and anti-intellectualism, and she targets his Eton education as the cause: "He is so deeply imbued with the idea that it is 'snobbish' to read and to know, and that nothing on earth is worth living for but animal pleasures. . . . I observe all the 'Eton fellows' of his age have exactly the same *baronial* views of life and hate the 'cads' who are base enough to read books" (352). Thus, she endeavors to persuade her husband to send Maurice to Dresden. Her husband, however, sends him to Brussels instead, a move of which she thoroughly disapproves: "I look upon Brussels as the *most* dangerous place possible with all the French and English vices and the idleness and *kleinstädlerei* [narrow mentality] of a provincial town" (294). Complaining to her mother she writes, "Oh! Why would he send him to such a sink of iniquity as Brussels?" (332).

Her husband's latest error of judgment only strengthens her resolve to take Maurice's education into her own hands, and her letters to her husband are increasingly filled with grim predictions about Maurice's future. After sustained battle, she triumphs, and Maurice comes to Egypt. Upon arrival, Duff Gordon attempts to liberate Maurice from his companion, Monsieur Soubre, a tutor hired by her husband to accompany Maurice to Brussels and Egypt. Though Duff Gordon has reason to attack M. Soubre's pedagogical practices, she instead focuses on the influences that he holds over her son's sexual practices. To this end, she drops all sorts of sexual innuendos, including one about the tutor's wife: "How was it, my dearest Alick, that you thought fit to have him with a tutor whose wife was like that?" (342). Again, she takes matters into her own hands, this time implementing a solution that reveals what she believes to be at the core of Maurice's education. When she learns that M. Soubre and Maurice are visiting prostitutes, she writes: "I told Maurice plainly that I dreaded the worst diseases and that if he *must* have an outbreak, I would give him a pound or two now and then to have a good dancing girl, rather than a lot of fourpenny women" (346). Thus, she redirects Maurice's tutelage by taking financial and aesthetic control of his sexual exploits. A few days later she discharges M. Soubre.

Immediately after she dismisses M. Soubre, she registers a notable improvement in her son. Maurice, whom she only ever depicted as idle, is newly active, as she writes to her husband: "I wish you could see your son bare-legged and footed, in a shirt and a pair of white Arab drawers, rushing about with the fellaheen. He is everybody's 'brother' or 'son'" (350). From this point on, Duff Gordon depicts her eighteen-year-old son as merely a child. It seems that he gains entrance into her Egyptian family at the expense of the control of his sexual appetites.

While Duff Gordon searches for a tutor to replace M. Soubre, she takes the opportunity to taunt her husband with the hypocrisy of his race prejudices:

> Would you be shocked if a nigger taught Maurice? One Hajji Daboos I know to be a capital Arabic scholar and he speaks French like a Parisian, and Italian also, only he is a real nigger and so is the best music-master in Cairo.... Maurice has no sort of idea why a nigger should not be as good as anyone else, but thinks perhaps you might not approve. (352)

Needling her husband about his failures in educating Maurice, she continues: "If you think Maurice would be better elsewhere I am not so selfish as to wish to keep him. Would he be less idle and might he not be dissipated if you again sent him to such places as Brussels?" (352), effectively silencing him on the matter. Yet Duff Gordon does not hire Hajji Daboos or any other well-qualified scholar; instead, she depends upon her own servant, Omar, to mind Maurice. And it is Omar, above all, whom she credits with Maurice's transformation: "You would rejoice to see his fat rose cheeks and increased breadth and vigor. I never beheld such a change for the better in a human being. Really Omar has done good service in keeping him out of mischief and teaching him to be more careful of money" (350). Duff Gordon had no intention of hiring a scholar to educate Maurice. Yet the question remains, why does Duff Gordon cajole her husband into sending his only son to Egypt to be educated by an illiterate Arab servant?

We can begin to formulate an answer to this question only by considering the historical context. It is during particular historical moments that the subaltern could be posed as a model for the colonizer. Duff

Gordon's keen sense of the period enabled her to pick up on one of its defining characteristics: an intensification of the competition for colonial resources. Many theorists of empire believe that the increased competition among industrial powers during the last quarter of the century propelled the "New Imperialism" that was characterized by the brutal grab for African land and resources during the 1880s. In *Letters from the Cape,* Duff Gordon shows how competition occurred on all levels in South Africa when she observes how the English, "Dutch, Malays, blacks, Africanders, and Hottentots" vied for resources (41), predicting that if the British could not learn to compete with these peoples, they would have no chance of economic success in the Cape. It is in this context that she first chastises the British for their laziness. She uses the example of the industrious Malays to discipline the idle British when she demonstrates how by dint of hard work the Malays gained a monopoly of the cart-hiring industry. If the English could not compete with the Malays, she proposes, it was their own fault. They needed to learn to work hard in the colonies. Duff Gordon continues this line of argument in *Letters from Egypt* by valuing a colonial work ethic and arguing against the importation of aristocratic behaviors. It is in this context that we can understand her desire to cure her son of his "baronial" views. And it is also in this context that we can see why she relied on Omar's guidance. She needed his example to teach her son how to be competitive in the newly competitive world.

II. Imperial Motherhood

1. Making the Family Work: Omar and Sally

Omar Abu Halaway stars in Duff Gordon's letters as her dearest child, her eldest son. While Duff Gordon mentions Maurice in approximately one in every ten letters, she does not pass up an opportunity to praise or relate an anecdote about Omar; he appears in nearly every letter. Omar is the character around whom her story unfolds. Upon arrival in Egypt, Duff Gordon employs Omar because she "found it quite impossible to get on without a servant able to speak English" (41). Originally he was hired to do the cooking and the shopping, but when she discovers how competent he is, he becomes her nurse, maid, language teacher, boat repairman, and navigator. "Omar turns out a jewel," she brags, as she narrates the story of how Omar managed to procure her just the right Nile boat at a quarter of the going price (44). In addition to taking care of the household management, Omar fills Duff Gordon's days as they shop, eat, and travel together.

When he visits his wife and child in Alexandria, she accompanies him and stays with his family. They rarely separate, and at times they seem more like husband and wife than son and mother.

Duff Gordon represents Omar to her family as a young son, in spite of the fact that he is already a father. When Omar chooses to stay with Duff Gordon in Luxor to nurse her through an illness instead of going home to visit his wife after the birth of their second child, Duff Gordon praises him, writing: "I don't know why he is so devotedly fond of me, but he certainly does love me as he says 'like his mother,' and moreover as a very affectionate son loves his mother" (272). She incorporates Omar into her British family circle, depicting him as anxiously awaiting news about her children, writing to her husband: "Omar wanted to hear all the news you sent about the children" (66). Further, "You would be amused to see Omar bring me a letter and sit down on the floor till I tell him the family news, and then *Alhamdulillah,* we are so pleased, and he goes off to his pots and pans again" (127). Her mother, Sarah Austin, even writes a letter to Omar, which he "kisses" and keeps as a "talisman" (314).

Moreover, Duff Gordon depicts Omar as the centerpiece of her Egyptian family. While slaves and servants come and go, he remains with her throughout her seven years in Egypt, nursing her through every illness till the bitter end. Early in her stay, she represents him as comfortably at home in her Luxor apartment with her and her British maid, Sally, who accompanied Duff Gordon from England: "I am now writing in the kitchen, which is the coolest place where there is any light at all. Omar is diligently spelling words of six letters, with the wooden spoon in his hand and a cigarette in his mouth, and Sally is lying on her back on the floor" (175). She boasts that he has come to feel so comfortable there that he prays in front of them: "It is only lately that Omar has let us see him at prayer, for fear of being ridiculed, but now he is sure that it is not so, I often find him praying in the room where Sally sits at work, which is a clean, quiet place" (134). Her cozy depictions of family life stop abruptly, however, when to her surprise and dismay Sally has Omar's baby. Even Duff Gordon was fooled by her portrayal of their familial relationship. Duff Gordon proves her love for Omar by immediately forgiving him. Sally she dismisses and sends back to England, accusing her of seducing Omar. She takes away Sally's baby and gives it to Omar, for whom she arranges to have it put out to nurse with an Egyptian woman.

Given the prevalence of native rapist stories, it is surprising to learn that Sally was solely blamed for the affair. Why didn't Duff Gordon accuse Omar? Sally, after all, was her beloved servant who had been with her for ten years. Sally's case is important to consider because it shows that colonial oppression was based upon more than just the racial oppression that the native rapist stories expose. Gordon's decision to expel Sally from her family, while keeping Omar, demonstrates that Gordon was able to fall back upon a narrative that punished Sally's class and gender at the same time that it upheld racist attitudes.

The narrative that Duff Gordon used to guide her understanding of Sally's affair has to do with the sexual proclivities of working-class women: they were seen to desire sex with black men. According to McClintock, commentaries like that of Edward Long were not out of the ordinary: "[T]he lower class of women in *England* are remarkably fond of blacks" (23). Indeed, Sally's fondness of blacks was what made her such a good servant in Duff Gordon's eyes: "Sally has been an excellent traveling companion, and really a better companion than many more educated people; for she is always amused and curious, and is friendly with the coloured people" (*Letters from the Cape* 135). That Duff Gordon sees "friendliness" to blacks as a class trait becomes clear when Sally's pregnancy causes Duff Gordon to swear off English maids for good, saying, "I find that these disasters are wonderfully common here—is it the climate or the costume I wonder that makes the English maids ravish the Arab men so continually?" (187). Soon thereafter, she intimates that Sally's German replacement, Maria, is also fond of blacks and dismisses her because of her flirtations. Yet, to see her dismissal of Maria only in terms of her flirtatious behavior would be to miss the point. While Duff Gordon discharges Maria because she fears that Maria may repeat Sally's indiscretion, she also knows that Maria disturbs the status quo by refusing to cooperate with Duff Gordon's family ideal: "An educated, coarse-minded European is too disturbing an element in the family life of Easterns; the sort of filial relation, at once familiar and reverential of servants to a master they like, is odious to English and still more to French servants" (265). Maria actively stirs up trouble, and she incites other servants to follow suit: "The European style of abusing me and making faces behind my back, and trying to set my household against me—in short, the vulgar servant view of the master as a natural enemy—struck absolute dismay among my hangers-on, paid and unpaid" (254). Maria is the last female to work for Duff Gordon.

Still another case to consider is that of Zeyneb, an eight-year-old African slave whom Duff Gordon gives away not long after acquiring her. Melissa Lee Miller uses the case of Zeyneb to support her theory that the function of the mother in the colonial setting is to "create or recreate the other in the British/parental image" (230). She argues that Duff Gordon seeks to create Zeyneb in her own image, but when the child asserts her Muslim identity by refusing to eat pork, Duff Gordon gives her away. The problem with Miller's reading, however, is that it ascribes Duff Gordon's actions to cultural racism alone. Yet Duff Gordon permits her other slaves and servants to maintain their dietary and religious practices. Omar, for instance, remains a practicing Muslim throughout his employment. Zeyneb's dismissal can be more fully understood if we consider it in terms of gender and class as well as race, for Duff Gordon dismisses not only Zeyneb, but all her female European servants. Shortly before Duff Gordon gives Zeyneb away, she also complains that Zeyneb has become sullen all of a sudden, saying: "[T]o keep a sullen face about me is more than I can endure, as I have shown her every possible kindness" (98). I am suggesting that Zeyneb was discharged for reasons similar to Maria's dismissal: both refused to work with a smile, shattering Duff Gordon's fiction of a happily working family.

Sally, who Duff Gordon reports worked even better after she gave birth, threatened Duff Gordon's ideal in similar ways. Even though Sally was reported to be a good worker, Sally was even more of a threat than Maria and Zeyneb. Duff Gordon affectionately called Sally a real Arab, a compliment that meant that Sally, like herself, relished the company of Arabs. Until the incident with Omar, Sally reinforced Duff Gordon's liberal ideals of inclusion. But afterward, Sally blurred the line between being a "real Arab" and being a real Arab. Sally represents the threat of the female domestic servant that McClintock outlines—the ability to cross lines imperceptibly and exist in two worlds simultaneously. Just as the female domestic servant challenges the neat notions of the public and private, a fantasy upon which the Victorian economy thrived, Sally threatened to break down the lines between the colonizer and the colonized. What is most disturbing is that she did it without detection. Duff Gordon had no idea that Sally, whom she saw every day, was pregnant until a week before the baby was born. She failed miserably in policing Sally's body, showing just how uncontrollable the working-class body could be. Sally's situation also warrants consideration alongside Maurice's. On the one hand, Maurice's case illustrates Stoler's argument: Duff Gordon succeeds in making Maurice into the colonizer by seizing control over his sexuality. Sally, however, proves to be a much more slippery subject. Duff Gordon fails to control her sexuality, and thus fails to mark her colonial status. Sally is neither colonized nor colonizer. Duff Gordon has no option but to return her to England where her status is less ambiguous.

Duff Gordon may have had an additional motive for ridding her family of its women workers. While upper- and middle-class European males flocked to Egypt to profit from Ismail Pasha's modernization schemes, working-class European women came in droves to be servants in the new

European households. There, they labored alongside Egyptians. We have little evidence of how these households functioned, yet Duff Gordon's depiction of Omar and Sally suggests that relations may have been good: "You would be amused to hear Sally when Omar does not wake in time to wash, pray, and eat before daybreak now in Ramadan. She knocks at his door and acts as Muezzin. 'Come, Omar, get up and pray and have your dinner'" (133). Maria also befriends her Muslim coworkers. Moreover, she allies herself with them, taking their side over her European masters': "She and little Ahmad are on the most affectionate terms and keep up a continual giggle. She won his heart by blazing at Ellen who beat the child" (235). Yet, soon after Maria leaves, Duff Gordon begins to revise the harmonious picture that she had been painting of labor relations in her household, claiming instead that the European servants tormented their Egyptian counterparts. While this may have been true, it is also clear that Duff Gordon feared the product of good labor relations: Sally and Omar's "howling baby," whom she swiftly had removed from the household, and Maria's transmission of knowledge about class relations in Europe that menaced the status quo of her household. Even Zeyneb begins to assert her rights only after she returns from Janet Ross's household, where Duff Gordon complains that she had too much contact with her daughter's European maids.[7]

2. THE COMFORTS OF FAMILY: OMAR AND MAURICE

After Duff Gordon sweeps the women from her home, she settles into a comfortable life with her new family composed of boys. She represents this family as consisting of three children: Omar and a pair of slave boys. In this way, her Egyptian family mirrors her English one, with an older sibling, Omar/Janet, minding two much younger ones. Duff Gordon represents this part of her life as ideal, never depicting the type of strife that caused her to discharge Zeyneb, Sally, and Maria. Instead, she writes that her "little boys" comfort her: "I am better again now and go on very comfortably with my two little boys. Omar is from dawn till night at work at my boat, so I have only Mabrook and Ahmad, and you would wonder

---

[7] I am not suggesting that the passing of knowledge between household workers was unidirectional. The British servants had to have learned as much, if not more, from their Egyptian counterparts as they learned from the British. I do, however, wish to call attention to the difference in the histories of labor movements in the two countries. See Joel Beinin and Zachary Lockman for an excellent account of the history of workers' movements in Egypt.

to see how well I am served. Ahmad cooks a very good dinner, serves it and orders Mabrook about" (276). She makes their tireless work seem like child's play: "You would delight in his [Mabrook's] guffaws, and the merry games and hearty laughter of my *ménage* is very pleasant to me" (276). She carefully intertwines scenes of work with scenes of play, and even when she is describing her slaves at their most industrious, her writing is characterized by a playfulness of tone: "What would an English respectable cook say to seeing 'two dishes and a sweet' cooked over a little wood on a few bricks, by a baby in a blue shirt?" (276). In this manner she familiarizes child labor, domesticating it and turning it into a family affair.

Omar plays the role of a big brother/mother who successfully teaches his younger siblings/children how to work:

> It is surprising how fast the boys learn, and how well they do their work. Ahmad, who is quite little, would be a perfectly sufficient servant for a man alone; he can cook, wash, clean the rooms, make the beds, do all the table service, knife and plate cleaning, all fairly well, and I believe now he would get along even without Omar's orders. (303)

Ahmad, under Omar's tutelage, has become nearly as efficient as Omar. Indeed, it is Omar who reproduces the labor in the household. Not only does he do so by having a child with Sally, but he trains the new boys to do the work of the women servants that Duff Gordon adamantly refuses to replace: "I have not got a woman-servant, but I don't miss one at all; little Ahmad is very handy. . . . Omar irons and cleans the house and does housemaid" (258). Claiming that she has no need for a woman servant, for "[l]ittle Ahmad has grown very clever and Omar has developed a talent for ironing of which I was unaware, and we do very well indeed" (253), she insists that her "boys" can do the women's work: "I go on very well with my two boys. Mabrook washes very well and acts a *marmiton*. Darfur is housemaid and waiter in his very tiny way" (330). Duff Gordon constructs an all-male family that not only does the work of women but works like women: they labor in the household where their work remains hidden and uncompensated.

Thus, when Maurice arrives in Egypt in November of 1867, he sees a smoothly running household of boys, headed by his mother. This well-working family is the crowning achievement of Duff Gordon's philosophy of rule. Early on she had complained, "What chokes me is to hear English people talk of the stick being 'the only way to manage Arabs'" (86), and now she has demonstrated that there is another way. Maurice is there to bear witness to it. Moreover, he learns its practice when he joins her household, and, like her other boys, prospers from Omar's teachings. While they learn, among other things, to make work look like play, Maurice learns to make play look like work: "Maurice has got back his old round boyish face; he eats like an ogre, walks all day, sleeps like a top, bathes in the morning and has laid on flesh so that his clothes won't button" (349). Portraying Maurice as a child, Duff Gordon disarms him of his sexuality. She also makes it easier to imagine his tutelage under Omar.

Omar teaches Maurice the benefits of his mother's model of colonial rule. He demonstrates the value of ruling like a mother, and he inculcates the advantages of implementing the family model of governance. Mothering ensures cheap and loyal labor at the expense of a little kindness only. Nobody demonstrates this better than Omar, whom Duff Gordon pays £3 a month, which is by her own admission the lowest wage in the region. She sheepishly explains that the low rate is *his* wish: "I really feel as if I were cheating Omar to let him stay on for £3; but if I say anything he kisses my hand and tells me 'not to be cross'" (162). When the traveler and author of *Cradle Lands,* Lady Herbert, attempts to lure Omar away by offering to triple his wages, Duff Gordon brags that he refuses to go. That Omar stays is a testament to the success of Duff Gordon's model. One wonders why Omar works for so little, and one afternoon while he rubs her feet, the answer becomes apparent. When she tells him that foot care is beneath his dignity, he sings in response, "The slave of the Turk may be set free with money, but how shall one be ransomed who has been paid for by kind actions and sweet words?" (164). On a similar occasion, he says, "I am your mameluke not your servant—your mameluke" (153).[8] Duff Gordon, who understands "mameluke" to mean "white slave," demonstrates throughout her text that her filial relationship with Omar extends the "kindness" of whiteness to him—in turn for his labors of love. Duff Gordon extracts more work from Omar with her "sweet words" than Baker ever obtains from his 1,645 Egyptian conscripts with all of his lashes.[9]

The mothering model of rule is a communicative one. In place of the inflexibility of Baker's stick, it offers the subtlety of language. Duff Gordon learns Arabic from Omar, who then becomes Maurice's language tutor. Articulating the connection between Maurice's linguistic training

---

[8] Although a "mameluke" is a member of the regime established by freed white military slaves which ruled Egypt from 1250 until 1517, and continued as a ruling military class under Ottoman rule until 1812, by the mid-nineteenth century, many British travelers used the word to mean only "white slave." This popular use of the term is employed throughout Burton's translation of *One Thousand and One Nights.*

[9] In 1869 Samuel White Baker came to Egypt on a mission to stop the slave trade. Ironically, he conscripted 1,645 Egyptians into his army in his war against slavery.

and his colonial career, Duff Gordon writes: "He is beginning to pick up a little Arabic, and has got a fancy to stay on with me and learn French, Arabic, and Turkish with a view to the Foreign office" (347). Indeed, learning Arabic is Maurice's primary accomplishment in Egypt: "I had had ideas about colonial life for Maurice for decidedly the animal predominates so utterly over the intellectual activity that he will never be fit for any desk or book work. Not that he is stupid; he talks Arabic quite fluently which is rather a feat to achieve in seven or eight months" (353).

Omar also demonstrates the importance of a model of rule that relies upon the logic of the nuclear family. Household laborers are incorporated into the family, and in turn they are expected to be "at once familiar and reverential" to their masters/mothers (265). Duff Gordon's familial model offers an antidote to labor relations at home, or what she calls the "vulgar servant view of the master as a natural enemy" (254), where servants are segregated from the family and taught to accept their difference. It also ensures that there would be only one source of female authority. In addition to all the other threats that Sally posed, she raised the specter of polygamy. With Sally's dismissal, Duff Gordon makes it clear that there could only be one mother in the modern Egyptian family.[10] By enforcing modern Western family practices, Duff Gordon participates in colonizing Egypt in the way that Timothy Mitchell describes. Whereas Mitchell argues that Europeans colonized Egypt by representing European institutions there such as the military and education, I am suggesting that Duff Gordon's representation of the nuclear family was equally important to the process of colonization, for through the family, Duff Gordon imagines a way for workers in the colonies to amicably receive their colonizers, as opposed to their labor counterparts in Europe, who were increasingly forming political organizations to fight their oppressors.

That Duff Gordon's model had applications beyond Egypt becomes clear with a story that she relates about a "queer little Indian from Delhi" whom she meets near Luxor:

> I sent for him, and he came shaking in his shoes. I asked why he was afraid? "Oh, perhaps I was angry about something, and he was my *rayah*, and I might have him beaten." I cried at him, "Ask pardon of God, O man.

[10] It has been argued that during the nineteenth century, elite Egyptians increasingly chose Western and modern styles of marriage, defined by monogamous behaviors, nuclear families, educated wives, and affectionate and companionate relations. See, for example, Lisa Pollard, Beth Baron, Eve Troutt Powell, and Mona L. Russell for arguments about the adoption of modern marital relations, familial behaviors, and household habits in nineteenth-century Egypt.

How could I beat thee any more than thou couldst beat me? Have we not laws? And art thou not my brother, and the *rayah* of our Queen, as I am and no more?" "*Mashallah!*" exclaimed the six or eight fellaheen who were waiting for physic, in prodigious admiration and wonder; "and did we not tell thee that the face of the Sitt brings good fortune and not calamity and stick?" (325)

With half a dozen fellaheen as her witnesses, Duff Gordon demonstrates the benefits of her style of rule. The Egyptian peasants get a glimpse of what it would be like to be a colonial subject when they see that Duff Gordon treats the Indian as a "brother" and equal. That Duff Gordon has slipped into the role of the child and sister, reverential to her queen mother, exposes the ultimate use of her familial model, and recalls her story of the two sheiks who begged her "to communicate to the Queen of England that they would join her troops if she would invade Egypt" (245). The fellaheen also witness the Indian's reaction to Duff Gordon's kindness, for she concludes her account by relating that the Indian was "miserable when I left and would have liked me to have taken him as a volunteer servant" (325). Indeed, throughout her letters Duff Gordon offers a method for obtaining volunteers, from Omar who learns to iron and teaches her child Arabic without ever intimating a desire to earn more, to the many Egyptians whom she meets, who, like the sheiks, volunteer to fight in the queen's army on the condition that she invade Egypt. In the end, Duff Gordon employs maternal methods of communication and cooperation learned in the family to invent a novel recipe for a volunteer colony.

Works Cited

Baker, Samuel White. *Albert N'yanza, Great Basin of the Nile, and Explorations of the Nile Sources.* London: Macmillan and Company, 1866.

Baron, Beth. *The Women's Awakening in Egypt: Culture, Society and the Press.* New Haven: Yale University Press, 1994.

Beinin, Joel, and Zachary Lockman. *Workers on the Nile: Nationalism, Communism, Islam, and the Egyptian Working Class, 1882–1954.* Princeton: Princeton University Press, 1987.

Burton, Richard Francis, Sir. *The Arabian Nights: Tales from One Thousand and One Nights.* New York: Modern Library, 2001.

———. *Personal Narrative of a Pilgrimage to Al-Madinah & Meccah.* New York: Dover Publications, 1964.

Buzard, James. "Victorian Women and the Implications of Empire." *Victorian Studies* 36.4 (1993): 443–53.

Cromer, Evelyn Baring. *Modern Egypt.* New York: Macmillan Company, 1916.

Duff Gordon, Lucie. *Letters from Egypt, 1862–1869.* Ed. Gordon Waterfield. New York: Frederick A. Praeger, 1969.

———. *Letters from the Cape.* Ed. John Purves. London: Humphrey Milford, 1921.

Edwards, Amelia Ann Blanford. *A Thousand Miles up the Nile.* Leipzig: Bernhard Tauchnitz, 1878.

Herbert, Mary Elizabeth. *Cradle Lands.* New York: Catholic Publication Society, 1869.

Martineau, Harriet. *Eastern Life Present and Past.* London: E. Moxon, 1848.

Matus, Jill. "The 'Eastern-Woman Question': Martineau and Nightingale Visit the Harem." *Ninteenth-Century Contexts.* 21:1 (1999): 63–87.

McClintock, Anne. *Imperial Leather: Race, Gender, and Sexuality in the Colonial Contest.* New York: Routledge, 1995.

Melman, Billie. *Women's Orients: English Women and the Middle East, 1718–1918, Sexuality, Religion, and Work.* Ann Arbor: University of Michigan Press, 1992.

Miller, Melissa Lee. "The Imperial Feminine: Victorian Women Travelers in Egypt." In *White Women in Racialized Spaces: Imaginative Transformation and Ethical Action in Literature.* Ed. Samina Najmi and Rajini Srikanth. Albany: State University of New York Press, 2002. 22–41.

Mitchell, Timothy. *Colonising Egypt.* Berkeley: University of California Press, 1988.

Nightingale, Florence. *Letters from Egypt, 1849–1850.* New York: Weidenfeld and Nicolson, 1987.

Pollard, Lisa. *Nurturing the Nation: The Family Politics of Modernizing, Colonizing, and Liberating Egypt, 1805–1923.* Berkeley: University of California Press, 2005.

Powell, Eve. M. Troutt. *A Different Shade of Colonialism: Egypt, Great Britain, and the Mastery of the Sudan.* Berkeley: University of California Press, 2003.

Pratt, Mary Louise. *Imperial Eyes: Travel Writing and Transculturation.* New York: Routledge, 1992.

Ross, Janet. *Last Letters from Egypt. To Which are added Letters from the Cape. By Lady Duff Gordon. With a Memoir by her Daughter Mrs. Ross.* London: Macmillan, 1875.

Russell, Mona L. *Creating the New Egyptian Woman: Consumerism, Education, and National Identity, 1863–1922.* New York: Palgrave, 2004.

Shereen, Faiza. "Lucie Duff Gordon." *Dictionary of Literary Biography.* Vol. 166. Detroit: Bruccoli, 1996.

Stoler, Ann Laura. *Carnal Knowledge and Imperial Power: Race and the Intimate in Colonial Rule.* Berkeley: University of California Press, 2002.

PART IV

The Maternal Body

CHAPTER 13

The Text as Child

Gender/Sex and Metaphors of Maternity at the *Fin de Siècle*

BRENDA R. WEBER*

The American humorist Fanny Fern quipped in 1867, "A woman who wrote used to be considered a sort of monster" (371). By "monster" Fern referenced a widely held belief that women of intellect and public fame had unsexed themselves, becoming "three-quarters men" due to their turn toward professional careers and their ostensible turn away from families. Fern's characterization drew on widely held Victorian investments in sex and gender ideologies on both sides of the Atlantic. The prevailing prescriptive code dictated that sex and gender were synonymous and that men, masculinity, and maleness existed separate from and situated against women, femininity, and femaleness. Both the imagined conflation of sex/gender and the rigid polarization of male/female signaled what Cynthia Eagle Russett has called a "near-total absence of information in the field of sex differences" (183). Yet the prescriptive solidity of the sex/gender ideology did not translate easily into everyday lives. Particularly at century's end, the charge that educated and New Women had become "unsexed" and the consequent efforts to police and punish disruptions of conventional sex/gender categories indicate fault lines in the prevailing social codes.

Because women's engagement in professional authorship threatened investments in gendered and sexed behaviors, the woman writer and her

---

* This essay is reprinted from *Feminist Studies* 32.3 (Fall 2006), by permission of the publisher, Feminist Studies, Inc.

text are rich sites for analysis. As the nineteenth century waned and more women claimed identities as professional (and public) authors, the writer and her work were often vilified through a public smear campaign that denigrated them both as trash. Women writers responded to this coercion in multiple ways—some acquiesced to traditional values, continuing to write but undermining the power of female characters; some rebelled and were branded bluestockings and New Women; some played a bit of both games, seeming to adhere to the dominant ideology but offering opportunities for subversion within their texts. It is this third category that interests me in this essay, for the professional writer was at once able to offer the patriarchal culture a "docile body," as Foucault terms it, perfectly in keeping with the cultural imperatives of feminine appropriateness, while also depicting a discursive "deviant body," which was too fluid, too plural, too different to be fully restrained by patriarchal representation.

In such a deterministic order where intellectual work stems from male faculties, a biological woman who crosses into masculinist behavior violates ideological symmetry, interrupting social prescriptions by announcing a third man-woman category. This third category is logically invalid in a binaried order. Indeed, as both Judith Lorber and Anne Fausto-Sterling note through the figure of Herculine Barbin, a French hermaphrodite whose life ended in suicide, the nineteenth century provided limited possibility "of living socially as both a woman and a man even if it is physiologically possible" (Lorber 80). The distinction between male and female presumed that biology ordered social arrangements, a logic evident, in particular, through the cult of motherhood. The mother, already a figure of some mythic proportion, became the critical signifier of sex/gender appropriateness, a sign that read as domestic, nurturing, and other-oriented. These markings were important, since at century's end, as Bram Dijkstra notes, the Victorian male establishment had become "obsessed" with women's degeneration, which it attributed to excessive stimulation, both sexual and intellectual. The corrective was clear: "Only complete absorption in the practice of motherhood was considered a fit activity for women" (74).

This indexical link between sex/gender and motherhood came with its own dilemmas. Obviously, not all women were mothers, some by choice and others by circumstance. For professional women, motherhood was often not an option sought or desired, and their very resistance to "maternal instinct" unsexed them. The sort of semiotic power afforded to women through the trope of the mother was, consequently, not equally available to all women. In this essay, I examine how three professional women writers turned what might have been a symbolic deficit to their advantage. They did this by creating women writer characters who conceived, birthed, and nurtured a textual child. In so doing, they were able to fuse idealized conceptualizations of Victorian womanhood (expressed through the trope of the mother) to the *fin-de-siècle* woman writer, thus expanding sex/gender categories and subversively appropriating monologic logics to support pluralistic outcomes.

In the small but insistent body of Victorian literature in which women writers created characters who were also women writers, the cultural mandate that good women be good mothers underwent multiple displacements and relocations. As with most abstractions, the mothering metaphor was slippery, particularly since the textual progeny were viewed by the larger culture as not only a writer's child, but often as a societal pollutant requiring regulation and elimination. Looking specifically at three texts authored in the 1890s—Mary Cholmondeley's *Red Pottage*[1] (1899), Rhoda Broughton's *A Beginner* (1894), and Elizabeth Robins's *George Mandeville's Husband* (1894)—I demonstrate how these writers imbued their author characters with the signifiers of motherhood as a way to bolster cultural legitimacy.[2] Rather than seeing the insistent mothering metaphors as only salutary, I suggest that the text-as-child metaphor functioned as a complicated disciplinary trope to pull women more tightly into hegemonically sanctioned roles. Since, as Russett notes, Victorian women were never "permitted to forget that their essence was reproductive," the text-as-child metaphor participated in a critical form of didactic instruction (43). Rhetoric about the natural obligation of the woman's womb placed Victorian women writers in a discursive straitjacket, disciplining the possibilities of the mind by restricting the representations of the physical body.

Yet this imperative connection between a woman's reproductive body and her imaginative offspring when portrayed in fiction could be conveyed with great complexity (and ambiguity). In Mary Cholmondeley's *Red Pottage,* for example, Hester Gresley's text is embodied as the "child of her brain," which is then "murdered" at the hands of her poor-reading brother. In Rhoda Broughton's *A Beginner,* if the text is child, we can see the novel authorizing nothing short of infanticide. In Elizabeth Robins's

---

[1] Cholmondeley's title is an allusion to the biblical tale of Esau, who sold his birthright to his brother Jacob for a meal of bread and pottage of lentils (Genesis 25:30–34). In Cholmondeley's hands, the allusion refers to one of her emasculated characters, Hugh Scarlett, whose disregard for his own birthright and consequent infatuation with a married woman leads to his eventual downfall.

[2] The text-as-child trope is not by any means exclusive to these three texts or to the *fin de siècle*, nor is it a metaphor employed only by or about women. Indeed, it was quite common for Romantic and Transcendentalist poets, in particular, to talk of their fathering vis-à-vis the text, a move that allowed them to placate "womb envy" and to claim roles as both creators and procreators.

George Mandeville's Husband, tropes of the mother's body and her "natural" responsibilities to both daughter and text are interrupted by a volley of referents that refute the naturalness of sex/gender categories, coding male bodies feminine and female bodies masculine, while leaving pubescent bodies dead in a pool of their own (menstrual?) blood. In these books, the representation of mothering allows for significant alteration of the overriding sense of what mothering might mean, and, hence, of a woman's "natural" role in late-nineteenth-century Britain. As such, these books perform an important countercultural work in their articulation and circulation of crucial debates about women's participation in a public commercial sphere. They do so in a way markedly different from most New Women texts in that they seemingly underscore dominant values while also necessitating a discursive realignment of the woman writer's role and thus a shift in the prevailing ideology.[3] This authorizes, as Wendy Parkins notes, "new forms of knowledge and new subject positions for women" (48). My examination seeks to reveal the ways in which Cholmondeley, Broughton, and Robins were both confined by the cultural straitjacket and able to wiggle free of it.

Pregnant with Meaning: Issues of Sex and Gender in Birthing the Text

Before thinking specifically about each of the novels I consider, it's important to map out a brief usage of the text-as-child metaphor. One example can be seen in Charles Dickens, who begins *David Copperfield* with an image that illuminates the debate about sex/gender and writing. "I was," he says, "born with a caul, which was advertised for sale, in the newspapers, at the low price of fifteen guineas" (9–10). A caul is the fetal membrane that most typically covers the head of the infant at birth. It is offered for sale in young Davy's case for its ability to guard against death by drowning. With no suitable bidders, the caul is stored away until ten years later it is "put up in a raffle." Copperfield recalls, "I was present myself, and I remember to have felt quite uncomfortable and confused, at a part of myself being disposed of in that way" (10).

---

[3] A more standard trope for narratives about women writers was failure. In her introductory essay to *Red Pottage,* Elaine Showalter argues, "It took a great deal of self-esteem to allow one's writer-heroine to succeed in the 1890s, and Cholmondeley could not quite bring herself to be so optimistic" (xiii), so that represented failure is the result of lack of self-esteem and of pessimism. Penny Boumelha, by contrast, strikes a more optimistic interpretive note, arguing that to make the woman writer fail is the only way to assert her artistry. See Pykett and Ardis for additional discussion on this issue.

It is not too great of an interpretive leap to connect the fetal membrane wrapped around the author's infant skull and later offered for sale with the text itself, the issue of his brain, packaged and sent into the world in exchange for money. Though David refers to the caul as "a part of myself," it is more accurately a part of his mother. By itself, the caul symbolizes female procreative power, specifically the woman's ability to produce within herself the fluids, membranes, and nutrients necessary to sustain life. Wrapped around the head of the author, the caul signifies his creative power, for it allows the male author to appropriate the womb by draping it around, and thus conflating it with, his mind.[4] He is at once creator and procreator. The membrane lends him female generative powers that he can confer on his male womb, the brain, yet it underscores his own absence, or lack, of the biological apparatus for creation.[5] Dickens's metaphor indicates that the penis may be the male organ of procreation, but the brain is his womb for creation, and any concretizing of the metaphor necessitates the displacement of mother's membrane onto son's mind.[6] This underscores the rightness of ontological separation—of women being linked to the body and to nature, of men being linked to the mind and to culture. It also reifies a perceived rightness of sex/gender sameness since it is impossible for male/masculinity to enact female/femininity except through appropriation and performance.

Such a division has implications for women's authorship, for as Gaye Tuchman observes, the "authority of the woman [as author] is based on her feelings, her intuitions, her connection with the earth and nature, in short, on her reproductive body; the authority of man is based on his will, his reason, his name which both identifies him with the patriarchal good and distinguishes him from other men in short, his productive mind" (25). So, though David Copperfield can here claim access to the procreative powers of the female womb, he does not disturb his male/intellectual situatedness, thus erasing his connection to "lack" through privileged right of entry to both metaphors.

---

[4] In this particular instance, the image of the caul also allows the abandoned David Copperfield a form of symbiosis with his idealized, though incompetent, mother, Clara. As critics of the novel have noted, a central preoccupation of the text is its working through of mother issues. Mary Poovey notes that the idealized mother figure "takes the form of a series of substitutions that exposes and punishes the mother's guilt without jeopardizing the idealized woman she retrospectively becomes" (*Uneven* 92).

[5] The notion of the brain as the male womb is, of course, nicely reinforced through the myth of Zeus bringing forth a fully formed Athena from his head.

[6] The idea that men can access women's generative power by appropriating female reproductive organs offers a nice corollary to the "pen as penis" metaphor considered particularly by Gilbert and Gubar in *The Madwoman in the Attic*.

As this suggests, the "creation as birth" metaphor is rife with hermeneutic complexity. Many literary-historical scholars have engaged with and critiqued the metaphor, suggesting that it can be both elucidating (for the discursive empowerment it allows) and essentialist (for the way it forever links the woman to the procreative body).[7] It is a metaphor deeply vexed, internally incoherent, occasionally essentialist, and potentially empowering. In short, a metaphor of considerable richness and complexity. In particular reference to the sex/gender overlap in the construction of the late-Victorian woman writer, the metaphor evokes other questions. These include: Does the body function as a reliable source of self-knowledge? Does female sexuality exist prior to social construction? Do women experience their bodies outside of acculturation?

My particular task is not to reconcile the debate about whether it is appropriate to invoke the body and mothering as metaphors for describing the writing process, nor is it necessarily to sort out how fully these images presuppose a biological essence. As a trope about Victorian literary production, the metaphor functions as a political concept that shapes cultural norms. The use of the childbirth metaphor compels imaginative coherence to an economy of sameness that represents all women as heterosexual, able-bodied, and premenopausal. It is hegemonic in that it appears to command consent "naturally." In short, it normalizes the body and the sexuality of a woman so that she is in all circumstances able and willing to function as a mother, and the metaphor pushes to the margins the "odd women" who risk "physical and emotional" disease and a "shorter lifespan," not to mention social ostracism, by refusing the natural call of their maternal "destiny" (Smith-Rosenberg 336).

The gendered and sexed implications for writing are profound. Given the prevailing Victorian stance that artistry is largely male and masculine, we see a cultural imperative for the male writer to appropriate (female) procreative powers, while the woman who writes must appropriate (male) intellectual ability. Though, as we see illustrated in the case of Dickens's *David Copperfield,* it is possible for the man to wrap the procreative membranes of the woman's body around his brain without compromising his gendered and sexed identity, a similar reversal is not allowed the woman. The woman who writes is "unsexed"; she is "three-quarters male" as a character in Robins's *George Mandeville's Husband* says about George Eliot. To perpetuate her gendered identity, the woman who writes must undergo several contortions in order to reconcile her behavior with her body. Like a woman pretending to be a transvestite, she must be a woman acting like a

---

[7] See Susan Stanford Friedman, Margaret Wise Petrochenkov, Sandra Gilbert and Susan Gubar, Nina Auerbach, Elaine Showalter (*A Literature*), and Margaret Homans.

man, borrowing from a woman—all of which underscores larger cultural ideologies that imagine sexed binaries as normative even as they expose the fluidity of gendered experience in everyday lives.[8]

When sex identity exists in such simultaneous overlap and contradistinction to gender roles—in this case, when behavior (artistic creation) is taken to be identical with biology (physical procreation)—the enforcement of both concepts is potentially at risk. We can see some evidence of that imbalance in the cultural anxiety operative at the end of the nineteenth century as demonstrated through Cholmondeley, Broughton, and Robins.

Red Pottage: The Author as (Masculinized) Mother

Mary Cholmondeley's representation of the woman writer in Hester Gresley codes her in cultural signifiers (such as thinness, frailty, and obedience) that underscore her conventional femininity. At the level of the body, she is most pointedly not a threat. Yet Hester possesses access to "imagination" and thus to an artistry that borders on the spiritual sublime, and this marks her as deviant for the way she embodies masculine expression in a female body. Hester's first book, *An Idyll of East London,* is moderately well received but, to many characters in the book, troubling for its commentary on poverty and urbanization. As Cholmondeley depicts it, the manner in which Hester tackles pressing social issues devolves for those who discuss her work into tedious debates of autobiography versus imagination, a larger cultural criticism lobbed at other Victorian woman writers, in particular the Brontë sisters. Essentially, the question is: how can a "protected" woman possibly imagine degradation? The answer suggests that any woman capable of imagining vice is no (true) woman at all.

Cholmondeley deploys Hester's body as a sort of corrective, her frailness standing in feminine compensation for the masculine aggression of her mind. The novel's early pages work to emphasize Hester's diminutive stature. Contrasting Hester with the novel's other heroine, Rachel Ward,[9] Chomondeley writes, "Rachel was physically strong. Hester was

[8] Robins's "Woman's Secret" (1913) makes evident the self-aware gender play necessary to appease expectations about masculine writerly output. She writes: "Contrary to popular impression, to say in print what she thinks is the last thing the woman-novelist . . . is commonly so rash as to attempt. In print, even more than elsewhere (unless she is reckless), she must wear the aspect that shall have the best chance of pleasing her brothers" (5). This includes, Robins notes, "doing her level best to play the man's game, and seeing how nearly like him she can do it" (6).

[9] I am not able to do full justice to the complexity of this novel here, but it is important to note, even if briefly, that the trope of dual heroines, who support and complement one

weak. The one was calm, patient, practical, equable, the other imaginative, unbalanced, excitable" (36). Subsequent scenes reinforce Hester's slight body and impetuous nature, by calling the reader's critical gaze to Hester's "white exhausted face" (36); her "small slight figure" (52); her "innocent, childlike face" (77); her "slight graceful figure" (155); her "thin hands" (320), all of which, in terms of artistic output, follow the dictates of "blind instinct" (335). The narrator notes, "Her irregular profile, her delicate pointed speech and fingers, her manner of picking up her slender feet as she walked, her quick alert movements, everything about her was neat, adjusted, perfect in its way" (54).

This sense of Hester's "perfection" (or rather, her perfect alignment with white, heterosexual, upper-class femininity) makes of Hester a multiple signifier of idealized femininity. The hyperarticulation of her femininity is particularly pronounced in the novel's mothering tropes. Though Hester challenges convention by being unmarried and not a biological mother, she is given the primary maternal role in the novel as articulated through her status as the mother of books. When her brother James discovers, surreptitiously reads, and then destroys the manuscript for her second novel, *Husks,* Hester responds with what seems obviously intended as a mother's fury. When her nephew, Regie, was ill, she tells her brother, "I did not let your child die. Why have you killed mine?" (276). The young Regie immediately enters this scene of confrontation, carrying a potato he has baked in the dying embers of the bonfire made of her manuscript, and Hester "turn[s] on him like some blinded infuriated animal at bay, and thrust[s] him violently from her" (277). Her capitulation to a more bestial form is justified, we are led to believe, by the murder of her own child. She later tells the bishop:

> "If I had a child . . . and it died, I might have ten more, beautiful and clever and affectionate, but they would not replace the one I had lost. Only if it were a child," a little tremor broke the dead level of the passionless voice, "I should meet it again in heaven. There is the resurrection of the body for the children of the body, but there is no resurrection that I ever heard of for the children of the brain." (344)

Here Cholmondeley turns the text-as-child metaphor so that the textual child possesses greater value than a biological son or daughter. The loss of the issue of the brain is represented here as irreparable, beyond a mother's

---

another and who end the novel by fleeing England together, functions as a significant turn on "conventional" plotting and thus opens the possibility for same-sex attachments and revised domestic paradigms.

grieving. Hester has been told that the "pang of motherhood is that even your children don't seem your very own. . . . [But] spiritual children, the books, are really ours" (334–35). Because Hester has gone a step further than the mother ideology allows, because she has claimed and sustained a belief that the text is her "very own" (and autogenously conceived) child, Cholmondeley's characterization of Hester pushes against a dominant and limiting trope, reconfiguring the value conferred on women through motherhood. As a consequence, not only has the author Hester the right to wear the mantle of mother, it is creation rather than procreation that makes her worthy of that honor.

Even so, Hester's relationship to her art plays out largely according to the terms of Victorian motherhood, for she sacrifices her well-being, her presence of mind, and her good health so that the textual more-than-child might prosper. She says of her text:

> "I loved it for itself, not for anything it was to bring me. . . . It was part of myself. But it was the better part. The side of me which loves success . . . had no hand in it. My one prayer was that I might be worthy to write it, that it might not suffer by contact with me. I spent myself upon it." Hester's voice sank. "I knew what I was doing. I joyfully spent my health, my eyesight, my very life upon it. I was impelled to do it by what you perhaps call a blind instinct, what I, poor simpleton and dupe, believed at the time to be nothing less than the will of God." (335)

In language that mirrors the cult of motherhood, Hester suggests that her call to artistry supersedes all. This is an interesting use of the self-sacrificing ideology, for it displaces the body of the child with the body of the text, yet it underscores the same values—womanly sacrifice to a duty that is greater than oneself.

Cholmondeley's (per)version of the mother ideology allows for alteration and difference. In this case, the written work moves to center stage in a woman's motherly responsibility. Hester is allowed to fulfill the dictates of a culture hungry for motherly devotion, but she does so by spending her fragile body so that her writing might live. Her frail, delicate, and slender body—all of which underscore her situatedness in patriarchal codes—refuses the signifying system it is placed within. Giving birth to a text rather than to a child, Hester alters the code of expectation, so that professional determination overrides biological determinism. This model, in which (woman's) will exerts more power than genetics, is an important reorganization of the prevailing phallocratic order, allowing possibilities for change in both ideology and social arrangements. By contrast, Rhoda

Broughton's *A Beginner,* though constructing its writer heroine in much the same way as Cholmondeley's *Red Pottage,* offers curtailed possibilities for change.

A Beginner: Cautionary Tale to the Lady Novelist and Would-be Mothers

Emma Jocelyn is *A Beginner's* literary protagonist, and the title of Broughton's novel points to both Emma's status and identity, for she is a beginner when it comes to textual production and she adopts the name "a beginner" as the nom de plume of her book *Miching Mallecho.* Like Hester in *Red Pottage,* Emma's body bears the signs of upper-class white heterosexual femininity. Emma is described as a "charming white nymph, who looks at once so fresh and so high bred" (69); characters are continually asked, "Why can't you sit and stand and walk as Miss Jocelyn does?"(58); her physical form, her "bow and gait," unlike her literary offspring, are beyond criticism (255). Though Broughton offers unfailing praise of Emma's physically feminine and whitened features, particularly those parts of Emma's body responsible for touching the text—her "affectionate white hand" (120), her "pink palm" (63), her "long white hands like lilies" (243)—Broughton is relentless in demonstrating the utter uselessness of Emma's book, the "offspring of her brain" (122). *Miching Mallecho* may well be the child of Emma's white, delicate, and upper-class body as fashioned by her lily-like hands, and she may indeed watch over that "beloved offspring" with "gnawing anxiety" (20), but Broughton makes clear that Emma's ambition is misplaced and her book is ill-developed and irrelevant, or, as a particularly sadistic London review echoing Samuel Johnson notes, her book is "ill-fed, ill-killed, ill-kept, ill-dressed, and ill-carved" (126). Already we can see the body metaphors piling up, as the text becomes both child of the lady novelist's mind and animal for slaughter and consumption.

Emma seeks to defend her child/text throughout the course of Broughton's novel, arguing that she writes in order to be a "teacher and a benefactor to her kind!" (79). Yet the stronger evidence of the novel's content comes through the response of its greatest advocate, Lesbia Heathcote, a second cousin to Emma. Lesbia finds the novel enchanting, and when reading, she becomes so absorbed that she is "unconscious of [her children's] clamour or even of their presence" (105). Further, Lesbia uses the novel to justify dalliances in extramarital romantic adventures. So we see that Emma's efforts to "benefit her kind" actually encourage her cousin to abandon her joint roles of mother and wife, a consequence completely unintended by the naive author. "How frightfully you have misunderstood me!" Emma says to Lesbia (112). Indeed, though Emma's novel is defended throughout the course of Broughton's novel, it is never quoted. Readers never gain access to (or are corrupted by) Emma's ideas; the ray of light never shines upon our brains.[10] Instead, the novel receives the response it purportedly merits: it is ridiculed and castigated, tossed on the floor, figuratively killed (the critic's hand is "red with her infant's blood" [166]), pulled from circulation, and ultimately destroyed.[11]

Through it all, Emma is both conflated with and distanced from the text. As "mother" of the novel, it is an extension of her body.[12] And though "perfect prosperity" is written on "every detail of her appearance" (252), Emma's own body cannot be separated from the public scorn accorded to her text. When Lesbia's husband throws Emma's book to the floor in disgust, for instance, Emma feels as if "some degrading physical indignity had been inflicted on herself" (114). Though the text makes insistent references to *Miching Mallecho* as the "offspring of her brain" (122), Emma's "beloved offspring" (20), her "literary infant" (122), it so castigates novel writing for unfeminizing Victorian women, for making a "good, if rather foolish, woman neglect her duties to God and man" (115), that the *A Beginner* ends with Emma becoming persuaded of her textual child's dangers and mournfully agreeing to burn the entire printing, save five copies lost in the circulating libraries.

Lest we think that the metaphor of child has receded at this point, Broughton depicts Emma as in "tragic dejection as she stands motionless" (390) and watches as the "whole little family" (391) is dumped upon the bonfire. The fire then "assert[s] its supremacy, and is licking and shriveling and crackling the gaily coloured boards, and tossing up the exultant brutality of its flames above their crumbling paper and vanishing type" (390–91). As a final act of "expiation," Emma steps forward with her original manuscript in hand, "the beloved, the much-treasured, the sole" (391)

---

[10] This, in fact, was one of the criticisms raised by an 1894 *Anthenaeum* review: "We are told little about the volume (*Miching Mallecho*) except that it is concerned with 'passion.' Yet it is the principal feature of 'A Beginner'" (574).

[11] There is some poetic justice in the fact that though the fictional text-child *Miching Mallecho* is destroyed, its material counterpart, *A Beginner,* survives intact.

[12] Pamela Gilbert and I disagree somewhat on just what body *Miching Mallecho* occupies. While I have argued here for it being a textual child, she sees Emma Jocelyn's novel as "the woman's body entering the realm of exchange—although 'innocent' and 'virginal' in its purposes, to the extent it succeeds in the market, it becomes dangerous, contagious, and seductive" (114). In both cases Broughton incorporates the text as an extension of the female body that must be contained through a figurative death by fire. Mary Poovey offers a compelling reading of a different infanticide metaphor in her contention that mid-Victorian rationales for colonization and capitalism are expressed in Dickens's *Our Mutual Friend* as the narrator's "offspring" that must be killed or sacrificed for the good of materials exchange (*Making* 163–64).

and she "tosses" this as well into the "funeral pyre." The act is occasioned with much sadness on Emma's part, and as she walks away from the burning mass of her literary children, Lesbia endeavors to cheer her up: "'Do not cry,' says Lesbia soothingly. 'At least, cry as much as you please, for there is no one near—no one, that is, except George!'" (393).

And who, pray tell, is George? None other than a tertiary character who, we are told in the afterword, emerges to marry Emma. This is an important development, as it must surely be deduced that one of the problems inherent in positing the text as child and the lady novelist as its mother is the absence of the father. Without a "father" to assist in the creation of the baby/text, that offspring is illegitimate and must be discarded to protect reputations. The textual baby is even more troubling than would be an actual "bastard child," moreover, because no man, whether husband or lover, is needed for its conception. The textual baby, then, is not only illegitimate, it is somehow monstrous, the offspring of a woman who can reproduce without a man. The comparisons to Christian lore cannot be overlooked, since the concept of a child without a father (and so conceived without sex) is akin to the virgin birth. The woman writer's progeny, however, is nowhere close to a conception without intercourse, for it is the woman's unsexed position, her crossing over from feminine practices to masculine behaviors that "fertilizes" the seed that will become her book. As such, the woman writer can impregnate herself: she is not a virgin, waiting for divine seed, but a monster, simultaneously man and woman, able to displace and replace both the phallus and the penis. She does not blur categorical boundaries but refutes the categories altogether.

What we see in *A Beginner*, then, is a story of a woman writer, depicted as physically delicate and intellectually naive, unable to control the destructive power of her own creation repetitively referred to as her monstrous child (an interesting echo of Mary Shelley's claim that *Frankenstein*, like Victor Frankenstein's monster itself, is her "hideous progeny"). In *A Beginner*, the text functions as an elaborate testing ground for the woman writer's product, and it eventually depicts her as saddened, humiliated, and recommitted to the values of middle-class Victorian culture through the contract of marriage and the promise of "real" (legitimate) rather than textual (illegitimate) children.

George Mandeville's Husband: Refusing the Mother, Refusing to Mother

In Elizabeth Robins's *George Mandeville's Husband,* we are presented with a startling departure from the delicate and chastened author characters constructed by Cholmondeley and Broughton. According to her effeminate husband, for whom the novel is named and through whom most perspective is focalized, George Mandeville is vulgar and unwomanly, her body is overlarge and unappealing, and her novelistic output (perhaps as a consequence of her physical excesses) is meaningless tripe (to clarify this characters' shifting-identities mechanism, "George" is the author-character's celebrity persona, "Lois" is the author-character, and "George/Lois" is the inevitable collapsing between the two). In this sense, Elizabeth Robins's George Mandeville is no true woman at all, her deviance announced by a body completely opposite Hester's and Emma's. Scene after scene portrays Lois Wilbraham—to the public, George Mandeville—increasingly obsessed with her persona as author. Gorged on food and flattery, George Mandeville becomes a spectacle of excess, not even the death of her daughter calling her to her womanly duties.

Plumpness may well be an articulation of maternal characteristics—an accentuation of breasts, hips, and the body fat needed to sustain pregnancy—but on the body of George Mandeville, plumpness turns to obesity, maternal ability to dysfunction, ambition to aggression. Thus Robins's representation here is in stark contrast to the positive relation between maternity and fatness discussed by Lilian Craton.[13] As such, Robins effectively converts what might be read as feminine and maternal into that which is masculine, monstrous, and terrifying. George/Lois is further "de-sexed" in that her maternal obligation is expressed in only the remotest forms of distracted interest. Though she is the only "real" mother of the three author characters considered here, Robins makes clear that her protagonist is a bad mother whose child has "few illusions as to her place in her mother's life" (8).

George/Lois's life is consumed not with the nurturing of children but with the production of text—hack novels and bad plays. What little maternal investment she possesses takes the form of talking to her slender, docile, and fragile daughter, Rosina, about "sordid" topics such as (we can only assume) menstruation and coming womanhood. This topic between Rosina and her mother, which is both addressed and not addressed,[14] is precisely

---

[13] See Craton in this volume.

[14] I borrow this concept from Catherine Wiley, who notes Robins's refusal of representation in her 1893 play *Alan's Wife* (cowritten with Florence Bell, though produced and published anonymously). Indeed, across the Robins canon, it is a common device to refuse to represent a controversial topic or theme, even as she insists that the reader acknowledge its presence. In Robins's 1894 unpublished play *The Mirkwater*, for instance, Robins leads us to believe that Felicia Vincent may well be responsible for her never-represented sister's disappearance, but ultimately, though obliquely, we learn that the sister weighted herself with stones and threw herself into a river when she discovered she had breast cancer. We see this same technique at work in *The Convert* (1907), Robins's novelized version of the stage

Rosina's maturation into puberty, a fact that biologically links Rosina's girl's body to the woman's body of the mother. Rosina is deeply insulted that her mother takes great liberties by asking her invasive questions about her health. She complains, "It might do if you've always told your mother every blessed thing from the time you were a baby. But if she's left you to yourself till you're fourteen, she can't suddenly—suddenly—tell you things—without a girl's feeling like murdering her" (138). These "things" her mother tells her are "facts of existence" that Rosina finds "so ugly, so ugly" (136). In Rosina's repulsion of her mother (and the coming womanhood of her own body), we see the results of her gender-skewed parenting, for the brusque and disinterested (masculinized) mother frightens the child away from a body that the overly fastidious (effeminate) father cannot fathom.

Though it is surely not unusual to make the rites of menstruation so secretive that they become taboo, Robins points to the presence of Rosina's blood, and her telling death marked by a large hemorrhage that stains her white sheets "bright with new-spilt blood" (211), through euphemisms that point to nothing at all. This functions as an effective sleight of hand that compels the reader to fill in the gap. In this case Robins points to the fissure between ideology and practice. George Mandeville is physiologically capable of having a child, but she does not possess maternal instinct, a contradiction that erodes an ideological belief connecting female bodies and motherly love. Likewise, her more tractable and seemingly "natural" daughter, who should theoretically flourish due to her congruence with the dominant bodily ideal, ultimately recoils at the realities of her own body and dies. The gap suggests, then, that biological sexed capacity does not necessarily determine embodied gendered behavior.

This disconnect between sex and gender is announced most pointedly in the figure of Ralph Wilbraham, Rosina's father and Lois's husband, a male character who is decidedly unmasculine. One significant result of depicting George Mandeville in such graphic and extreme terms is that the mother's excessiveness cements the "dysfunctional" bond between father and daughter. Rosina goes to Ralph for comfort, compassion, and commiseration. She turns to her father for a mother's support. If this were merely a novel of role reversal, Rosina would find succor in the mothering she receives from her father. Yet the kind of haven Ralph offers Rosina is rife with peril, precisely due to Ralph's entrenchment in and commitment

---

play *Votes for Women* (1907). In both, Vida Levering crusades for suffrage, but only after Robins has made clear that she carries some mysterious secret from the past. We discover in elliptical references that she was seduced, impregnated, and lost the child, whether through miscarriage, stillbirth, or abortion we don't know.

to gendered ideologies that suggest men work and have public identities while women sacrifice themselves to families.

Rosina's anxiety about what she shall "do" manifests itself repeatedly through the latter half of the novel. "'Suppose, father,' she asks, 'nobody ever loved me but you, and suppose I lived the longest—I might, you know—and suppose I was very poor—what then?'" (85). With this Rosina asks Wilbraham the question of the age: If a woman does not or cannot compete in the marriage market, and if she is not trained or prepared to earn a living for herself, and if her father is not in a position to support her, what kinds of options are open to her? Ralph assures her that "a dozen womanly things" await her, like tending to small children or keeping house or sewing, but he is adamant that she shall never be an artist or a writer. As she approaches death, Rosina hits on a vocation that will support her. She tells her father, "There's something I could do for my living, that even you would say was quite 'seemly'—that is, of course, if I live to be very old and very poor, and you aren't here to take care of me" (196). Her brainstorm? "[M]ending's my great accomplishment" (201). It's a rather pitiful prospect, even to Ralph.

We see here the consequences that result when a young girl is disallowed autonomy by the patriarchal structure that governs her: with professions that feed her creativity barred to her and virtually no other viable path open, she literally undergoes a transformation from embodied character to idealized image, dying upon her invalid's couch in a death scene worthy of any consumptive heroine. Consider the language Robins uses to describe Rosina on her deathbed: "What tiny little hands she had! Her face, with the small, regular features, was even unusually pretty to-day. Her creamy skin had that look common to her type, as though a soft light shone behind it—that pale, luminous quality which is the peculiar compensation of complexions that are very fine, and yet not fair or ruddy. No one ever saw that light in a face of 'lilies and roses,' but these for whom it shines are not bereft of beauty" (196). The resulting death scene is the quintessence of high-Victorian sensibility, yet it is also the most subversive moment in Robins's novel, for she turns the code of the passive consumptive askew so that it registers less as a moment of peaceful apotheosis and more as proof of the failure of ideology.

This repetition of a literary trope in a way that refuses to conform to familiar ideological registers is a discursive process Nancy Cervetti has identified in numerous literary texts. Drawing on Judith Butler's idea of "subversive repetition," Cervetti gives a more specific sense of its relevance to literature. She notes that similarity offers a form of cultural legibility; at the same time "a subversive repetition disrupts old ways through differences in tone, in recontextualization and location, and in deviant endings. A repetition with a difference displaces the old through ambiguity, irony, hyperbole, parody, and dissonance" (4). Robins's ending to *George Mandeville's Husband* operates in just this manner.

I've already noted that Rosina dies in a pool of blood, and given the undercurrent of whispered conversations, the scarlet stain on Rosina's white bed sheets resonates with sexual meaning. It is not particularly innovative to imbue a death scene with sexual implications, particularly to the Victorians. It is innovative, however, to undercut the erotics of such a scene by averting the reader's gaze from the death itself. When Rosina dies, both Ralph and the reader are in George Mandeville's parlor, entertaining her "insufferable" literary throng. Rosina's death is told, then, not by the sometimes-present narrator or through the more common focalization of Ralph, but by the great lady of popular rubbish herself, George Mandeville.

In her hands, Rosina becomes nothing other than representation, her image adjusted to fit her novelist mother's purposes. In essence, Rosina transforms from biological child to textual child, a move depicted in the novel as unjust and dehumanizing. The novelist's idealized stories erase the conflicted relationship between Lois and Rosina and create, instead, an account of perfect love between mother and daughter (as well as a daughter whose unruly brown hair has suddenly become flaxen and ringletted). Though this whitewashing through memory is surely common as human experience, Robins emphasizes that George Mandeville's fictionalization of her daughter tragically erases the "real" Rosina. Unlike a character in a book who can live in "a thousand homes" where there is "still some sign of them" in the material reality of the book itself, Robins notes, Rosina is truly gone in both body and memory, particularly since George Mandeville's evocation of Rosina is discursive and never fixed in a published characterization (219).

In these final images, Robins offers a different, and more insidious, version of the death of the innocent, for this girl's end figures as a tragic waste, built upon the sandy foundation of vanity and weakness. Her legacy in memory is not stable, and her life is overshadowed by her mother's textual children. We also see a different orientation of the text as child than that suggested by Cholmondeley or Broughton. Whereas Hester and Emma consider the "child of the brain" more real (and thus more tragically dead) than a child of the body might be, Robins suggests that the dead child of the body experiences a finality in mortality that a textual character, who can live on in the material reality of books, never quite possesses.[15]

---

[15] The obvious irony: Rosina is also a fictional character, so though she dies, she can be resurrected simply by rereading the novel.

Rosina's complete erasure—both in being misunderstood during life and in her reappropriation as a heroine after death—is her true tragedy. It's a tragedy made all the more poignant by the self-awareness, the ability to read her own suffocation, that Rosina possesses. To finally die not because she is too sweet, good, and pure for this world—the standard fate of the Victorian heroine—but because she has been ill-prepared and disallowed from any kind of meaningful activity, must strike the reader as an injustice most foul.

So not only does Robins engage in subversive repetition through this death of the consumptive, which works against Victorian idealizations of illness, she participates in a subversive repetition by seeming to revere motherhood, only to finally undercut it. We see the character of George Mandeville/Lois Wilbraham failing as both artist and mother, and we also witness her daughter failing to mature into adolescence. In effect, by refusing her mother, Rosina refuses to mother, and her impending puberty—signified by the menstrual blood that marks her as ready to uphold the symbolic weight of a fecund female body—gives way to physical collapse and a final hemorrhage into death. Though it is significant that Robins both points to and effaces Rosina's development into a body capable of bearing children, it is, ultimately, more significant that, in killing the character, Robins refuses to represent Rosina's life. She kills her off rather that let her be co-opted by Ralph Wilbraham's symbolic order, which disallows meaningful work for women, or a larger social order that idealizes and disempowers women, in effect, depriving them of personhood and turning them into text.

Conclusion

The novels I examine here suggest a range of representation laying out who the professional woman writer is, what she looks like, and how her work should be valued, all conveyed through the "cult of motherhood." As I have noted, each novel differently imagines author-characters who conceive and birth their child-texts, only to see those children die (whether through murder, neglect, or outright infanticide). For *Red Pottage*'s Hester the author is represented as physically feminine but intellectually masculine. Her textual child is misunderstood and ultimately murdered, leaving the author/mother shaken and mourning, consolable only by same-sex friendship. For *A Beginner*'s Emma, her own body is refined, whitened, and elite, but her textual baby is hideous. Emma must be coerced into offering her deformed baby to a funeral pyre in a public rite of symbolic cleansing. Her "reward" for doing so is realignment with heteronormative codes through promises of a "real" husband and "real" children. In *George Mandeville's Husband* the characterization of George/Lois heightens the tension between author and mother roles. She is the only biological mother of the three characters considered here, yet she is also the least sympathetic character. Her yellowed fingers, her over-large body, her loudness and indiscrete behavior all signify excess. Her appropriation of a male pseudonym, primary role as breadwinner, and consequent emasculization of her husband equally suggest a freakish "unnaturalness," underscored by her complete lack of what all women are supposed to instinctively know: how to mother. The author's self-absorption leads to her biological daughter's death, a death she exploits by turning her daughter's memory into idealized fiction.

Given this range in which none of the author characters here ultimately comes off well or produces literary or biological children that are allowed to remain alive, how can I argue that these representations are ultimately salutary? I do so because whether the author/mother characters be murderess, monster, or naïf, the sheer range of possibility problematizes a seemingly monologic construct. The representations here redefine both motherhood and womanhood, two roles intertwined at this time, two roles that are supposedly so natural that no clear articulation of their meaning is necessary. In so doing, these representations interrogate unmarked categories, ultimately giving the power for definition to the author behind the author, to Cholmondley, Broughton, and Robins.

In these novels, the representation of mothering alters who mothers are, what they look like, and what they do. This necessarily influences prescriptive ideologies about woman's "natural" role in late nineteenth century Britain. As such, these books perform an important countercultural work through a subversive repetition that expands sex/gender categories. These outcomes are not actualized in the conclusions of the texts themselves but, I believe, in the minds of the readers who are invited to interrupt "naturalized" presumptions about gender and sex differences as guided by a new multivalent form of "natural woman," the writer.

Works Cited

Ardis, Ann. *New Women, New Novels: Feminism and Early Modernism*. New Brunswick: Rutgers University Press, 1990.

Auerbach, Nina. "Artists and Mothers: A False Alliance." *Women and Literature* 6 (Spring 1978): 1–17.

Boumelha, Penny. "The Woman of Genius and the Woman of Grub Street: Figures of the Female Writer in British Fin-de-Siècle Fiction." *English Literature in Transition* 40 (1997): 164–90.

Broughton, Rhoda. *A Beginner.* London: Bentley and Sons, 1894.

Cervetti, Nancy. *Scenes of Reading: Transforming Romance in Brontë, Eliot, and Woolf.* New York: Peter Lang, 1998.

Cholmondeley, Mary. *Red Pottage.* 1899. New York: Virago Press, 1985.

Dickens, Charles. *David Copperfield.* 1850. New York: W. W. Norton & Co., 1990.

Dijkstra, Bram. *Idols of Perversity: Fantasies of Feminine Evil in Fin-de-Siècle Culture.* New York: Oxford University Press, 1986.

Fausto-Sterling, Anne. *Sexing the Body: Gender Politics and the Constitution of Sexuality.* New York: Basic Books, 2000.

Fern, Fanny. *Ruth Hall.* Ed. Joyce Warren. New Brunswick: Rutgers University Press, 1992.

Friedman, Susan Stanford. "Creativity and the Childbirth Metaphor: Gender Difference in Literary Discourse." In *Speaking of Gender.* Ed. Elaine Showalter. New York: Routledge, 1989. 73–100.

Gilbert, Pamela. *Disease, Desire, and the Body in Victorian Women's Popular Novels.* Cambridge: Cambridge University Press, 1997.

Gilbert, Sandra M., and Susan Gubar. *The Madwoman in the Attic: The Woman Writer and the Nineteenth-Century Literary Imagination.* New Haven: Yale University Press, 1979.

Homans, Margaret. *Bearing the Word: Language and Female Experience in Nineteenth-Century Women's Writing.* Chicago: University of Chicago Press, 1986.

Jones, Ann Rosalind. "Writing the Body: Toward an Understanding of l'Ecriture Féminine." In *Feminisms: An Anthology of Literary Theory and Criticism.* Ed. Robyn R. Warhol and Diane Price Herndl. New Brunswick: Rutgers University Press, 1993. 357–70.

Lorber, Judith. *Paradoxes of Gender.* New Haven: Yale University Press, 1994.

Parkins, Wendy. "Home and Away: The New Woman and Domesticity in Mary Cholmondeley's *Red Pottage.*" *Women: A Cultural Review* 10.1 (1999): 47–55.

Petrochenkov, Margaret Wise. "Pregnancy and Birth as a Metaphor for Literary Creativity." PhD diss., Indiana University, 1992.

Poovey, Mary. *Making a Social Body: British Cultural Formation, 1830–1864.* Chicago: University of Chicago Press, 1995.

———. *Uneven Developments: The Ideological Work of Gender in Mid-Victorian England.* Chicago: University of Chicago Press, 1988.

Pykett, Lynn. "Portraits of the Artist as a Young Woman: Representations of the Female Artist in the New Woman Fiction of the 1890s." In *Victorian Women Writers and the Woman Question.* Ed. Nicola Diane Thompson. Cambridge: Cambridge University Press, 1999. 135–50.

Robins, Elizabeth. "Woman's Secret." *Way Stations.* New York: Dodd, Mead, 1913.

———. (as C. E. Raimond). *George Mandeville's Husband.* New York: D. Appleton and Co., 1894.

Russett, Cynthia Eagle. *Sexual Science: The Victorian Construction of Womanhood.* Cambridge: Harvard University Press, 1989.

Showalter, Elaine. "Introduction." In *Red Pottage.* By Mary Cholmondeley. New York: Virago Press, 1985.

———. *A Literature of Their Own: British Women Novelists from Bronte to Lessing.* Princeton: Princeton University Press, 1977.

Smith-Rosenberg, Carroll. *Disorderly Conduct: Visions of Gender in Victorian America.* New York: A. A. Knopf, 1985.

Suleiman, Susan Rubin. "Writing and Motherhood." In *The (M)other Tongue: Essays in Feminst Psychoanalytic Interpretation.* Ed. Shirley Nelson, Garner, Claire Kahane, and Madelon Sprengnether. Ithaca: Cornell University Press, 1985. 352–77.

Tuchman, Gaye. *Edging Women Out: Victorian Novelists, Publishers and Social Change.* New Haven: Yale University Press, 1989.

Wiley, Catherine. "Staging Infanticide: The Refusal of Representation in Elizabeth Robins's *Alan's Wife.*" *Theatre Journal* (December 1990): 432–46.

CHAPTER 14

The Widest Lap

Fatness, Fasting, and Nurturance in Nineteenth-Century Fiction

LILLIAN E. CRATON

> She, too, was stout, but it was with the plumpness of a vigorous matron; and an eager vitality was everywhere visible—in her energetic bearing, her protruding, enquiring glances, her small, fat, capable and commanding hands.
> —Lytton Strachey, *Queen Victoria* (chap. 6, pt. 4)

In this 1921 description of the middle-aged Queen Victoria, Lytton Strachey offers a physical image of nineteenth-century womanhood rarely considered in literary and cultural studies. Ironically implying that Victorian culture was overly feminized, Strachey contrasts the rotund, robust monarch with her frail husband to hint that Victorian femininity (or at least Victoria's femininity) did not always conform to the docility and affectionate self-sacrifice we have come to associate with the middle-class Angel in the House. While Victoria was among the nation's advocates of female domesticity, her own social role and physical presence defied conventional boundaries. In her maturity, Victoria's physical weight grew to match her importance in England's political and cultural life, and Strachey here uses the excess of Victoria's body to suggest excesses of character. Even her glances are "protruding"—an image that allows Strachey to poke fun at one of Victoria's prominent features, but also to reflect her dynamic presence. Victoria's ample flesh reveals energy and authority: Strachey invites us to see the queen as competent, aggressive, and fat.

This essay will argue that the value placed on nurturance within women's role in Victorian culture also sows seeds for revision of unhealthy extremes within the middle-class feminine ideal. Female fatness, as a sign of plentitude and inexhaustible reserves of nurturance, offers a tool with which some fiction writers subtly enrich and expand the prevailing gender role prescribed nineteenth-century women. While England's queen (and thus its public face) had a double chin and a temper, the sentimental novels and advertising that often served as mouthpieces of Victorian popular culture tended to prize a more tightly laced brand of femininity. Given the iconic, atypical social role her royalty demanded, Victoria shared certain qualities with another familiar figure in nineteenth-century popular culture: the fat lady of the carnival freak show.[1] In addition to their excessive bodies, both monarch and fat lady performed their roles for public consumption, and both tended to be presented through the rhetoric of idealized femininity.[2] Together, these figures straddle the culturally dominant middle class, the aristocratic matron mirroring the folk performer whose carnival venue grew from working-class culture. Their extreme bodies help illustrate contradictory expectations for both female strength and female self-abnegation within nineteenth-century ideology, as well as unhealthy extremes of self-abnegation produced by the gender code of the self-conscious Victorian middle class.[3]

Though the feminine ideal was often imagined as ephemeral and disembodied, the responsibilities incumbent upon women demanded real physical strength in addition to nurturing compassion. On one hand, the middle-class idealization of female domesticity elevated the moral status of women and conferred great honor on the work of motherhood: successful performance of nurturance was a woman's finest achievement.

---

[1] Noting the elaborate nature of royal ceremonies, and that folk performances (including a freak show) were featured in the queen's coronation festivities, Michael Diamond suggests: "The great royal occasions showed clearly the link between royalty and showbusiness" (7). Though American audiences tend to locate the heyday of the freak show in the Depression-era traveling circus, the ancient tradition of bodily spectacle flourished in early and mid-Victorian England.

[2] As Robert Bogdan and other disability theorists have explored, freak shows generally included narrative accompaniment that either aggrandized or exoticized performers. Female performers were described as unusually beautiful or as devoted wives and mothers, in order to contrast (and thus emphasize) their extreme physical traits.

[3] For reasons of space, I have omitted a lengthier discussion of the freak show and Mikhail Bakhtin's notion of the grotesque. Like all aspects of the medieval and renaissance carnival tradition that Bakhtin describes in *Rabelais and His World,* the grotesque aesthetic is a tool for social regeneration and the revision of dominant ideals, and thus enables the notion that open, excessive bodies (as well as grotesque imagery of excessive consumption) are a long-standing tool for social criticism. Though Bakhtin saw nineteenth-century realism as an enemy of the grotesque, he finds a plentitude of grotesque imagery in the work of Dickens. Of the characters discussed at length here, Mrs. Jarley and Boule de Suif are presented with particularly grotesque imagery.

On the other hand, the selflessness associated with motherhood was often exaggerated and stylized within Victorian culture to an unhealthy degree. The hourglass figure cultivated by women throughout most of the century demonstrates the contrast between these two forces. An ample bosom and wide hips, physical traits associated with the comfort and plentitude offered by mothers, are emphasized by a tightly corseted waistline—a bodily emblem of self-restraint.[4]

Today the typical mid-Victorian silhouette seems plump and curvy, a comparison which leaves many of us nostalgic for a time of greater tolerance of bodily variation. Yet as Peter Stearns, Joyce Huff, and others have remarked, nineteenth-century culture was not wholly accepting of fat.[5] While Stearns argues that American fat-phobia matured in the twentieth century, he suggests that it took its shape from nineteenth-century anxieties about consumer culture, religious skepticism, and social diversity. Joyce Huff cites the writing of William Banting, leader of a mid-nineteenth-century British diet movement, as evidence that fat-fighting was an active concern within Victorian culture. Banting, whose personal narrative of weight struggle characterized fat as disabling and demoralizing, recommended a low-carbohydrate diet that sparked medical controversy and put weight-control at the center of a passionate debate. Like Stearns, Huff suggests that our contemporary perception of fat grew out of Victorian concerns about self-control, heightened by the growing abundance of consumer goods and advertising.

Among the fundamental values of Victorian norms for women, Anna Silver's *Victorian Literature and the Anorexic Body* lists "an understanding of the body as an entity that must be subordinated to the will and disciplined as an emblem of one's self control," along with a resulting "aesthetic validation of the slender female form as the physical ideal of beauty and a concomitant fear of fat as ugly and/or unfeminine" (27). She assures us that "the slim-waisted hourglass figure occupied fashion's spotlight throughout the nineteenth century" and required corseting and an anxious relationship with food from those women who hoped to achieve the ideal (35). Silver counters the common belief that Victorians valued plumpness with the claim that plump arms and hips serve primarily as foils for the true mark of nineteenth-century womanhood—the tiny "wasp" waist. As physical evidence of self-control over one's appetites, the slender waist was a symbol of proper middle-class womanhood, and fat thus was a failure to live up to the ideal.

---

[4] Susan Bordo makes a similar point in *Unbearable Weight*.
[5] See Peter Stearns's *Fat History* and Joyce Huff's unpublished dissertation *Conspicuous Consumptions*.

Yet fat is too supple to conform to a single rigid interpretation.[6] Victorian culture also cherished a range of positive associations for excessive fatness. While some excessive bodies seem to have been fed by the poverty of less fortunate characters, Victoria's fat is a comforting sign of the grandeur and plentitude of the empire, and reassurance of her capacity to nurture an entire nation. Similarly, Arbuthnot's iconic John Bull, reproduced in advertising and cartoons throughout the nineteenth century as a symbol of the ordinary Englishman's stalwart strength, draws his characteristic firmness from his extra weight. The fat displayed within bodily spectacles is jolly and entertaining, and reassures the viewer of his or her own normality. For disability theorist Sander Gilman, fat adds gravitas and sensitivity to the characterizations of late-century male detectives.[7] Clearly, the ideological implications of fatness (like those of femininity) shift radically from context to context. Even within the work of a single author, Charles Dickens, critics identify competing images of excess: Joyce Huff and Juliet McMaster each point out that Dickens blends positive and negative forms of fat characterization, what McMaster refers to as "jolly" fat and "bloated" fat. Here I focus on one particular aspect of nineteenth-century fat: the ability of physical excess to fuel nurturance within stories of poverty and social vulnerability. Beginning in the periodicals and novels of Charles Dickens before branching out to an 1880 work of Guy de Maupassant, the essay will explore the positive potential of fat to push back against extreme images of self-abnegation also resonant in Victorian gender ideology.

---

[6] As disability theorist Rosemarie Garland-Thomson has observed, unusual bodies attract ideological interpretation. Fat theorists Kathleen LeBesco and Jana Evans Braziel remind us that interpretations change, but the need to interpret an unusually fat body continues over time: "[F]at is a malleable construct that has served dominant economic and cultural interests, to the detriment of all people" throughout history (3). For LeBesco and Braziel, the meanings of "fat as an encoded surface" shift, but are generally negative: "Fat equals reckless excess, prodigality, indulgence, lack of restraint, violation of order and space, transgression of boundary" (3).

[7] Interestingly, Gilman argues that fatness helps by feminizing male detectives and putting them in touch with premodern instincts and intuition:

> The fat detective's body is of a different sort than that of the skinny philosopher. Huge, ungainly, sedentary, it houses the brain of a detective.... It is not a "modern" body, if by modern we imagine the body as trained, lithesome, strong, active, and thus supremely masculine. Such an obese body seems more feminine, but certainly not female; it is expressive of the nature of the way the detective seems to 'think.' His thought processes strike us as intuitive and emotional rather than analytic and objective. (*Fat Boys* 155)

I. Fat People and Fasting Girls[8]

If fatness was not fully accepted within nineteenth-century social norms, it nonetheless provided the Victorians some entertainment value. An examination of the corpus of Charles Dickens reveals contradictory attitudes about extremes of self-indulgence and self-abnegation in its description of real and fictional bodies. Dickens's *All the Year Round* explores this fascination in the unsigned 1864 essay "Fat People," a consideration of fat men and women who have exhibited themselves publicly. The essay confers a certain grandeur on large bodies. Extreme thinness does not satisfy: "It is observable that very thin people do not announce their thinness abroad. We speak, truth to tell, somewhat contemptuously of them. . . . Scarcely any man, except the Living Skeleton, ever exhibited himself on account of his thinness. What a poor object that same Claude Ambrose Seurat was!" (353). While it is unpopular to make a spectacle out of one's thinness, "many have done so for their stoutness. It is those who grow largely in excess, and not those who lag far behind the average of eleven stones, who claim for themselves a place in history" (353). The article goes on to describe several cases of dramatic obesity that captured the public imagination, and ends with a description of famous fat man Daniel Lambert's shoes as a mind-expanding object of contemplation. They are "[t]oo broad to be conceived by any narrow mind" (355).

Yet thinness seems more entrenched than fatness in the imagery of Victorian womanhood. Five years later, another unsigned *All the Year Round* essay entitled "Fasting Girls" provides a more skeptical view of another form of bodily spectacle while reinforcing the idea that thinness and self-starvation generally lack nobility. The article observes the phenomenon of young women who starve themselves, and catalogues a number of cases in which girls have publicly claimed to exist without sustenance. The author's tone is doubtful: "[F]asting women and girls have made more noise in the world than fasting men, and there has been more suspicion of trickery in the cases recorded" (442).[9] The article attributes each case to fraud or attention seeking, thus implying that society rewards girls for pretending to survive without food and affirming the notion that social roles value

---

[8] Joyce Huff also discusses the two *All the Year Round* essays from which I borrow my section title.

[9] The increase of skepticism here may also reflect the growing taboos placed on bodily spectacle as a form of entertainment. Though the second half of the nineteenth century saw the freak show coded as tawdry and limits enforced on venues and performances, unusual bodies continued to exert their shock and wonderment in the sensational fiction of the 1860s and beyond.

such self-starvation. The article clearly views fasting as a performance, and links the girls it describes to the bodily spectacle of the "hunger artist" enshrined in freak show tradition. By inviting readers to see such behavior as artificial, attention-seeking (and perhaps even feigned) performances of extremes, the author undermines any sense of wonder attached to such starvation. The skeptical outlook offered by this article echoes the negative perspective offered in "Fat People" on the pitiful Claude Seurat.

Female self-denial is a pressing issue for Victorian culture. "Fasting Girls" clearly identifies this brand of performance as largely feminine, and women's fashions reinforce the idea that displays of self-control are an imbedded part of nineteenth-century gender code. The corset, with its offer of an artificially thin waist, gives us a material image for the more general value placed on female containment and bodily control in nineteenth-century middle-class culture. In her history of the Victorian corset, Leigh Summers suggests that the corset serves as a foundation, not just for fashion, but for nineteenth-century womanhood itself: "Few garments other than the corset could claim such an intimate, influential and popular place in the material culture of Victorian womanhood. The corset was (for many women) a lifetime companion, fitted in early childhood and worn until death" (4–5). The corset demonstrated the self-control and, by extension, the moral continence of the wearer. The meaning attached to the narrow waist reflected on a woman's social status as well as on her personal character. A narrow waist served as a mark of her social class, and the tighter she could draw her laces, the more her body illustrated a privileged social position. Working-class bodies were already imagined as robust, so middle-class ladies (and, as manufacturing made corsets cheaper, working-class women with ambitions) used bodily control as a status symbol.[10]

Both Anna K. Silver and Gail Turley Houston have emphasized the importance of self-starvation to Victorian gender ideology. Silver places the confining physical norm at the center of Victorian femininity and argues for a link between the voluntary starvation of anorexia nervosa (first diagnosed in the nineteenth century) and the values of middle-class femininity:

[10] As Helena Michie argues, "While middle-class women were imagined—at least ideally—to be delicate and refined, working-class women were traditionally seen as coarse and robust" ("Under Victorian Skins" 410). Susan Bordo notes the different expectations for men and women in the middle class. While a protruding male stomach could indicate bourgeois success, a slim wife served as another male status symbol: "[I]f [the middle-class man] could not be or marry an aristocrat, he could have a wife who looked like one, a wife whose non-robust beauty and delicate appetite signified her lack of participation in the taxing 'public sphere'" (*Unbearable Weight* 117).

> Anorexia nervosa, I argue, is deeply rooted in Victorian values, ideologies, and aesthetics, which together helped define femininity in the nineteenth century. . . . One can thus "read" Victorian gender ideology through an anorexic lens. . . . The anorexic woman's slender form attests to her discipline over her body and its hunger, despite the persistence of that hunger, and indicates her discomfort with or even hatred of her body and its appetites, which may or may not include her sexuality. If one reads the disease metaphorically, then, it becomes evident that the pathology of anorexia nervosa and predominant Victorian constructions of gender subscribe to many of the same characteristics. (3)

Control over the appetite for food analogizes the control over sexual desire, and thus points to limitations on sensuality imbedded in nineteenth-century expectations for women. Silver argues that the self-sacrifice and self-control often idealized in middle-class femininity easily took a sinister turn into self-starvation, and that anorexia nervosa therefore serves as a metaphor for unhealthy extremes within Victorian gender ideals.

In *Consuming Fictions,* Gail Turley Houston makes a similar suggestion targeted specifically at Dickens's fiction: "Dickens's representations of Victorian ideologies about the consuming practices of the sexes and classes indicate that codes of consumption were so extreme, complicated, and disjunct, they translated into medically defined consumptions, or what we now refer to as eating disorders" (xiii). She argues that women and the working class share the tendency for noble self-starvation in Dickens's work, particularly in sentimentalized characterizations. While these characterizations can serve as social criticism, they often reinforce notions that women and the poor enact a "noblesse oblige" by denying themselves life's comforts, literalized in the relationship to food: "Dickens both endorses and dismantles Victorian ideologies about class and hunger while he inculcates a similar ideology of abstinence when it comes to gender" (12). In her discussion of gender, Houston affirms the metaphorical significance of anorexia and extends the discussion of the disease to the mother figures that concern this study: "Because anorexia nervosa was diagnosed in nineteenth-century Britain, the Victorian cult of motherhood—which Dickens's fictions helped to create and subvert—underwrites its nosology" (that is, its classification as a disease) (52).

For Silver and Houston, the need to control one's appetite and body shaped the life of a Victorian woman. This code illuminates the middle class's unhealthy discomfort with physical appetites, both gustatory and sexual, or possibly suggests an expectation for unequal distribution of resources that overlaps class discourse. To embody the ephemeral morality and spirituality expected from the idealized womanhood, one eschews creature comforts to the point of starvation. From this viewpoint, self-control, self-abnegation, and respectability go hand in hand. A woman is measured by the size and shape of her waist, and thus also by her tolerance for hunger and constrictive pressure. Certainly, many of Dickens's characters support a positive reading of voluntary hunger, particularly among women. Self-abnegating young women like Little Nell and Amy Dorrit, both of whom forgo shelter or food to leave more for their family members, are among Dickens's loftiest characters.

Yet the ironic tone of "Fasting Girls" offers an alternative reading of self-starvation, far from noblesse oblige. The article's emphasis on fraud suggests that fasting behavior is fundamentally unhealthy and ignoble, and that no woman would starve herself without clear motive. It imagines fasting girls as selfish, or at least hungry for fame and fortune. In that light, the small, disadvantaged girls of *The Old Curiosity Shop* and *Little Dorrit* are crafted to earn our pity and respect, but do not necessarily represent Dickens's endorsement of voluntary starvation. Little Nell's hunger and habitual sacrifice for her weak-willed grandfather seem tied to the gradual wasting that leads to her death. We mourn her, not as a mature woman making a reasonable sacrifice for her children, but as a girl whose life was cut short because of insufficient nurturance from others. Like much of Dickens's fiction, *The Old Curiosity Shop* serves as an indictment of a social system that tolerates poverty and the neglect of the vulnerable. The suffering Nell endures with her grandfather contributes to her idealized presentation, but the novel's tragedy lies in the fact that such a young woman has no better caretaker. As part of a host of child victims and orphans within Dickens's novels—figures who drive Dickens's social criticism—Nell does not represent an ideal to which other girls should aspire so much as an extreme, sentimental representation of the burden society allows its most vulnerable citizens to bear. Little Nell starves in her adolescent transition from girlhood to womanhood, not to enact an anorexic feminine ideal, but because she has not been sufficiently nurtured to build the strength required for her adult role.

Perhaps for that reason, a similar wasting illness—outwardly resembling anorexia—seems far less tragic when it afflicts an adult woman or biological parent. Nurturance requires strength, and those charged with the care of children must first keep themselves alive to perform their duty. As the next section argues, even Nell requires fat nurturance to sustain her brief time in the world, and finds it during her time with the jolly Mrs. Jarley. Similarly, orphan David Copperfield depends on extensive nurturance to meet his childhood needs. David's mother, Clara, is presented in terms more closely resembling the vanity of *All the Year Round*'s fasting girls than noblesse oblige, while the fat housekeeper Clara Peggotty provides young David with some of the best and most loving care. In the roles they play in the lives of their novels' protagonists, as well as in the light they shine on the novels' leaner characters, these fat ladies provide an important alternative image of the nurturing ideal for Victorian womanhood.

Dickens's corpus contains a vast and varied cast of characters. In the subtle similarities and differences within Dickens's network of characterizations, his reader finds a range of variations and repetitions of any given social type, and thus the ideological implications of Dickens's work are most often revealed in the intersections of its descriptions or the juxtaposition of its characters.[11] In his orphan-centered novels, Dickens condemns the economic and social vulnerability of children and tracks their journeys of sorrow or self-discovery, but must keep them alive for a time to do so. To that end, he introduces supplemental nurturers—representations of the kinder forces within society—to shelter these children along the way.[12]

And that is where fat ladies offer their contribution. The robust, hardworking, stout body (conventionally expected of the working-class woman, but also a mark of hedonism and personal excess) is better suited to the demands of nurturance than the slim body of the fasting girl. In *The Old Curiosity Shop* and *David Copperfield,* Dickens introduces fat nurturers who seem to balance the novels' propensity toward hunger, particularly in the weak, thin parent figures whose wasting is presented as more selfish than noble. In the lean world of the Dickensian orphan, fictional fatness offers a respite from suffering and models a more fruitful form of nurturance: one which can continue because it espouses self-nurturance, too. The energy contained in the plump body of Queen Victoria, for example, assures us she has strength to mother an empire, and so the nation's welfare depends on her health and willingness to self-nurture—after all, "God save the Queen!" is the paramount cry of English patriotism. Fat mothering is supplemental. It meets excessive need with excessive means,

---

[11] I echo Alex Woloch's idea of "character-systems" here. In *The One v. The Many,* Woloch argues that the interplay of characters give minor figures in a novel a key role in determining how we read the novel's protagonist and overall significance.

[12] Though I use the term "supplement" in a conventional sense here, Jacques Derrida's philosophical explanation of the supplement in *On Grammatology* provides a useful framework for understanding the process through which a cultural ideal is deconstructed and, thus, revised through supplementation. As a practice or an idea that is added on to an original practice or idea, the supplement reconstitutes the whole. Whether the supplement is "a plenitude enriching another plenitude," or whether it "adds only to replace" (Derrida suggests that both relationships are possible), the supplement creates space for imaginative play with absence and substitution (144).

and demonstrates that such means are first gained through aggressive self-nurturance.

II. Dickens's Supplemental Mothering

This section explores Dickens's use of nurturing fat ladies as a supplement for various forms of thinness in *David Copperfield* and *The Old Curiosity Shop*. In particular, *David Copperfield* creates a pronounced dichotomy between thin and fat motherhood, self-abnegation and self-nurturance. The Copperfields' housekeeper and David's most affectionate mother figure, Clara Peggotty, embodies the excess and warmth of the fat-mother alternative to more restrictive gender ideals. Her supplemental role in the Copperfield household fills David's early needs for nurturance, and the comparison readers form between Clara Peggotty and Clara Copperfield, David's biological mother, emphasizes the weakness within some versions of middle-class femininity and the child's urgent need for supplemental care.

Clara Peggotty shares a first name with her employer, David's biological mother Clara Copperfield, and the parallel names invite readers to contrast the characters. David himself seems to link the two women in his mind. He states: "[T]he first objects I can remember as standing out by themselves from a confusion of things, are my mother and Peggotty" (*DC*, chap. 2, 15). Indeed, David's "earliest impressions" include his comparison of the distinctive beauties of both women:

> When my mother is out of breath and rests herself in an elbow-chair, I watch her winding her bright curls round her fingers, and straightening her waist, and nobody knows better than I do that she likes to look so well, and is proud of being so pretty.
>
> That is among my earliest impressions. That, and a sense that we were both a little afraid of Peggotty, and submitted ourselves in most things to her direction....
>
> I thought her in a different style from my mother, certainly; but of another school of beauty, I considered her a perfect example. (*DC*, chap. 2, 20–21)

Clara Copperfield is delicate, smooth, pale, and passive in appearance—an ideal Victorian woman. Clara Peggotty, on the other hand, is sturdy, rough, florid, assertive, and fat—far too big, aggressive, and full of working-class vigor to reach the middle-class ideal. Yet young David finds her beautiful, if unconventionally so. Of David's two early mother figures, Peggotty becomes David's best source of nurturance, and has the fuller role to play in his life.

While Peggotty thrives, Clara Copperfield wastes away. David's mother presents a self-effacing extreme of middle-class feminine ideal as she repeats the cant of Victorian domesticity: "I ought to be very thankful to him, and very submissive even in my thoughts" (*DC,* chap. 8, 123). She remarries the seemingly respectable Mr. Murdstone, thereby disrupting young David's sense of stability and security, only to find Murdstone cruel and inflexible. David's stepfather dominates his wife's impressionable personality. He revokes her household authority, interferes in her friendship with Peggotty, and, worst of all, rejects David and expects his wife to do the same. Torn between husband and son, David's mother weakens. After giving birth to another child, she sickens and dies (along with her infant), leaving David vulnerable. Returning from school, David marks her physical wasting: her face is "too delicate," and her hand "so thin and white that it seemed to me to be almost transparent" (*DC,* chap. 8, 120). From David's point of view, his mother's physical self-destruction is catastrophic. She does not starve so that he may eat, as Amy Dorrit does for her family, but instead wastes away from a lack of strength to defend her son. Had Clara Copperfield nurtured herself more successfully, she might have lived to protect David from his stepfather. Certainly, David's mother achieves her own brand of asceticism through her submission to Murdstone's abuse and her wasting illness, but her decision to remarry seems to grow out of vanity and desire for romantic love, which in this case conflict with the maternal love that Dickens and David Copperfield most value. While seeking an ideal middle-class domestic existence—married life, more children, and a strong patriarchal presence—Clara Copperfield in fact appears weak, even selfish, rather than self-sacrificing. Her figurative starvation and early death are a failure in her maternal responsibilities.

Unlike her employer, Clara Peggotty clearly rejects asceticism and abstinence, at least in terms of diet. Her excessive intake (as revealed through her excessive weight) renders her an inexhaustible source of nurturance and affection. Because she is not self-denying, she thrives as a nourishing mother figure. Even Clara Copperfield compares their parenting ability, joking that "Peggotty's love is a great deal better than mine, Davy" (*DC,* chap. 2, 23). The largesse of Peggotty's affectionate nature, hinted at by the largeness of her body, supplements Clara Copperfield's frailty. David describes Peggotty in terms of a personal magnitude that becomes even vaster in his moments of his greatest vulnerability, such as just before sleep: "I had reached that stage of sleepiness when Peggotty seemed to swell and grow immensely large" (*DC,* chap. 2, 19). Enveloped in the reassuring vastness of Peggotty's presence, David finds moments of peace in a turbulent childhood.

As a working-class servant, Peggotty faces a different set of physical and social expectations than Clara Copperfield, but the child-centered structure of Dickens's novel emphasizes her role as David's nurturer. On the one hand, Peggotty represents the middle-class fantasy of a loving servant, whose robust body is an inexhaustible source of nurturance to be used indefinitely without risk of injury or emaciation. Houston emphasizes Peggotty's compensatory role in the household, and notes that she serves to prop up David's relationship with Clara Copperfield: "Dickens's magnification of Peggotty's bodily economy allows David to split the nurturing role between his two mothers, and David avoids consciously recognizing the inadequacy of his real mother" (102). Indeed, Peggotty compensates for Clara Copperfield's weaknesses and proves capable of great self-sacrifice in the name of love. On the other hand, Peggotty does not seem to be primarily a figure of self-sacrifice, and need not be read in terms of class exploitation. In fact, her position in the Copperfield household is one of significant personal power, and her role in David's life aligns her with strong-willed women of the middle class. Ultimately, the different physical norm tied to the working class, in which cultural expectations lean toward female robustness instead of a tightly controlled waistline, offers a healthier image of femininity that, in Dickens's novel, outperforms middle-class beauty. Peggotty's fatness implies reserves of strength and energy and, by extension, suggests that the excessive output expected from Victorian mothers can best be met through an equally excessive intake.

While Dickens endows Peggotty with a remarkable affection for her middle-class "superiors," he does not emphasize self-abnegation or meekness in his description of this ideal servant. Consider Peggotty's explosive embrace:

> [S]he laid aside her work (which was a stocking of her own), and opening her arms wide, took my curly head within them, and gave it a good squeeze. I know it was a good squeeze, because, being very plump, whenever she made any little exertion after she was dressed, some of the buttons on the back of her gown flew off. And I recollect two bursting to the opposite side of the parlour, while she was hugging me. (*DC,* chap. 2, 20)

In this passage, David specifically notes that Peggotty's sewing project is "a stocking of her own," an unlikely detail for a child to remember, but an important reflection of Peggotty's overall character. For Peggotty, self-assertion and self-nurturance go hand in hand with dedicated mothering. She rules the Copperfield household with an iron (if loving) fist. Often treating Clara Copperfield like an errant child, Peggotty inverts the usual class relationships and takes on far more authority within the family than her position would normally allow. Her role is inflated to the point that, as cited earlier, David and his mother "were both a little afraid of Peggotty, and submitted ourselves in most things to her direction" (*DC,* chap. 2, 20). This unusual level of authority draws attention to the failure of David's mother to meet her own responsibilities, but it also creates an alternative image of a grand, bossy nurturer whose success in the parenting role stems from self-assertion rather than self-denial. Just as Queen Victoria herself exercises power beyond the usual station of women, Peggotty exercises an authority far beyond the usual station of servants: perhaps that is why David promises to make Peggotty "as welcome as a queen" in any of his future homes (*DC,* chap. 8, 120).

Beyond her obvious pairing with Clara Copperfield, Peggotty's connections to the novel's other characters emphasize the brand of nurturance that makes her so valuable to David, and undercuts the idea that only the working class needs vigorous femininity. In the interest of space, though, I will offer only a broad survey. Peggotty eventually marries the miserly (but otherwise good-hearted) Mr. Barkis, and lovingly pushes him to spend money both for his own care and, at times, for David's. In this sense, she again defends self-nurturance over pointless asceticism. The reader discovers Barkis's attraction to Peggotty when she springs from the hedgerows to ambush Barkis's cart, which was carrying David away to school, to force a wealth of food and some rough embraces on the boy before departing "without a solitary button remaining on her gown" (*DC,* chap. 5, 68). The scene, in which Peggotty's abundant love seems nearly violent in intensity as she literally "crammed" the food into David's pockets, suggests that excess is the root of Peggotty's appeal.

The analogous nurturing roles played by Peggotty and David's abrasive Aunt Betsy Trotwood also draw attention to the importance of sustainable lifestyles for Victorian nurturers, and the value of supplementary excess in nurturing relationships. David's Aunt Betsy assumes the role of primary caregiver for his young adulthood. As a representative of the middle class, Aunt Betsy calls into question the idea that Peggotty's rough, rugged nurturing is simply a reflection of her social class. If Peggotty's position in the family breaks the boundaries of the usual servant's role, Aunt Betsy crosses gender lines to assert her authority: this "formidable personage" is the "principal magnate" of David's family (*DC,* chap. 1, 4). Far from selfless,

Betsy asserts her rights aggressively (by, for instance, leaving a failed marriage and famously chasing marauding donkeys from her yard). Both Peggotty's fat body and Betsy's fat ego provide shelter for David. Dickens takes pains to bring Betsy and Peggotty together for comparison. They both vie for power in the Copperfield family, provide shelter for David when he needs it, and accept his reciprocal support later in life. When he wins Agnes's hand in marriage, they celebrate together: "The moment my aunt was restored [from happy hysterics], she flew at Peggotty, and calling her a silly old creature, hugged her with all her might" (*DC,* chap. 62, 904).

As David chooses a mate, readers apply the lessons of his early life to the young women he loves, and thus find a broader implication for the lessons taught by the novel's excessive mother figures. We recognize in David's first wife, Dora, an image of his mother. Like Clara Copperfield, Dora is too fragile and helpless to care for a household. Though not ascetic, Dora cannot nurture herself—for instance, she incurs sizeable grocery bills without producing edible meals. Like the fasting girls of *All the Year Round,* she seems to feel that sustenance is unnecessary. When David suggests to her that "we must work, to live," she responds skeptically:

"Oh! How ridiculous!" cried Dora.
"How shall we live without, Dora?" said I.
"How? Any how!" said Dora. (*DC,* chap. 37, 571)

Ultimately, as in the case of Clara Copperfield, Dora cannot fulfill her domestic role and dies young, leaving David bereft. In contrast with Dora, David's second wife, Agnes, seems defined by her capability. She guides David's decisions and manages his household with all the authority allotted to the domestic role. Like Peggotty, Agnes pairs affection with strength, and survives to nurture David and his children. By repeating his juxtaposition of a strong and a weak woman, Dickens drives home the value of strength and self-care and aligns Agnes, his most direct expression of the feminine ideal, with those female characters who go to extremes of self-nurturance rather than extremes of self-abnegation. By creating double-wives as well as double-mothers for David, Dickens explores alternative models of femininity that reshape the normative ideal at the center of Victorian womanhood. The anorexic extremes of middle-class femininity appear here as a failure, and Dickens instead asks us to value the strength, even the supplemental excess, required for successful mothering.

While *David Copperfield*'s Agnes is offered as an idealized image of female nurturance, *The Old Curiosity Shop* presents its heroine Little Nell as an idealized image of female self-sacrifice. Nell serves as the paragon of a certain brand of fragile Victorian femininity and, like Dora, is doomed to a short life. A young teenager, Nell is pretty, small, meek, and affectionate, and inspires strong impulses to either nurture or exploit in the novel's older characters. Her trials as she flees the villainous Quilp include pronounced hunger, and her physical wasting leads to her death at the novel's end. Houston examines Nell's contrast with the all-consuming Quilp (whose voracious appetite extends to boiling liquids and eggshells), and claims for Nell the redemptive power of self-starvation in the face of consumerism run amuck. While the novel certainly valorizes Nell's self-sacrifice—her story criticizes a neglectful society by granting female self-sacrifice the affective quality of pathos—her death ultimately points to flaws in the social system and calls for better nurturance of society's vulnerable members. However noble, Nell's brand of self-abnegation is impracticable as a way of life. Yet *The Old Curiosity Shop* also offers a series of characters whose experiences shape our reading of Nell's. For instance, the spunky and demanding Marchioness—a girl roughly Nell's age and also a victim of poor or absent parenting—manages to exhibit fine nurturing ability and also to carve out a fine life for herself with Dick Swiveller. The inclusion of such a character in the story provides a happy counterpoint to Nell, and suggests that a more aggressive attitude might better serve those in need. It is Nell's parent figures that concern me here, though. Her gambling-addicted grandfather is both self-abnegating (as evidenced by his emaciated frame and constant avowals to sacrifice all for his granddaughter) and selfishly consumed by vice (a problem even Nell must acknowledge when he steals from her in a dreamlike trance). Like the "Fasting Girls" of *All the Year Round,* his character links the language and bodily experience of self-sacrifice with images of weakness and wasteful consumption. Most importantly, fat lady Mrs. Jarley provides the best nurturing Nell receives in the novel, and does so with constant reference to self-care and self-nurturance.

Mrs. Jarley, proprietress of the novel's waxwork, serves as an alternative image of femininity in whom consumption is presented as positive. Jarley, "stout and comfortable to look upon," meets Nell and her grandfather on the road, takes them in, and gives them food and work (*OCS,* chap. 26, 222). She first appears in the novel at repast and eats throughout the majority of her scenes. Spotting Nell and her grandfather among the other travelers, she summons the girl between gulps: "'Hey!' cried the lady of the caravan, scooping the crumbs out of her lap and swallowing the same before wiping her lips," as Nell looks on with "modest but hungry admiration" (*OCS,* chap. 26, 222). Seeing Nell's hunger, she invites the pair to join her for tea and urges self-indulgence: "Now hand up the teapot for a little more hot water, and a pinch of fresh tea, and then both of you eat and drink as much as you can, and don't spare anything; that's all I ask of you" (*OCS,* chap. 26, 225). Jarley's doctrine is consistently one of self-care through excess: she assures Nell, "[I]t does you good, when you're tired, to sleep as long as ever you can" (*OCS,* chap. 28, 238).

Mrs. Jarley's behavior is far from ideal and her habits of traveling with nonrelative male companions and drinking alcohol by the tumbler verge on scandalous. She does not vie with Nell for the novel's idealized feminine role. Yet Jarley is a warm, positive character who offers a necessary supplement to Nell's asceticism, and her nurturance keeps the young woman alive for a significant portion of the novel. Jarley operates a traveling waxwork depicting history's most excessive figures, including "the fat man, and then the thin man, the tall man, the short man, the old lady who died of dancing at a hundred and thirty-two, the wild boy of the woods," and a host of famous criminals (*OCS,* chap. 28, 242). Roving the countryside in tandem with a range of other folk entertainments including a live freak show, Jarley's waxwork provides a direct link to the bodily spectacles considered in *All the Year Round.* The waxwork seems an extension of Jarley's excess. Wax is a combustible fuel like fat itself, and the combination of Jarley's personal fat and the waxwork's profusion of artificial bodies (controlled and arranged by Jarley) seems to put an unlimited supply of real and waxen flesh—and hence, stored energy—at her disposal. According to its promotional poster, the waxwork "enlarges the sphere of the human understanding" (*OCS,* chap. 28, 244). It presents a spectacle of freakish extremes in order to encourage philosophical contemplation and a broadened perspective for its onlookers (not unlike Daniel Lambert's shoes mentioned in the essay "Fat People"). Jarley, too, offers a spectacle of extreme self-nurturance that encourages examination of the self-sacrifice presumably expected from mother figures and freely given by Nell to her grandfather. In the show she makes of hearty eating and self-care, and in the encouragement she gives Nell to follow her lead, Mrs. Jarley offers a supplemental image of hearty femininity.

Mrs. Jarley forces the novel's reader to question whether selflessness is the key requirement for good nurturance. The lady of the waxwork feeds Nell, offers her shelter and affectionate care, and yet doesn't hesitate to profit from Nell's skills as promoter. As the attractive Nell draws crowds to the waxwork, the two women share a mutually beneficial relationship. Jarley is both consuming and giving, with the natural procreative ability of a businesswoman: her "inventive genius" brings income and bon temps to the entire waxwork party (*OCS,* chap. 29, 245). In this case, a judicious and balanced selfishness goes hand in hand with hearty nurturance, and forms a stable middle ground between the extreme greed of the novel's villain Quilp and the extreme self-sacrifice of Nell.

Jarley's active consumption renders her a far better nurturer than Nell's grandfather, the child's official caretaker. The grandfather's compulsive gambling makes him at once all-consuming and nonconsuming. The grandfather's gambling is both a form of sacrifice (in this case, sacrificing the present comfort for the hope of a better return) and a destructive brand of selfishness. He justifies his habit with the belief that his winnings will be for Nell rather than himself, and mourns that "God knows that this one child is the thought and object of my life, and yet he never prospers me—oh, never!" (*OCS,* chap. 1, 8–9). Ultimately, Nell's grandfather provides neither protection nor sustenance for the object of his love. Quilp purchases the old man's debts and uses that leverage to push his way into the household, forcing the man and child to flee. Unable to provide for his family, Nell's grandfather starves alongside the child he loves.

Mrs. Jarley supplements the nurturance provided by Nell's official guardian, and thus offers nurturing excess and self-care as antidotes to the grandfather's unusually selfish brand of starvation. Fat ladies feed themselves in order to produce for their dependants, while failed parents squander resources in the name of self-sacrifice.

III. Fat Sexuality in Maupassant's "Boule de Suif"

If the corset and thinness serve as an emblem of self-restraint that extends, metaphorically, to sexual continence, then the excess and self-indulgence hinted at by a fat body are likely to suggest libidinous sexuality. Indeed, Anna Silver suggests that the corseted waist is idealized specifically because it forecloses any suspicion of pregnancy. Though Dickens suggests a general moral laxity for *The Old Curiosity Shop*'s Mrs. Jarley, nineteenth-century connections between fatness and sexuality are scarce in British literature as cultural taboos ensured that sexuality itself is often relegated to the subtext of Victorian fiction. The more flexible moral code of French Naturalism offers a useful extension for an examination of how fatness enables both nurturance and the redefinition of ideology itself. In the case of Guy de Maupassant's 1880 short story "Boule de Suif," fatness carries nobility that allows it to interrogate restrictive and unhealthy moral codes. Maupassant's work echoes the social message of Dickens's fat lady imagery, but sets aside the demands of child rearing in favor of a more general consideration of community spirit and nurturance and forges connections between fat and sex as pro-social bodily transgressions that push the limits of women's roles.

Guy de Maupassant's story "Boule de Suif," literally, "Ball of Lard," centers on a egregiously fat prostitute, and thus marries fat to female sexuality in its title character. Maupassant crafted this work within the comparatively liberal culture of 1880s France. Like Dickens, though, Maupassant appreciates nineteenth-century concerns about consumption and sexual control, and recognizes the imagistic potency of fat within social criticism.[13] "Boule de Suif" chronicles the journey of a group of Normans trying to escape the ravages of the Franco-Prussian War by securing passage on an outbound coach. The passengers embody the wealth, religion, and ideological negotiation of bourgeois culture. They include three wealthy merchant couples, two nuns, a famous revolutionary named Cornudet, and the title character, an elite courtesan. Confined to the coach throughout the day, the unprepared passengers suffer greatly from hunger and thirst until Boule de Suif offers to share the ample picnic she brought for just such an eventuality. The "respectable" passengers put aside their prejudice against their "immoral" benefactor long enough to eat, and they pass the common cup (literally) in almost biblical fashion. Later, however, the coach is stopped by a Prussian officer and his men, who confine the passengers for several days. The officer will let them go, he insists, only if Boule de Suif makes love to him. Intensely patriotic, she refuses until her impatient companions assure her that such a sacrifice would be morally right and pressure her into accepting the officer for the common good. Against her judgment, she agrees, and the passengers are allowed to resume their journey. In spite of their prior assurances of gratitude, however, the upstanding citizens treat Boule de Suif with blatant scorn and, when they assemble an impromptu buffet from their meager food supplies, they refuse to share with her. Hurt and disgusted, Boule de Suif sobs while her ungrateful companions dine.

Like the amorous Prussian officer, Maupassant's omniscient narrator evaluates Boule de Suif with an appreciative eye and metaphors of food:

> Small, round and fat as lard, with puffy fingers choked at the phalanges like chaplets of short sausages, with a stretched and shining skin, an enormous bosom which shook under her dress, she was, nevertheless, pleasing and sought after on account of a certain freshness and breeziness of disposition. Her face was a round apple, a peony bud ready to pop into

---

[13] Zola and others share Maupassant's fascination with fat sexuality. I prefer this particular story because of its strongly positive presentation of excess.

bloom, and inside that opened two great black eyes shaded with thick brows that cast a shadow within; and below, a charming mouth, humid for kissing, furnished with shining, microscopic baby teeth. She was, it was said, full of admirable qualities. ("BDS," 6)[14]

Boule de Suif's extreme fatness is characterized as unusual but not unpleasant, and of a magnitude appropriate for her warm and outgoing personality. Her attractions, the narrator insists, are her "freshness and breeziness of disposition" and her "humid" sensuality. Her sausage-like fingers blur the line between food and body—they suggest that she, too, might be consumable. As critic Mary Donaldson-Evans argues, Boule de Suif and many of Maupassant's other female characters are treated as consumables and exploited by their society. This aptly characterizes the attitudes of the other passengers, including the story's narrator, yet in its entirety "Boule de Suif" resoundingly condemns such practice and shows that even women who commodify their sexuality are much more than objects. In Boule de Suif's physical description, the challenges to middle-class ideology posed by the potential for cultural transformation within the grotesque aspects of her body merge with narrative irony about the consumption of the prostitute's body by mainstream culture.[15]

Maupassant also mocks the presumption of a fat prostitute's lack of physical control to create ironic commentary on the nineteenth-century's ideological limits for both bodies and social roles. Self-starvation and corseting were valued in nineteenth-century middle-class culture as proof of bodily self-control, so Boule de Suif's transgression of physical and sexual norms should point to weak self-control. Yet Maupassant's characterization insists on a more complex reading of his character's bodily life. Boule de Suif is not a passionate amateur, but a sex professional who bases decisions about her body not just on emotion or desire, but also on experience, personal values, and business principles. Boule de Suif's sexual professionalism actually enables her control over her own body. While the other

[14] Petite, ronde de partout, grasse à lard, avec des doigts bouffis, étranglés aux phalanges, pareils à des chapelets de courtes saucisses, avec une peau luisante et tendue, une gorge énorme qui saillait sous sa robe, elle restait cependant appétissante et courue, tant sa fraîcheur faisait plaisir à voir. Sa figure était une pomme rouge, un bouton de pivoine prêt à fleurir; et là-dedans s'ouvraient, en haut, deux yeux noirs magnifiques, ombragés de grands cils épais qui mettaient une ombre dedans; en bas, une bouche charmante, étroite, humide pour le baiser, meublée de quenottes luisantes et microscopiques.

[15] The narrator's fixation on his character's bodily openings such as her mouth, and the extent to which his food imagery also blurs the boundaries between meat and person, death and life, draws attention to the short story's imagery. In context of Bakhtin's concept of carnival, the grotesque underscores the main character's role as a tool for social criticism.

characters blindly follow prescribed moral codes, the prostitute is free to give or withhold sex based on her own set of principles about politics and commerce. Her initial decision to withhold sex from her Prussian pursuer (and in an earlier scene, from Cornudet) foregrounds her moral and physical self-determination: she bases her decision on her political and ethical sensibilities, not on men's desire.[16] While Boule de Suif makes mature, reasonable sexual decisions and refrains from sex with ease, her cotravelers are preoccupied with sex and childishly titillated by the prostitute's sexuality. In the same manner, Boule de Suif casually shares her food and voluntarily skips meals during the passengers' confinement, while the others complain incessantly of hunger, devour her proffered rations, and then hoard their own supplies. Clearly, of all the characters, the fattest is best able to control her sexual and gustatory impulses. By conflating fat with sexual excess, and associating both with self-governance and an authentic moral consciousness (through his central character's prolonged deliberation of whether or not to barter sex for freedom), Maupassant presents the female body as something to be revered rather than restrained.

Like Peggotty and Jarley, Maupassant's prostitute demonstrates the interpersonal warmth and social responsibility valued by the emphasis on motherhood within nineteenth-century feminine ideals. Maupassant's story features only adult characters, but nevertheless ties bodily excess to caretaking and nurturance. Boule de Suif's sensual richness is urgently needed within the story's war-starved environment, in which the fleeing passengers cannot stop for food without risk of capture. One female passenger becomes ill with hunger before agreeing to partake of the prostitute's food: far from being the story's unhealthy eater, Boule de Suif instead resuscitates the flagging health of others. In contrast, the self-starving attitude of the other passenger seems narrow-minded rather than noble. Though excessive for one person, Boule de Suif's plentiful picnic offers a necessary counterbalance to the emptiness of the others' stomachs.

Like the bulk and excess of Dickens's supplemental mothers, Boule de Suif's fatness points to an almost limitless generosity and strength of character. Though Maupassant emphasizes that middle-class society is more willing to exploit such excess than validate it, he criticizes such a mentality and gives the fat prostitute a moral high ground. These images of inexhaustible women whose bodies store fuel for near-eternal mothering

---

[16] As Mary Donaldson-Evans notes in *A Woman's Revenge,* Boule de Suif and many other of Maupassant's heroines "preserve their self-respect by transferring their morality to a nonsexual sphere" and "play active and heroic roles" in spite of their socially stigmatized profession (14).

and lovemaking are deeply powerful. They have strength and resilience in stark contrast with scads of nineteenth-century wilting, swooning heroines, and the size of their bodies adds weight to their presence. They defy the notion that female self-sacrifice must come through self-denial, and instead find active roles to play in improving the lives of those around them. Most importantly, by exceeding the acceptable physical dimensions for women and (in Boule de Suif and Jarley's cases) transgressing the acceptable social limitations of womanhood, they challenge the idea that a woman should fit into a particular mold while still outperforming more conventional female characters at the valued work of nurturance. Peggotty redefines nurturance as an active, important role requiring as much self-care as self-sacrifice. Jarley helps us to distinguish between productive, nurturing excess and selfish asceticism. Finally, Boule de Suif insists on her right to determine her own sexual and ethical boundaries and weeps in frustration at a society's lack of appreciation for her valuable excess.

Exceptional fatness can hold myriad meanings, but in these works it guides our appreciation of a character's attitude toward consumption, pleasure, and self-nurturance. As an obvious physical signal of excess—excess that can also emerge as social nonconformity or open sexuality—fat supplements lean spots in nineteenth-century social norms. Such supplementation creates the possibility for revision of a troubling contradiction within Victorian femininity: the potential for self-starvation within some applications of the middle-class feminine ideal can rob women of their ability to nurture and, thus, to fulfill that ideal. Within *David Copperfield* and *The Old Curiosity Shop,* assertive women who feed their own physical and emotional needs make the best nurturers. Dickens invites us to break the connections between bodily conformity, social conformity, and successful motherhood. Dickens has his finger on the tool that succeeding generations of women would use to call for female social equality: the claim that since motherhood gives women authority and requires mental and physical strength, women should therefore be nurtured, educated, and allowed to speak their minds. Maupassant contrasts joyful consumption with mercenary consumerism and embraces fat female sexuality as metaphor for a more permeable, sharing society in which we all nurture each other. For both authors, fat pushes back against social restrictions to create breathing room for all women, as expansive female bodies produce expansive female lives.

Works Cited

Bakhtin, Mikhail. *Rabelais and His World.* Trans. Helene Iswolsky. Bloomington: Indiana University Press, 1984.

Bogdan, Robert. *Freak Show: Presenting Human Oddities for Amusement and Profit.* Chicago: University of Chicago Press, 1988.

Bordo, Susan. *Unbearable Weight: Feminism, Western Culture, and the Body.* Berkeley: University of California Press, 1993.

Braziel, Jana Evans, and Kathleen LeBesco. *Bodies Out of Bounds: Fatness and Transgression.* Berkeley: University of California Press, 2001.

Derrida, Jacques. *On Grammatology.* Trans. Gayatri Spivak. Baltimore: Johns Hopkins University Press, 1976.

Diamond, Michael. *Victorian Sensation, or The Spectacular, the Shocking, and the Scandalous in Nineteenth Century Britain.* London: Anthem, 2003.

Dickens, Charles. *David Copperfield.* 1850. New York: Oxford University Press, 1983.

———. *Little Dorrit.* 1857. New York: Oxford University Press, 1983.

———. *Old Curiosity Shop.* 1841. New York: Oxford University Press, 1983.

Donaldson-Evans, Mary. *A Woman's Revenge: the Chronology of Dispossession in Maupassant's Fiction.* Lexington: French Forum, 1986.

"Fasting Girls." *All the Year Round,* n.s., 2 (October 9, 1869): 442–44.

"Fat People." *All the Year Round,* o.s., 12 (November 19, 1864): 352–55.

Garland-Thomson, Rosemarie. *Extraordinary Bodies: Figuring Physical Disability.* New York: Columbia University Press, 1997.

Gilman, Sander L. *Fat Boys: A Slim Book.* Lincoln: University of Nebraska Press, 2004.

Houston, Gail Turley. *Consuming Fictions: Gender, Class, and Hunger in Dickens's Novels.* Carbondale: Southern Illinois University Press, 1994.

Huff, Joyce. "Conspicuous Consumption: Representations of Corpulence in the Nineteenth-Century British Novel." PhD diss., George Washington University, 2001.

Maupassant, Guy de. *Boule de Suif.* Ed. Ernest Flammarion. Paris: Bibliothèque Flammarion, 1928.

———. "Ball-of-Fat." *Short Stories of the Tragedy and Comedy of Life.* Trans. M. Walter Dunne. Akron: St. Dunstan Society, 1905.

McMaster, Juliet. *Dickens the Designer.* London: Macmillan, 1987.

Michie, Helena. "Under Victorian Skins: The Bodies Beneath." In *A Companion to Victorian Literature & Culture.* Ed. Herbert Tucker. Oxford: Blackwell, 1999. 407–24.

Silver, Anna K. *Victorian Literature and the Anorexic Body.* Cambridge: Cambridge University Press, 2002.

Stearns, Peter N. *Fat History: Bodies and Beauty in the Modern West.* New York: New York University Press, 1997.

Strachey, Lytton. *Queen Victoria.* New York: Harcourt Brace, 1921.

Summers, Leigh. *Bound to Please: A History of the Victorian Corset.* Oxford: Berg, 2001.

Woloch, Alex. *The One vs. the Many: Minor Characters and the Space of the Protagonist in the Novel.* Princeton: Princeton University Press, 2003.

CHAPTER 15

Mother Love

Edith Simcox, Maternity, and Lesbian Erotics

ELLEN BAYUK ROSENMAN

Edith Simcox (1844–1901) was an extraordinary Victorian woman by any measure. An avid trade unionist, founder and manager of the Women's Shirtmaking Cooperative for working-class women, she contributed to some of the major journals of her day and wrote two significant works of nonfiction: *Natural Law* (1877), an investigation of the supposedly natural foundation of ethics, and *Primitive Civilizations* (1894), a two-volume treatise on property laws in Egypt, China, Babylonia, and other ancient civilizations (1894). She was also the would-be sweetheart of George Eliot, immortalizing her unrequited passion in two very different works of life writing: the deceptively titled *Autobiography of a Shirtmaker* (1877–1895), a poignant account of her unrelenting struggle to gain Eliot's affection, and *Episodes in the Lives of Men, Women, and Lovers* (1882), a series of dreamlike, loosely connected fictional vignettes that encode and rewrite her erotic frustration. These works register the dissonance between her experience and the conventions of autobiography and fiction, founded on the dominant social and discursive plots of heterosexuality. They turn to the mother as the ultimate object of desire, refusing the Oedipal mandates of renunciation, substitution, and development that structure the family romance.

However, if mother love tantalized Simcox with the possibility of expressing her attachment to Eliot, it never fulfilled that promise. Drawn to approach-avoidance relationships with adoring female friends, Eliot could hardly have been a more frustrating object. But it was not only Eliot and Simcox's idiosyncratic relationship that guaranteed frustration. The stigma against lesbianism, the incest taboo that insists all infantile desire must find a substitute object, and the manifold contradictions within maternity created a defining "barrier" that both thwarted and structured Simcox's desire (*Autobiography* 47).[1] In her constant yearning, Simcox became an insightful critic of these obstacles, especially the categorical distinctions between erotic and familial or friendly relationships. In her life writing, *Autobiography of a Shirtmaker* and *Episodes in the Lives of Men, Women, and Lovers,* Simcox refuses to normalize "normal" roles and relationships, insisting on the claims of other affiliations and other logics of attachment. It was not that Simcox unfortunately chose an inhospitable object in Eliot, but rather that Eliot was the perfect object to enact her frustrated desire. While maternal love offered a template and guise for same-sex eroticism for a number of Victorian women, the relationship between Simcox and Eliot highlighted its intractable difficulties, staging the many intertwined impasses of both maternity and lesbianism in Victorian Britain. Her extended expression of illicit desire allows us to take the full measure of the complexities of the maternal icon.

Simcox's understanding of economics, moral philosophy, and anthropology provided the resources with which to critique and reimagine the conventions surrounding maternity, heterosexuality, and the family. Although her work in these areas does not always focus directly on gender or sexuality, it offers a critical perspective on the often conflicted relationship between individual desires and cultural norms. In the golden age of amateurism, women like Simcox had the opportunity to become experts in such fields, which required no credentials apart from curiosity, wide reading, an incisive mind, a strong work ethic, and the public connections necessary for publication. Through this work, she discovered other models of attachment aside from Victorian domesticity and found a vantage point from which to experiment with narrative conventions that did not rely on the family romance or the marriage plot. Paradoxically, maternity provided a model and guise for an illicit desire that challenged its heterosexist basis.

[1] I use the term "lesbianism" even though it is anachronistic. No such category existed in the nineteenth century, and it has tended to confine our understanding of female relationships within rigid sexual binaries of homosexual versus heterosexual, and licit versus illicit, as Sharon Marcus has ably demonstrated. However, I retain this term because it accurately conveys the explicitly sexual nature of Simcox's desire, directed exclusively toward women, as well as her self-identification on this basis.

Autobiography of a Shirtmaker, more accurately subtitled *A Monument to the Memory of George Eliot,* dwells on Eliot from its inception in 1877, five years after their first meeting, until its last reference in 1887, five years after the novelist's death.² Simcox clearly saw Eliot as a maternal figure, addressing her as "mother" and seeking her ethical counsel. The rhetoric of family love sanitized but preserved Simcox's attachment, folding its eroticism into devotion and veneration. Eliot was quite willing to take the role of maternal icon, accepting the title of Madonna within her intellectual circle and, for a time, signing her letters to Simcox "your loving mother" (Haight 494). It is equally clear that Simcox understood her attachment as sexual and forbidden, characterizing her feelings as a "restless heartache" and a "thirst" that can never be satisfied (47, 13). Simcox's adaptation of mother worship as a model for her passion has been noted before—indeed, it could hardly be missed. Gillian Beer and Rosemarie Bodenheimer provide nuanced accounts of its shifting currents of power and love, while Martha Vicinus persuasively argues that the mother-daughter relationship offered a recurring, strategically useful "metaphor" for same-sex love (*Intimate* xxvii).

What leads me to reconsider Simcox's relationship in the same terms is my sense that, while these critics provide rich, convincing accounts of Simcox and Eliot, they have left the mother-daughter relationship relatively untouched, taking it up as a safe template for same-sex desire rather than as a problematic in its own right. Mother love was not only a "metaphor," in Vicinus's terms, a linguistic approximation of the real thing; it was the original same-sex love that infused adult attachments. As Freud argues throughout his work, the parent-child relationship is the original human love affair, structuring and underlying the future relationships that are supposed to supplant it: the "genealogical history" of all adult love is incestuous (*Totem* 16).³ Foucault locates this paradigm historically: "[S]ince

---

² Ironically, although *Autobiography of a Shirtmaker* was not published in Simcox's lifetime, it is now the only work by Simcox in print, thanks to the hard work of Connie Fulmer and Margaret Barfield.

³ In its rendering of the pre-Oedipal stage and the resolution of the Oedipus complex, Freudian psychoanalytic theory provides the standard narrative of infantile sexuality, maternal attachment, and normative development. For all infants in the pre-Oedipal stage, the mother is the first erotic object, providing physical intimacy and emotional nurturance. The daughter must replace this first love with another object, the male lover she is "biologically destined" to choose, a substitution that involves both a change in the actual object and a change in the object's sex ("Femininity" 118). The desired endpoint in this theory of development is nonincestuous heterosexuality, but psychoanalytic theories of subject-formation also assert that infantile and childhood attachments persist in adulthood, so that this first maternal attachment underlies all future ones (105). Chodorow's influential feminist

the eighteenth century the family has been an obligatory focus of affects, feelings, love; . . . sexuality has its privileged point of development in the family; . . . for this reason sexuality is 'incestuous' from the start" (108–9). As marriage increasingly became a bond of love as well as expediency, the companionate family (so to speak) borrowed the gestures and rhetoric of romance to cement its loyalties, saturating kinship with desire. Most obviously, the mother represented an ideal of femininity for her sons that was later to be incarnated in a wife. When Tom Brown gapes at his friend Arthur's mother and wonders breathlessly "if Arthur's sisters were like her," we see the sexual connotations of the mother's body (Hughes 321). In "normal" development girls trade the mother for a male love object, a substitution that was supposed to occur in the erotic-maternal paradigm of Victorian same-sex attachments as well as the nuclear family. Vicinus says, "The mother-daughter metaphor was more common than the husband-wife metaphor, in large part because it seemed safer than the obvious eroticism of figurative marriage, but also because it implied a temporary stage. Just as a child grew up and left her natal home, so too would a young woman grow up and leave her older, maternal friend" (xxvii–xxviii).

But leaving the natal home, literally or figuratively, did not automatically erase the intensity or persistence of this first bond. The erotic potential of the mother's body raised awkward questions about the nature of mother-child attachments, for daughters as well as sons. On the one hand, advice literature is filled with moments of tender affection, often stressing the mother's endless availability through tropes implying physical proximity. Sarah Stickney Ellis, queen of Victorian conduct books, reminds the daughters of England "how every wish and want was whispered to her mother's ear, which was never turned away" (*Daughters* 178). Likewise, many of the daughter's responsibilities and privileges involved intimate gestures of caretaking, such as the "heart-thrilling" privilege of "combing back the mother's silvery locks" (*Female Excellence* 151, 137). Stressing the extent and multiple expressions of female eroticism, and persuasively detaching it from the homosexual/heterosexual binary, Sharon Marcus brilliantly demonstrates the elaboration of daughterly desire in doll tales, which routinely narrate "the erotic contentment of a girl in the arms of an adored mother" (161). Conduct books and doll tales set up physically affectionate and pleasurable interaction between mothers and daughters as a familial norm.

---

rethinking of the pre-Oedipal stage for women, along with the work of other psychoanalytic critics such as Melanie Klein and object relations theorists, develops the importance of maternal attachment for daughters, charting a distinctive developmental path in which the mother remains intensely present in the daughter's psychic life, in contrast to male development, which privileges autonomy.

However, such rhapsodies coexisted with a queasy concern about maternal duties. While advice books wondered explicitly whether mothers could maintain the serenity necessary for moral guidance if they involved themselves in the more exhausting, undignified aspects of child care, other sources suggest that such chores might cross the hazy boundary between the acceptable and disturbing eroticism.[4] Describing her relationship with her "perfect" mother, one Victorian woman noted with relief that the "intimate functions" of child care were left to her nurse, adding, "I did not like Mother to even see me in the bath," a comment that hints at the potentially excessive sensuality between mothers and children (Davidoff and Hall 95). Dressing and especially bathing children, which could involve intense intimacy, could be left to servants (in *My Secret Life,* Walter's first memory is of his nursemaid fondling his penis), but mothers also performed these tasks, and, according to Freud, unintentionally initiated their daughters into genital pleasure: "[T]he mother who by her activities over the child's bodily hygiene inevitably stimulated, and perhaps even roused for the first time, pleasurable sensations in her genitals" ("Femininity" 106).[5] However many mothers actively engaged in bodily contact with their daughters, and however inevitable genital arousal actually was as a result of this contact, it is clear that motherhood was a symbolically fraught category, as

---

[4] The mother's role in child care is a subject of debate. In "Below Stairs: The Maid and the Family Romance," Stallybrass and White cull a number of sources suggesting that upper-middle-class families delegated these functions to nurses (149–70), while Amanda Anderson finds a new model of parenting at midcentury, an "emergent conception of controlled and professionalized motherhood" calling for greater degrees of emotional and physical detachment (55). Davidoff and Hall, however, insist that middle-class families did not adopt the "aristocratic habit" of employing servants to care for their children (335). See Regagnion and Craton, in this volume, for a parallel discussion of the complex attitudes toward servant versus maternal care.

 We can also see the power of such concerns in the immensely popular *East Lynne,* which not only challenges the ideal of sexless maternity with the familiar plot device of the mother's sexual fall, but also suggests the far less common possibility that the mother-child relationship might itself be erotic. In addition to its overt thematizing of the mother's adultery, it also stages a debate about the physical responsibilities of the mother, "resolving" the conflict between physically distant maternal love and the physical intimacy of paid child care by returning the tragic heroine to her children in the guise of a governess, in which role she can indulge her craving for physical intimacy with the children she abandoned (indeed, she is able to involve herself much more intimately in their daily physical care as a governess than she ever could as a mother). In essence, the novel has it both ways, wringing pathos from the "impassioned manner" with which she caresses her children—but only when she is no longer recognized as their mother (533). Tacking back and forth between the fallen heroine's love for her husband and for her children, the novel represents these passions as interchangeable and almost indistinguishable motivations for her return.

[5] See Stallybrass and White for a discussion of the exchange of the servant for the mother as an object of desire (149–70); see also *My Secret Life* (I:13–15).

the ambiguous eroticism of the mother's body shadowed practical questions about caretaking. It may not be overreading to suggest that the cult of angelic motherhood was a reaction formation against the eroticization of the mother within the new intimacy of the bourgeois family, rearticulating the incest taboo at this critical historical juncture.[6] This ambiguity gave Simcox room to maneuver when she entered the Priory, the home Eliot shared with George Henry Lewes, and declared her symbolic daughterhood.[7] Although Simcox never realized her desire for a full-scale physical relationship, mother love proved indispensable as she negotiated a canny intimacy within the Lewes household. In the face of social taboos, she found it possible to claim embraces and kisses that were helpfully blurred by codes of familial intimacy. Simcox's diary is replete with reports of affectionate contact in which she takes the role of the "loving child" in order to encode her desire (*Autobiography* 97): "I kissed her hand" (7); "her dear cheek pressed itself caressingly on my lips" (86). (It is interesting that Eliot initiates contact in this unusual and perhaps wishful formulation.) In her dogged pursuit of Eliot, Simcox explicitly questioned the nature and the firmness of boundaries separating one kind of attachment from another. Her interest in moral philosophy supplied the enabling vantage point from which to question these norms: "Are the fixed rules concerning the relations of men [*sic*] to each other, observed in real communities, such as follow from the nature of men, or are they arbitrary inventions?" (*Natural Law* 19). She elaborated on this question in *Primitive Civilizations,* her anthropological history of ownership:

> There is not one of the leading traits of modern family life which can be put forward as so pre-eminently and absolutely natural as to be universal. Polygamy flourishes along with rarer experiments in monogamy, and has been practiced by women as well as men. Children are sometimes reared and sometimes abandoned or put to death by their parents. Marriage is sometimes a light relation during pleasure on both sides, sometimes an indestructible bond, trebly woven of duty, inclination, and convenience, and sometimes it rests on a one-sided utility, involving the

---

[6] Marcus's *Between Women,* which argues that female eroticism was a common, acknowledged, and broadly defined aspect of Victorian life, underscores my claim that Simcox could find acceptable models of same-sex affection close at hand through which to both express and disguise her desire.

[7] See also Marks's treatment of what she calls the "Sappho model" of same-sex attachment, which she sees as "reminiscent of a mother-daughter relationship" in its union of an older, more restrained woman and a passionate acolyte: "The conventions of this topos are simple and limited" (274). Bodenheimer briefly acknowledges the possibility that incestuous desire might accompany Simcox's symbolic daughterhood, though she does not develop this line of thought (419).

virtual slavery of wives; sometimes the authority of the father, sometimes that of the mother, and sometimes that of both parents over their children is unrecognized, while elsewhere the authority of one—or it may be of both—is carried to the point of almost fantastical absoluteness. Our notion of what is natural in family relationships is compounded of all those features of family life which, upon calm retrospect, appear to our present taste as useful and agreeable.... (9–10)

Meticulously tracing variations in family attachments as well as economic arrangements, Simcox was acutely aware of the relativism of family values and the behaviors that expressed them.

Drawing on this knowledge, she explores the potential fluidity of the categories that structured modern familial experience. As Beer notes, Simcox "refused to accept social taxonomies," and adds provocatively, "With her erotic daughterly self-representation the family becomes a swooningly dangerous set of relations rather than a rigid set of social roles" (177). Simcox's sense of cultural difference, her comparison of different kinship structures, her recognition that physical gestures had different meanings in different contexts, impelled an analysis of her own culture's regulatory categories and boundaries. Reflecting on her behavior with Eliot, Simcox surveys the rules that separate *kinds* of relationships, alert to what she can adapt from sexually innocent contexts. One "lawful way" in which she can love Eliot, she notes, is "with a child's fondness for the mother one leans on notwithstanding the irreverence of one's longing to pet and take care of her," registering the affection and the prescribed distance of the mother-child relationship (*Autobiography* 120). Specifying the other forms of lawful love—"idolatrously, as Frater the Virgin Mary, in romance wise as Petrarch, Laura"—she marks out not only alternative but related forms of devotion that she could subtly emulate (120).

> Like ways of loving, kisses can also take on many meanings: The fact is there are as many kinds of good kisses as there are of dear loves: friendly, filial or fraternal; a mother's, a lover's and those appropriate to any composite relation in law or love, provided always that two things separately lawful are not contaminated by an unavowed mixture, as when something amorous sneaks into the relation between two persons who are not lovers or who stand to each other in some other relation incompatible with that. (241)

Insisting that kisses stay in their proper place, Simcox clearly understands the likelihood that forbidden love might disguise itself as an innocent gesture of affection. "Unavowed mixture" is of course a perfect description of her strategy. At moments, Simcox crossed the line and revealed too clearly her carnal intentions: lying in front of the fireplace at Eliot's home, leaning her head on Eliot's knee like a dutiful daughter, Simcox is overcome and "gave the passionate kisses that filled my eyes with tears," receiving Eliot's rebuke (49). At some point, Eliot seemed to realize that honorary motherhood did not defuse Simcox's passion but simply disguised it. Withdrawing this privileged title, she told Simcox that "she did not like for me to call her 'Mother'" since "her feeling for me was *not* at all a mother's"—though not specifying how it was different (110). Expecting a more drastic rebuff, Simcox says "that the only name natural to me was darling and that I took the other as being less greedy, more dutiful," calling attention to illicit feelings that shielded themselves in family roles (110).

Eliot was something of an overdetermined object for category-blurring affection and maternal contradictions, since she was both the Madonna, sage dispenser of moral guidance, and the scarlet woman who had run off with a married man. As a spiritual counselor, Eliot heartlessly preached self-control and selflessness, urging Simcox to dampen her ardor and occasionally to find a husband. Renunciation, of course, was one of Eliot's favorite themes, and, as Bodenheimer observes, Simcox found herself perpetually trapped within it: "[O]ver and over Simcox tries, and fails, and tries again to force herself into a George Eliot plot, in which the heroine is granted love only if she relinquishes desire" (406).[8] Chafing against Eliot's benevolent advice-giving sessions, Simcox asks poignantly, "[H]ow can one keep one's mind and feelings set constantly and with practical effect upon the higher and not the lower? . . . Dearest, dearest every glimpse of the true truth turns to afterglow of grateful tenderness and the sweet worship of love" (*Autobiography* 111). In her "afterglow of great tenderness," one can discern the dream of postcoital pleasure that Simcox cannot quite relinquish. She oscillates between desire and renunciation, yearning for physical consummation yet striving to transform her lust into selfless devotion and productivity. In her despair, Simcox continually experienced the double bind that structured maternal eroticism: the mother who ministers to the child's needs must be tenderly cared for but must also be kept unsullied from physical contact to preserve her purity. Her relationship with Eliot seems designed to enact over and over again the theme of desire and loss, registering simultaneously the twin prohibitions against incest and homosexuality. While, as Vicinus demonstrates, mother love served as a useful model for other women, wrapping same-sex desire in an ideology

---

[8] See also Vicinus: "Ironically, her renunciation of reciprocal love turned her into a heroine worthy of Eliot" (*Intimate* 124).

of adoration and moral guidance, Simcox's frustration reveals the tensions and impossibilities implicit in this apparent solution.

Eliot was more than willing to keep desire in tension, never accepting it but subtly encouraging it. Acknowledging Simcox's desire in letters, Eliot seems to offer the hint of a response beyond moral exhortations about duty and heterosexuality, though in a teasing tone that rather heartlessly sidesteps Simcox's ardor. Eliot tells Simcox that their letters would "make a very pretty romance" and that "she [Eliot] wished my letters could be printed in . . . [a] veiled way . . . "The Newest Heloise"—referring to Rousseau's recent *La Nouvelle Heloise,* a sensation in Europe that depicted a love triangle involving a husband, his wife, and her former lover, written in epistolary form (*Autobiography* 104, 39). Eliot seemed to maintain a high emotional pitch in her relationships with spiritual daughters: another follower, a Mrs. Congreve, confessed to Simcox that "she had loved my darling lover-wise too," and recounted a scene in which she overcompensated for her desire with a cool demeanor, only to watch Eliot flee the room in tears (146). In Eliot's moral philosophy and her approach-avoidance female friendships, Simcox found the perfect unfulfilling object for her incest drama, the ideal lover who can never be loved but will not allow herself to be fully given up.[9] Even after she refused to be called "mother," Eliot continued to encourage Simcox's visits and correspondence (in fact, a week later she offers to introduce Simcox to Mrs. Congreve, as if to recommend a more acceptable model of incestuous affection).

In fact, for Eliot the mother-daughter relationship was ideal as long as its erotic component did not become too explicit; she preferred the "diffident or rather delicate reticence" of less demanding followers (Eliot, *Letters* 128). Eliot's identification with the figure of the mother offered a way of refusing sexual attraction. Exploiting the strand of moral guidance central to the maternal role, she exerted control over eroticized mentorship, which had frustrated and disempowered her earlier in her life. As a young woman, she had played the role of the adoring supplicant to seductive but unattainable father figures and felt the consequences of unleashing the sexual potential of family identifications. As an adult, she gained the protection of age, authority, and, at least in theory, a vastly diminished sexual component. The role of spiritual counselor exacted a devotion that she found irresistible, especially in light of her own torturous experience with the erotics of domesticity. Her ultra-respectable role as "iconic sage" (to quote Deirdre David's incisive phrase), allowed her to rewrite and control

---

[9] For discussions of Eliot's relationships with her female admirers, including Simcox, see Vicinus (*Intimate* 1525–26) and Polkey (68).

these relationships, and so led her to accept Simcox's problematic attraction, at least for a time (161).

Those familiar with Eliot's biography will recall her humiliating expulsion from the symbolic paternal home not once but twice. In 1843, when she was twenty-four years old, Dr. Brabant, father of an acquaintance, invited her to move into his home as a kind of replacement for a daughter who had recently married. Thrilled by the promise of reading, talking, and translating German with him, she was equally enamored of his pet name for her: "Deutera, which *means* second and *sounds* a little like daughter" (Ashton 48). But Eliot's delicious daughterhood soon alarmed even Brabant's blind wife, who insisted that Eliot leave the house. Eight years later she moved into the home of John Chapman, her urbane guide to the sophisticated culture of London and the owner of the *Westminster Review,* for which she was to serve as assistant editor.[10] Once again, Eliot's intellectual and erotic lives dovetailed disastrously. Consulting constantly on the journal, playing Mozart for Chapman in her room, perhaps, as Rosemary Ashton suggests, entering into a brief sexual relationship, Eliot aroused the anger of Chapman's wife and mistress, who, astoundingly, were also installed in the same house (Ashton 84). The two joined forces and, once again, Eliot was ejected from her mentor's home. Though Chapman's machinations can hardly be considered standard family practice, these painful scenes suggest how highly charged domestic space could be. Not only were inhabitants placed in close physical proximity and expected to cultivate strong affective ties, but, with its designation of public and private rooms, the middle-class home created secret places that made seclusion intrinsically suspicious. Eliot may well have been only playing the piano, but her refusal to do so in the parlor marked her performance as dangerously seductive.

In the role of spiritual mother, Eliot rescripted these encounters to affirm her own inviolate status, receiving adoration and safely doling out wisdom in return. In these relationships, Eliot was the superior figure rather than the supplicant, and her female followers were—at least in theory—not likely to stir up currents of desire. (Her male disciples tended to call her "teacher," avoiding both the infantilizing suggestion that they were her children and the potential incestuousness of their attachment,

---

[10] It is worth noting that both Simcox and Eliot are young adults during these erotic traumas, a correspondence that may have reminded Eliot of her own missteps and intensified her dislike of Simcox's advances: Simcox was twenty-eight when she met Eliot and thirty-three when she began *Autobiography*. As Bodenheimer notes, Simcox herself recycled the inequality of this relationship when she found herself the object of a younger woman's affection (411). Like Eliot, she may have found the image of her own youthful intensity disturbing and was not very sympathetic to her admirer.

which would have been more obvious in a heterosexual relationship.) Thus, same-sex friendships offered her controlled intimacy tempered by her superiority, as the hierarchy of mother and child, her considerable fame, and, above all, the incest taboo granted her an impregnable position.

I call attention to the significance of the incest taboo as a structuring device in Simcox's desire, not only because it defines mother love—and, as Freud and Foucault insist, all desire—but also because its solution of substitution, replacing the mother with another object, reiterates itself in Simcox's relationship with Eliot. Her relationship with Eliot seems designed to enact over and over again the theme of desire and renunciation that governs the incest taboo, protesting the inaccessibility of the mother's body as much as the ideological constraints against same-sex love. The power of this taboo looms over Simcox's passion at the very moment when she might fulfill it—that is, when Lewes dies. Without a figure of "mediation," as Bodenheimer says (409), Simcox pulls back, refashioning her desire into an identification with Eliot, grieving for Lewes and imagining Eliot's pain as if it were her own. She cries out, "I feel as if I would give my mother's life for this!" (50). In her extravagant mourning, Simcox offers up the maternal object so that Eliot can have her heterosexual paradise, a selfless acquiescence to Victorian sexual morality. At the same time, she acknowledges the ultimate prohibition, offering to destroy her own mother at the moment when the blocking father disappears and Eliot seems to be available to her. Psychic barriers as well as social prohibitions thwarted her desire, which was most insistent when she could depend on its ultimate frustration.

In this regard, Simcox's relationship to her own mother is poignantly revealing. In contrast to Eliot, Simcox's actual mother plays a very small role in her writing, although, or perhaps because, they lived together. For most of the autobiography, Eliot, in the role of iconic, unattainable maternal object, seems far more compelling than the actual mother. Most references to her are brief, involving arrangements for her health and welfare. In their few reported conversations, she is strikingly prosaic compared to the eloquent Eliot. Showing her mother a letter from a friend over which she has cried, Simcox reports her mother's reaction: "[I]t is a very nice letter" (*Autobiography* 40). Simcox may well have found Eliot an inspiring mother substitute, modeling public achievement and self-development, unlike her biological parent, who sought no visible distinction and fulfilled her traditional role with apparent contentment.[11]

---

[11] This is one other way in which the complexities of the mother-daughter relationship affected Simcox. As feminist revisionists have noted, the mother's limited social role can frustrate the daughter, leading her to resist or resent her identification with femininity through the mother (Chodorow; Flax); however much the daughter might love her particular mother, she may resent the contingent position ideology prescribes for her and, by

But the moment when Simcox must actually "give [up my] mother's life" occasions the autobiography's most heart-wrenching entry, in which she recasts her relationship with her mother as a marriage: "[Y]ou hear where people have been in love over 50 years—the time of a golden wedding, if they part, both are older than I, old enough to feel that it is not for long.... But I am widowed when not far past the prime of a modern life" (*Autobiography* 279). The next entry is the last. In this moment, it seems that Eliot is not the desired but forbidden mother but another stand-in, a safe substitute through which Simcox could stage and displace mother love. With the death of her actual mother comes the vanishing point of writing. Yet in returning her thoughts and heart to her mother—to her "real" mother—Simcox once again reveals the constraints of the mother-daughter relationship. If her desire for Eliot cannot fulfill itself directly but must be narrated in terms of daughterly devotion, here the mother-daughter relationship must be recast as a marriage. We return once again to a central contradiction of the bourgeois Victorian mother, who must be cherished and caressed with love but without passion. Simcox cannot describe her feelings for her mother without having recourse to another relationship, that of husband and wife, in which eroticism can be more openly expressed and the trauma of loss perhaps more publicly accepted. In a sense, then, her "real" mother is not real at all, but another unrealized possibility, another erotic phantom, grasped at through the substitution of Eliot's body and the analogy of marriage.

It should be obvious by now that the title *Autobiography of a Shirtmaker* hardly conveys the contents of the volume. In the first place, it is not an autobiography but a diary, composed of separate dated entries, with no attempt to create an aesthetic whole. *Autobiography* suggests that this obviously private confession, narrating an entirely unacceptable attachment to a revered public figure, is a public document. It also implies a tale of development, perhaps "a Comptean framework of human progress," as Linda Peterson describes one major strand of Victorian autobiography (64). *Autobiography of a Shirtmaker* also defines its author in terms of her work, perhaps detailing the acquisition of professional expertise and exemplary conduct along the lines of Samuel Smiles's *Lives of the Engineers*. From these perspectives, the title *Autobiography* is heavily ironic. But at the same time, the volume does constitute Simcox's life writing, dwelling on what she considered the defining personal experience of her life even if it did

---

extension, for the daughter herself, especially if the daughter has aspirations beyond domestic life. See also Marks's discussion of the Sappho model, which can be compelling because daughters find their real mothers "inadequate" (274).

not resemble conventional autobiographical material.[12] Entering the text is like moving quickly through the surface of a geological site, brushing aside the generic work-orientation of the title to find a rich, unconventional stratum of lived experience. In its contrast to the conventional expectations raised by the title, *Autobiography* is a cry of pain, the chronicle of an obsession. What is striking about it, in addition to its psychological and sexual content, are its generic and narrative implications. The text makes painfully clear the limitations of the traditional autobiography and the bildungsroman, its fictional counterpart, demonstrating their fealty to a notion of development that requires the erasure of the mother and the heteronormativity that is supposed to follow.

Simcox was well aware of the expectations associated with conventional autobiography, having surveyed them extensively in her essay "Autobiography." The expected structure of *bildung* does not hold sway; instead, Simcox's autobiography remains fixated on a single object. Carolyn Dever persuasively argues that both Freudian psychology and Victorian novels insist on the mother's death, symbolic or literal, as the precondition for normative subjectivity. In one sense, Simcox's pervasive sense of neglect honors that assumption; Eliot is as inaccessible as if she were lost or dead, while Simcox's reiterated desire may correlate to the obsessive search for personal origins and so to authentic identity that Dever identifies as one of the most defining features of realism, both fictional and autobiographical. Yet at the same time, *Autobiography* refuses the very notion of development in favor of an unswerving attachment coded as maternal. Dever's description of Victorian narrative shows, by contrast, the revisionism of *Autobiography:* "[T]he specter of the motherless, vulnerable child ... is the paradigmatic subject of nineteenth-century British narrative, the ensuing *Bildung* mapping the child's negotiation back into domestic space—and defining, along the way, the parameters of that domestic space and the male and female subjects that inhabit it" (2). Though Simcox often resembles the motherless, vulnerable child, she resolutely refuses to give Eliot up, to move on to a substitute attachment, to find a new focus for her writing, if not her life, to fashion a new domestic space from the acceptance of maternal loss, to place heterosexuality—the "male and female subjects that inhabit" the home—at the center of the story. Simcox's same-sex desire has forced a significant rewriting of conventional narratives in which the Oedipal paradigm does not hold sway.[13]

---

[12] The work's subtitle, "A Monument to the Memory of George Eliot," was added by the editors (Connie Fulmer, personal communication, October 11, 2007).

[13] Among other works analyzing resistance to conventional domesticity, including treatments of adoptive, composite, and constructed families, see especially Chase and Levenson's

This conspicuous resistance to Oedipal plotting is equally striking, if more implicit, in Simcox's *Episodes in the Lives of Men, Women, and Lovers* (1882).[14] In these strange, fablelike stories, a group of friends pays annual visits to the island home of a central figure identified only as "Master." After seven years, the guests are considered initiates: the Master invites them to compose stories about memorable moments in their lives and to read the stories composed by other insiders. Despite its lack of any direct reference to her experience, Simcox also considered *Episodes* a form of life writing: "every scrap of insight or feeling is taken direct from my own experience. . . . There is no imagination here, but one thing more I see goes to producing the effect thereof,—a sense of life's analogies, so that one can confess one's own hidden feeling undisguised in a new framework which disguises our part in it" (*Autobiography* 185). The complex reworking of Simcox's own experience is visible in her paradoxical description of her "hidden feeling" as both "undisguised" and "disguise[d]," a description reiterated in the Master's instructions to his disciples to narrate incidents "more entirely their [the disciples'] own because of the remoteness of such veiled confessions from the intercourse of ordinary life" (*Episodes* 15). As in *Autobiography,* the most meaningful experience eludes conventional narrative frameworks.

Episodes "disguises" Simcox's "part in it" with the self-consciously literary techniques that give the volume its ethereal qualities: the evocative and mysterious settings, the emphasis on interiority rather than event, the pastiche-like effect of the apparently unrelated episodes, and the dispersal of the narrative "I" into the personas of the stories. If *Autobiography* is one long unrelieved cry for Eliot's presence, *Episodes* dissolves emotion into a mist of otherworldly scenes and characters. While *Autobiography* responded to the chasm between deep feeling and public life with an unrelenting insistence on a single emotional state of longing for a single object, *Episodes* moves in the opposite direction, refracting Simcox's emotions into different character-narrators, different settings, and different plots. Julie Abraham has accused "the lesbian novel" of simply substituting lesbian lovers for heterosexual ones while leaving other aspects of the erotic plot

chapters "Tom Pinch: The Serpent beside the Dickensian Fireside" and "Love after Death: The Deceased Wife's Sister Bill" for treatments of the complicating eroticism of family ties.

[14] I make more positive claims for *Episodes* than Bodenheimer, but agree with her interest in the text as reflecting not only Simcox's frustration with Eliot, but also her frustration with conventional stories. The collection is heterogeneous, and our interest in different stories partly accounts for our different interpretations of the achievement of the collection as a whole.

intact, but in this strange text Simcox actually uses a cast of heterosexual lovers to challenge the conventions of realism and to undercut familiar Oedipal patterns.[15]

Implicitly, the frame narrative of *Episodes* offers an alternative to the unsatisfactory plot of the family romance. Rather than futilely attempting to fill the lonely void left by an absent parent or to accept maturity in a heterosexual dyad, the writers of the *Episodes* trade these highly fraught affective bonds for looser, lighter attachments, what the narrator calls "neighborliness" (*Episodes* 11). In this fantasy world, community replaces family, a cyclical structure replaces linear plotting, and gendering ignores the either/or binary of normative ideology. Master is an authoritative figure, masculine in his position and control but in other ways a perfect mother, performing on a public scale a series of feminine caretaking functions: he nurses shipwrecked sailors back to health, organizes communal harvests, maintains a fertile garden, and nurtures close relationships among the island's inhabitants; his six-month cycles of presence and absence may also evoke the mother goddess Demeter. Simcox invents a new society with its own rituals and structures of affiliation. Suspended between the heartache of isolation and the claustrophobia of the family, this island retreat, with its cycle of coming and going, provides a network of satisfying and manageable friendships. *Episodes* sketches a cooperative community, reflecting Simcox's interest in the quasi-communitarian arrangements recorded in *Primitive Civilizations,* such as the public feasts in Crete and Sparta, and the function of the Egyptian lord as a "giver of food" whose generosity

---

[15] In this heterogeneous text, Simcox also revises her relationship to Eliot in a variety of inconsistent but wish-fulfilling ways. Moving from story to story, the narrator is now an accepted male lover, now a rejecting female one, now a man who marries a woman named "Marian" (one of the spellings Eliot used for her first name), now a detached observed describing the experience of a love-struck character, now a man beloved by a woman called Diva and Diatoma (conjuring up Eliot's intertwined roles as queen bee and iconic sage) whom he rejects, saying, "Stay, sweet Goddess, on your pedestal"—a fictional dismissal of Eliot that must have given Simcox no little satisfaction. In the final story, the narrator acts as a "guide and philosopher" to a boy named Johnny, who soaks up the narrator's pronouncement that "the eternal marriage of love and duty" is the greatest good (271, 302). "Johnny" was the nickname of John Cross, longtime rival for Eliot's attentions who married her shortly after Lewes's death—"the fatal Johnny," Simcox called him (*Autobiography* 19)—while Simcox was in the midst of writing these stories (the rivalry was visible enough for Eliot to playfully accuse Simcox of conspiring to poison his clothing through the shirt-making cooperative (11). Simcox's fiction emphasizes Johnny's youth, his status as a literal Johnny-come-lately in this established community, and her own position as a trusted, mature insider of long standing in contrast to Cross's successful usurpation of Eliot in real life. Perhaps Simcox also enjoyed casting herself in Eliot's role of the sage dispenser of wisdom in contrast to her actual lot as a supplicant jockeying for position in the circle of admirers.

nurtures "the bond of common citizenship" (71, 67). We can also trace the outlines of Simcox's communitarian shirtmaking venture, for among his other accomplishments the Master organizes a spinning and knitting cooperative. It is surely significant that Simcox described her own organization in language suggesting its effective substitution for marriage: "[T]he firm and its present biographer were united in the bond of lawful partnership" ("Eight Years" 1040). Perhaps, too, Simcox's fiction talks back to Eliot as Simcox herself seems never to have done. In contrast to Eliot's denigrating insistence that Simcox marry, *Episodes* promotes the satisfaction of work and friendship; in contrast to Eliot's devotion to Lewes and her speedy marriage to John Cross after Lewes's death, the Master rejects a friend's suggestion that he find a wife.[16]

Speculating on the qualities of an "emancipatory" aesthetic that embraces play and pleasure, Isobel Armstrong writes: "[T]he further away some of our discourses are from everyday discourse through the transformation of categories, the nearer they are to critique" (184, 185). These strange tales that locate themselves in their "remoteness . . . from the intercourse of everyday life"—a virtual paraphrase of Armstrong's description—offer such alternatives. One of their most obvious characteristics is their lingering descriptions of moods that evoke Freud's oceanic consciousness, the infant's sense of pre-Oedipal union with the mother.[17] The story "Consolation" is paradigmatic, collecting many features of other stories into a single narrative. It begins with an apparently gratuitous recounting of the death of a mother and her children from diphtheria. Although the death of the mother opens the tale, this would-be origin takes place off-stage and is quickly forgotten. This apparent tragedy is relevant only because the narrator is recovering from the same illness. It is as if the story begins by clearing away the mother-child relationship, making way for other kinds of stories in which maternal loss, longing, and fulfillment are represented in safely symbolic forms. The narrator sits by the sea watching the waves crash onto the shore and then retreat, falling into a meditative unity with nature, the "Great Mother" who will speed his recovery (32).

---

[16] In so doing, she may have tacitly revised the recurring heterosexual resolutions of Eliot's novels. Of course, not all the novels end with this convention. In her last works, such conclusoins are either absent or severely qualified: *Romola* closes with the alliance of Romola and Tessa, while *Daniel Deronda* places Daniel and Mirah's happiness alongside Gwendolen's bewildered loneliness.

[17] It may also make sense to call these scenes and moods "melancholy," the term which Freud used to describe incomplete mourning for the lost maternal object, taken up by Butler as the key signifier of the costs of a "successful" development that requires adults to repress identifications and erotic objects that, if necessary to the *process* of constructing normative subjectivity, are ultimately defined as inappropriate to a stable, heterosexual adulthood.

The ocean obligingly provides two key images of the child's relation to the mother: the narrator regressively yearns to enter the "resting place" at the center of the womblike vortex of a whirlpool, while the waves allow the narrator to stage Freud's classic game of fort/da, in which the child symbolizes the mother with an object, hiding and retrieving it to exert imaginative control over her absence and presence. Watching the waves advance and retreat on the shore, the narrator, "like a child," asks the ocean, "Do it again, please," lulled by the rhythm of the waves' dependable return (37).

The story's ending is almost a parody of resolution. In contrast to the extended descriptions of his dreamy convalescence, the narrator notes his eventual recovery and marriage almost as an afterthought, dispatching his happy ending with unsettling brevity. A temporal and emotional chasm separates the two parts of the story, with intense feeling on one side, in the past, and a matter-of-fact present on the other. We never see the narrator falling in love with the woman who becomes his wife, a common pattern in the stories.[18] The movement into marriage and domesticity is completely uninteresting and entirely incommensurate with the emotions it is supposed to channel. These stories keep maternal erotics alive by dispensing with Oedipal dynamics, then switch abruptly to the normative ending of adult heterosexual romance, a poor and illogical substitute. As different as they are from *Autobiography,* they also protest the narrative of development, fashioning other conventions that, story after story, center their attention on diffuse sensual pleasures that are suddenly replaced by the marriage plot. In *Autobiography,* Simcox writes, "I should like to know how many women there are who have . . . some other story than the one which alone is supposed to count" (233). *Episodes* sketches such "other stories," offering fluctuating and implicit but nevertheless visible alternatives.

Having situated Simcox in the context of Victorian maternity and lesbian literature, I'd like to consider her briefly in the context of women's

---

[18] "Diptych" is one of the most interesting stories in this regard. The narrator describes two unsuccessful but intense love affairs (one in which he rejects an impressive woman with "an angel's voice . . . [and] a wise and tolerant tenderness" who is obviously a version of Eliot—a fictional role reversal that must have given Simcox some satisfaction). Again, the narrator falls in love with and marries a woman without describing either the process or the partner, except to say that his wife is an artist and has painted portraits of both women, whom she has encountered in different settings; hence the diptych of the title. Once again, compelling emotional experience is relegated to the past, even more emphatically closed by the framing of the past lovers. But in a further twist, the wife herself has been painted by a friend of the narrator, creating a triptych of beloved women who are now reduced to static images. The present is a time of detachment and calm description, with passion relegated to the past.

literary history, as a recovery project. Her life and writing offer significant cultural insights because they complicate some familiar paradigms that, as the introduction to this volume observes, seem to have a preternatural tenacity—separate spheres, the Angel in the House, the sanctity of domesticity.[19] Highlighting this tenacity, Mary Poovey performs a mock recovery of novelist Ellen Pickering, who can be shown to have written into her plots the obligatory conflicts of "the woman writer"—living under the sway of cultural imperatives but struggling toward resistance. Margaret Homans comments drily, "You can tell Poovey is getting tired of her old themes" (456). Simcox is interesting, in part, because she escapes from the subversion/containment model in her pursuit of the significantly different plot of communal life. In our current literary history, there are few examples of similar works from which such formulas could be drawn. In the nineteenth century, I can only think of Sarah Orne Jewett's *The Country of the Pointed Firs* and Elizabeth Gaskell's *Cranford,* though there may well be others.[20] Certainly Victorians experienced these affiliations, described in Vicinus's *Independent Women,* Judith Walkowitz's *City of Dreadful Delight,* and Seth Koven's *Slumming.* Perhaps there is another literary history of women writers, underdeveloped by our current critical interests, that fashioned conventions for narrating community and shared work. Further, Simcox holds our attention as a writer in multiple genres and a social activist, not only because this is interesting work in itself but because it extends our sense of "women writers" to consider the importance of nonfiction in the history of women's authorship. Our valorization of the novel as the richest, most telling form of women's writing, and perhaps of Victorian writing as a whole, sometimes obscures the power and uses of other genres. Amanda Anderson calls for investigations into the "available practices of self-reflection" that writers might have had at their disposal to challenge dominant beliefs (63). In Simcox's case, the disciplines of anthropology and moral philosophy, along with the activism of trade unionism and cooperative economic enterprise, provided just such practices. Commitments beyond fiction writing helped Simcox see past the conventions of realism and the marriage plot to experiment with other forms.

[19] See "Gender Studies in the Twenty-First Century," Alison Booth and Christopher Lane's interview in *Nineteenth-Century Gender Studies*.

[20] Eliot's *Romola* might be another candidate, though its female community is more like another nuclear family (especially as Romola and Tessa are particularly dedicated to raising the son Lillo), and takes shape only at the end of the novel. See Pauline Nestor's *Female Friendships and Communities,* which traces the shifting interplay of the heterosexual plot and female same-sex ties in Brontë, Eliot, and Gaskell. Deborah Morse also proposes the less-well-known author Hesba Stretton, the subject of her essay in this volume on a different aspect of mothering.

That Simcox's formal experiments dovetail with Freud's theory of human development and the imagery of "oceanic" feeling also has suggestive implications for literary history. Their parallel thinking identifies one consequence of maternal loss as psychological impoverishment, imposing on a potentially more expansive subject the straitjacket of the ego-self with its firm boundaries, outer-directed energies, and legible public face. Despite obvious differences in the motivations behind and scope of their ideas, both writers reformulate subjectivity and sexuality as layered and discontinuous, widening the gap between accepted social roles and psychodynamics. Writing out of this understanding, Simcox is a kind of bridge figure between nineteenth- and twentieth-century narratives. In *Episodes*, she reaches toward new representational strategies that, though they have counterparts in nineteenth-century novels, strongly anticipate modernist techniques: pastiche; the ventriloquism of multiple voices; the fragmentation of continuous linear time; the liberal use of the atmosphere of dreams and fantasy; the sketchy treatment of external details and description; and a lyricism designed to capture alternative mental states that resembles the style of Virginia Woolf's *The Voyage Out,* another novel saturated with maternal erotics. This last connection raises a question that I have been unable to answer: are the pre-Oedipal metaphorics employed by Simcox, Freud, and Woolf historically specific? Is there something distinctive about the Victorian bourgeois family that called forth rhapsodic, tactile descriptions of the ocean? Countering idealizations of the pre-Oedipal period as a primeval attachment predating patriarchal imperatives, Diana Fuss reminds us that "pre-oedipality is firmly entrenched in the social order and cannot be read as before, outside, or even after the symbolic; the mother-daughter relationship, no less than the father-daughter relationship, is a Symbolic assertion completely inscribed in the field of representation, sociality, and culture" (73). Metaphorically, of course, it is easy to connect the ocean to boundlessness, to amniotic fluid, and to the origins of life, as countless critics have done. These links are transhistorical (at least to the extent that womb was understood as a watery environment for the fetus). But perhaps because of the distinctive idealizations and ambiguities that shaped Victorian motherhood, the fantasy of perfect communion took on a special urgency and so was harnessed to the natural world, "inscribed in the field of representation," as Fuss puts it, in a way that naturalizes its imaginary satisfactions.

Simcox's unrequited love for Eliot gave her a distinct perspective on Victorian society, transforming the icon of the mother into an alluring, frustrating, and contradictory presence. As an experimental writer, she turned the master-narratives of maternal loss, individual development, and heterosexual happiness inside out. Her unconventional life and the texts she made of it are part of the "historical lineages" of lesbianism as she struggled to articulate and imaginatively overcome the multifaceted barrier that blocked her erotic fulfillment (Moore 11). At the same time, her role as a public intellectual stretches the definition of female literary history, insisting on its intersection with other, apparently tangential discourses that offer resources for cultural critique. An anthropologist of her own culture, Simcox insistently defamiliarized the categories and conditions of family life, along with some of the most commonplace conventions of Victorian narrative.

Works Cited

Abraham, Julie. *Are Girls Necessary? Lesbian Writing and Modern History.* New York: Routledge, 1996.
Anderson, Amanda. *The Way We Argue Now: A Study in the Cultures of Theory.* Princeton: Princeton University Press, 2006.
Armstrong, Isobel. "So What's All This about the Mother's Body? The Aesthetic, Gender, and the Polis." *Women: A Cultural Review* 4 (Autumn 1993): 172–87.
Ashton, Rosemary. *George Eliot: A Life.* London: Penguin, 1996.
Beer, Gillian. "Passion, Politics, Philosophy: The Work of Edith Simcox." *Women: A Cultural Review* 6 (1995): 166–79.
Bodenheimer, Rosemarie. "Autobiography in Fragments: The Elusive Life of Edith Simcox." *Victorian Studies* 44 (2002): 399–422.
Butler, Judith. *Gender Trouble: Feminism and the Subversion of Identity.* New York: Routledge, 1990.
Chase, Karen, and Michael Levenson. *The Spectacle of Intimacy: A Public Life for the Victorian Family.* Princeton: Princeton University Press, 2000.
Chodorow, Nancy. *The Reproduction of Motherhood: Psychoanalysis and the Sociology of Gender.* Berkeley: University of California Press, 1978.
David, Deirdre. *Intellectual Women in Patriarchy: Harriet Martineau, Elizabeth Barrett Browning, George Eliot.* Ithaca: Cornell University Press, 1987.
Davidoff, Leonore, and Catherine Hall. *Family Fortunes: Men and Women of the English Middle Class, 1780–1850.* Chicago: University of Chicago Press, 1987.
Dever, Carolyn. *Death and the Mother from Dickens to Freud: Victorian Fiction and the Anxiety of Origins.* Cambridge: Cambridge University Press, 1998.
Eliot, George. *Letters from George Eliot to Elma Stuart, 1872–1880.* Ed. Roland Stuart. London: Simkin, Marshall, Hamilton, Kent, and Co., 1909.
Ellis, Sarah Stickney. *Daughters of England: Their Position in Society, Character and Responsibilities.* London: Fisher, Son and Co., 1842.
Female Excellence; or, Hints to Daughters by a Mother. London: Religious Tract Society, 1838.
Flax, Jane. "The Conflict between Nurturance and Autonomy in Mother-Daughter Relationships and within Feminism." *Feminist Studies* 4 (1978): 171–89.

Foucault, Michel. *History of Sexuality: An Introduction*. Vol. 1. Trans. Robert Hurley. New York: Vintage, 1990.

Freud, Sigmund. "Femininity." In *New Introductory Lectures on Psychoanalysis*. Trans. James Strachey. New York: Norton, 1965.

———. *Totem and Taboo*. Trans. James Strachey. New York: Norton, 1950.

Fuss, Diana. *The Identification Papers*. New York: Routledge, 1995.

"Gender Studies in the Twenty-First Century: An Interview with Christopher Lane and Alison Booth." *Nineteenth-Century Gender Studies* 3.1 (Spring 2007). http://www.ncgsjournal.com/issue31/rosenman.htm.

Haight, Gordon. *George Eliot: A Biography*. New York: Penguin, 1985.

Homans, Margaret. "A Response to Mary Poovey's 'Recovering Ellen Pickering.'" *Yale Journal of Criticism* 13 (2000): 452–60.

Hughes, Thomas. *Tom Brown's Schooldays*. Oxford: Oxford University Press, 1989.

Koven, Seth. *Slumming: Sexual and Social Politics in Victorian London*. Princeton: Princeton University Press, 2004.

Marcus, Sharon. *Between Women: Friendship, Desire, and Marriage in Victorian England*. Princeton: Princeton University Press, 2007.

Marks, Elaine. "Lesbian Intertextuality." In *Sexual Practice/Textual Theory: Lesbian Cultural Criticism*. Ed. Susan J. Wolfe and Julia Penelope. Oxford: Blackwell, 1993. 271–90.

Moore, Lisa. *Dangerous Intimacies: Toward a Sapphic History of the British Novel*. Durham: Duke University Press, 1997.

My Secret Life. 2 vols. New York: Grove Press, 1966.

Nestor, Pauline. *Female Friendships and Communities*. Oxford: Oxford University Press, 1985.

Peterson, Linda. *Traditions of Victorian Women's Autobiography: The Poetics and Politics of Life Writing*. Charlottesville: University of Virginia Press, 1999.

Polkey, Pauline. "Recuperating the Love-Passions of Edith Simcox." In *Women's Lives into Print: The Theory, Practice and Writing of Feminist Auto/Biography*. Ed. Pauline Polkey. New York: St. Martin's, 1999. 61–79.

Poovey, Mary. "Recovering Ellen Pickering." *Yale Journal of Criticism* 13 (2000): 437–52.

Simcox, Edith. *Autobiography of a Shirtmaker*. Ed. Constance M. Fulmer and Margaret E. Barfield. New York: Garland, 1998.

———. "Autobiographies." In *Prose by Victorian Women: An Anthology*. Ed. Andrea Broomfield and Sally Mitchell. New York: Garland, 1996. 528–63.

———. *Primitive Civilizations, or Outlines of the History of Ownership in Archaic Communities*. 2 vols. London: Swan Sonnenschein and Co., 1896.

———. "Eight Years of Cooperative Shirtmaking." *Nineteenth Century* 15 (June 1884): 1037–54.

———. *Episodes in the Lives of Men, Women, and Lovers*. London: Trubner and Co., 1882.

———. *Natural Law: An Essay in Ethics*. London: Trubner and Co., 1877.

Stallybrass, Peter, and Allon White. *The Politics and Poetics of Transgression*. Ithaca: Cornell University Press, 1986.

Vicinus, Martha. *Intimate Friends: Women Who Loved Women, 1778–1928*. Chicago: University of Chicago Press, 2004.

———. "'The Gift of Love': Nineteenth-Century Religion and Lesbian Passion." *Nineteenth-Century Contexts* 23 (2001): 241–64.

Vince, Norma. "The Fiddler, the Angel and the Defiance of Antigone: A Reading of Edith Simcox's 'Autobiography of a Shirtmaker,'" *Women: A Cultural Review* 6 (1995): 143–65.

Walkowitz, Judith R. *City of Dreadful Delight: Narratives of Sexual Danger in Late-Victorian London.* Chicago: University of Chicago Press, 1992.

Wood, Ellen. *East Lynne.* Ed. Andrew Maunder. Peterborough, ON: Broadview, 2000.

CONTRIBUTORS

Mary Jean Corbett is the John W. Steube Professor of English and an affiliate of the Women's Studies Program at Miami University in Oxford, Ohio. She is the author of *Representing Femininity: Middle-Class Subjectivity in Victorian and Edwardian Women's Autobiographies* (Oxford University Press, 1992) and *Allegories of Union in Irish and English Writing, 1790–1870: History, Politics, and the Family from Edgeworth to Arnold* (Cambridge University Press, 2000). Her new book, *Family Likeness: Sex, Marriage, and Incest from Jane Austen to Virginia Woolf*, is published by Cornell University Press (2008).

Lillian Craton is assistant professor of English at Lander University in South Carolina. Her essay in this collection grew out of research at Emory University for her doctoral dissertation, "Odd-Bodied: Physical Difference and Ideology in Nineteenth-Century Popular Fiction" (2006), which examines intersections between disability theory, women's studies, and Victorian fiction. Other research efforts include past contributions to an Emory-NEH digital text library of Victorian pulp fiction, a forthcoming essay on teaching with digital texts, and a forthcoming book on physical difference in literature. She is a married mother of three cats.

Deirdre d'Albertis is associate professor of English at Bard College and the author of *Dissembling Fictions: Elizabeth Gaskell and the Victorian Social*

Text (Palgrave Macmillan, 1997). She is currently studying the concept of work outside the home in the writing lives of Hannah Cullwick, Eliza Lynn Linton, Margaret Oliphant, and Margaret Harkness.

Ginger Frost is professor of history at Samford University in Birmingham, Alabama. She is the author of *Promises Broken: Courtship, Class, and Gender in Victorian England* (University of Virginia Press, 1995) and *Living in Sin: Cohabiting as Husband and Wife in Nineteenth-Century England* (Universtiy of Manchester Press, 2008). She is currently working on a study of growing up illegitimate in England, 1870–1940.

Laura Green is associate professor in the Department of English at Northeastern University. She is the author of *Educating Women: Cultural Conflict and Victorian Literature* (Ohio University Press, 2001). Her current book project, "Transforming Fictions," concerns relations of literary identification among authors, readers, and characters in the realist novel; she has published articles on this topic in *Tulsa Studies in Women's Literature, Twentieth-Century Literature,* and *Victorians Institute Journal.*

Claudia C. Klaver is associate professor of English at Syracuse University and is the author of *A/Moral Economics: Classical Political Economy and Authority in 19th-Century England* (The Ohio State University Press, 2003). She has also published articles on Charlotte Brontë, Charles Dickens, Harriet Martineau, and Indian Mutiny memoirs and is currently working on a project on the Crimean War.

Teresa Mangum is associate professor of English at the University of Iowa. She is the author of *Married, Middlebrow, and Militant: Sarah Grand and the New Woman Novel* (University of Michigan Press, 1998) and numerous articles on nineteenth-century animals, aging, and novels. She was also guest editor of a recent issue of *Victorian Periodicals Review* on magazine pedagogy.

Deirdre McMahon teaches in the English and Philosophy Department of Drexel University. She is currently completing a monograph entitled *Strange Family Stories: Race and Domesticity in Nineteenth-Century British Literature* and is co-editing a collection, *Material Possessions: The Objects and Textures of Everyday Life in Imperial Britain.*

Heather Milton is lecturer at the University of California, Davis. She has authored articles on women's confessions in the Victorian novel and the formation of subjectivity in working-class women's autobiography.

Deborah Denenholz Morse is professor of English at the College of William and Mary. Her books include *Women in Trollope's Palliser Novels,* (UMI Research Press, 1987; reprinted Rochester/Boydell & Brewer, 1991); *The Erotics of Instruction,* edited with Regina Barreca (University Press of New England, 1997); *Victorian Animal Dreams: Representations in Victorian Literature and Culture,* edited with Martin Danahay (Ashgate, 2007); and *The Politics of Gender: Anthony Trollope in the Twenty-First Century,* co-edited with Margaret Markwick and Regenia Gagnier (Ashgate, 2008). Her current projects include *Narrative and Tolerance in the Novels of Anthony Trollope.* Morse's recent articles are on Trollope, Elizabeth Gaskell, Kay Boyle, Elizabeth Coles Taylor, and Hesba Stretton. She is currently essay submissions editor for *Victorians Institute Journal.*

Cara Murray is assistant professor at University of Houston–Downtown where she teaches Victorian and postcolonial literatures. In her book *Victorian Narrative Technologies in the Middle East* (Routledge, 2008), she considerers the novel, alongside roads and canals, as one of the technologies of imperialism. She is currently working on a manuscript on catastrophe in the nineteenth-century novel.

Deirdre Osborne is a lecturer in drama and theater arts at Goldsmiths, University of London. She most recently edited and contributed critical essays to *Hidden Gems* (Oberon Books, 2008), an anthology of plays by black British dramatists. Her published work in the field of black British writing and theater history includes essays on Kwame Kwei-Armah, Lemn Sissay, debbie tucker green, and Roy Williams. Other research includes representations of women in espionage in World War II France and gender and the prison space.

Dara Rossman Regaignon is assistant professor of English at Pomona College, where she also directs the Program in College Writing. In her current project, she uses rhetorical genre theory to understand how images and anxieties about motherhood are generated and transmitted in fiction, advice literature, and life-writing. She has also published articles in *Victorian Literature and Culture, Women's Writing,* and *Pedagogy.*

Ellen Bayuk Rosenman is professor of English and a faculty affiliate of the Gender and Women's Studies Program at the University of Kentucky. Her most recent book is *Unauthorized Pleasures: Accounts of Victorian Erotic Experience* (Cornell University Press, 2003). She is currently working on a manuscript on penny dreadfuls and their relationship to working-class politics.

Lucy Sussex is a senior research fellow at Melbourne University. She gained her PhD from Cardiff University in 2005. Her special interest is Victoriana, specifically crime, Australian, and women writers. She has produced editions of writing by Mary Fortune and Ellen Davitt, and is currently completing a study of the first women writers of crime and mystery fiction. She is also an award-winning writer and editor, producing four anthologies, three collections of short stories, five books of fiction for younger readers, and the novel *The Scarlet Rider* (Forge, 1996). In addition she reviews weekly for the *Age* and *West Australian*.

Brenda R. Weber is an assistant professor in Gender Studies and an adjunct assistant professor in English, American Studies, and Cultural Studies at Indiana University. Her present book projects include "Subject to Change: Becoming a Self on Makeover TV" and "Figuring Fame: Women, Gender, and the Body in the Transatlantic Production of Literary Celebrity."

INDEX

(Page numbers in italics refer to illustrations.)

A

Abraham, Julie, 326
absent mothers, 8, 11, 58–59, 61, 70, 216–17. *See also* maternal loss; orphan stories/novels
Acrobat's Girlhood, An (Stretton), 104
Adam Bede (Eliot), 36n2, 63, 126
Adams, Maurianne, 243–44
"Address to Working Men, by Felix Holt, The" (Eliot), 56–57, 72
adoption, 16, 232–35
adulterous mothers. *See* fallen women
advice literature, 3–4, 9–10, 28, 203, 209–10, 316–17; opium warnings in, 125–33, 136, 142
Advice to a Mother (Chavasse), 128, 132–33, 142
"African Queen's Lament, The" (C. Brontë), 232–33
agency and power, female, 4–5, 7, 18, 69–70, 152, 195, 206–7, 303
Allen, Judith, 165
Alone in London (Stretton), 104
Anderson, Amanda, 5, 33, 58, 330
Andrews, William L., 184n3
"Angel in the House," 2–3, 5–6, 10–11, 113, 138, 291, 318, 330. *See also* maternal ideals
anorexia nervosa, 296–98
Antony and Cleopatra (Shakespeare), 88, 93–94
Arbuthnot, John, 294
Armstrong, Isobel, 328
Armstrong, Nancy, 2, 57
Arnot, Margaret, 146
Ashton, Rosemary, 322
aunts, maiden, 140–41
Aurora Leigh (Browning), 36n2, 55, 59, 67
Austen, Jane, 241
Austin, Sarah, 253, 259
Australian Baby, The (A. Ellis), 215, 219
autobiographical writing, 36–37, 41–43, 184, 313, 325
Autobiography of a Shirtmaker (Simcox), 17, 313–15, 318–20, 323–26, 329
autonomy, 33, 285, 316n. *See also* agency and power, female
Azim, Firdous, 234, 235

B

baby farmers/farming, 107n24, 153, 163–64, 166, 169–70

339

baby sweaters, 170–71
Baker, Samuel White, 249
Bakhtin, Mikhail, 292n3, 309n15
Banting, William, 293
Barret-Ducrocq, Françoise, 6
Barrett, Thomas, 127
Barros, Carolyn, 38n4
Baucom, Ian, 199
Bawarshi, Anis, 142
Baynton, Barbara, 205, 207–8, 211–23
Bede's Charity (Stretton), 104, 105, 110n30
Beer, Gillian, 315, 319
Beetham, Margaret, 3
Beginner, A (Broughton), 273–74, 280–82, 287–88
Behlmer, George, 147–48, 153
Bell, William, 151
Benjamin, Walter, 25
Benson, A. C., 50n12
Bentley, Colene, 58
Berridge, Virginia, 129, 130nn6–7
Berry, Laura, 104
Bleak House (Dickens), 36n2, 67, 104, 108, 110n29, 114
Blenkner, Margaret, 78
Blessington, Marguerite Gardiner, Countess of, 88
Bode, Rita, 71
Bodenheimer, Rosemarie, 315, 318n7, 320, 322n10, 323
Boehmer, Elleke, 203
Boer War (1899–1902), 208
Book of Beauty (Countess of Blessington), 88
Booth, Alison, 4, 19, 56n3, 69
Bordo, Susan, 296n10
"Boule de Suif" (Maupassant), 307–11
Boumelha, Penny, 232, 239, 246, 274n3
Braziel, Jana Evans, 294n6
breast-feeding/breast milk, 9, 132, 136, 147, 194
"British Hotel," 183, 188, 199
British Inter-Departmental Committee on Physical Deterioration (1903), 210
Britishness, ideals of, 2, 15; construction of, 200; cultural reproduction and, 196; imperialism and, 181–84; race and, 185–92
Brody, Jennifer, 7
Brontë, Anne, 36n2, 108, 228
Brontë, Charlotte, 16; "The African Queen's Lament," 232–33; *Caroline Vernon,* 235; "The Foundling," 229–30; "The Green Dwarf," 234–35; *Jane Eyre,* 230–35, 239–46; "A Leaf from an Unopened Volume," 233–38; *The Professor,* 236, 239n6; "Roe Head Journal," 235; *Shirley,* 227–30, 239; *Villette,* 238–39
Brontë, Emily, 235
Brought Home (Stretton), 119–21
Broughton, Rhoda, 16, 273–74, 280–82, 287–88
Browne, Hablot "Phiz," 80–*81, 88–89*
Brownell, David, 134n9
Browning, Elizabeth Barrett, 36n2, 55, 59, 67
Buckwalter, Kathleen, 78, 94
Bull, John (symbolic character), 294
Bull, Thomas, 127–29, 132–33, 137, 142
Burdett-Coutts, Angela, 101
Butler, Judith, 285

C

Cannon, Michael, 164
care at a distance, maternal, 126, 132–33, 135–38, 141–42, 248, 253–58, 317
Caroline Vernon (C. Brontë), 235
Cassy (Stretton), 104, 105
Cervetti, Nancy, 285–86
character development, 55–58, 64, 70; the "climacteric" and, 96–97; masculinity and, 55–56, 65–66, 72; parent care and, 14, 77–80, 94–95
Chase, Karen, 3, 125n2
Chavasse, Pye Henry, 128, 132–33, 142
Chenery, Thomas, 188
Chepaitis, Elia Vallone, 136
childbirth. *See* pregnancy and childbirth
children: domestic workers and, 125–28, 130–33, 136; legal protections for, 101–5, 147–48; maternal excess and, 49–51, 60, 62, 65, 67n12; in neglect

cases, 147–53, 159–60; violence against, 146–47, 153–59. See also infanticide
"Children's Employment" (Parliamentary Report, 1843), 136
Chodorow, Nancy, 315n3
Cholmondeley, Mary, 16, 273–74, 277–80, 287
Christian imagery, 86, 105, 107–8, 111–13, 116, 119–22, 164, 231–32, 282
Clarissa (Richardson), 140
Clayton, Jay, 26n2
Cleopatra, 88, 90–91, 94, 206, 217
climacteric periods, 96–97
Coghill, Annie, 41
Cohen, William, 159
colonial contexts, 15–16, 18–19; constructed family in, 248–51, 258–66; domestic workers in, 260–62; gender roles in, 203; infanticide in, 165, 169; of national identity, 184, 202–23; of race, 2, 7, 16, 186, 196–97, 206n9, 210; sexuality/reproduction, control over, in, 256, 261; of slavery, 186, 192, 195–97, 242, 254–55; writing from, 212
conduct books. See advice literature
Congreve, Mrs., 321
consumerism, 28–29, 293, 305, 311
Convert, The (Robins), 283n14
Corbett, Mary Jean, 3, 16–18, 37, 38n4, 45
Country of the Pointed Firs, The (Jewett), 330
courts, attitudes of, 145–47, 149–50; in infanticide cases, 145–47, 153–54, 163–77; in neglect cases, 147–53, 159–60; in violence against older children cases, 154–59
Craik, Dinah Mulock, 59–60
Cranford (Gaskell), 79, 330
Craton, Lillian E., 16, 17, 18, 283
Creaghe, Emily Caroline, 204n7
Crimean War (1854–56), 182–83, 188, 197, 199–200
Cromer, Evelyn Baring, 251n3
Crooke, Stan, 116

Cross, John, 327n15
"Cross Line, A" (Egerton), 205–7, 211–23
Cullwick, Hannah, 6
cult of motherhood/true womanhood, 27, 272, 279, 287, 297, 318
cultural reproduction, 196
Cutt, Nancy, 105, 109n28

D

Daisy Chain, The (Yonge), 14–15, 126, 133–41
d'Albertis, Deirdre, 13, 18, 39n4
Daniel Deronda (Eliot), 37n3, 328n16
David, Deirdre, 321
David Copperfield (Dickens), 109n27, 111n31, 126, 274–76, 298–304, 311
David Lloyd's Last Will (Stretton), 104
Davidoff, Leonore, 2, 10
Davin, Anna, 208
dead mothers. See maternal loss
death narratives, 111–13
demonic mothers. See transgressive mothers
Derrida, Jacques, 299n12
despairing mothers, 105, 114
detective fiction, 166–67, 294
Dever, Carolyn, 8, 27n4, 36, 61, 70, 138, 140, 229, 325
Diamond, Michael, 292n1
Diaries of Ethel Turner, The (Turner), 204n7
Dickens, Charles, 294, 297–98; *Bleak House*, 36n2, 67, 104, 108, 110n29, 114; *David Copperfield*, 109n27, 111n31, 126, 274–76, 298–304, 311; *Dombey and Son*, 14, 75–97; "Fasting Girls," 295–96, 298; "Fat People," 295; *Little Dorrit*, 298; *The Old Curiosity Shop*, 298–300, 304–7, 311; *Oliver Twist*, 104; *Our Mutual Friend*, 281n12
Dijkstra, Bram, 272
DiQuinzio, Patrice, 26
dirt, Victorian obsession with, 114n37, 148–52, 159–60
Disraeli, Benjamin, 164–65

distance mothering. *See* care at a distance, maternal
docility. *See* passivity and docility, ideals of
doll tales, 316
Dombey and Son (Dickens), 14, 75–97
Dombey and Son (Taylor), 81–82
domestic fiction, 36, 125, 241
domesticity, 40; masculinity and, 153; performance of, 25–34; war and, 187–92. *See also* femininity, ideals of
domestic workers, 26; child care and, 125–28, 130–33, 136; in colonial contexts, 260–62; race and, 250
Donaldson-Evans, Mary, 309, 310n16
Donzelot, Jacques, 133
Dover, Margaret, 151
Doyle, Laura, 194
"Dreamer, A" (Baynton), 205, 207–8, 211–23
drunken mothers, 101–22, 146
Duff Gordon, Lucy: *Letters from Egypt*, 16, 18, 248–66; *Letters from the Cape*, 253, 258

E

East Lynne (Mrs. Wood), 36n2, 317n4
Egerton, George, 205–7, 211–23
Egypt, modernization of, 251
elderly mothers, 75–97
Eliot, George, 17, 43, 313–15, 318–24; *Adam Bede*, 36n2, 63, 126; "The Address to Working Men, by Felix Holt," 56–57, 72; *Daniel Deronda*, 37n3, 328n16; *Felix Holt*, 14, 36n2, 37n3, 55–72; *The Mill on the Floss*, 37; *Romola*, 328n16, 330n20
Elliott, Dorice Williams, 3
Ellis, Annie Everett, 215, 219
Ellis, Sarah Stickney, 10, 18, 316
Engels, Friedrich, 113n36
English Society for the Prevention of Cruelty to Children, 169
Episodes in the Lives of Men, Women, and Lovers (Simcox), 17, 313–14, 326–30, 331

Evans, Julie, 223

F

fallen women: absent mothers and, 58–59, 70; drunken mothers as, 107; iconography of, 111; men's responsibility for, 68; redemption of, 55, 59–61, 66–69, 116, 119–22. *See also* unwed mothers
families and kinship: constructed, 17, 109–10, 191, 196, 199, 248–51, 258–66; determination of, 241–43, 246; mother's importance to, 106; orphan stories and, 79, 95–96; providers/breadwinners for, 151–53, 159–60, 288; sexual attachments in, 313–32
"Fasting Girls" (Dickens), 295–96, 298
fatness/plumpness, 283, 291–311
"Fat People" (Dickens), 295
Fausto-Sterling, Anne, 272
Felix Holt (Eliot), 14, 36n2, 37n3, 55–72
"female nature," essentialist, 3, 26n1, 37, 215, 218, 276
femininity, ideals of, 1–2, 6–7; appropriation of Britishness through, 181–200; the courts and, 160; modesty, 204, 219, 221; passivity/docility, 5, 215, 272, 291; public expression of, 4; self-control, 56–61, 293, 296–98, 309, 320; self-sacrifice, 2, 33, 37, 62, 149, 193, 204, 279, 291, 297, 301–2, 305–7, 311; sympathy, 56–58, 60, 72
feminist theory, 27, 193
Fern, Fanny, 271
Fineman, Martha, 193
Flanders, Judith, 28
Fortune, Mary, 167
Foucault, Michel, 140, 272, 315–16, 323
"Foundling, The" (C. Brontë), 229–30
foundling plots, 229, 231
Frankenstein (Shelley), 282
freak shows, 292, 295n9
Freud, Sigmund, 8, 51, 315, 317, 323, 328–29, 331
Friedman, Susan Stanford, 203n6

Frost, Eleanor Hannah, 148–50
Frost, Ginger, 6, 15, 106
Frost, Lucy, 216
Fuss, Diana, 331

G

Gaboriau, Emile, 169
Gager, Valier, 88
Garland-Thomson, Rosemarie, 294n6
Gaskell, Elizabeth: *Cranford,* 79, 330; "Libby Marsh's Three Eras," 110n29; *Mary Barton,* 110; *Ruth,* 36n2, 55, 59, 62, 67, 110n29
Gaskell, William, 102
gender-crossing motherhood. *See* male mothers
gender roles: in colonial/imperial contexts, 15, 203–4, 221–22, 250; essentialist views of, 3, 26n1, 37, 218; as family providers/breadwinners, 151–53, 159–60, 288; separate spheres ideology and, 2–6, 7, 11, 56, 188; women writers and, 271–73, 275. *See also* femininity, ideals of
George Mandeville's Husband (Robins), 273–74, 276, 282–88
Gikandi, Simon, 185, 191, 192n5
Gilbert, Pamela, 281n12
Gilbert, Sandra, 2
Gilman, Sander, 294
Goldstein, Vida, 202n2
Gonne, Maud, 12n11
governesses, 3
grandparenthood, 96
Green, Laura, 13–14, 62
"Green Dwarf, The" (C. Brontë), 234–35
Greenwood, Kerry, 175
Grimshaw, Patricia, 223
Gubar, Susan, 2

H

Hall, Catherine, 2, 10
Hardy, Thomas, 36n2
Harris, Wendall, 206
Hein, Hilde, 203n6, 223

Her Only Son (Stretton), 102, 104, 117–19
heterosexuality, 4, 7, 313
Hewson, Isabella, 155
Hicks, Neville, 210
Holledge, James, 164
Holt, John, 150
Homans, Margaret, 330
Hopkins, Ellice, 59
Houston, Gail Turley, 296–97, 305
Howard, John, 151–52
Howitt, Mary and William, 45–46
Huff, Joyce, 293–94
Hughes, Winifred, 67
Hughes-Hallett, Lucy, 88, 90
Hume, Fergus, 169

I

I Don't Know How She Does It (Pearson), 13, 27–28
imperialism, 2, 7, 182–84, 208–9, 221–22; critiques/justifications of, 248–49, 251, 255; "New," 258. *See also* colonial contexts
India, 165, 169
individualism, 27, 72. *See also* agency and power, female
infanticide, 15; court cases on, 145–47, 153–54, 163–77; fictional treatments of, 63, 107, 165, 167, 273, 281n12, 287
In Memoriam (Tennyson), 48
In Prison and Out (Stretton), 102, 104
insanity, 60, 153–54, 174
Inter-Departmental Committee on Physical Deterioration, British (1903), 210

J

Jaffe, Audrey, 96
Jaggs, Donella, 166
Jane Eyre (C. Brontë), 230–35, 239–46
Jay, Elisabeth, 39, 39n4, 41–42, 47, 49, 52
Jeanne d'Arc (Oliphant), 42
Jessica's First Prayer (Stretton), 102, 103, 104, 110–11

Jessica's Mother (Stretton), 104, 107, 111–12
Jeune, Mary, 59
Jewett, Sarah Orne, 330
John Bull (symbolic character), 294
Joseph, Gerhard, 95n10, 111
Jusova, Iveta, 206n10, 207, 214

K

Kilgour, Maggie, 132
kinship. *See* families and kinship
Knorr, Frances, 15, 163–64, 166–77
Knox, William, 116
Kreilkamp, Ivan, 114–15
Kristeva, Julia, 204, 207

L

Lamb, Margaret, 88
Langbauer, Laurie, 39n4
Langland, Elizabeth, 3, 5, 37, 65, 68n13
Laster, Kathy, 174–75
Lawrence, Annie, 156–58
Lawson, Nigella, 25, 29
"Leaf from an Unopened Volume, A" (C. Brontë), 233–38
LeBesco, Kathleen, 294n6
lesbianism. *See* same-sex attachments
Letters from Egypt (Lady Duff Gordon), 16, 18, 248–66
Letters from the Cape (Lady Duff Gordon), 253, 258
Levenson, Michael, 3, 125n2
Levine, Caroline, 11
Lewes, George Henry, 91–92
"Libby Marsh's Three Eras" (Gaskell), 110n29
Little Dorrit (Dickens), 298
Logan, Deborah Anna, 60
Logan, Thad, 29
London Society for the Prevention of Cruelty to Children (LSPCC), 101, 103
Long, Edward, 260
Lorber, Judith, 272
Lost and Saved (Norton), 36n2

Lost Gip (Stretton), 103, 104, 107–9
lower classes, 104, 105–6, 112, 121–22. *See also* working classes
LSPCC. *See* London Society for the Prevention of Cruelty to Children

M

MacDonald, George, 102
McClintock, Anne, 6, 7, 250, 260–61
McCullogh, Kate, 214
McMahon, Deirdre, 15–18
McMaster, Juliet, 294
Magdalen's Friend and Female Homes' Intelligencer, The, 60
Makin, John and Sarah, 166, 168, 173
male mothers, 17, 108, 111
male violence/neglect, 145–46, 150–51, 160
Mancini, Michelle, 81n4, 83
Mangum, Teresa, 14, 17–18
Marcus, Sharon, 5, 10, 316, 318n6
Marks, Elaine, 318n7
marriage plots, 27, 36
Marsh, Joss, 77n2, 82, 95–96
Mary Barton (Gaskell), 110
masculinity, 4, 7; autonomy and, 316n3; character development and, 55–56, 65–66, 72; the courts and, 160; domesticity and, 153; failure of, 39–40, 51–52; female/femininity performance and, 275; imperialism and, 183; maternal excess and, 49–51, 62, 65; providing for family and, 151–53, 159–60, 203, 288; self-control and, 56; sympathy and, 56, 65–66, 97. *See also* male mothers
maternal body, 9–10, 16–17; eroticism of, 5–6, 8–11, 212–14, 217, 297, 315–19, 325, 328–29, 331; fatness/plumpness and, 283, 291–311; race and, 193–95
maternal failure, 1, 8–9, 13–14; care at a distance and, 126, 132–33, 135–38, 141–42; excess as, 49–51, 60, 62, 65, 67n12; gender roles reproduction and, 37–52; insanity and, 60, 153–54, 174; nurturance, lack of,

as, 14, 298, 301, 304, 307. *See also* transgressive mothers
maternal ideals, 1–2, 13–14, 18, 105–6; critiques/analyses of, 3–11; cult of motherhood/true womanhood and, 27, 272, 279, 287, 297, 318; institutionalization of, 192–97, 200; nurturance, 28, 63, 126, 138, 145, 152, 195, 272, 292–93, 298–307, 310–11; performance of, 25–34, 292–93; redemption and, 55–72, 85, 116, 119–22; reorientation in study of, 11–13, 17–19. *See also* femininity, ideals of
maternal loss, 8, 36, 61, 138–41, 325. *See also* absent mothers
Maternal Management of Children in Health and Disease (Bull), 127–29, 132–33, 137, 142
Matus, Jill, 8–9
Maupassant, Guy de, 307–11
Mavor, Carol, 6
medical literature. *See* advice literature
men, as writers, 275–76
Mendelson, Cheryl, 25
Meredith, George, 34, 253
Mermin, Dorothy, 5
Meyer, Susan, 230
Michie, Helena, 296n10
middle classes: Christian duty and, 119–21; differentiation from other classes by, 125–26, 129, 132; dirt obsession of, 114n37, 149, 159–60; superiority of, 2, 7
Miller, Melissa Lee, 251, 260–61
Milligan, Barry, 128–29
Mill on the Floss, The (Eliot), 37
Milton, Heather, 13–14
Mirkwater, The (Robins), 283n14
Miss Marjoribanks (Oliphant), 40, 44
Mitchell, Sally, 19
Mitchell, Timothy, 265
M'Neil, Mary, 153–54
modesty, 204, 219, 221
moral growth. *See* character development
Morant Bay Massacre (1865), 197
Morrison, Elizabeth, 150–51

Morse, Deborah Denenholz, 14–15, 17
motherhood, as an institution, 192–97, 200
Mugglestone, Lynda, 56n3
Mumm, Susan, 59n7
Munby, Arthur, 6
Murray, Cara, 16–18

N

national identity. *See* Britishness, ideals of
National Society for the Prevention of Cruelty to Children (NSPCC), 147–48
nature, 215–16, 218, 275, 328
Needle, Martha, 164
neglect, court cases on, 147–53, 159–60
Nelly's Dark Days (Stretton), 116–17
Nestor, Pauline, 62n10
New Imperialism, 258
Newlin, George, 79
Newsom, Robert, 91
New Woman figure, 215, 216, 219, 271
Nightingale, Florence, 4–5, 183, 200, 249
Nora, Pierre, 199
Nord, Deborah Epstein, 3, 106, 145, 229
Norton, Caroline, 36n2
Nouvelle Heloise, La (Rousseau), 321
NSPCC (National Society for the Prevention of Cruelty to Children), 147–48
Nunokawa, Jeff, 90
nursemaids. *See* children: domestic workers and
nurturance: fatness/plumpness and, 292–93, 298–307, 310–11; ideals of, 28, 63, 126, 138, 145, 152, 195, 272; imperialism and, 251; male mothers and, 17; maternal failures in, 14, 298, 301, 304, 307; poorer classes and, 145, 152; violence and, 153

O

Old Curiosity Shop, The (Dickens), 298–300, 304–7, 311

Oliphant, Margaret, 18; *Autobiography*, 13–14, 38–52, 62; *Jeanne d'Arc*, 42; *Miss Marjoribanks*, 40, 44; *Phoebe, Junior*, 44
Oliver Twist (Dickens), 104
opium warnings, 126–33, 136
orphan stories/novels, 103, 227–46, 299
Osborne, Deirdre, 15–16, 18
Our Mutual Friend (Dickens), 281n12

P

paid child care. *See* domestic workers
Paquet, Sandra Pouchet, 184n3
parent care, 14, 77–80, 94–95
Parkins, Wendy, 274
passivity and docility, ideals of, 5, 207–8, 215, 219, 272, 291
Patmore, Coventry, 10
Payne, Mary Ann, 150
Pearson, Allison, 13, 27–28
Perera, Suvendrini, 90
performance, 25–34, 292–93
Perry, Ruth, 241, 244
Peterson, Linda, 3, 37, 39n4, 44, 51, 324
Phillips, A. A., 221
Phoebe, Junior (Oliphant), 44
Pickering, Ellen, 19, 330
Pilgrim Street (Stretton), 102, 104
Plasa, Carl, 235n4, 236
police procedural novels, 169
Pollard, Lisa, 251
poor, the. *See* lower classes
Poovey, Mary, 2, 4–5, 8–9, 19, 40n5, 187, 275n4, 281n12, 330
Potter, Beatrice, 114n37
power. *See* agency and power, female
pregnancy and childbirth: bodily form and, 307; empire and, 208–10, 221–22; as metaphor for creativity, 16, 204–5, 271–88; passivity and, 207–8, 219
premarital motherhood. *See* unwed mothers
Primitive Civilizations (Simcox), 313, 318–19, 327
Professor, The (C. Brontë), 236, 239n6
providing for family, 151–53, 159–60, 203, 288

psychoanalytic theory, 8, 51, 315n3
public/private spheres, ideals of. *See* separate spheres ideology
Punch, 130–31, 196

R

race, 17; Britishness, ideals of, and, 2, 15, 181–82, 185–92; colonial contexts of, 7, 16, 186, 196–97, 206n9, 210; domesticity and, 187; domestic workers and, 250, 260; the maternal body and, 193–95; in orphan stories, 236–38, 242; social class and, 6–7, 260
redemption, 55–72, 85; drunken fathers and, 116, 119; drunken mothers and, 107, 116, 119–22
Red Pottage (Cholmondeley), 273–74, 277–80, 287
Regaignon, Dara Rossman, 14–15, 18
Religious Tract Society (RTS), 101–3
rhetorical genre theory, 142
Richardson, Samuel, 140
Rickard, Suzanne, 104
Robins, Elizabeth, 16; *The Convert*, 283n14; *George Mandeville's Husband*, 273–74, 276, 282–88; *The Mirkwater*, 283n14; "Woman's Secret," 277n8
Robinson, Amy, 184n3, 192n5
"Roe Head Journal" (C. Brontë), 235
roman policier fiction, 169
Romola (Eliot), 328n16, 330n20
Rosenman, Ellen Bayuk, 16–18
Ross, Ellen, 10, 105–6, 105n16, 115n39
Ross, Janet, 252, 253
Rousseau, Jean-Jacques, 321
Rowley, Sue, 203n4, 210
Royal Commission on the Decline of the Birth Rate, New South Wales (1903), 210
RTS (Religious Tract Society), 101–3
Ruskin, John, 10, 18, 28
Russell, W. H., 188
Russett, Cynthia Eagle, 271, 273
Ruth (Gaskell), 36n2, 55, 59, 62, 67, 110n29
Rye, Maria, 108

S

same-sex attachments, 5, 17, 313–32
Sandbach-Dahlström, Catherine, 134n9
Schaffer, Talia, 134n9, 141
Scheckter, John, 212
Scottish Temperance League, 103
Seacole, Mary, 11n11, 15, 181–200
Sedgwick, Eve, 12
self-assertion. *See* agency and power, female
self-control, 56–61, 293, 296–98, 309, 320
self-denial, 16, 56, 60, 185, 296. *See also* self-sacrifice
self-restraint. *See* self-control
self-sacrifice, 2, 33, 37, 62, 149, 193, 204, 279, 291, 297, 301–2, 305–7, 311
sensation fiction, 67
Sense and Sensibility (Austen), 241
sentimental literature and sentimentality, 77, 82, 189–91, 198, 292
separate spheres ideology, 2–6, 7, 11, 56, 188, 330; domestic workers in, 250. *See also* maternal ideals
servants. *See* domestic workers
Sexualities in Victorian Britain (Miller, ed.), 5
sexuality: control over, in colonial contexts, 256, 261; fatness and, 307–11; female, 5–6, 8–11, 212–14, 217, 297; same-sex attachments and, 5, 17, 313–32
Shakespeare, William, 88, 93–94
Shelley, Mary, 282
Shereen, Faiza, 249
Sheridan, Susan, 212
Shirley (C. Brontë), 227–30, 239
short story form, 208
Showalter, Elaine, 221, 274n3
Shuttleworth, Sally, 8–9, 49, 51, 58n5, 60, 67n12
Silver, Anna, 293, 296–97, 307
Simcox, Edith, 17–18, 313–32; *Autobiography of a Shirtmaker,* 17, 313–15, 318–20, 323–26, 329; "Autobiography," 325; *Episodes in the Lives of Men, Women, and Lovers,* 17, 313–14, 326–30, 331; *Primitive Civilizations,* 313, 318–19, 327
Simpson, Sarah Ann, 150
slavery, colonial contexts of, 186, 192, 195–97, 242, 254–55
Smiles, Samuel, 185
social class, 6–7, 10, 15; bodily manifestations of, 296; redemption and, 60, 119–22. *See also specific types (e.g., working classes)*
Spence, Catherine H., 202n2
Spender, Dale, 205
Spillers, Hortense, 195
Spivak, Gayatri Chakravorty, 139
Starr, Elizabeth, 71n17
Stearns, Peter, 293
Steer, Mary H., 60n8
stepmothers, 148–49
Stewart, Martha, 25–26
Stoler, Ann Laura, 2, 7, 249, 251, 256, 261
Storm of Life, The (Stretton), 112–13
Strachey, Lytton, 291
"street arab" fiction, 103. *See also* orphan stories/novels
Stretton, Hesba, 17, 101–22; *An Acrobat's Girlhood,* 104; *Alone in London,* 104; *Bede's Charity,* 104, 105, 110n30; *Brought Home,* 119–21; *Cassy,* 104, 105; *David Lloyd's Last Will,* 104; *Her Only Son,* 102, 104, 117–19; *In Prison and Out,* 102, 104; *Jessica's First Prayer,* 102, 103, 104, 110–11; *Jessica's Mother,* 104, 107, 111–12; *Little Meg's Children,* 103; *Lost Gip,* 103, 104, 107–9; *Nelly's Dark Days,* 116–17; *Pilgrim Street,* 102, 104; *The Storm of Life,* 112–13; *A Thorny Path,* 104, 105, 112–16
Struve, Laura, 58n6
suffrage, women's, 40, 56, 202n2, 219
Summers, Leigh, 296
Sunday at Home, 103
Sussex, Lucy, 15
Sutton, Margaret, 155
Swift, Jonathan, 169
Sybil (Disraeli), 164–65
Sybylla, Roe, 97
sympathy, 56–58, 60, 65–66, 72, 97

T

Taylor, Thomas Prochlus, 81–82

Tenant of Wildfell Hall, The (A. Brontë), 36n2, 108, 228
Tennyson, Alfred, Lord, 48
Tess of the D'Urbervilles (Hardy), 36n2
Thackeray, William Makepeace, 13, 27, 29–34
Thaden, Barbara, 38
Thorny Path, A (Stretton), 104, 105, 112–16
Tilt, Edward, 97
Toise, David, 96
Tompkins, Jane, 191
transgressive mothers, 14–15, 156; drunken mothers as, 101–22, 146; maternal excess and, 49–51, 60, 62, 65, 67n12; unwed mothers as, 36, 145–60, 165–66
travel narratives, 15
Tuchman, Gaye, 275
Tucker, Herbert, 111
Turner, Ethel, 204n7

U

unwed mothers, 36, 145–60, 165–66
upper classes, 104

V

Vallone, Elia, 130n7
Vanity Fair (Thackeray), 13, 27, 29–34
Vicinus, Martha, 2, 5, 207, 216, 315–16, 320
Victoria, Queen of England, 4, 12n11, 291–92, 294, 299
Villette (C. Brontë), 238–39
violence: infanticide, 15, 63, 107, 145–47, 153–54, 163–77; against women, 145–46; by women, 146–60, 163–77
Voyage Out, The (Woolf), 331

W

Walkowitz, Judith, 3
Warner, Judith, 26, 28
Waterfield, Gordon, 253
Weber, Brenda R., 16, 18
Weiner, Martin, 146
Weinroth, Michelle, 66
Weiss, Barbara, 198
Wiley, Catherine, 283n14
Williams, Merryn, 40
Williams, Raymond, 185
Wohl, Anthony S., 130, 136
Woloch, Alex, 299
"Woman's Secret" (Robins), 277n8
women as writers, 5–6, 14, 16, 18, 45–46, 51, 212, 223, 271–88
Wonderful Adventures of Mrs. Seacole in Many Lands (Seacole), 15, 181–200
Wood, Mrs. Henry, 36n2, 317n4
Woolf, Virginia, 331
working classes, 6; bodily form and, 296, 299, 302; maternal failure and, 106, 112, 209; opium warnings and, 129–32; race and, 260; rights for, 56–58, 72, 262; self-control and, 57, 72; violence and, 15, 147–60
working mothers, 130, 136, 145, 152
Wuthering Heights (E. Brontë), 235

Y

Yonge, Charlotte, 14–15, 126, 133–41

PR 468 .M596 O75 2008

Other mothers

AUG 3 1 2009